A Woman's Life

IN THE COURT OF THE SUN KING

A Woman's Life

Letters of

IN THE COURT
OF THE SUN KING

Liselotte von der Pfalz, 1652-1722
Elisabeth Charlotte, Duchesse d'Orléans

Translated and introduced by

ELBORG FORSTER

THE JOHNS HOPKINS UNIVERSITY PRESS

Baltimore and London

This book has been brought to publication with the generous assistance of the Andrew W. Mellon Foundation.

Based on a text originally published in German in 1958 by Langwiesche Verlag, Ebenhausen, as *Liselotte von der Pfalz, Elisabeth Charlotte von der Pfalz, Duchesse d'Orléans, Madame, Briefe* © 1958 by Langwiesche-Brandt Verlag

English translation and new material © 1984 by The Johns Hopkins University Press

The Johns Hopkins University Press, Baltimore, Maryland 21218

The Johns Hopkins Press Ltd., London

The paper in this book is acid-free and meets the guidelines for permanence and durability of the Committee on Production Guidelines for Book Longevity of the Council on Library Resources.

Library of Congress Cataloging in Publication Data

Orléans, Charlotte-Elisabeth, duchesse d', 1652–1722.
  A woman's life in the court of the Sun King.
  Translation of: Liselotte von der Pfalz, Duchesse d'Orleans, Madame, Briefe.
  Includes index.
  1. Orléans, Charlotte-Elisabeth, duchesse d', 1652–1722. 2. France—History—Louis XIV, 1643–1715. 3. France—Court and courtiers. 4. France—Princes and princesses—Correspondence. I. Forster, Elborg, 1931–   . II. Title.
DC130.O7A4 1984   944'.033'0924   84–5718
ISBN 0–8018–3159–8

End papers: Wing of the Château of Saint Cloud, with View of Horseshoe-Fountain. Engraving by J. Rigaud. Bibliothèque Nationale, Paris. Photo by N. D. Roger-Viollet.

For Marc

⚜ Contents

Preface *ix*
Acknowledgments *xiii*
Introduction *xv*
Cast of Principal Characters *xxxv*
Plates *li*

To 1671: YOUTH *1*

1672–1701: MARRIAGE *5*

1701–1715: WIDOWHOOD *131*

1715–1722: MOTHER OF THE REGENT *201*

Index *279*

 # Preface

Elisabeth Charlotte, Duchesse d'Orléans (1652–1722), known in Germany as Liselotte von der Pfalz and in France as *Madame* or *La Palatine,* was a prodigious letter-writer. Married at the age of nineteen to the only brother of Louis XIV, she spent fifty years at the French court, writing about forty long letters a week, most of them to relatives in her native Germany. Much of this correspondence has been lost, but several major collections, containing the letters to her favorite aunt, Electress Sophie of Hanover, to the members of the Degenfeld family, to Caroline of Wales (née Princess of Ansbach), as well as scattered letters to others, have been published in scholarly editions. Friedrich von Schiller already considered Elisabeth Charlotte's letters important enough to include many of them in his *General Collection of Historical Memoirs* (1791–93), and Leopold von Ranke appended large extracts to his history of France (1868–70). Selections of Madame's letters were translated into French in the nineteenth century, and English translations also appeared, under such lurid titles as *The reign and amours of the Bourbon régime, a brilliant description of the courts of Louis XIV, amours, debauchery, intrigues, and state secrets, including suppressed and confiscated manuscripts, the correspondence of Madame . . . Unexpurgated rendition into English* (New York, 1889). Two English translations of Elisabeth Charlotte's letters have been published in the twentieth century, both of which are now out of print. They are Gertrude Scott Stevenson, *The Letters of Madame,* 2 vols. (London and New York, 1924–25) and Maria Kroll, *Letters from Liselotte* (London, 1970). Several French editions also exist, the most recent being *Lettres de Madame, Duchesse d'Orléans, née Princesse Palatine,* ed. and annotated by Olivier Amiel, pref. by Pierre Gascat (Paris, 1982).

The present, entirely new, translation is based on a selection edited by Margarethe Westphal and published by Langwiesche Verlag in 1958. It differs from the previous ones in several respects, the most important being the selection itself. A greater emphasis on Elisabeth Charlotte's German background situates her development in a cross-cultural context, thereby adding an extra dimension to the lively description of the outward life of the French court—its ceremonies, buildings, gardens, furnishings, clothes, and political events. The Langwiesche selection stresses Madame's personal reflections on life and letters, human destiny, religion, the role of princes in society, the health of body and mind, and the education of children. In this sense, it is more than a source of information about the court of Louis XIV, for it amounts to a document in intellectual, social, and even literary history. A careful reading of the scholarly editions of the German texts has persuaded me that this selection is representative indeed of Madame's entire German correspondence.

The attentive reader will soon realize that this book can be read as a kind of *Bildungsroman,* tracing the transformation of a bright, eager, and innocent girl into a thoughtful observer of human folly and a seasoned writer. The splendor and squalor of a great court provide an exciting setting for such a novel, and the presence of well-known historical figures will arouse the curiosity of many readers. Anyone who has ever studied the history of seventeenth-century Europe will be fascinated by the first-hand accounts of monarchs, mistresses, and ministers. Here is Louis XIV in triumph and in crisis, playing his roles as statesman, paterfamilias, and object of craven hero-worship; here are his mistresses, especially the all-powerful, uncrowned queen of France, Madame de Maintenon, and that "desperate woman," Madame de Montespan, the mother of the King's bastard children; here are powerful ministers, Louvois, Colbert, Torcy, and Dubois, along with the King's confessors, Père Le Tellier and Père de la Chaise, and his physician, Monsieur Fagon. Here also is James II of England, living and dying in exile at Saint-Germain; his rival, William of Orange, fighting for the crown of England; Peter the Great of Russia being derided by Louis XIV for learning the shipbuilding trade; George I of England sorting out his marital troubles; and Pope Clement XI suffering from his hernia. Here are the great marshals of the age, Turenne, Marlborough, and Prince Eugene of Savoy. We even hear about the birth of a Prussian prince who was to become Frederick the Great. Moreover, Madame also provides her opinions about many of the great events and issues of her age: Louis XIV's campaigns, many of the descriptions complete with battle accounts; the Spanish succession; the devastation of the Palatinate; the revocation of the Edict of Nantes; the papal bull *Unigenitus;* Quietism and Jansenism; the censorship of the mails; the famine and the horrendous winter of 1709; and John Law's financial "system." All of this sounds—and is—very serious, but there is a wonderful surprise in store for the reader of Liselotte's story: it is the delightful humor—ranging from the simple pleasure in reporting a funny incident and a sense of subtle irony to biting satire and broad scatological jokes—that pervades almost every page. It is this quality that accounts for the enduring popularity of the letters of Liselotte von der Pfalz among German readers. May this translation enable the English-speaking reader to share their pleasure.

A word about this translation. There is no question that some of the appeal of Madame's prose resides in the flavor of her seventeenth-century language. Yet is was out of the question to produce a prolonged pastiche of seventeenth-century English; it would too easily have assumed a ponderousness that is totally inappropriate. Thus, the challenge was to find a level of style that preserves a certain formality along with an extreme informality. It would not do, for example, to drop Madame's insistence on ceremonial forms of address, such as "Your Grace," "His Majesty," or "His late Grace," for it would have been a shame to destroy the comic contrast in a sentence like "Then Oncle will ask again . . . what Your Grace wants with this crap." I therefore decided to adopt a somewhat old-fashioned American idiom and, in many cases, to use expressions marked *ant.* or *F.* in the dictionaries. This seemed particularly appropriate in view of the fact that Madame's language must soon have appeared somewhat old-fashioned to her German correspondents, since she had left her homeland at the age of nineteen and necessarily missed some of the mutations in the German language over the next fifty years. Every effort has been made to convey the different levels of style adopted by the author, depending on the subject discussed in the letter and on the recipient.

Another fundamental decision concerning the translation involved the many French expressions with which the text is peppered and the reported conversations in French. The Langwiesche edition from which this translation was made quite properly leaves all of them intact as an integral part of Madame's language and, indeed, of the German language of the seventeenth century. As a help to the German reader who is unfamiliar with French, the Langwiesche edition provides a glossary of all French terms at the end of the volume and a translation of reported conversations at the end of each letter. Since in English, however, most of these French words (e.g., *coiffure, collation, gravité, farce, passion*) evoke a Latin-root word that may or may not be a so-called false friend, I decided to translate them in order to render their meaning as precisely as possible. The reported conversations are translated in the course of the letters. The historical and biographical notes at the end of each letter are intended to facilitate the understanding of the text and have been written especially for this English-language edition; headnotes explaining certain major historical developments have been added.

A special problem is raised by the many German and French proverbs cited throughout the letters. Some of these dicta have an exact equivalent in

English, but occasionally the equivalent English proverb changes the image. The idea of *Gleich und gleich gesellt sich gern, sprach der Teufel zu dem Kohlenbrenner* ("Like and like will go together, said the devil to the charcoal burner"), for example, is expressed in "Birds of a feather flock together." In this case I regretfully gave up a suggestive image for the sake of familiarity; after all, the point of citing a proverb is to "ring a bell." Many German proverbs, of course, have no equivalent in other languages. These, alas, cannot ring a bell, and here the translator falls back on the old maxim that a good translation must allow the original to shine through to some extent.

Another problem are folksongs and church hymns. The former I have translated as best I could into some kind of jingle, and the tone of the latter was suggested by Lutheran hymnals.

In this, as in every translation, certain features of the original cannot be reproduced at all. This is the case with the dialect words that Madame used with great pleasure, often expressly calling attention to them. But since each of these words evokes a particular region of Germany (*geheyt* is from the Palatinate, *geknottert* from Osnabrück, *wat wie fuligte Käs* from Mecklenburg, and *met Verlöff* from Westphalia), it would be pointless to find an equivalent from the dialect of, say, Scotland or Northumberland. Nor is it possible to render the gradations in familiarity that were so important to our duchess beyond the distinction between the "persons of quality," who are addressed in the third person as "Your Grace" or "Your Majesty," and the others, who, in English, are addressed as "you." Yet, in the German text, important differences in status and familiarity are expressed by the use of *Du, Ihr,* and *Er.* In one of the letters, much of Madame's playful banter in writing to her young half-brother, alternately calling him *Ihr* and *Du,* is lost. Missing also is the respect expressed in referring to *Mein Herr Vater* or *seine Gross Frau Mutter.* It would not be possible to translate *mein Herr* ("my husband") as "my lord," even though the husbands of ordinary women are not referred to in this manner.

But, as Madame was so fond of saying, "What can't be cured must be endured," and if these letters give the reader half as much pleasure as they have given the translator, the frustrations inherent in this enterprise will have been well worthwhile.

❧ Acknowledgments

I would like to express my gratitude to several persons who have been helpful in the preparation of this translation and who have taken time to comment on the introduction. Katherine Stern Brennan, Joseph Claits, Linda Clark, Nicholas Fessenden, Emmet Kennedy, Sharon Kettering, Robert Kreiser, Ane Lintvedt and Alexander Sedgwick came to a special seminar at my house to explore the issues raised by these letters; Lieselotte Kurth discussed the language and the literary merits of her illustrious namesake with me, made valuable suggestions for the introduction, and invited me to present a sample of the translation to her translation seminar at The Johns Hopkins University; Orest Ranum and Mack Walker helped me understand the historical context of these letters. A special thanks goes to my husband, Robert Forster, who painstakingly read the entire manuscript and patiently listened to innumerable Liselotte stories.

❧ Introduction

*I believe that the histories which will be written
about this court after we are gone will be better and
more entertaining than any novel, and I am afraid
that those who come after us will not be able to believe
them and will think that they are just fairytales.*

The letters of Elisabeth Charlotte, Duchesse d'Orléans, Louis XIV's
sister-in-law, have long enjoyed the status of a literary classic
in Germany and a valuable historical source in France. In the
present translation I hope to acquaint a wider English-speaking
public with a most engaging writer who, possessed of keen intelligence,
strong feelings, uncompromising frankness, and a wonderful sense of humor,
commented for fifty years on the private and public life of the French
court under Louis XIV and during the Regency, and, indeed, on courtly and
popular culture throughout Europe from the perspective of an insider who
was also an outsider.

What do we know about the family background of Liselotte von der Pfalz?
Following a long exile during the Thirty Years' War (1618–48), her father,
Elector Karl Ludwig von der Pfalz, regained possession of the lands he had
inherited, but the Pfalz (Palatinate) was devastated and impoverished. Professing the Reformed (i.e., Calvinist) faith but pragmatic in his approach to
religious matters, Karl Ludwig set about rebuilding his country by tireless
planning and personal frugality, which earned him the loyalty of his subjects. Destroyed towns were rebuilt and the fertile land gradually regained its
past prosperity. From his marriage to Charlotte von Hessen-Kassel two children were born—in 1651 a son, Karl, and on 27 May 1652 a daughter, Elisabeth
Charlotte. But the Elector and Electress were ill matched, for the latter
had looked forward to a lively and carefree court life and had no understanding of her husband's austere conception of the princely calling; nor did
she share his taste for art and learning. After years of constant dissension,
the Elector repudiated his unwilling wife and contracted a marriage "to
the left hand" (i.e., a marriage whose offspring were excluded from the succession) with Luise von Degenfeld, one of the Electress's ladies-in-waiting,
on whom he conferred the title "Raugräfin von der Pfalz." Of the fourteen

children born from this union, five survived; these half-sisters and -brothers figure prominently in the subsequent correspondence of Elisabeth Charlotte. In fact, the letters in the possession of the Degenfeld family, published between 1867 and 1881 by Ludwig Holland, fill no fewer than seven volumes.

The repudiated Electress refused to leave Heidelberg for several years after the de facto divorce. In order not to expose the seven-year-old Liselotte to the conflict between her parents, the Elector sent her to live with his sister Sophie and her husband, Duke Ernst-August von Braunschweig-Lüneburg, subsequently Elector of Hanover and, much later, father of the Hanoverian line of English kings. Liselotte spent four happy years at Hanover with "Ma Tante" and "Oncle." The style of his court was easy and unaffected, and Duchess Sophie saw to it that the child (who later described herself as "willful and forward") was well brought up. More than once in these letters we hear of strict discipline, great emphasis on physical robustness, writing and language teachers, dancing and music masters, as well as religious instruction, but we are also told of games and laughter, walks and journeys, pageants and concerts. The little girl was already developing her talent as a letter-writer, for in 1661 Duchess Sophie assured her brother that "no one but herself touches Liselotte's letters. The last one she sent to you was so well written that if I had not seen her do it, I would not have believed that she had written it herself." Liselotte remembered these four years as a very happy time of her life, and her aunt Sophie remained her most intimate friend and confidante until the death of the Electress.

After Liselotte's mother had retired to Kassel, her father sent for her to return to Heidelberg. Between the ages of eleven and nineteen she thus lived in the lively household of her father's second, young family; this was the time when she formed a deep attachment to the towns and villages, vineyards and forests, of her beloved Palatinate.

As the daughter of an important sovereign of impeccable lineage (her paternal grandmother was a Stuart), Elisabeth Charlotte was demanded in marriage by several sons of German princely houses, but, for one reason or another, all of these proposals were rejected. In 1671, however, her father eagerly accepted a plan mediated by his sister-in-law, the intelligent Anna Gonzaga, who had been living for many years at the French court, where she was known as the Princesse Palatine. Liselotte was to marry the recently widowed Monsieur, Philippe d'Orléans, the only brother of Louis XIV. Karl Ludwig hoped that by establishing a close kinship relation to the French royal family, he could protect his country and his people from a powerful and aggressive neighbor. Many years later Elisabeth Charlotte would gently remind her aunt Sophie, who had also advocated this strategy, that she, Liselotte, had not believed at the time that the ploy would work—as indeed it did not—but that she had agreed to go to France "from a sense of duty and filial obedience." Her father, she felt, had been so eager to conclude this prestigious alliance that he had agreed to certain unusual clauses in his daughter's marriage contract that jeopardized her widow's rights. "From this I conclude," she wrote after the death of Monsieur in 1701, "that my late Papa must not have understood this matter properly when he made me sign such a thing; but Papa had me on his hands and was afraid I might become a little old maid, and so he got rid of me as quickly as he could."

Marrying into the French royal family also involved conversion to Catholicism. Liselotte, who had a keen understanding of religion, as these letters show, had been brought up to embrace a universal Christianity and to consider confessional difference as "priests' squabbles" of no concern to "persons of quality." She was "impatient" with James II of England, who "lost three kingdoms through bigotry" and considered him "a good, honest man, but the most simple-minded person in the world." Having been secretly instructed in the Catholic faith by her father's French secretary, Urbain Chevreau, and examined by Père Jourdain, who subsequently became her confessor, she formally converted at Metz, just before the marriage was concluded by proxy. In 1707, Elisabeth Charlotte recalled the conversion ceremony: "They simply read something to me, to which I was to answer 'yes' or 'no,' which I did according to my own mind, and a few times I answered 'no' when I was supposed to say 'yes,' but it went through anyway; I had to chuckle to myself. I protested so vigorously against the condemnation of the parents that nothing was said about it in my case. I listened most attentively and answered quite according to my own mind." Her father publicly registered his disapproval of the conversion.

And then she met Monsieur, the thirty-one-year-old widower of the charming and beautiful Henrietta of England, who had died the year before, many said of poison. At first Elisabeth Charlotte tried to put up a brave front. "I say only this," she wrote to her aunt, "that Monsieur is the best man in the world. We get along quite well; he does not resemble any of his portraits." But a more ill-matched couple could hardly be imagined: Monsieur, a blatant homosexual, was interested in jewels, parties, and court intrigues; Madame was full of intellectual curiosity and loved to "reason" with learned men. She also enjoyed the outdoors and cared nothing about her own or anybody else's appearance, having concluded that she was and always would be homely. Monsieur once tried to put make-up on her face, but she simply could not stand it. Nonetheless, the couple managed to produce three children between 1673 and 1675; the oldest son died before the age of three.

Her son's death was only the first of the many blows that in 1682 prompted Madame to ask the King's permission to retire permanently to a convent. In these first years of her marriage, the cabal of Monsieur's friends and lovers, led by the Chevalier de Lorraine, the Marquis d'Effiat, and Madame de Grancey, had gained complete control over him. They eventually mounted a complicated intrigue, designed to prove that Madame was having an affair with a minor courtier, in order to discredit her with her husband and the King. Louis XIV did not believe a word of it—and neither does the reader of her letters—and he adamantly refused to let her leave the court: it was her duty as a member of the royal family and as his own sister-in-law, he pointed out, not to cause a public scandal by leaving. And since "duty" was a word she understood in her Protestant, German heart, she accepted a formal reconciliation with Monsieur and stayed—although in moments of great homesickness she sometimes talked of "simply running away." The marriage was over for all practical purposes. As we learn from Madame's letters, Monsieur had left her bed after the birth of their third child, rather to her relief, since she "did not like the business very much." In fact, she continued, if Monsieur had not squandered so much of *her* money on his boys, she would gladly have said to these young fellows, "You are welcome to gobble the peas; I don't like them."

Henceforth, Monsieur and Madame lived separate lives: he in a continual round of feasting, drinking, and partying; she, increasingly absorbed in her correspondence, in a small circle of French and German friends. Meanwhile, the children—Philippe, the future regent, and Elisabeth Charlotte, the future Duchesse de Lorraine—were growing up, their upbringing and especially the arrangement of their marriages giving rise to periodic crises.

The greatest source of Elisabeth Charlotte's unhappiness in these years before Monsieur's sudden death in 1701, however, was the devastation of her homeland, the Palatinate, to which Louis XIV laid claim in her name after the death of her father and her brother, who died childless in 1685. When their successor refused to accept French rule, Louis XIV and his minister of war, Louvois, instituted a policy of scorched earth, and the towns and the countryside of the Palatinate were systematically put to the torch. No pleading for mercy was of any avail, and Madame vividly describes her despair and the nightmares in which she saw her beloved Heidelberg, Mannheim, and Schwetzingen in flames.

On 10 June 1701 Monsieur suddenly died of a stroke. Madame and her children faced an uncertain future, for it looked as if Monsieur had ruined the family's finances, although recent research has established that, in fact, his and his advisers' investments had laid the foundations for the subsequent immense wealth of the house of Orléans.* Swallowing her pride, Elisabeth Charlotte sought the help of Madame de Maintenon, the King's mistress and

---

*Nancy N. Barber, "Philippe d'Orléans, Frère unique du Roi: Founder of the Family Fortune," *French Historical Studies* (Fall 1983).

secretly wedded wife—whom she detested—to obtain the King's largesse, which would provide the means to maintain her and her children in the position to which their rank entitled them. She felt that she had to stay in France and at the court since her "calling" and her destiny had brought her there. In the years between the death of Monsieur and that of Louis XIV in 1715, Madame lived almost in retirement in the midst of the court, but her eyes and ears, like those of the Duc de Saint-Simon, were wide open, and she recorded everything—daily events, the weather, illnesses, deaths, scandals, anecdotes, unusual occurrences, her own reading—in an increasingly prodigious correspondence.

After the death of Louis XIV, her son became Regent of the realm. Many courtiers now cultivated her in hopes of gaining the Regent's favor, but Madame steadfastly refused to meddle in affairs of State because "I have never learned the art of governing . . . and am much too old to learn such a difficult thing" and also because "this kingdom, to its detriment, has been ruled for too long by old and young women." Her son's regency was a source of great maternal pride but also of constant anxiety for her, for the country's public finances were in terrible disorder after Louis's many disastrous wars; moreover, there was dissension within the royal house itself and constant threat of rebellion from the great lords of the realm (*les Grands*) who, as Elisabeth Charlotte put it, "have always gotten too big for their breeches when there was a regency."

By now she had grown quite old by the standards of her time, and though for many years she had enjoyed remarkably good health—in spite of her "monstrously fat shape" and no doubt because of her avoidance of the court's medical services—her health began to fail. During a "precautionary" bleeding her barber fainted, causing him to bandage the arm improperly so that the wound opened twice, with additional loss of blood each time. It was the beginning of the end. Despite her weakness, Elisabeth Charlotte attended the coronation of young King Louis XV at Reims, where she saw her daughter and her grandchildren of Lorraine one last time. A few weeks later, on 8 December 1722, she died at the age of seventy, "without regrets and without grief, happy to leave this world in the hope that my Redeemer, who died and rose to heaven for me, will not forsake me in my final hour."

The life of this German princess at the French court, then, was not a happy one, despite the high rank in the court hierarchy she enjoyed as a member of the immediate royal family. The first rank in this hierarchy was occupied, of course, by the King, the absolute master over the entire royal family. The Queen and the Dauphin also had ceremonial precedence over everyone else. As the wife of Monsieur, the King's brother, Elisabeth Charlotte ranked among the "Sons and Daughters of France," along with the King's younger children and his first cousin, Mademoiselle de Montpensier (the "Grande Mademoiselle") a granddaughter of Henri IV. Certain honorific privileges, such as the right to have a military honor guard or that of standing on a special altar cloth during mass, "do not go further than to the Sons and Daughters of France," Madame proudly informs her half-sister. This rank gave Madame precedence over the next category, the "Princes of the Blood," which included the members of the Bourbon, Condé, and Conti families, all of whom were descended in the direct male line from Hughues Capet. The lowest category of the "Great" living at the court consisted of the "Dukes and Peers," scions of houses that had held the kingdom's great fiefs in the past, as well as the "Foreign Princes," such as the Dukes of Lorraine, Savoy, Mantua, and Rohan (descendants of the House of Brittany). Toward the end of Louis XIV's reign, the King's illegitimate children, traditionally ranked between the Princes of the Blood and the Dukes and Peers, were elevated to the rank of "True Princes of the Royal Blood" and even declared eligible for the succession to the throne. This royal decision profoundly shocked Madame and that *homo hierarchicus,* the Duc de Saint-Simon.

Also in residence at the court were the highest military officers—marshals, admirals, and so forth—and the great officers of the State—ministers, chancellors, secretaries of State, controllers-general, intendants of finance, and so on. Furthermore, all the members of the royal family, from the King to the Princes of the Blood, had separate households, each with a full complement of "officers": almoners, intendants, masters of the horse, masters of the hunt, mistresses of the wardrobe, ladies-in-waiting, equerries, master pantlers, coachmen, valets, lackeys, and dozens of others. All these people owned their offices and usually served *par quartier,* that is, three out of twelve months, so that each function was divided among four office holders. Foreign visitors, ambassadors, ordinary courtiers looking for royal or princely favors, musicians, actors, workmen, tradesmen, and adventurers came and went, and it has been estimated that more than 15,000 persons lived and worked at the great palace of Versailles in the heyday of Louis XIV's reign.*

Versailles, however, was only the principal residence of the court. Whenever its restless master, following the pattern of his ancestors, decided to visit another of the royal chateaux—Paris, Saint Germain, Marly, Fontainebleau—the entire royal family and the more prominent courtiers had to follow, whether it was convenient or not. This policy was actually more than

*The preceding two paragraphs are based on Gillette Ziegler, *At the Court of Versailles: Eyewitness Reports from the Reign of Louis XIV,* trans. Simon Watson (New York, 1968), 32–33. See also Nancy Mitford, *The Sun King* (London, 1966).

a royal whim; in the aftermath of the great rebellion of the Fronde, which had pitted the high aristocracy against the King under the leadership of his own cousin, it was essential to keep tight control over potential rebels at all times. It is true that each branch of the royal family was free to spend time at its private residence, which is why many letters in this volume are dated from Saint Cloud, the sumptuous property of the Orléans family; but no member of the royal family was permitted to travel without the King. Elisabeth Charlotte thus never returned to Germany to visit her family, nor was she permitted to visit her married daughter in Lorraine or even to travel to a hot-water spa to seek relief for her arthritic knees. This was one of the issues that repeatedly prompted her to complain bitterly about the "tyranny" under which she was obliged to live. The royal family also owed strict obedience to the King in all matters pertaining to major appointments in their households and especially to the arrangement of marriages. Not that Elisabeth Charlotte objected to the principles of royal absolutism and paternalism, even as they affected the King's family; she only felt that Louis XIV was often unreasonable and misguided, namely by "old women and wicked priests," in the application of these sacred principles.

Her German upbringing had imbued her with a most inflexible conception of the hierarchical order of society—princes were princes, nobles were nobles, bourgeois were bourgeois, peasants were peasants, and so forth—and although she respected a "good honest person" as long as he stayed within the station to which he was born, "mishmash" of any kind was anathema to her, for it amounted to a rebellion against the order God had instituted in the world. We can therefore believe her claim that her life was ruined when this kind of "disorder" was brought into her own family through her son's marriage to Mademoiselle de Blois, an illegitimate daughter of Louis XIV and Madame de Montespan. Her unreasonable, visceral hatred for Madame de Maintenon can be explained in part by the Maintenon's role in arranging this marriage, which "the old trollop" favored as the former governess of the Montespan's children. In addition, Madame found it deeply galling to see this woman of "low birth" occupying the position of uncrowned queen of France; yet one suspects that these two women—the robust, outspoken Madame with her keen sense of the comic, and the fragile, calculating Maintenon with her profoundly ascetic piety—would have been hostile to each other under any circumstance.

Part of the routine for the royal family was daily attendence at mass. In writing to her German, Protestant relatives, Elisabeth Charlotte could rarely forego some irreverent remark about the cult of the saints, about the "eternal blabbing of Latin," and about her knack for escaping the excruciating boredom of sermons (especially in the afternoon) by promptly falling asleep. She considered the Catholicism practiced at the French court shallow, deploring the ignorance in religious matters she observed all around her; at the same time, she made gentle fun of her pietistic German half-sister Amelise, who assumed that French Catholics were not really Christians at all. Although Madame had many harsh things to say about the "confounded vermin of priests, who will ruin everything in which they become involved," she never stopped going to mass, which was part of excerising her "*métier* of being Madame"; nor did she ever stop arguing with her succession of confessors. Her letters make it abundantly clear that she remained a Protestant at heart throughout her life—not in any narrow, sectarian sense (both Dr. Luther and Calvin, she felt, would have done more good if they had gone on teaching without causing an uproar) but in her earnest endeavor to understand and accept the will of God. As a good Protestant she regularly read her German Bible, sang the Lutheran hymns in private, and speculated in her own way about such things as the meaning of certain biblical passages, reincarnation, and the immortality of the soul. She was troubled by this last concept, being, as she put it, so coarse that she could not conceive of enjoying anything beautiful without the help of her senses.

Many of the letters in this volume are inspired by pure nostalgia and pure homesickness. A place or a person casually mentioned by Madame's correspondents conjures up a flood of memories: where to find the best huckleberries in Heidelberg; the view from her window at Schwetzingen; what fun it was to deceive her governess; how her father punished a presumed caprice of hers (see, for example, the appalling episode described in the letter of 1 January 1719); or how she loved to read, sitting on a fallen log near a bubbling stream, sometimes interrupted by peasants who came to talk to her, and how this was "more entertaining than the duchesses in the *cercle*." To the reader these memories convey a glimpse into the style of life at a small German court that complements the more immediate view of the splendors and miseries of Versailles and Paris.

One learns, for example, that Liselotte was brought up bilingually, unlike, for example, Frederick the Great, who spoke mainly French as a child. Sometimes the reported conversations with Liselotte's father, her aunt, or her governesses are cited in German, sometimes in French. One also learns that certain courtiers spoke a dialect, and that this was perfectly acceptable, although the eternal *met verlöff* ("by your leave") of a certain Frau von Wolzogen is always cited in these letters with a smile, as it were. Elisabeth Charlotte's constant use of proverbs and proverbial sayings, her familiarity with fairytales, popular farces, and almanacs, and her attitude toward medical science indicate that the court at Heidelberg was imbued with what we now call popular culture, which, as we shall see, meshed at many points with learned culture.

Proverbs and proverbial expressions occur at every turn in Elisabeth Charlotte's letters, and the indexes of the scholarly editions have long entries referring to them. Some of these, we learn from the author herself, came from the "writing books" from which Liselotte, like every literate child of her age, learned reading and writing. In this category are proverbs like "What can't be cured must be endured," or "Stretch your legs according to your coverlets." But surely a proverb like "He who dies of threats must be buried with donkey farts" did not come from any writing book! Many others have a distinctly rural flavor, which also places them in an oral tradition. "Patience will get the better of buttermilk," for example, is not immediately understandable to modern readers, unless they know that the farmer's wife must turn the handle of the churn for a long time before the buttermilk releases the butter; to be as tired of something "as if one had been stuffed with it by the spoonful" refers to the force-feeding of geese; "When the goat gets too frisky she goes dancing on the ice and breaks a leg" is applied to people who overstep the bounds of common sense; and to "throw a sausage at a side of bacon" uses the image of a thief in a smokehouse to express the idea of giving up a small thing in order to obtain a more valuable one. A busy person is "as busy as a mouse in her nest," and a person in bad humor—including Louis XIV and Madame herself—is "as cranky as a wall-bug." Even as aristocratic a concern as the disapproval of mismarriages is couched in terms of the proverb "Mousedroppings always want to mix with the pepper"; this saying was so well known that Elisabeth Charlotte could end a long complaint about her daughter-in-law's personal shortcomings by saying, "and to think that with all of this she is nothing more than mousedroppings, I must confess is a bit upsetting." Indeed, she frequently referred to her son's wife as "our mousedroppings." These proverbs and proverbial expressions seem to flow spontaneously from Madame's pen, yet a humorous little aside shows an awareness of their use as a literary device: "I am citing so many proverbs that Your Grace will end up thinking that I am Sancho Panza; I already have his shape, and perhaps his simplemindedness as well."

Fairytales were another genre that was appreciated both by the people and the high aristocracy. "I can remember more than a dozen [fairytales] that were told to me in my youth, and I remember them better than other, serious things I have heard," writes Elisabeth Charlotte. In addition to the orally transmitted fairytales, she also knew and enjoyed written fairytales, such as *Rübezahl* or *Mélusine*, as well as the many French collections of fairytales that burst upon the scene starting with Charles Perrault's *Contes de ma mère l'oie* in 1694 (which, incidentally, were dedicated to Madame's daughter).

Twenty volumes of fairytales, most of them written by women, were published in France between 1694 and 1702, and Madame, a voracious reader, was well prepared by upbringing and temperament to enjoy them. Images from fairytales often helped her to characterize people around her. A particularly pretty example is her allusion to the story of Mélusine: "When the women wear wimples, they look just like Mélusine as I saw her painted in an old book. . . . I think that in the end the train on their skirts will turn into a snake, as she did. If this happened to the Grancey [a member of the *cabal* that troubled her so much] I would not be surprised at all, for she already has a snake's and adder's tongue with which she stings me only too often." Another person reminds her of "a woman who had been a cat and jumped out of her husband's bed to catch a mouse."

Familiarity with fairytales may have shaped Elisabeth Charlotte's life and attitudes in an even more profound way. As Bruno Bettelheim shows in *The Uses of Enchantment,* the universe of the fairytale is an ordered one, where good always wins out over evil and where the highest reward for virtue is to become a king or a queen. Kingship thus has a magic aura, and for all of Madame's intimate knowledge of the personal shortcomings and the flaws of the many crowned heads she had known in her life, and despite the realization, on a rational level, that "a crown, though it shines beautifully, is often a heavy burden and causes its wearer headaches," this magic never paled in her imagination. For a modern reader it is almost painful to read her description of the lackluster, dull, and fainthearted widowed Dauphin, presumably the next king of France, followed by bitter regrets that intrigues have prevented the arrangement of a marriage between this Dauphin and her own daughter. In the fairytale world, moreover, the King stands for absolute power, and Elisabeth Charlotte was quite prepared at times to see Louis XIV's power in magical terms: At Marly his will could transform a stagnant pond into a lovely, full-grown forest between one visit and the next and make pools full of beautiful, shining fish appear overnight. Indeed, the King would have the power to right all wrongs, if only he could be extricated from the evil influence of "old women and wicked priests," rather like the fairytale prince who, bewitched and turned into a bear or a loathsome toad, is brought back to his true self through the love of a true princess or a faithful servant. Liselotte had fantasies of "opening his eyes" and making him see the errors of his ways, and this complex mixture of mythic thinking about the magic of kingship and devotion to the prince who rightfully occupied the highest rank in the God-given hierarchy may well account for Madame's unwavering devotion to Louis XIV, of whose foibles and shortcomings in real life she was only too well aware. Facile gossip about a romantic attachment certainly fails to do justice to her feelings for him.

Popular German plays (*Volksschauspiele*), like the "Comedy of Dr.

Faustus," and farces (*Possenspiele*), performed in dialect and featuring such characters as *Pickelhering* the clown or *Mutter Anneke,* were also part of a German princess's heritage. They were performed at the court of Heidelberg, and our duchess could still cite lengthy passages twenty years after her arrival in France "even though I do not rehearse them very often."

Popular beliefs concerning witches and ghosts were also well known to Elisabeth Charlotte, but for the most part she did not share them. François I, for example, who was said to haunt the château of Fontainebleau, "never did me the honor of showing himself to me," and she gently made fun of Lenor, the friend of her youth who spent several months with her every year: "She says I cannot see ghosts because I do not want to believe that they might come; this, she says, annoys the ghosts and therefore they do not want to come to me." As for witches, "it is a foolish opinion to think that women and men can hide in the clouds and make hail in order to ruin everything." She was less sure about certain other occult phenomena, however, such as the gift of "second sight," the "marking" of an unborn child by what its mother has seen, or the ability of the dying to prophesy. Whenever such phenomena came to her attention, she examined them one by one, sometimes accepting and sometimes rejecting them. When one of her German correspondents sent her an almanac indicating, among other things, the best day of the year for a bleeding, she tried to take comfort in this prediction but anticipated that the bleeding planned for that day would make her feel terrible, as usual.

A profound distrust of medical science, coupled with a belief in the healing powers of nature, was another attitude Elisabeth Charlotte shared with the people. One of the first pieces of gossip Madame de Sevigné reported about the new Madame on her arrival in France in 1671 was that "she has no use for doctors and even less for medicines. . . . When her doctor was presented to her, she said that she did not need him, that she had never been purged or bled, and that when she is not feeling well she goes for a walk and cures herself by exercise." This was perfectly true, and the many medical disasters Madame had to report in her letters only confirmed her in her attitude. Again and again she told her correspondents how she had cured herself by exercise, diet, and simple remedies, by drinking lots of water and having patience. "My illnesses must go away as they have come, for I cannot bring myself to take medicines and go in for doctoring." On one occasion she chides her half-sister for experimenting with too many remedies; "this is not what you have learned at Heidelberg." The remedies that Elisabeth Charlotte did recommend show what she had learned at Heidelberg. Here are just a few samples: a few spoonfuls of Mosel wine is a light and not disagreeable medicine; English flannel put on arthritic knees is better than smearing on the smelly stuff that the barbers give you; black bread with laurel baked into it and held against a throbbing ear as soon as the bread comes out of the oven will break up an abscess; an egg beaten with boiling water and cinnamon and sugar will keep a cough down during the night. Cataplasms made with frogs' eggs, unfortunately, were not available in France, where the apothecaries carried nothing but clysters, quinine, emetics, and opium. However, Elisabeth Charlotte was even selective in her approval of popular remedies from Germany and would rather have died than drunk "cow piss" or rubbed her hurting knees with human fat.

Given this attitude, it is no wonder that Madame fought a running and, as it turned out, ultimately losing battle with the court physicians, whose art for the most part consisted of prescribing such violent remedies as bleeding, purging, emetics, and antimony, a highly toxic metal compound similar to arsenic. Well might she mock them for claiming that she, Madame, was sicker than anyone else because she did not even know it; when it was time to bleed and purge her as a precautionary measure, especially as she grew older, she was put under so much pressure by the doctors and everyone else at court that she eventually had to give in "just to have peace." But the reason for her compliance may well have been deeper. It has recently been argued by Emmanuel Le Roy Ladurie that at the court of Louis XIV, bleeding, and especially purging, fulfilled the function of a ritual of royal purity, comparable to the constant washing and bathing incumbent on the highest Brahmin circles in the Indian caste system. Perhaps this is why Elisabeth Charlotte, imbued with the mystique of kingship, felt compelled to transcend her own common sense, as it were, and to submit once again to what was represented to her as her duty.

Liselotte von der Pfalz has sometimes been characterized, especially by French authors, as a "child of nature," an earthy, headstrong, if not altogether coarse, character, totally out of place in the refined atmosphere of France's classical age. German authors of the nineteenth century, on the contrary, have praised her for upholding the purity of German womanhood amidst the profound corruption of the French court. Both assessments must certainly be taken with more than a grain of salt. In many respects, Madame adhered passionately to the ideals of *bienséance* of *la cour et la ville,* and often her undeniable *furor teutonicus* was directed precisely at those who failed to live up to these ideals. She railed, for example, against women of the court, like her daughter-in-law, who were too lazy to have themselves laced up properly and went around in loose-fitting gowns; she also frequently asked persons of lower rank who were sitting down in her presence to stand up, and she was shocked to hear that certain gentlemen of the court were in the habit of sprawling on the settees at Marly. Her castigation of truly dissolute behavior—"gorging, guzzling, whoring," and worse—has been likened by no less a critic than Sainte-Beuve to the stern condemnations of the Old Testament patriarchs.

In keeping with the ideal of the *honnête homme,* which to some extent she liked to apply to herself, and with her own temperament, Madame was not learned. Learning, she felt, was a good thing for a person of quality but had to be balanced by social accomplishments, "lest it come out too doctorish." She frequently protested her ignorance in philosophy, religion, arts and letters, and affairs of State, but it is obvious that she was filled with a lifelong intellectual curiosity. She deeply regretted that no member of the royal family was permitted to leave the kingdom or even to travel at all without the King, for she would have loved to visit foreign places, "especially Rome . . . because of all the paintings and antiquities there"; and when her half-brother was in Greece, she asked him to send her a detailed description because she was "extremely curious to find out what *Athene* and *Corintho* look like now." She "could have listened all day long" to a much-traveled merchant who told fantastic stories about Egypt and Judea. As it was, she had to make do with little outings to local exhibits of "fine Indian curiosities," excavations under Parisian churches, or private art galleries. She had her own portrait gallery and print collection and was a knowledgeable collector of medals; toward the end of her life she proudly reported that her series of Roman emperors was complete—every piece in good condition, too—and she even exhibited that telltale mark of the true collector, the glee at having obtained an important item at a reasonable price!

Madame's interest in literature was nurtured above all by the theater, and this was one pleasure in which she could indulge to her heart's content, since her schedule usually included three or four plays, operas, or ballets a week. "I am never tired of the verses of Corneille or Racine, or of the comedies of Molière, as long as they are played well." Unlike in church, she never slept in the theater, she informed her half-sister, but did so quite often in the opera. It was a heavy blow indeed to have to forego the theater during the two years of formal mourning for Monsieur, and Madame de Maintenon's attempt to have stage plays forbidden was just one more black mark against her. Many of Elisabeth Charlotte's letters include critiques of new plays and of the actors who performed them, along with her personal reactions. She found it quite natural to be moved to tears by a tragedy, but her likes and dislikes were highly personal. *Tartuffe* was her favorite among Molière's comedies because of her intense dislike of the *dévôts* at court, and *Bérénice* was her least favorite among Racine's plays because she felt that Bérénice's conduct was unworthy of a princess: "I do not like it that Bérénice still loves Titus when she sees that he is tired of her and sends her away with his rival. All the howling she sets up about this makes me impatient. She should just simply have taken and King of Commagene and despised Titus.''

Despite Madame's many self-disparaging remarks about her lack of sophistication, her ignorance, and her naiveté, the reader soon becomes aware of Elisabeth Charlotte's familiarity with many of the principal works of European literature of the past as well as with the ''bestsellers'' of her own time. Her letters contain references to Ovid's *Metamorphoses,* to Virgil, Ariosto, Petrarch, Montaigne, Rabelais, and Cervantes, to *Amadis de Gaule,* Andreas Gryphius, and to the fashionable novels of her distant cousin, Duke Anton Ulrich of Braunschweig-Wolfenbüttel. Even Shakespeare's plays, which were performed—albeit in more or less popularized translations—by English comedians at German courts and in Holland throughout the seventeenth century were known to her, as the allusion to ''shrewish Kate'' indicates.

Elisabeth Charlotte always had a lively interest in philosophy and theology. One letter included in the present collection (28 July 1701) describes how, as a young girl, she reduced her religion teacher to silence by her persistent questioning, and we also hear that in the days when she was on reasonably good terms with Monsieur, he would bring her philosophers, savants, and theologians so that she could ''reason'' with them. But her interest in philosophy and theology, like her appraisals of literature, was very personal in character: she wanted to know above all about the immortality of the soul because the idea of total extinction, which she considered a distinct possibility, was abhorrent to her. It would be most reassuring, she wrote, to think that she would meet all her loved ones, including her little dogs, in the next world. But neither the writings of the mystic Franz Mercurius Helmont nor those of the philosopher Leibniz convinced her that human reason is capable of fathoming the ultimate secrets, and so she fell back on a simple faith in God, ''who knows what is best for me.'' Meanwhile, however, she consistently advocated the use of reason and common sense in all matters pertaining to life in this world, and she was fascinated and delighted by the new scientific and technical discoveries of her age, such as magnifying glasses and microscopes, ''in which a louse looks so big,'' and which would enable man to understand nature better. She heartily approved of her son's spending considerable amounts of money on scientific apparatus and of the experiments he conducted in his own laboratory with Monsieur Humberg, his physician and a noted chemist.

Liselotte von der Pfalz, then, was more than a child of nature who poured out her impressions and her feelings pell-mell. Hers was a rich life of the mind and the imagination that demanded expression. She was, in a word, what we today would call a "closet writer." Frustrated in many aspects of her outward life—the most profound frustration, perhaps, being that she was born a woman rather than a man—Madame increasingly withdrew into quasi-solitude, spending many hours of each day alone in her apartments, playing with her spaniels, reading, looking at her copper engravings, and writing. "Writing," she declared, "is my principal occupation," and although this was true for a number of French aristocratic women—Madame de Sévigné, Madame de La Fayette, Mademoiselle de Scudéry, Madame de Sablé, Comtesse d'Aulnoye, Comtesse de Murat, and others—it would not do for a member of the royal family to publish anything. And so she wrote letters.

"Not a day passes," she wrote in 1707, "that I do not write at least four letters, and on Sundays I often write twelve." She wrote when she was not feeling well ("I have a headache today, yet I have already written five letters, not counting this one, and must do two more"); she wrote while waiting for her carriage; as a young woman she wrote while her children were beating on drums right next to her desk; later she wrote while people were playing cards in her room, occasionally interrupting herself to give someone advice on how to play a hand; she wrote at five o'clock in the morning and at midnight; she wrote when it was so cold that she could barely hold the pen and when it was so hot that her sweaty hand stuck to the paper. She wrote her last letter on her deathbed. Many of these letters describe her daily routine, her animals, her food and drink, the weather, the view from the various châteaux where she lived. Her "*métier* of being Madame," however, involved participation in formal ceremonies such as royal weddings, baptisms, funerals, and receptions of foreign dignitaries, as well as in the royal hunts; but one has the impression that all these contacts with the world served primarily to gather material for her writing. "I must tell Your Grace something pretty that my son told us today at table," she might write, or "yesterday at table they talked about . . ." or "Not much is new here at court right now, but one hears some strange stories from Paris." Thus she was always on the lookout for funny, touching, or simply unusual stories, which she would lovingly polish and send to her correspondents. A new face at court, brought by the arrival of the ten-year-old Marie-Adélaïde de Savoie, the future bride of the King's grandson, the Duc de Bourgogne, is the occasion for a full-length *portrait,* a genre much in vogue in French literature at that time. Another *portrait* is prompted by the departure of the Duc d'Anjou, the King's second grandson, who became King of Spain in 1700, and this time Madame adds the portraits of all his brothers for good measure. There are several *portraits* of Madame's son and daughter as children, adolescents, and adults, and the most artful of these is a character sketch of her son, twenty-six years old at the time, couched in terms of a well known fairytale: My son, Elisabeth Charlotte says, is like the child in the tale of the fairies who are asked to the christening: six of them present him with wonderful qualities, but the seventh, who has not been invited, vows to pursue him throughout his life with such hostility that all his good qualities will come to nought. The result is a playful yet also deadly serious display of maternal pride and maternal concern about a son who fails to live up to his potential and permits himself to be led astray by bad company. It should be added that the most merciless portrait of anyone's physical appearance is her own (see 22 August 1698 and 10 October 1699).

Motivated at first, no doubt, by homesickness and the need to stay in touch with family and friends in Germany, Elisabeth Charlotte soon developed a great facility for writing. "It does not cost me much trouble to write," she assures one of her correspondents in 1706, "for I do not ever write anything that is difficult and demands a lot of thinking about." Yet one must realize that by that time she had lived in France for more than thirty years and spoke and heard almost nothing but French in her everyday life. Perfectly capable of speaking and writing in French (even French poetry, "all of it very bad"), she insisted on writing in German to her German correspondents, some of whom initially felt that it would be more elegant and more appropriate to address Her Royal Highness in French. It is a measure of her nostalgic patriotism as well as of her seriousness as a writer that she wanted to do her share to counteract the growing degradation of the German language about which Leibniz spoke so forcefully in his *Exhortation to the Germans to Make Better Use of Their Reason and Their Language*. Elisabeth Charlotte had lived in France and close to some of the greatest French writers of her age long enough to have absorbed some of their preoccupation with language as the expression of a great culture. But it was her genius to understand that writing good German was an entirely different matter from writing good French.

The German language had not undergone the "classical muting" that Karl Vossler has detected in the language of Racine. In Germany the outstanding model for good writing was still Martin Luther's Bible translation in which Luther, as he said himself, "kept his eye on the people's mouth." Elisabeth Charlotte often told her correspondents that she read her German Bible almost every day, and indeed many biblical citations and images are there to prove it. Elisabeth Charlotte understood and practiced what Leibniz pointed out in his theoretical treatise, namely, that the German language was rich and forceful in its ability to express "everything that is apprehended with the five senses and is also known to the common man, particularly in matters concerning the body and the arts and crafts." Leibniz deplored "a certain decline" in the German language in dealing with abstract moral and psychological concepts, and one notes that Elisabeth Charlotte often uses French when speaking about such matters: *éloquent, debauchiert, politesse, particularité, affectation* are some of the words that occur again and again in her letters. Yet Elisabeth Charlotte was extremely inventive in using the imagery of the human body to convey emotions or abstractions: The sight of the King's bastards "makes her blood boil," the French way of bringing up children "makes her burst out of her skin," the persecutions to which she is subjected "squeeze the very marrow out of her bones," two people who are very close are "but one soul in two bodies," her father had her "on his hands" (literally "around his neck"), a quiet person "never opens his mouth," the priests "cannot see further than their noses," her accident has "loaded her down" with a lot of tiresome visitors, on Easter one is "stuck" in church all day long, and the list could go on and on. In speaking of Elisabeth Charlotte's style, it should be pointed out that there are times when her anger and her frustration are so great that her syntax falls apart; the words tumble forth so quickly that the author loses control over them. The translator feels that such occasional weaknesses are characteristic of the Duchess's style and has therefore made no attempt to "correct" them.

Her claim to the contrary notwithstanding, Elisabeth Charlotte did think about the use of language. Sometimes there is a note of the writer's frustration: "this cannot be described as comically as he did it." Her greatest personal worry was, of course, that she might forget her German altogether, and in later years she realized that the German language had changed since her departure. She thought about language in a more impersonal manner as well. "It is true that French is shorter than German," she wrote, and: "In my day it was already the custom to mix French words with the German ones; I sometimes do this myself, for after all one must follow the custom in this. But what annoys me is when it is done from *affectation*. This last word I cannot possibly say differently in German; in fact, I do not think there is another word for it in German." Yet as late as 1715 she reported with obvious pleasure that "Herr Leibenitz, to whom I write sometimes, flatters my vanity by saying that I write German rather well; that is quite a comfort to me."

Remembering Leibniz's postulate that good writing in German involves the five senses, one can cite many examples for the use of each of them in the Duchess's letters. One is struck above all by her keen interest in color. For all of her professed dislike of ceremonies, she loved to describe them; partly, to be sure, to show their folly, but partly, no doubt, because of their visual appeal. A ceremony in which she received the formal condolences of the King and Queen of England following the death of Monsieur, for example, is a picture in black and white: black dress, white band around the forehead, black belt, white wimple, black veil, black cape lined with white ermine, black-draped room and bed, white candles; and although "all of this looked perfectly awful," she describes it in exquisite detail. It takes a true writer to transform such a stressful occasion into a memorable image. In the letter of 17 September 1719, reporting the ceremonial installation of her granddaughter as abbess of Chelles, Madame expressly calls attention to the "amusing" constrast between forty black-clad nuns and the colorful, magnificently laid table at which they are eating lunch. One of the prettiest examples of the use of color is found in the letter of 23 November 1719, in which the thick fog Madame sees from her window at the château of Saint Cloud naturally leads her to a description of her friend Mademoiselle de Chausseraye who, pale and wan from a long illness, tall and thin, and clad in white from head to foot, looks like a ghost. The examples cited here suggest that Elisabeth Charlotte's uncompromising, forceful personality was attracted to strong visual impressions, to the contrast between black and white, black and color, or to unmitigated white. Similarly, she was delighted by the vivid primary colors of the famous carp in the pools at Marly.

With respect to hearing, her pleasure was also sharpened by contrast; in the letter of 26 April 1704, for example, the song of the nightingales is "all the sweeter after one has heard the great noise of dogs and hunting horns," and one of her objections to the singing of Latin in Catholic churches was the monotony of the Latin chants, "nothing but vowels, like aaa eee ooo iii, which is enough to make one burst out of one's skin with pure impatience." The sense of smell, too, is evoked frequently, usually in the negative sense. Elisabeth Charlotte refers to several people as "smelly," or even "stinking as he-goats," and she associates Monsieur's strong perfumes with his memory long after his death. Except for one reference to the pleasure of scratching an itching back, the evocation of tactile sensations is curiously lacking in these letters, perhaps owing to Madame's intense dislike of intimate personal contact, particularly sex. The sense of taste, on the other hand, is celebrated in vivid commentary about food and drink.

A lively intelligence, a rich cultural heritage, a strong sense of self, and keen sensual perceptions were the mainsprings of Elisabeth Charlotte's art as a writer. If historians appreciate her letters as a valuable, albeit not always reliable, source, it is precisely because of their literary character. Especially in her later years, Elisabeth Charlotte constantly related real-life situations to situations she had read about or seen in the theater. "This reminds me of the opera of Alcestis," she might write, or "this strikes me like watching a tragedy." Conversely, as we have seen, she also applied her personal standards to such literary protagonists as Racine's Bérénice. Imperceptibly, life and literature merged into one for this lonely woman.

Indeed, the very relationships with her correspondents increasingly became a kind of literary fiction. Except in the case of her beloved "Ma Tante," Electress Sophie of Hanover, who had played an important role in forming the character and deciding the destiny of young Liselotte, Elisabeth Charlotte had only very tenuous personal relations with her correspondents. Some of them, like Freiherr von Goertz, occasionally called on Her Royal Highness, while others, like Herr and Frau von Harling, never saw her again after she left Germany. Most striking is the absence of personal contact with three of her principal correspondents. Her half-sisters, the Raugräfinnen Luise and Amelise, were children when Elisabeth Charlotte was married, and in view of the duchess's constant assurances that they were "near and dear" to her, one is rather surprised to come upon the draft of one of "dearest Luise's" letters to Elisabeth Charlotte: replete with such phrases as "humbly begging Your Royal Highness's forgiveness for presuming to express my pleasure at the recovery of His Royal Highness, the Duc de Chartres," it suggests that the social realities did not correspond to the fiction of a warm personal relationship. As for Caroline of Wales, with whom the duchess entered into a voluminous correspondence after the death of the Electress, Madame had never met her at all, and the correspondence was initiated as part of the Regent's policy of seeking closer ties with England. Yet for many years Elisabeth Charlotte shared her most intimate thoughts and memories, all the big and little events of her existence, with these three women.

"Writing is my principal occupation," then, is an understatement. In fact, it was Elisabeth Charlotte's whole life, her way of mastering a destiny that was forced upon her by transforming her loneliness, her frustrations, and her anger into literature.

ELBORG FORSTER

✣ Cast of Principal Characters

(Recipients of letters are indicated by *)

ELISABETH CHARLOTTE'S RELATIVES IN GERMANY

Karl Ludwig, Elector of the Palatinate* (1617–80), Elisabeth Charlotte's father: "Papa." The oldest surviving son of the Palatine Elector and "Winter King" of Bohemia and his wife Elizabeth Stuart, Karl Ludwig was brought up in precarious circumstances during his parents' exile in Holland. He did, however, receive an excellent education at Leyden University, where he engaged in the study of philosophy, theology, law, history, literature, and even mathematics. Fluent in German, French, Italian, English, and Latin, Karl Ludwig had a lifelong interest in arts and letters and occasionally referred to himself as "a prince and a philosopher." Finally restored to his position as Elector of the Palatinate by the Peace of Westphalia (1648), which ended the Thirty Years' War, he devoted all of his energy to rebuilding a devastated country. His tolerant attitude in religious matters proved a great asset in this undertaking, since his protection of various sects, such as the Anabaptists or the "Sabbatarians," attracted settlers to refurbish the Palatine population. Parsimonious in his administration and in his personal life, Karl Ludwig nonetheless made great efforts to bring renowned scholars to his court and to Heidelberg University.

A man of fierce temper (during the deliberations over electing a new emperor in 1685, he threw an inkwell at the envoy of the Bavarian Elector), Karl Ludwig was admired but also feared by his family. His legitimate spouse, who fought him, was publicly repudiated by him for her "willful, stubborn, and disobedient" behavior; his morganatic wife cringed at every reprimand; his son and successor was so terrified that he was unable to discuss any serious subject with his father; and Liselotte herself, although she "passionately loved" her father, reported that "he knew how to make himself feared." Exhausted by his long struggle to keep his country out of the clutches of the *"Roy peu chrétien,"* embittered by the failure to receive help from the Emperor and the other German princes, and disappointed by the incompetence of his son and heir, who did not even seem able and willing to produce an heir to the Electorate, Karl Ludwig died at the age of sixty-two.

Charlotte of Hessen-Kassel (1627–86), Karl Ludwig's repudiated wife and Elisabeth Charlotte's mother. A rather hazy figure, Charlotte is rarely mentioned by her daughter. Unflattering anecdotes about her temper, her love of lavish expenditure, her selfishness, and her coquetry have come down to us from her husband's correspondence with his sister and his second wife. A few of Charlotte's own letters, written toward the end of her life, are whining in tone; but perhaps a repudiated wife, forsaken for a younger woman, separated from her children, and sent back to her family without status and without money had reason to feel sorry for herself.

Karl, Elector of the Palatinate* (1651–85), Elisabeth Charlotte's brother. Unlike his sister, Karl was a sickly and nervous child. Nevertheless, his father was determined to give him an upbringing that would make him physically and mentally tough. Among his tutors were the famous jurist Pufendorf and the diplomat Spanheim. But he was still treated as a child by his governor, Monsieur de Wattewille, who would strike the sixteen-year-old when the prince's hair was tousled or his clothing in disorder. Above all, Karl was completely crushed by his father's forceful personality, much to the disgust of the latter, who would have liked to live on an easy, comfortable footing with his son. In his late twenties Karl became extremely pious, also to the disgust of his father. Upon becoming Elector in 1680, Karl restored the strictest Calvinist discipline to the local church, relaxed the financial discipline imposed by his predecessor, and turned a deaf ear to the pleas of his half-brothers and -sisters. Ruled by his favorites, the court preacher and his personal physician, and suffering from consumption, Karl was unable to stand up against the French incursions. He died without heirs at the age of thirty-four.

Wilhelmine Ernestine of Denmark* (1650–1706), Karl's wife. Daughter of the King of Denmark, Wilhelmine Ernestine was considered an excellent match for the Electoral Prince of the Palatinate. She was a reticent and rather plain young woman, and her stand-offish attitude toward the Elector's second wife and her children soon earned her the hostility of her father-in-law. She was also blamed for failing to produce a child, even though indications are that her husband considered sexual intercourse dangerous to his physical and spiritual health. Elisabeth Charlotte's letters to her show that the young princess took refuge from her many misfortunes in a deep, ascetic piety.

Luise von Degenfeld, Raugräfin von der Pfalz* (1637–77), morganatic wife of Elisabeth Charlotte's father. As a modest, twenty-year-old lady-in-waiting to Electress Charlotte, Luise von Degenfeld, daughter of a respectable old noble family, was caught in the whirlwind of the Elector's passion for her. Fearing that her reputation was ruined anyway, she agreed to the morganatic marriage, a decision that was made a little easier when the Elector found a pastor who was willing to admit her to the sacraments and to unite the couple in marriage. Her married life with the jealous, moody, and domineering Karl Ludwig cannot have been easy; the published correspondence between the couple affords frequent glimpses of jealous reproaches by the Elector, humble justifications by his wife, and hurt feelings on both sides. The Raugräfin died at the age of thirty-nine during the birth of her fourteenth child. She left eight living children, among them:

Raugraf Karl Ludwig* (1658–88), Elisabeth Charlotte's favorite half-brother: "Carllutz," "black-curls." Fourteen years old when Elisabeth Charlotte was married, Carllutz was a member of the party that accompanied the bride to the French frontier. In subsequent years he visited the French court several times but, to the disappointment of his family, was not given a military commission in the French army. He eventually commanded a regiment in the Imperial army and died of fever during the siege of Negroponte, deeply mourned by his half-sister.

Raugräfin Karoline* (1659–96), married to Count Mainhard von Schomberg, the scion of a prestigious military family, who established himself in England. Elisabeth Charlotte had little contact with this branch of the family.

Raugräfin Luise* (1661–1733). Intelligent and industrious, Luise was one of Elisabeth Charlotte's favorite correspondents. She was too poor to attract a husband of proper status and became the spokeswoman for her brothers and sisters in the protracted and largely unsuccessful efforts to obtain incomes from the electors who succeeded their father, who, owing to his untimely death, had failed to provide adequately for the children of his second marriage. Having spent several years in England, where she was able to arrange advantageous marriages for the children of her deceased sister, Raugräfin Luise eventually became first lady-in-waiting and a kind of secretary to her aunt Electress Sophie of Hanover. Significantly, the Electress offered her this position only after she had become a widow, for her husband had insisted that his mistress have ceremonial precedence over the Raugräfin. A straightlaced and, as she put it herself, "old-fashioned" spinster, Luise was the last surviving link to Elisabeth Charlotte's German family. Receiving long letters from her illustrious half-sister every week without fail for thirty years was a great source of pride to her, but one can only speculate about her disappointment at Madame's constant laments about her inability to provide material support for her "dearest Luise."

Raugräfin Amalie Elisabeth* (1663–1709): "Amelise." Rather less worldly and energetic but prettier than her sister Luise, with whom she lived, Amalie Elisabeth also remained unmarried. In poor health throughout her life, she was given to an enthusiastic piety, and her letters frequently assumed the character of sermons. Elisabeth Charlotte took a somewhat malicious pleasure in enlightening her about the evil ways of the real world.

Raugraf Karl Moritz* (1670–1702). An orphan since the age of ten, Karl Moritz was educated at private schools in Leyden and then at the *Ritterakademie* in Braunschweig. His plans for a miliary career were thwarted by an almost dwarflike stature, and his looks were further ruined by a protruding fleshy growth in one eye. A poet and a philosopher, he was a sparkling conversationalist, but by the time he was in his mid-twenties, his sisters and his aunt had realized that he was a confirmed alcoholic. The disease so undermined his health that he died at the age of thirty-two.

Three other Raugrafen also died young, all in 1691: **Karl Casimir** was killed in a duel, **Karl Eduard** lost his life in a battle, and **Karl August** died of an illness. Very little is known about these three young men.

Sophie, Duchess of Braunschweig-Lüneburg*, after 1692, Electress of Hanover (1630–1714); sister of Elisabeth Charlotte's father: "Ma Tante." Foster mother to young Liselotte for four impressionable childhood years, Sophie was her role model for the rest of her life. Growing up as the youngest in a group of talented siblings had sharpened Sophie's wits at an early age; her correspondence and her letters are a delight to read and reveal many of the attitudes that also inform the correspondence of Elisabeth Charlotte. Married at the age of twenty-eight to Duke Ernst August of Braunschweig-Lüneburg, a younger son of the house of Hanover with limited expectations, she was determined to love her husband and to enjoy everything that life had to offer. Luck aided the young couple who, through various inheritances, eventually became the heads of the house of Hanover. Seven sons and one daughter were born to the couple, even though Sophie realized that "for a younger branch it is not politic to have so many children." As the only Protestant descendant of the house of Stuart through her mother, Elizabeth Stuart, Sophie would have inherited the English crown had she not died three months before Queen Anne. It was therefore her oldest son, Georg Ludwig, who became King George I of England. Her daughter, Sophie Charlotte (Madame's godchild), also became a queen when her husband, the Elector of Brandenburg, founded the kingdom of Prussia as King Frederick I.

Ernst August, Duke of Braunschweig-Lüneburg, after 1692, Elector of Hanover (1629–1698); Sophie's husband: "Oncle." As the youngest of four brothers, Ernst August's prospects seemed limited to becoming the Protestant bishop of Osnabrück, but by a series of fortunate circumstances he ended his days as Elector of Hanover and an ancestor of the royal houses of England and Prussia. He was a pleasure-loving prince who traveled to Italy almost every winter without his wife, spent a great deal of time hunting, and could never resist the enticements of beautiful women. After a very few years of marriage, he established an official mistress, Countess Platen, at his court. Elisabeth Charlotte often commiserated with her aunt about the inevitability of such behavior in the men of her world. Despite the frivolity of his lifestyle—he did not share his wife's interest in philosophy, religion, and the arts—Ernst August was a shrewd and lucky politician who, having become the head of the house of Hanover, obtained the electoral dignity for his family. As one of the eight electors of the Holy Roman Empire (a position that was said at the time to have cost him a million *Louis d'or*), he became the most powerful prince in northwestern Germany.

Georg Wilhelm, Duke of Celle (1624–1705), Ernst August's older brother: "Godfather." Duke Georg Wilhelm was originally betrothed to Elisabeth Charlotte's aunt Sophie; when he decided that he was not suited for marriage (Sophie contended that a Venetian courtesan had rendered him so!), his younger brother Ernst August agreed to take over the bride in exchange for a promise that Georg Wilhelm would never marry and would leave his fortune and his dukedom to the future children of the young couple. Some twenty years later, however, Georg Wilhelm did marry his mistress, *Eléonore d'Olbreuse;* Elisabeth Charlotte's outrage at this misalliance—a theme that is sounded over and over in her letters—was therefore reinforced by concern for the material welfare of her beloved aunt's family.

Eléanore d'Olbreuse (1639–1722), Georg Wilhelm's mistress and eventual wife; French lady-in-waiting to the Princesse de Tarente. The offspring of Eléanore and George Wilhelm, a legitimated daughter, Sophie Dorothea, was married to the oldest son of Duke Ernst August and Duchess Sophie in order to consolidate the patrimony of the house of Hanover. This marriage was dissolved when the young woman was caught in a scandalous adultery. To Elisabeth Charlotte this was proof that "misalliances never work out in the end."

Louise Hollandine, Abbess of Maubuisson (1622–1709), another sister of Elisabeth Charlotte's father. Born during the Dutch exile of her parents, the "Winter King" of Bohemia and his wife, Elizabeth Stuart, Louise Hollandine was given her unusual name because she was the godchild of the Dutch Estates General. This Protestant body failed, however, to provide an adequate livelihood for the daughter of the head of the German Protestant Union, and since no suitable husband could be found, Louise Hollandine migrated to the court of France, where her brother Edward, known as the Prince Palatine, had been established for some time. Like her brother, Louise Hollandine converted to Catholicism and thus became eligible for the headship of the prestigious convent of Maubuisson, which provided her with an excellent livelihood, a responsible occupation, and leisure to pursue her own interests. Among these were painting and work on behalf of the unification of the Christian churches, about which she corresponded with the German philosopher Leibniz. Elisabeth Charlotte greatly admired her aunt the Abbess and often visited her at Maubuisson. Another of her father's sisters, the learned Elisabeth, had become abbess of the Protestant convent of Herford in Germany. Clearly, a pragmatic attitude in matters of religious confession was a necessity in this hard-pressed family, and Elisabeth Charlotte's tolerant attitude had more than only philosophical roots.

PERSONALITIES AT GERMAN COURTS

Anna Katherina von Offeln* (died 1702), Elisabeth Charlotte's governess during the Hanover years.

Christian Friedrich von Harling*, Master of the Horse; later, councillor at the court of Hanover; Anna Katherina von Offeln's husband.

Eberhard Ernst Franz von Harling, Christian Friedrich von Harling's nephew; page; later, captain of the guards in Madame's household; and field marshal in the French army: "my Harling." In 1719, when von Harling aspired to the position of her *chevalier d'honneur,* that is, supervisor of her entire household, Madame had to tell him that his birth was not high enough.

Friedrich Wilhelm Freiherr von Goertz* (1647–1728), court official at Hanover.

Eleanore von Ratsamhausen, friend of Elisabeth Charlotte's youth: "Lenor," "the Rotzenhäuserin." Eleanor spent several months each year in France as Madame's lady-in-waiting.

Gottfried Wilhelm von Leibniz* (1646–1716), one of the great philosophers of the age; friend of Sophie of Hanover. The author of important treatises in metaphysics, mathematics, logic, and linguistics, Leibniz was also a political adviser to the dukes of Hanover, who commissioned him to write the history of the house of Braunschweig-Lüneburg. His *Theodicee: An Essay on The Goodness of God, the Freedom of Man, and the Origin of Evil,* preceded by *Discourse on the Conformity between Faith and Reason* (1710), grew out of discussions with Electress Sophie and her daughter, Queen Sophie Charlotte of Prussia, and he even copied the Electress's memoirs, correcting her French grammar and spelling. Echoes of Leibniz's political thought, which stressed the notion of natural law as the foundation of the common good, placed great faith in the potential of human reason and, in practice, led him to work for the reunification of the Christian churches, are found throughout Elisabeth Charlotte's correspondence.

Franz Mercurius van Helmont (1618–1699). The son of a famous Belgian chemist, Helmont also learned chemistry, along with many other arts and crafts. During extensive travels in his youth he pursued cabbalistic studies, and his activities caused him to be incarcerated by the Spanish Inquisition. In 1663, he found refuge at the court of Elector Karl Ludwig in

Heidelberg, where he further pursued his study of the Cabbala. Helmont was a mystic who believed in reincarnation, in the Universal Panacea, and in the Philosophers' Stone. He called himself a "seeker." Electress Sophie always felt that Helmont was confused on a very high level, but Leibniz had respect for him and composed his eulogy.

ELISABETH CHARLOTTE'S FRENCH RELATIVES

Philippe I d'Orléans (1640–1701), Elisabeth Charlotte's husband; only brother of Louis XIV; widower of Henrietta of England: "Monsieur." Many historians are convinced that Monsieur's upbringing was a political crime. His mother, Anne d'Autriche, and Cardinal Mazarin, who ruled France during the minority of Louis XIV, were so traumatized by the uprising of the royal princes during the Fronde, in which Gaston d'Orléans, the brother of Louis XIII, had played a major role, that they were determined to keep political and military power out of the hands of all royal princes but especially out of the hands of the King's brother. The best way to achieve this goal was, on the one hand, to give him no more than a minimal education and, on the other, to keep him occupied with frivolous pursuits, pleasures, and conspicuous consumption. In his childhood and during the fragile adolescent years, Philippe's mother and the Cardinal encouraged his friendships with known homosexuals at court, who delighted in dressing him up in sumptuous female clothing and jewelry, complete with beauty-spots and makeup. He was known as a chatterbox, and his expert advice was sought by all and sundry when it came to fashions, jewelry, court ceremonial, and genealogy. This conscious policy was continued when Louis XIV began his personal reign. Monsieur was given no governorship of a province, no place in the Council of State, and no military command, even after he won a brilliant victory at the battle of Cassel in 1676. By way of compensation, he received huge pensions and grants from the King to supplement the income from his *appanage,* or personal landed property. At the time of his marriage to Elisabeth Charlotte, Monsieur's annual income from the crown was about 1,212,000 livres, or 80 percent of his total income. As Louis XIV said in his memoirs, "The sons of France must never have any home but the court nor any resource but the love of their brother." Monsieur was an obedient brother to the end of his days.

Henrietta of England, Duchesse d'Orléans (1644–70), Philippe I's first wife: "the first Madame." Monsieur's first marriage was even more unhappy than the second because Henrietta, unlike Elisabeth Charlotte, was beautiful and ambitious, and so *coquette* that neither his jewels nor his lovers were safe from her. When she died very suddenly at the age of twenty-six it was widely believed—as she herself believed—that she had been poisoned by Monsieur's favorites, the Chevalier de Lorraine and the Marquis d'Effiat. An autopsy revealed, however, that her liver was completely diseased, and historians today attribute her death to natural causes. In any case, Henrietta's health was so bad that most of her eight children were stillborn. Only two daughters survived and became, respectively, Queen of Spain and Duchesse de Savoie. Elisabeth Charlotte was very fond of both these step-daughters.

Alexandre Louis, Duc de Valois (1673–76), Elisabeth Charlotte's first son, who died at the age of two years, nine months.

Philippe II d'Orléans (1674–1723), Elisabeth Charlotte's second son; Duc de Chartres until the death of his father, then Duc d'Orléans; Regent of France during the minority of Louis XV: "My son." Well-educated—thanks to his mother—and of a skeptical turn of mind, he was a talented amateur painter and musician and a knowledgeable art collector. Philippe also dabbled in scientific experiments (an activity that was suspect at a time when alchemy and chemistry were not yet separate in the popular mind) and kept up with the latest in scientific and philosophical literature. Deeply frustrated by his existence as a useless courtier—for he, like his father, was systematically deprived of any administrative or military responsibility—Philippe increasingly withdrew into a round of pleasures ("gorging, guzzling, and whoring," his mother called it) that earned him the displeasure of his uncle, the King. In 1706, Philippe was finally given a military command in Italy, where he lost the battle of Turin, and in the following year he commanded an army in Spain. There he plotted to obtain for himself the succession to the Spanish throne, which Louis XIV's grandson, Philip V, seemed about to lose. When the plot was discovered, the Duc d'Orléans was recalled to France and made to sign a formal renunciation of all claims to the Spanish crown.

Despite his misgivings about his nephew's behavior, Louis XIV before his death formally appointed him as Regent of the realm (albeit with the stipulation that he was to share power with a regency council) during the minority of young Louis XV. Philippe d'Orléans deployed all of his considerable energy to acquit himself of this difficult task, for the country was exhausted and impoverished by years of warfare. Although the "system" of the Scottish financier John Law, to whom the Regent entrusted the management of the financial affairs of the realm, ended in failure, the moderate and flexible policies of the new administration served to stimulate commerce and the arts and, above all, kept the country at peace. The Regent himself kept up a frenetic pace, working "like a soul in damnation," as his mother put it, during the day and spending his nights in revels that became legend. In 1723, a year after the coronation of Louis XV, he died in the arms of his mistress at the age of fifty.

Françoise Marie de Bourbon, Mademoiselle de Blois (1677–1749), legitimized daughter of Louis XIV and Madame de Montespan; Philippe II's wife. A handsome woman despite a slight deformity, she was rather reticent in her dealings with everyone but her brothers—also legitimized children of the Montespan—whose "glory" and well-being seems to have been her principal concern. In keeping with the court mores of the time, her husband's extramarital affairs left her indifferent; even before her marriage she was heard to say, "I do not care whether he loves me; I care that he marries me." Elisabeth Charlotte was fiercely opposed to this marriage, which she considered a gross "misalliance." In Madame's eyes, Mademoiselle de Blois was the offspring of a double adultery and nothing but a bastard who contaminated the bloodline of the house of Orléans.

Grandchildren on the Orléans side

Marie-Louise, Mademoiselle d'Orléans (1695–1719), married to the Duc de Berry, grandson of Louis XIV.

Louise-Adélaïde, Mademoiselle de Chartres (1698–1743), abbess of Chelles.

Charlotte-Aglaë, Mademoiselle de Valois (1700–61), married to the Duke of Modena.

Louis, Duc de Chartres, after his father's death, Duc d'Orléans (1703–52); married to Augusta-Marie of Baden.

Louise-Elisabeth, Mademoiselle de Montpensier (1709–42), married to Luis de Asturias, crown prince of Spain.

Philippine-Elisabeth, Mademoiselle de Beaujolais (1714–34), betrothed to a son of the King of Spain but sent back to France.

Louise-Diane (1716–36), married to Louis, Prince de Conti.

For Madame's assessment of these grandchildren, see her letter of 31 March 1718.

Elisabeth Charlotte (1676–1744), married to Duc Leopold de Lorraine in 1698: "Mademoiselle," "my daughter." Vivacious and amusing as a child, the Duchesse de Lorraine was, according to her mother, the very epitome of a virtuous princess. No rumors of *galanterie* were ever attached to her name before her marriage, and her marriage was "good" because she gracefully put up with her husband's mistress, who ruled him completely and fleeced him to the best of her ability. Fourteen pregnancies were another sign of a good marriage, and Madame was delighted (see the letter of 5 November 1722) with her five surviving grandchildren of Lorraine.

Grandchildren of Lorraine

Leopold Clemens (1707–23).

Franz Stephan (1708–65), married Empress Maria Theresa and became German Emperor.

Anne Charlotte (1714–44), abbess of Rémiremont.

Elisabeth Theresa (1711–41), married to King of Sardinia.

Karl Alexander (1712–41), Austrian general and governor of the Austrian Netherlands.

PRINCIPAL PERSONALITIES AT THE FRENCH COURT

Louis XIV (1638–1715): "the King," "the great man." King of France at the age of four, assuming the reins of government at twenty-three, and ruling with an iron hand until his death at seventy-four, the "Sun King" or "Most Christian King" was admired, feared, and aped by every European monarch of his time. An energetic and loyal group of ministers, an expanded, paid bureaucracy, a series of policies mobilizing the country's resources, a standing army under the direct command of the royal government (replacing the quasifeudal armies raised and financed by the great princes of the realm), and above all an ambitious and ruthless policy of conquest made Louis XIV the most powerful monarch in Europe.

Louis ruled under the motto *Un roi, une loi, une foi* ("One King, One Law, One Faith"). "One King" implied the need to "domesticate" the great nobles of the realm by dispensing large royal favors to them, but only if they were in regular attendance at court, where they incurred huge sumptuary expenses and lost whatever local preeminence they had enjoyed in the past. "One Law" implied the replacement of local regulations and customs with a single national law and also led the Crown to curtail the powers of the parlements, or courts of law, which had traditionally claimed the right to interpret the fundamental French law and to limit the power of the monarch. "One Faith" was incompatible with the existence of "heretics"—that is, Protestants, Jews, or atheists—within the body politic; the Edict of Nantes (1598), which had granted a large measure of tolerance to French Protestants in the previous reigns, was therefore interpreted in a more and more restrictive manner from the very beginning of Louis's reign and finally revoked altogether in 1685. In addition, Louis XIV's insistence on certain royal prerogatives regarding the Catholic hierarchy made the French, or "Gallican," Church almost independent of the Pope in Rome.

Having assembled a formidable machine of State, Louis XIV embarked upon a series of aggressive wars, especially against the Spanish Netherlands, the Dutch Republic, and the German principalities, which pushed the French frontiers further north and east toward the Rhine River. His power and glory were at their height when Elisabeth Charlotte arrived in France in 1672: the building of Versailles neared completion; brilliant architects, landscape artists, writers, painters, and musicians glorified the person of the monarch; crowds of fawning courtiers spent their lives practicing the "cult of the King"; and when, in subsequent years, a son, then three grandsons, and eventually two great-grandsons were born to the King, the continuity of the dynasty seemed amply assured.

Yet, like the hero of a tragedy, Louis XIV overreached himself. Continuous warfare against almost all of Europe and relentless spending to keep up the splendor of the most sumptuous court in Christendom exhausted his country's resources. In addition, the country suffered a series of crop failures and food shortages. The severe winter of 1709 was the climax of many years of bad harvests, high bread prices, and mass starvation. Yet the war dragged on. In 1711–12, when within eleven months the King had lost his son, his oldest grandson, and his oldest great-grandson, so that the succession fell to a sickly two-year-old boy, it seemed to him that God was punishing him for his sins, and indeed even the modern observer is awed by this spectacle of hubris brought low.

Yet despite the misfortunes of his declining years, and despite the various ailments that even a man of his robust constitution could not avoid, Louis XIV never permitted the world to see him in anything but the role of the splendid King in full possession of his God-given powers.

Marie-Thérèse (1638–83), Spanish infanta; wife of Louis XIV: "the Queen." Married to Louis XIV as the crowning token of the Peace of the Pyrenees (1659), Marie-Thérèse was never at home in France. Brought up amidst the oppressive piety and the rigid ceremonial of the Spanish court, and so poorly educated that she barely spoke French, she was neither bright nor adaptable enough to play her rightful role at the "Court of Apollo," where beauty, wit, and stamina were indispensable qualities. In her somber apartments and in her private chapel, she spent long, regular hours in austere devotions at the foot of the crucifix, attended by elderly duennas, priests, and monks. Her entertainment was provided by a half-dozen dwarf-fools and numerous dogs. Aside from drinking innumerable cups of coffee and chocolate, the only worldly pleasure she enjoyed was gambling, but she played so badly that certain courtiers were said to make their living from the Queen's gambling losses. A stout and plain little lady with milk-white skin and rotten teeth, she was humbly devoted to her dashing husband and was always the last to find out about a new mistress. Memoir writers tell us that it was common knowledge that the King had "commerce" with the Queen at least twice a month, for she loved to talk about his attentions and always had a special mass said on the morning after in order to ask God for children. Her prayers were only partially answered, for although she gave birth to five children (two sons and three daughters), only one of them survived early childhood. Except for the servants of her household, who lost their lucrative positions, no one cared much when she died at the age of forty-five.

Louis, the Grand Dauphin (1661–1711), only surviving son of Louis XIV and Marie-Thérèse; "Monseigneur," "the first Dauphin." Resembling his mother physically as well as in intelligence and personality, the Dauphin was never given a chance to emerge from the shadow of his powerful father, whom he feared and revered to his dying day. A careful education, directed by Bishop Bossuet, who wrote his *Histoire universelle* expressly for the Dauphin's instruction and edification, did little to open the mind of the young man, who even in maturity spent most of his days hunting, eating, and supervising his gardeners. The military commanders who "served under his orders" did not even pretend that he was directing the operations, and on the rare occasions when he participated in the Council of State he only spoke when expressly called upon to do so. Although he became the center of a coterie that looked ahead to the next reign as Louis XIV grew older, the Dauphin never cared to involve himself in high politics; as Madame put it, "he does not care about anything in the world." Nor, apparently, did he care when he became a widower at the age of twenty-nine. Believing that he had done his duty by the Crown by begetting three sons, he settled down to a comfortable life, secretly marrying his mistress, Mademoiselle Choin, an unassuming woman who never made any demands on him. The son of one king, Louis XIV of France, and the father of another, Philip V of Spain, the Grand Dauphin did not live to become a king himself.

Maria Anna Christine of Bavaria (1660–90), the Grand Dauphin's wife: "Madame la Dauphine," "the first Dauphine." Although the Dauphin's marriage to this German princess was a disappointment to Madame, who had hoped to have his "place" given to her cousin and godchild, the Hanoverian princess Sophie Charlotte, Elisabeth Charlotte soon made friends with her compatriot. A plain, pious, and sensitive young woman, Madame la Dauphine shared Elisabeth Charlotte's disapproval of the mores of the French court; another bond between them was their shared dislike of Madame de Maintenon. In poor health even before her marriage, the Dauphine spent her life in France "being bored and pregnant." Yet the fact that she provided three living sons to the Crown gave her a modicum of royal favor. She died at the age of thirty.

Louis XIV's Legitimate Grandsons, Children of the Grand Dauphin and the First Dauphine

Louis, Duc de Bourgogne (1682–1712), the second Dauphin for one year after the death of his father. Intelligent, alert, well-educated, and afflicted with a slightly hunched back, the young Duc de Bourgogne struggled throughout his short life to control his fierce temper. When he reached his early twenties, his grandfather gave him major responsibilities in the royal council and in the army, but the young prince, who had been converted to a deep and thoughtful piety by his beloved teacher, Bishop Fénelon, was more interested in theology and pious works than in power and conquest. He was married to Marie Adélaïde of Savoy (1685–1712); Monsieur's granddaughter by his first marriage, a lovely and spirited young woman who was the pride and joy of Louis XIV's old age. The King and the court were devastated when, eleven months after the death of the Grand Dauphin, the second Dauphin and Dauphine and their oldest son, the five-year-old Duc d'Anjou, died of measles within a week of one another, leaving only their youngest son, the two-year-old Duc de Bretagne, as successor to the Crown of France.

Philippe, Duc d'Anjou (1683–1746), King Philip V of Spain after 1700. A repressed and docile youth of seventeen when his grandfather accepted the Spanish crowns for him in 1700, Philip V almost immediately found himself engaged in a war to save his kingdom from partition by a powerful European coalition. This situation was entirely beyond his abilities, and his dependence on French help was complete in the early years of this "war of the two crowns." Yet in the course of the war, which lasted thirteen years, Philip gradually achieved independence from his grandfather's tutelage and convinced the ruling circles of Spain that he was first and foremost the King of Spain. In no small measure his success was due to the influence of two women, his wife, **Marie-Louise-Gabrielle of Savoy** (1688–1714), another granddaughter of Monsieur's, and the **Princesse des Ursins** (1642–1722), the favorite of the royal couple, who practically ruled Spain until the death of Queen Marie-Louise in 1714. A year later, Philip V married the Italian princess Elisabeth Farnese, who promptly banished the Princesse des Ursins and soon achieved greater influence over her husband than his first wife ever had. Philip V founded a dynasty of French Bourbons that has ruled in Spain, with interruptions, until today.

Charles, Duc de Berry (1686–1714). Vivacious and amusing as a child, the third of the Grand Dauphin's sons grew up to be a happy-go-lucky epicure who refused, according to Madame, to worry about anything as long as his pleasures were provided for. He was married to **Marie-Louise d'Orléans** (1695–1719), Madame's eldest and somewhat unbalanced granddaughter. The first child to be born from this marriage lived only a few hours, and the second died a few weeks after birth. Having sustained internal injuries in a hunting accident, the Duc de Berry died without heirs. Madame reports that after his death containers full of blood, which he had hidden from his attendants in order to conceal the seriousness of his condition, were found under every piece of furniture in his room.

Louis XIV's Legitimized Children

> *By Madame de la Vallière*

Marie-Anne de Bourbon (1666–1739). Married to Louis-Armand, Prince de Conti, and widowed at the age of nineteen, she was a famous beauty. She was known as "the beautiful Princesse de Conti," to distinguish her from her sister-in-law.

> *By Madame de Montespan*

Louis Auguste, Duc du Maine (1670–1736): "the limping bastard." His governess, Madame de Maintenon, found the cure that permitted the lame child to walk when he was five years old. Despite his handicap, the Duc du Maine was handsome; he was also witty and well educated, and his charm was such that he was his father's favorite throughout of his life. The Duc du Maine was married to **Anne-Louise-Bénédicte de Condé** (1676–1753), the diminutive bluestocking who, at the time of the regency, led the conspiracy against the Regent and attracted many of the most brilliant intellectuals of the age to her lavish fêtes at the château of Sceaux.

Louise-Françoise de Bourbon, Mademoiselle de Nantes (1673–1743), married to Louis III de Condé: "Madame la Duchesse."

Françoise Marie de Bourbon, Mademoiselle de Blois (1677–1749), married to Madame's son, Philippe II d'Orléans, the Regent: "our mousedroppings."

Louis Alexandre, Comte de Toulouse (1678–1737).

All of Louis XIV's children by Madame de Montespan, except the Comte de Toulouse, had some physical deformity; two others died in early childhood.

The Princes of the Blood

Louis II de Bourbon, Prince de Condé (1621–86): "the Grand Condé," "Monsieur le Prince." Condé had been the leader of the Fronde of the Princes, the rebellion that almost cost the adolescent Louis XIV his throne. Defeated, exiled, and finally pardoned, Condé was stripped of all personal power and henceforth loyally served the Crown as one of the ablest generals of his generation. His wife, a niece of Cardinal Richelieu, was a dwarf and a hunchback, whose grotesque appearance was passed on to several generations of Condés.

Louis III de Bourbon, Prince de Condé (1668–1710), grandson and heir of the Grand Condé: "Monsieur le Duc." He married **Louise-Françoise de Bourbon**, eldest daughter of Louise XIV and Madame de Montespan, "Madame la Duchesse."

Louis Armand de Bourbon, Prince de Conti (1661–85), married to **Marie-Anne de Bourbon**, daughter of Louis XIV and Madame de la Vallière. He died young and left no offspring.

François Louis de Bourbon (1664–1709), *Prince de Conti* after the death of his brother. He was married to Marie-Thérèse de Condé, the favorite granddaughter of the Grand Condé. Louis XIV never liked or trusted the Prince de Conti, an ambitious young man of great promise who was extremely popular with the Parisians, cultivated the Grand Dauphin, and was too obviously planning to play a great role in the next reign. The King's plan to get rid of Conti by forcing him to accept the crown of Poland failed when the Polish nobility preferred August the Strong, the Elector of Saxony. Conti was delighted and returned to France, but there was no outlet for any of his talents, and he gradually sank into idleness and debauchery.

Louis XIV's Official Mistresses

Louise de la Vallière (1644–1710). A young and inexperienced lady-in-waiting to the first Madame, Louise de la Baume le Blanc was dazzled by the handsome young King and would not have dreamt of escaping his attentions, especially since her parents had no objections to seeing her as the mistress of the King. But she did not have enough intelligence and verve to hold him for very long. After she had borne him three children, two of whom lived long enough to be legitimized, her beauty faded and the King's passion was transferred to Madame de Montespan. Louise was rewarded for her services by being made Duchesse de la Vallière and retired to a convent in 1674.

Françoise Athénaïs de Mortemart, Marquise de Montespan (1641–1717). Strikingly beautiful, cultivated, extravagant, and versed in all the social graces, Madame de Montespan was the very symbol of the Sun King's lavish court in the early part of his reign. Born into one of France's greatest families, she—unlike almost everyone else—was not afraid of Louis XIV and indeed often treated him to fierce temper tantrums. Despite the open criticism voiced by Bossuet, Bourdaloue, and other great preachers of the day of this doubly adulterous affair—after all, both Louis and Athénaïs were married—the reign of La Montespan lasted for about twelve years. When the King, inspired in part by Madame de Maintenon, began to worry about his soul in earnest, and as the years and six pregancies began to take their toll, Madame de Montespan seems to have had recourse to love potions, magic powders, and black masses. All of this was hushed up, however, when the infamous *affaire des poisons*—a veritable wave of poisonings—implicated some of the greatest names in France. In 1691, long after the King had ceased to care for her, Madame de Montespan finally left the court and spent the rest of her life occupied with devotions and good works.

Marie Adélaïde Scorailles de Roussilhe, Duchesse de Fontanges (1661–81). As Madame recalled many years later, La Fontange was "beautiful as an angel, with an excellent heart, but no more brains than a little bird." And Madame would know, since La Fontange started her life at court as a lady-in-waiting in Madame's own household. Here La Fontanges realized her ambition of becoming an official mistress of the King, and a duchess to boot. Her rise to royal favor was the first serious challenge to the reign of Madame de Montespan, but La Fontange's glory was short-lived: A year after the liaison began, she had a baby that died. "Wounded in the service of the King," as the cruel wags put it, she never regained her health, became despondent, and was soon packed off to a convent, where she lingered on for a few weeks before she died. She was only twenty.

Françoise d'Aubigné, widow Scarron, Marquise de Maintenon (1635–1719): "the old trollop," "the great man's old woman," "old pruneface," "the old ragbag," "the Pantocrate," etc. It is doubtful that Madame de Maintenon was ever Louis XIV's mistress in the carnal sense of the word; on the other hand, historians today are agreed that he secretly married her after the Queen's death in 1683; some think that the marriage took place as early as 1684.

The life of this uncrowned Queen of France is an altogether unlikely story. Although she came from a long line of provincial nobles, she was born in a debtors' prison, where her father, the ne'er-do-well son of the brilliant Protestant poet Agrippa d'Aubigné, happened to be incarcerated. Baptized a Catholic, Françoise then spent several of her childhood years in Martinique before she found herself, at the age of sixteen, a penniless orphan living in the households of various Protestant relatives, who briefly converted her to their faith. Reconverted by the sisters of the Ursuline convent where she was educated, Françoise became an earnest Catholic who—Madame's cries of "hypocrisy" notwithstanding—struggled throughout her life to reconcile the demands of the "world" with the imperatives of her religion.

The material circumstances of her youth had not prevented her from receiving an excellent education which, in conjunction with native intelligence and exquisite manners, permitted the young Françoise d'Aubigné to move in the most fashionable literary circles of Paris. It was there that she met Paul Scarron, a minor poet, playwright, and pamphleteer, who was willing to marry her without a dowry. Since the only alternative was life in a convent, Françoise, at the age of eighteen, decided to become Madame Scarron, even though her husband, her senior by twenty-four years, was severely crippled—his legs were permanently folded back behind his back. Until his death eight years later, Madame Scarron kept a modest salon and established herself within a respectable and cultivated circle of friends, among them Madame de Sevigné, Madame de La Fayette, and Madame de Coulanges. These connections in turn helped her secure a small pension when she became a penniless widow, burdened with her husband's debts. They also caused her to be "discovered" by Madame de Montespan, who was desperately looking for a discreet and genteel governess for the children she was bearing the King in rapid succession.

As the governess to the royal bastards, to whom she became deeply and sincerely attached (as even Elisabeth Charlotte had to admit), Madame Scarron needed considerable social skill and a cool head to maneuver her way between the temperamental Madame de Montespan and the King who, as the years went by, was almost unconsciously looking for a way out of this strenuous relationship. Madame Scarron's cool and quiet personality was a relief, and so she gradually became his friend and confidante. In 1675 a royal grant enabled her to buy the handsome estate of Maintenon, and the King himself introduced her as the Marquise de Maintenon. Her fortune was made, and she knew how to hold on to it.

A great deal of ink has been spilled over the question of why Louis XIV married Madame de Maintenon when he became a widower. The answer seems to be that, with the succession assured by a son and two grandsons, the King did not wish to start a second family, which was liable to bring nothing but trouble within the royal house; moreover, a marriage with a foreign princess could have upset the system of alliances. On the other hand, the promiscuous sexual activity of the past was also out of the question, now that Louis had become a pious, middle-aged man. Madame de Maintenon was also middle-aged and could not be expected to have any children, yet she was well-preserved, handsome, and slender, and she attracted Louis as a woman. He also knew that Madame Scarron was discreet and that she would never become extravagant and hysterical, as so many of his mistresses had been—he called her "*Votre Solidité.*" In short, he liked her and counted on her to be his companion in old age. As for Elisabeth Charlotte's unreasonable and visceral hatred of Madame de Maintenon, an attempt has been made in the Introduction of this translation to elucidate its motives.

Ministers and Courtiers

François-Michel Le Tellier, Marquis de Louvois (1641–91). The son of Michel Le Tellier, Chancellor of France, Louvois was an "apprentice" in the war ministry before he became Louis XIV's minister of war as well as superintendent of the postal system, Master of the Hunt, and administrator of the orders of Saint-Lazare and Mont-Carmel. He was a hard driving, ruthless, even brutal man, a thorough professional who never permitted human considerations to interfere with the most efficient way to achieve a goal. It was Louvois who suggested the policy of scorched earth by which the towns and countryside of the Palatinate were devastated in order to prevent the region from becoming a staging area for any aggression against France; it was Louvois who ordered the infamous *dragonnades,* the conversion of recalcitrant Protestants by military force, and it was he who, as superintendent of the postal system, organized the "black chamber" for the purpose of spying on the correspondence of all foreigners (including Madame and the Bavarian Dauphine). No one liked Louvois, not even the King, who on one occasion was so irritated with Louvois's overbearing manner that he almost struck him. Indeed, there were rumors that Louvois was about to be dismissed when he died, probably of a stroke, at the height of his career.

Jean Baptiste Colbert, Marquis de Torcy (1665–1746). A nephew of Louis XIV's great minister, Torcy served in various ambassadorial posts before he became treasurer-general of the realm. At the beginning of the War of Spanish Succession, he succeeded his father-in-law, Pomponne, as secretary of State for foreign affairs, a post that gave him a voice in the royal council. At this time, Torcy also became superintendant of the postal system and in this capacity continued the censorship of the mail. An accomplished diplomat, he negotiated a separate peace with England in 1709. In the latter part of the regency, Torcy lost the confidence of the Regent, who replaced him with Philippe's former tutor, Abbé Dubois.

Guilleaume Dubois (1656–1723), abbé, archbishop, and cardinal; prime minister under the regency. The son of an apothecary at Brives-la-Gaillarde, Dubois arrived in Paris as a scholarship student. The brilliant and ambitious young abbé worked as a tutor to bourgeois and noble children and in this capacity made the acquaintance of a subtutor to

Madame's son, the Duc de Chartres. This was his entry into the Orléans household, where he made his fortune. He was an excellent teacher for the talented young duke. At first Madame appreciated him for his scholarship and for his devotion to her son's *gloire,* but her feelings changed when she found out, years after the fact, that Dubois had been instrumental in persuading the Duc de Chartres to marry Mademoiselle de Blois. Under the regency, Philippe d'Orléans named his former tutor councillor of State for foreign affairs and then prime minister. An extremely adroit diplomat, Dubois negotiated the rapprochement with England that culminated in the Quadruple Alliance between France, England, the Empire, and the Netherlands. It is a measure of his skill that his cardinal's hat was bestowed on the recommendation of both the Protestant King George I and the Catholic Pretender.

Antoine René, Marquis d'Effiat (1638–1719), a favorite of Monsieur, rumored to have had a hand in poisoning the first Madame.

Charlotte de Grancey, a favorite of Monsieur and mistress of the Chevalier de Lorraine; briefly governess of Madame's children.

Philippe de Lorraine-Armagnac, Chevalier de Lorraine (1643–1702), the handsome and wily favorite of Monsieur who has been called his "evil genius." He, too, was suspected of poisoning the first Madame.

Anne Marie de la Tremouïlle, Princesse des Ursins (1642–1722), widow of Adrien Blaise de Talleyrand, Duc de Chalais, and the Italian prince Flavio Orsini, Duc de Bracciano. Enjoying the confidence of Louis XIV as a close friend of Madame de Maintenon, the princess used her Italian connections to work for the Bourbon succession to the Spanish Crown as early as 1693–98; at that time she also won the friendship of Archbishop Portocarrero of Toledo, who made the dying King of Spain sign his will in favor of the French prince. When Philip V mounted the Spanish throne, the Princesse des Ursins became his main political adviser and practically ruled Spain until the death of his first wife.

FURTHER READING

Barine, Arvède. *Madame: Mother of the Regent.* Translated by Jeanne Mairet (New York, 1909).

Chandernagor, Françoise. *The King's Way.* Translated by Barbara Bray (New York, 1984).

Henderson, Ernest F. *A Lady of the Old Regime* (London, 1909).

Mitford, Nancy. *The Sun King* (London, 1966).

Norton, Lucy. *First Lady of Versailles: Mary Adelaide of Savoy, Dauphine of France* (Philadelphia, 1978).

Wolf, John B. *Louis XIV* (New York, 1968).

Ziegler, Gillette. *At the Court of Versailles: Eyewitness Reports from the Reign of Louis XIV.* Translated by Simon Watson (New York, 1968).

Elector Karl Ludwig von der Pfalz. Portrait by J. B. Ruel. Kurpfälzisches Museum, Heidelberg (permanent loan from the Ministry of Culture of Baden-Württemberg). With kind permission.

Madame en habit de chasse. Engraving, ca. 1675. Collection Viollet, Paris.

Philippe d'Orléans, Monsieur. Portrait by unknown artist. Collection Viollet, Paris.

The Château of Versailles in the Seventeenth Century. Engraving by Perette. Bibliothèque Nationale, Paris. Collection Viollet.

Louis XIV. Portrait by Van der Meulen, Musée de Dijon. Photo by N. D. Roger-Viollet.

Wing of the Château of Saint Cloud, with
View of Horseshoe-Fountain. Engraving by
J. Rigaud. Bibliothèque Nationale, Paris.
Photo by N. D. Roger-Viollet.

Madame de Maintenon. Engraving. Bibliothèque Nationale, Paris. Photo by N. D.
Roger-Viollet.

Philippe d'Orléans, the Regent. Engraving by Santerre and Chéreau. Bibliothèque Nationale, Paris. Photo by N. D. Roger-Viollet.

Liselotte von der Pfalz. Portrait by Pierre Mignard (?). By permission of Historisches Museum der Pfalz Speyer.

Elisabeth Charlotte, Duchesse d'Orléans. Portrait by Rigaud. Herzog Anton Ulrich-Museum, Braunschweig. With kind permission.

A Woman's Life

IN THE COURT OF THE SUN KING

To 1671:

Youth

The eight letters from Liselotte's childhood and youth in this first chapter are usually not included in published selections from her correspondence. Their content is slight, the style is undeveloped, and they serve only to mark the contrast between the innocent young princess and the forceful personality that was to emerge later. Much more information about Elisabeth Charlotte's childhood and youth can be gleaned from the reminiscences she included in her letters to the Princess of Wales and her half-sister Luise toward the end of her life.

To ELECTOR KARL LUDWIG

The Hague,[1] *November 1659*

My dearest Papa, I believe Your Grace will already have heard from Ma Tante that we safely arrived here a week ago. Her Majesty the Queen is very kind to me; she has already given me a little dog; tomorrow I will get a language master and the dancing master has already come to see me twice. Ma Tante says that if someone who sings well can be found I am to have singing lessons as well. So I will become very clever and hope that when I once again have the honor to kiss Papa's hands, Your Grace will find that I have learned a lot. I have not yet been able to deliver the little bowl for the Queen because my things are still on the ship and some of our people are still missing. God grant that they have not been drowned; that would not be funny at all. Now I am to go with Ma Tante to the Princess of Orange, therefore I must close and herewith submissively kiss Your Grace's hands, humbly begging my dear Papa to keep me in his good graces and to believe that I will always remain with . . . all due respect my dearest Papa's most obedient and devoted daughter and servant Elisabethe Charlott.

1. Where Duchess Sophie and Liselotte spent the winter with Liselotte's grandmother, the exiled Queen of Bohemia.

To ANNA KATHERINA VON UFFELN

Amsterdam,[1] *19 May 1661*

My dearest Mistress Offelen, I am bound to let you know that I am thinking more of you than you expected, and I hope that you too will think of me. Enough of this. I also must complain to you that the mosquitoes have bitten me so much. Madalenchen[2] sends her respects. Our journey was quite jolly. I must also ask how things are with my little cousin.[3] I hope that we will see you again soon. I must not make excuses that this is not well written since you know very well that I am not yet able to do better. Adieu to my dearest mistress Offelen until I see you soon; I remain always your affectionate friend Elisabethe Charlotte.

1. Written during a later stay in Holland. 2. Liselotte's maid. 3. Georg Ludwig, eldest son of Duchess Sophie, later King George I of England.

To FRAU VON HARLING[1]

Frankenthal, 15 September 1663

My best dearest Mistress Offelen. That I have not written to you for so long has not happened from forgetfulness but because I have been so busy and also because with the journey to Frankenthal and now this journey I have missed the mail. Will mistress Offel please respectfully kiss Ma Tante's hands for me and also please make my excuses to my little cousin for not answering him; I shall remember and not forget to do it by the next mail. Would my dear mistress Offelen also please give all my good friends my regards, especially Monsieur Harling. Please also tell Landen[2] that I have heard that she is expecting a little one; I wish her all the best. I also thank her very much for all the pretty things she has sent me. Meanwhile I assure my dear Mistress Uflen that I shall always be fond of her and that I will remain Mistress Ufelen's good friend Elisabethe Charlott.

1. Anna Katherina von Uffeln had married Herr von Harling, Master of the Horse at the Hanover Court. 2. Fräulein von Landas, lady-in-waiting to Duchess Sophie.

Friedrichsburg, 26 October 1668

I was very glad to hear that Ma Tante had a little princess.[1] . . . Your letter must have taken a very long time, since I only received it the day before yesterday. . . . Papa also has already had a letter from Ma Tante, though it was written with a red chalk pencil. . . . I would like to write more, but I do not know anything new for this time, except that right now I am going to send to the pantry for some grapes; I wish the princess and Frau Harling were here to eat grapes with me, since this is more rare there than for us here.

1. Sophie Charlotte, later married to Friedrich I of Prussia.

Friedrichsburg, 4 November 1668

I was cordially pleased when I heard that Ma Tante and Oncle have done me
the honor to choose me as one of the godparents, particularly because I know
that they are so fond of my godchild, since Ma Tante was hoping for a
princess. I also thank Frau Harling for the trouble she has taken in standing
in for me; I would love to see my godchild and play with her. But now my
hopes have fallen into the well, for I had hoped that I would have the honor
to greet Ma Tante here; but since, as I see from Frau Harling's letter, she is
off to Lüneburg, I am afraid it will not be for some time. . . . Please kiss my
godchild for me, and also the princes. Adieu then, and best of luck for the
journey to Lüneburg.

Heidelberg, 4 March 1670

And now I must tell my dear Frau Harling how my brother and I have been
short-changed: for carnival we were all to be gods and goddesses, and because
at the time it was still too cold, the festivities were put off for ten days and
were to have taken place a week ago yesterday; our clothes were all ready to
go. My brother was Mercurius and I Aurora, Landas Diana, Mistress Kolb
Ceres; summa summarum we were all gods, goddesses, shepherds, and nymphs.
The triumphal chariots were in readiness and we were only waiting for
Thursday to play it, and then on Wednesday came the news that the King of
Denmark died. So all the gods were turned into mortals. However, we were
told to be patient for six weeks and then, if nothing goes wrong, Frau Harling
will only have to tell me whether she likes to rise early or not, for then I
will have power over the gates of day and will not open them until she wants
me to. When we play this, I will send her a list of the participants and of
the parts they take. —I beg my dear Frau Harling to tell the oldest prince how
afraid I am that the little Princess of Hanover, when she gets a little bigger,
will step into my shoes and that I am already beginning to vie with her for the
prince, but that he should remember that I have the first promise.

Schwetzingen, 12 April 1671

Yesterday my brother protested that I should not cry as I did last time when
he left, because he is going to such a fine place where he so much wants to
go. So I answered him, "I am not going to cry because you are going to Osnabrück but because I am not allowed to go along. . . ." I believe you will not
recognize my brother because he has changed so much since he had smallpox.
. . . I am afraid the marks will be permanent. The Princess of Denmark[1] will
now have to look more to his good nature than to his face, and a good nature
she will surely find. This Frau Harling will also see when he has been with
her for a while. He has also told me that he is counting on her to tell him, for

old acquaintance's sake, if he makes any mistakes, and to continue to act a bit as his governess. All the news from here will be told by my brother and his companions.

1. Wilhelmine Ernestine, Karl's future wife.

Schwetzingen, 26 May 1671

From your kind letter I see that my brother has now arrived in Osnabrück. How sorry I am that I cannot be there myself I think my dear Frau Harling can imagine on her own, without my having to describe it at length. At least I am glad that I am missed; but I am bound to think that Our Lord deals with me as He did with a certain rich man: I received my inheritance some years ago, while my brother is getting his only now. Still, I continue to hope to see everyone there soon and must dine on that hope, although it is rather meager fare. I am told that my brother is taking my place in all things, except that he is not washed as thoroughly as Frau Harling used to wash me. And yet as a bridegroom he certainly needs that, so that when he goes to his bride he will sparkle like a carbuncle in the fireplace. My brother cannot say enough to me about all the grace and honor that is bestowed upon him, and how he loves the life he is leading. Nor is he talking foolishness, for I know very well what it is like. He has sung the praises of the oldest prince, telling me how well he can already ride toward the ring and pick it off right in the center; summa summarum, his whole letter is all about how well content he is and how he is having such a fine time; he also greatly enjoys dancing and playing games. . . .

My dear Frau Harling must not talk of old age yet, for since she is still so hale and hearty and can join in the fun, she must not imagine that she is old; I certainly hope to see a great deal of her in the next twenty years and to have good times with her. I think my brother will be very pleased to become a tutor under the title of councillor, and so would I if only I could be there. I beg my dear Frau Harling to help me remain in Ma Tante's and Oncle's good graces and also to see to it that my brother, who is present, will not altogether outshine me, who am absent.

1672-1701:

Marriage

Elector Karl Ludwig and his family had been casting about for an advantageous marriage for Liselotte for some time when "the place of Madame fell vacant" at the French court through the sudden death of Henrietta of England, the wife of Monsieur, only brother of Louis XIV. Twelve days later, Karl Ludwig was contacted by his sister-in-law, widow of his brother Eduard, about the possibility of marrying his daughter to Monsieur. Anna Gonzaga (known as the Princesse Palatine) was one of the cleverest women at the French court and a longtime confidante of Monsieur. Karl Ludwig was extremely eager to conclude an alliance with the French royal house, for he hoped that such a marriage would not only establish his daughter in great splendor but also permit him, the Elector, to play the role of mediator between the German Empire and France and, above all, to shield his own country from the potential aggression of its most powerful neighbor.

It is not as clear why Louis XIV agreed to this marriage between his brother and a rather poor and reputedly plain German princess, for in 1670 there was no reason to believe that the line of Pfalz-Simmern would die out in the foreseeable future, thereby giving Monsieur's family claims to an inheritance in the Palatinate. It has been suggested that Monsieur was attracted by the jewels, objets d'art, and table and toilet accessories in gold and silver that Elisabeth Charlotte would bring with her. These articles, however, were valued at only 10,400 livres, which was a very modest trousseau, and the dowry was no better. After a great deal of evasion on the part of the Elector, the dowry was fixed at 64,000 livres, a positively paltry sum when one considers that Monsieur's income at the time was almost two million livres a year!

However that may be, the negotiations proceeded apace, and by August 1671 the Princesse Palatine had informed Karl Ludwig that the only obstacle from the French side was the matter of religion: The bride's conversion to Catholicism was not negotiable. Over Liselotte's timid objections, a plan was subsequently worked out by which she was "secretly" instructed in the Catholic faith by her father's French secretary, Urbain Chevreau, and taken to Metz, ostensibly to pay a visit to her aunt, the Princesse Palatine, but in reality to be examined by a group of French theologians and to sign a declaration stating that she had embraced the Catholic faith. Thereupon the Elector publicly registered his disapproval, adding, however, that since he believed in freedom of conscience, he would not impose his religious views on anyone, least of all on his daughter. Thus the way was cleared for the marriage by procuration. The ceremony took place on 16 November 1671.

The marriage contract stated that the new Madame would receive a widow's jointure of 40,000 livres per year and a widow's seat in keeping with her dignity if Monsieur should die first. Even before the marriage, the Princesse Palatine had informed her brother-in-law that a magnificent apartment was being prepared for his daughter, that the annual expenses for her household of about 120 persons would be 250,000 livres (to be paid by the King), and that Monsieur's wedding present would be jewelry valued at 50,000 livres. In addition, Madame would receive a personal allowance of about 30,000 livres a year. These were heady prospects for a nineteen-year-old princess brought up at a provincial German court where money was such a problem that the Elector himself had his shoes mended when they wore out. Yet Elisabeth Charlotte reported that she "bawled" all the way to Châlons after she had taken leave of her father at Strasbourg. On the way to Paris the bride and her retinue were chaperoned by the Princesse Palatine, who had seen to it that Elisabeth Charlotte's coat-of-arms was put on her carriage and that French clothes were made for her, including a white wedding-gown. During this journey the Princesse Palatine made one shocking discovery: The bride had only six shifts and six nightgowns. This, she informed the Palatine chargé d'affaires in France, must be remedied immediately, lest it become known through her chambermaids or other French attendants and Madame be made the laughing-stock of the French court. Three to four thousand livres, she said in her urgent message, would take care of everything needed; nor should the chargé bother about the bracelet he was supposed to send, since all the jewelry would be provided by Monsieur.

These, then, were the circumstances under which Liselotte von der Pfalz became Madame and found herself in a position to observe and describe in countless letters a world that fascinated her contemporaries as much as it still fascinates posterity.

To DUCHESS SOPHIE

Saint Germain, 5 February 1672

My dearest Ma Tante will not receive a portrait through Madame de Wartenberg since even the one for Papa was not yet dry enough to send along, so I hope that when I send Papa's I can send those for Your Grace by the same mail. But I would be a thousand times happier if I could bring it myself or if Your Grace and Oncle had to fetch it here. But I am afraid that neither will happen, since I can hardly hope that Your Grace and Oncle will come here, nor is it likely that I will go to the army with the King, since the Queen[1] is great with child and will be brought to bed by that time. It is not that I am taking more or more strenuous walks here than I used to do, but the people here are as lame as geese, and except for the King, Madame de Chevreuse,[2] and myself there is not a soul here who can do more than twenty steps without sweating and puffing.

1. Of France, Marie-Thérèse.   2. A duchess, Colbert's daughter.

To FRAU VON HARLING

Versailles, 23 November 1672

My dearest Frau von Harling. I have not heard from you in such an eternally long time that I almost imagined my dear Frau von Harling had completely forgotten her pupil here in France, and therefore asked monmaistre's[1] wife whether she knew the reason for it. . . . So she told me that you are not at Osnabrück but had taken a journey to Oldenburg. That is why I waited to write until you might be back at Osnabrück. I would have liked to have written even earlier, but I was very sick for two months, as you have probably heard from my letter to Ma Tante. —O my dear mistress Uffel! What an outlandish thing for a merry little leaf-rustler not to be permitted to run and jump, not even to ride in a coach, but to be carried around in a sedan chair all the time. And if it were to be over soon, that would be one thing, but that it will have to go on like this for a full nine months, that is a wretched situation, and I would fain say as little Prince Gus[2] used to say at Heidelberg, "Great mistress mine, I would like to have patience, please give me patience," for that is what I now need most of all. But once this egg is hatched, I wish I could mail it to you in Osnabrück, for you are better at this craft than anyone in this entire country, and I am assured from my own experience that it would be well cared for; but here no child is safe, for the doctors here have already helped five of the Queen's to the other world; the last one died three weeks ago, and three of Monsieur's, as he says himself, have been expedited in the same way. But apropos of pupils: If you want to give me someone to bring up, you will have to send him soon, namely a page, for tomorrow or the next day one of my pages will receive his arms[3] and I will keep the position open until I hear from you whether you want to send me one of your cousins or not; but there is one thing I must not hide from you: I cannot guarantee that, if he is not a Catholic, he will keep his religion. If this should make you decide against sending me one of your kin, please be kind enough to ask President Hammerstein[4] whether he wants to send me someone, for I promised him as well. I have mentioned this matter of religion only so that you will not think that I want to deceive you in any way, but I would like to do you this favor. What else can I say, I do not know anything new; the old news you know as well as I do, and lying is a sin, so that all that is left to me is to beg you to deliver my warmest and prettiest compliments to all the princes, and the princess as well.

1. Her former dancing master, Jeme, who had accompanied her to France. 2. Friedrich August von Hanover. 3. The German expression *wird wehrhaft* refers to the ancient ceremony of the *Schwertleite* ("receive his arms"). 4. A high official at the Hanover court.

To DUCHESS SOPHIE

Saint Germain, 3 December 1672

I only say this, that Monsieur is the best man in the world. We are getting along very well together, he does not resemble any of his portraits.

To FRAU VON HARLING

Saint Cloud, 30 May 1673

I thank you for the kind confidence you and Monsieur Harling have in me to send me your little cousin.[1] Be assured that I will take care of him to the best of my ability. He surely is a very cunning child; not only Monsieur and I but everyone is fond of him. He already serves like one of the others and is beginning to speak and understand French. I have had him lodged apart from the others in a house where the mistress of the household takes care of him, combs his hair every day, washes his linen, and makes him say his prayers. I will also have a little bed with curtains made for him, so that he sleeps alone, and he eats at the table with my maids of honor. I therefore hope that he will not lack in anything. So that you can see that he has not yet forgotten how to write German, I herewith send you a letter from him, which will no doubt sound very fine. He will also write to you how he likes it here. His first service was that he had to wait at table on one of the prettiest young ladies in this country, which he rather liked, for several times at the end of the meal the young lady kissed him. This he would have liked to have made a habit; and once when she did not think to do it, the little man planted himself before her and held up his cheek. She told him that he was just too cunning and that she could not refuse him, and then kissed him. So you see that he has already become quite *galant* here in France. Everybody wants his company, for people find him delightful. Once he went for a ride with Monsieur and myself; we found him playing in the garden and Monsieur was afraid he might become too hot and get sick, therefore he had him caught and brought to us in the carriage; in this manner he stayed with us for the whole ride. At other times when the young ladies also go along on rides, he sits in their carriage and whistles the whole way. All the little girls, down to monmaistres's daughter, are in love with him, but he is quite cruel and does not want to have anything to do with them. He tells me lots of things about his brothers and says he has one who is very, very beautiful, has beautiful red cheeks, a beautiful high nose, and pretty eyes, but one trouble withal, namely a harelip on his mouth that keeps him from talking. I often have long conversations with him, for he is just too cunning; when he tells me something, he puts on such a serious little face, it always makes me laugh. I wish I could be so clever to bring forth as cunning a little man as young Harling, I would be very proud indeed. Very soon now the big blast is going to take place, for I am three weeks into my ninth month. If I still have time and have not yet delivered before monmaistre leaves, I shall write again to my dear Frau Harling through him.

1. Her six-year-old nephew, Eberhard Ernst Franz von Harling, who served as a page to Madame and later became a very capable military officer.

To RAUGRAF KARL LUDWIG

30 June 1673

From my bed, at ten in the morning. My dearest black-curls, it makes me happy right in my heart that you, my dear boy, have arrived. No excuses! You must come here this evening, I do not care how you do it, for I am just too eager to see you and embrace you; nowhere but here will I tell you what you have to do.

To DUCHESS SOPHIE

Saint Cloud, 5 August 1673

As for my little one,[1] he is so terribly big and strong that, begging your leave, he rather resembles a German and a Westphalian than a Frenchman, as Your Grace will see from his picture as soon as it is painted, for I will send it to Your Grace right away. Meanwhile, monmaistre will bring my bear-cat-monkeyface[2] with him. People here all say that my little boy looks like me, so Your Grace can imagine that he is not exactly a pretty fellow, but so long as he pleases my godchild, Your Grace's little princess, everything will be well since, as Your Grace writes to me, they are to be a pair in good time. . . . Also want to tell Your Grace how glad I am that I will now learn how to ride a horse; this is a fine thought for Liselotte's rustle-bustle head, as Ma Tante knows very well. For if the truth be known, I have not changed all that much.

1. Her first son, Alexandre Louis, born 2 June 1673. 2. Her portrait. This expression seems to have been coined by Liselotte's father and remained an in-joke within her family.

To RAUGRÄFIN LUISE[1]

Paris, 26 August 1673

I was happy to see from Frau Raugräfin's letter that Carllutzchen is so content with the outcome of the journey he so much wanted to make. Carllutz is well aware that I am very fond of him and therefore has been pleased with everything that has happened to him here, which does not deserve particular thanks; I hope to deserve Frau Raugräfin's gratitude better if he comes again and stays longer which, I hope, will be soon. Meanwhile I wish to assure Frau Raugräfin that I am his, as well as her, affectionate friend, Elisabeth Charlotte.

1. Her father's second wife.

To DUCHESS SOPHIE

Saint Cloud, 10 October 1673

I am very glad to learn from Your Grace's welcome letter of 22 September that Your Grace is pleased with Monsieur's and my portrait which Jeme has brought along. As for my little lad, he does not (as the lady said) have a smelly head but, begging your leave, his ears do smell a bit like rotten cheese; but I trust he will have gotten over it by the time he marries my little god-child because she finds him pretty enough after all. When I look at him I sometimes remember how Godfather, Duke Georg Wilhelm, once said to me that I would be good enough to eat if I were roasted like a suckling pig, for my little one is so fat and round, thank God, that I am afraid he will soon be as wide as he is long. But this I do not fear as much as that he will lose only too much flesh and become quite skinny when he starts teething. I would not dare speak to Your Grace of this child for so long if I did not know that Your Grace loves children. . . .

Next week I hope to go hunting on horseback with the King. Jourdan[1] is a most sincere, honorable man. Hinderson[2] also thinks very highly of him. She has been ill with a touch of the red flux, but is now quite well again, and I believe that her health is in better condition than her marriage plans. This is a pity, for she is an excellent person, as Your Grace knows so well, and I am very fond of her and therefore am sorry that despite her great piety things do not seem to be moving as smoothly as they should. . . .

Your Grace's letters are the most valued of my relics and I am keeping good care of them, for Your Grace is the only saint through whom God has bestowed great favor upon me, and who has helped me more than any other.

1. Père Jourdan, Madame's confessor. 2. One of her ladies-in-waiting.

During the Dutch war (1672–79), William of Orange led the Dutch against the French troops, commanded by the so-called Great Condé. In the course of this war French troops under the command of Marshal Turenne repeatedly devastated the Palatinate.

Saint Cloud, 22 August 1674

If my wishes could come true, I would wish that Your Grace's little princess, my godchild, could have Monsieur le Dauphin[1] rather than my son, for this would be a better catch and also just right with respect to their ages; and then Your Grace should have another daughter and give her to my son. . . . God grant that our princess at Heidelberg[2] will soon begin to follow our good example. But my first wish for Heidelberg must be that God may restore the blessed peace to us, else the porridge will become very dear in the good Palatinate if Monsieur de Turenne[3] keeps taking away more cows, although I hope that Godfather[4] will now put a stop to this. . . .

Just now I am being called to go downstairs, for the King, the Queen, and the Dauphin wish to call on me in passing; they are coming from Paris where a Te Deum was sung today for the battle Monsieur le Prince won; he defeated the Prince of Orange's rear guard and took all the baggage trains and many prisoners. . . . All of this is very well and good, but to speak quite plainly, I would prefer a good peace to all of this, for if we had that, our good Palatinate and Papa would find some rest.

> 1. The King's first son, Louis, born in 1661. 2. Wilhelmine Ernestine, Elisabeth Charlotte's sister-in-law, who was and remained childless. 3. Henri de la Tour d'Auvergne, Vicomte de Turenne (1611–75), one of the great generals of the age. He had been a loyal defender of the monarchy during the uprising of the Fronde, and Louis XIV considered him the "father of the country." He died in this war. 4. He and his troops had come to the aid of Elector Karl Ludwig.

Paris, 22 May 1675

Praise and thanks be to God, not so much for delivering me from death as for giving me, for once, a day when I can express to Your Grace my humble gratitude for her most gracious message, in which Your Grace so kindly manifests her affection and the sadness she and Oncle have felt during my great illness.[1] I firmly believe that Monsieur, Papa, Your Grace, and Oncle have done more to abate my fever and to restore me to full health than Messieurs Braye, Baylay, Tissot, and Esprit,[2] and I do believe that the joy of feeling the sympathy of the former has done more to purge my spleen than the seventy-two clysters the latter had administered to me. The unbelievable crowd of people who came to see me every day has kept me from writing before now. Then I went to court, where for eight days in a row there were leave-takings for those who joined the army. And with all that, one only arises at half past ten around here; around twelve one goes to mass; after mass one chats with those who have attended, and around two one goes to table. After dinner the ladies come; this lasts until six, and thereafter come those of the men of quality who are still here. At this time Monsieur plays *bassette* and I also have to play at another table. . . . or I must take the others to the opera, which lasts until nine. When I return from the opera, I must play again until ten or half past ten, and then to bed. So Your Grace can imagine how much time I have had to myself. But henceforth I shall be more assiduous. Saturday next we shall go to Saint Cloud, where I will not have so much company that keeps me from writing.

1. Smallpox. 2. Court physicians.

Versailles, 22 August 1675

I must confess (and this is said just between us) that I have not been too sad about the battle that Marshal de Crécy lost against Oncle and Godfather.[1] I have here two wild characters who all day long make such noise with their drums that one can neither hear nor see; however, in the last two weeks the oldest[2] has become a little more quiet, for in this time he has cut five teeth, including the eye-teeth. This autumn he is to be weaned, for he already can happily devour a big chunk of bread from his fist like a peasant. The littlest one[3] is even stronger, he is already beginning to walk on his leash and wants to jump like his brother, but he is still a bit scaly-pated. But I think this is enough talk of the little fellows. Monday next we will go to Fontaine-bleau, where the King wants to take me because I have never been there. I hope we will have a good time, for all the hunting equipment is being sent there, as well as the comedians. The lovely weather we are having also makes me hope that we will take many carriage rides.

1. On 11 August, Duke Georg Wilhelm of Celle ("Godfather") and his brother Duke Ernst August of Braunschweig-Lüneburg ("Oncle") had defeated the French near Trier. 2. Alexandre Louis. 3. Philippe, born 4 August 1674.

Saint Cloud, 14 September 1675

I wish to express to Your Grace my joy that God Almighty has mercifully protected Oncle, Godfather, and the Prince[1] before Trier. When I learned of this news I could not jump for joy as I did when I heard of the victory in battle, for I was told of the taking of Trier by the King himself, who had extraordinary praise for Oncle and Godfather and also said that the prisoners were full of admiration for the generosity as well as the bravery of those who had captured them. Thereafter, when I told the King and Monsieur how generously our Prince had acted in the battle, where he not only charged against the enemy but also saved so many men's lives, and that he is barely fifteen years old, they marveled exceedingly. I know that Your Grace too would not have minded a bit to hear how all and sundry admired him.

I must admit that I had a fine time at Fontainebleau, but I have since paid bitterly for this pleasure, for when I arrived here I found my oldest child nearly at death's door. I told Monsieur that if the decision were mine to make, I would send my children to board with Frau von Harling at Osnabrück, for then I would be sure that they would not die or be brought up too delicately, as they are wont to be in this country, which makes me burst right out of my skin.

1. Georg Ludwig, Duchess Sophie's oldest son.

Your Grace's most welcome letter, which I received yesterday, has gladdened my heart, for I see from it, first of all, that Your Grace has had the joy of seeing the safe return—thanks be to God—of Oncle, the Prince, and Godfather, and also that Your Grace does me the honor of being pleased with me. The day before yesterday I had much pleasure listening to Monsieur de la Trousse speaking about the great admiration he has for these three lords and to hear him sing their praises, not only to me but to everyone here. Every day now the courtiers bring me prisoners who have been captured by our dukes to pay, as they say, their respects to me, for everyone has learned that it gives me great pleasure to hear about them. . . . Nay, Monsieur himself brings them to me, knowing that it gives me pleasure. Indeed, people suddenly think that I must be very special because I have lived with Your Grace for five years, whereupon I reply, so as not to bring disgrace upon Your Grace, that if I had been there longer I would undoubtedly have been brought up better . . . but that, alas, I had to leave when I was too young. This has made me very conspicuous at court, and as I pass people, I hear them say, "these princes who are praised so much are Madame's uncles and her first cousin." I am quite conceited about it, too, and when I receive a letter from Your Grace I read it three and four times, particularly in places where I see a lot of people, for usually someone will ask me from whom this letter has come, and then I casually throw out over my shoulder, "from Ma Tante, the Duchess of Osnabrück," and then they all stare at me as a cow stares at a new barn door.

To FRAU VON HARLING

I have been quite unable to answer you before now, for I was too stricken by the unexpected disaster God Almighty has visited upon me;[1] I simply cannot get over it. Now you see that it was not for nothing that I wished my children were in your hands, for I saw my misfortune come from afar. They have strange ways here with children, and unhappily I was only too aware that they would not work out well in the long run. My misfortune is that I have no idea how one must handle children, having no experience in this matter, and therefore I must believe all the drivel they tell me here. But enough of this, for the more I think about it, the sadder it makes me; and now there is no one here to comfort me, for last Thursday Monsieur left with the King for the army. All of this will not do my spleen any good, and however cheerful I may be by nature, this is no help in such dreadful sorrow. I do not believe that one can die of excessive sadness, for if this were the case I would undoubtedly have been done for; what I felt within me is impossible to describe. Unless God Almighty gives very special help to the child I am carrying now, I feel that its prospects for life and health are very poor indeed, for it is impossible that it should not have been affected by the pain within me. But speaking of pain: I hope that you will have regained perfect health and no longer feel your arm, especially in this lovely spring weather. But here they are calling me to the table, therefore I can say nothing more than that Monsieur Harling finds my greetings in this letter and that I am sure that if he saw me now he would not recognize me, for I am no longer a merry little leaf-rustler; in a dreadful way I no longer feel like rustling.

1. On 16 March her first son had died at the age of two years, nine months.

To RAUGRAF KARL LUDWIG

Saint Cloud, 27 April 1676

Dearest Carllutzchen, believing that you have returned home and that therefore my old nurse will see you, I did not want to let her go without giving her a little note for you to remind you that you must always love me, for I am very fond of you, my black-curls, and remain ever your affectionate friend Elisabeth Charlotte.

To FRAU VON HARLING

Saint Cloud, 30 May 1676

As for my great misfortune,[1] I am sure that you feel pity for me; I confess that for my part I have trouble digesting it, it has hit me just too hard. You are so very right, my dear Frau von Harling, in saying that the older one grows the more one comes to know the world and to feel all the miseries to which we are subject. Even now, when I have not yet gotten over this distress, Monsieur has left for the army, where he has already made me suffer a thousand frights by exposing himself to terrible dangers, as I am told in letters from all sides, in Condé's two sieges and then in that of Bouchain. This last siege was started and, thanks be to God, brought to a speedy and successful conclusion by Monsieur himself. And now I have even more worries, for we are told that many people in the army are falling ill, and since Monsieur fatigues himself no less than the others, often staying on horseback for twenty-four hours and going without sleep, I am afraid that he will end up getting sick too, for they say that the campaign will not be over soon and that the King is not even thinking about returning. O what a wearisome, wretched business. It is enough, as I wrote before, to make me forget all thought of rustling and to bring on a disease of the spleen before my time. I do wish from the bottom of my heart that we might soon have a good peace, for I am as tired of this war as if, by your leave, I had been stuffed with it by the spoonful, as the saying goes.

No one could have been more astonished than I was when I heard the story about Godfather,[2] and if I had not been told about it in a letter from Ma Tante, I would have refused to believe it and would have thought that this is something Godfather's enemies had laid on his doorstep. I wrote a story about this newly baked duchess to Ma Tante, who might pass it on to you: she [the new duchess] wanted to marry one of my husband's valets; his name is Colin and his son is still in service here to this day. Very befitting for a duchess of Celle. . . .

I wish that I could send you my remaining de Chartres[3] in a letter, for then I could be sure that he would stay alive, but, as it is, I am in constant fear and would like to be some three or four years older so that I could see this child safely weaned, for this is something they do not know how to do in this country; nor do they want to take any advice and so send an incredible lot of children into the other world. Perhaps, considering the strange things that are going on in this world, they do it to spare the poor children the trouble of contemplating the wretched state of the world; but I rather believe that it happens because of stupidity and negligence, for which I can cite a very strong example.

1. Her son's death.   2. Eléanore d'Olbreuse had been the mistress of Duke Georg Wilhelm of Celle for some years when he married her in 1676, making her the ruling Duchess of Celle.   3. Her second son, Philippe, Duc de Chartres.

To RAUGRAF KARL LUDWIG

Saint Cloud, 6 June 1676

My dearest Carllutz, I no longer say Carllutzchen, for if one is so capable an officer that he can last all through winter quarters, he is no longer a child, and so it would be insulting if I continued to treat you as a child. But I do believe that if you were here I might still sometimes call you my dear black-curls, which have surely not been bleached in the snowy mountains of the Tyrol. I can well understand if you say that you were quite bored down there, and I am sorry to hear it. But sometimes one finds more pleasure in a peasant hut and at a rural dance than in the greatest palaces and at the finest ballets and balls. However that may be, I wish you a happy and contented life wherever you may find yourself, for you know that I have always been very fond of you since you were a child, and still am. I have not written to you since the letter I sent through my old nurse because I believe that you are again on campaign and must be as busy as a mouse in her nest, which is why I felt that you might not have time to read my letters. However, your Mama has sent me a dose of swallow water[1] for convulsions, and so I want to make you my envoy, asking you to make my prettiest compliments to your Mama (if you should be at home) or otherwise give her my thanks by letter. Don't you forget it now, lad! Else I shall dreadfully box your ears. I wish we had peace, for I am very tired of war, and time hangs heavily on my hands. It is now nearly two months already that the King and Monsieur have been off to war without even thinking of returning, that is why there is little news, and what there is is nothing but foolishness. Adieu, dear Carllutz! Believe that I remain always your affectionate friend!

1. Probably water from the spa at Langenschwalbach.

To FRAU VON HARLING

Saint Cloud, 10 October 1676

Although today I have already written a long letter to Ma Tante, one of the first I have written since my confinement,[1] I do not wish to let this mail pass without thanking you for all the good wishes you sent me and my newborn child. As for me, I have been feeling exceedingly well, thanks be to God, ever since I was delivered and so far have not suffered the slightest discomfort, although this time the labor was harder than the other two times; I was in strong labor for ten hours and this, to tell the truth, has so put me off that I do not wish to build up a set of organ pipes, as you say in your letter; it is just too painful a business. And then if they stayed alive, that would be one thing, but if one sees them die, as I sadly experienced this year, there is no pleasure in it at all. As for my remaining de Chartres, whom I so often wish to be with you, he is now, thank God, in quite perfect health, as is his baby sister, who is as fat as a stuffed goose and very big for her age. On Monday last both of them were christened and given Monsieur's and my names, so that the boy is now Philippe and the girl Elisabeth Charlotte. Now there is another Liselotte in the world; God grant that she may not be more unhappy than I am, for then she will have little to complain about. As for the rest, I am much obliged to you for wishing as I do that my son were with you. If Ma Tante could see him now, he would give her a moment's amusement, for he can now speak in full sentences and walk by himself, and he babbles on all day long, it is enough to make one's head spin; he always converses with the King and the Queen when they come here.

1. On 13 September, Madame had given birth to a daughter, later the Duchesse de Lorraine.

To DUCHESS SOPHIE

Saint Germain, 14 December 1676

I humbly beg Your Grace's forgiveness for having failed in my duty to write for such an eternity. . . . After I arrived here, I meant to answer every day, but every time something kept me from doing it, especially a lot of tiresome visits with which I was loaded down after my fall from the horse. But this is a story I must tell Your Grace: We had already caught a hare and flushed out a magpie and were therefore riding along slowly. I felt that my dress was not under me properly, and so I stopped and bent down to straighten it out, but just at the moment when I was in that position a hare burst forth and everyone gave chase. My horse, seeing the others rush off, wanted to follow and jumped to one side, and in this way, not being firmly in the saddle, I slid all the way to one side, but I quickly grasped the pommel and kept my foot in the stirrup, hoping to lift myself back into the saddle; but as I grasped the pommel, I let go of the reins. I called out to a rider in front of me to stop my horse, but he galloped toward me so furiously that he frightened my horse, which lost no time turning to the other side and then bolted. Yet I held on as long as I saw that the other horses were close to me, and as soon as I found myself alone I slowly let go and dropped onto the green grass. This came off so well that I have not, thank God, hurt myself in the slightest. Your Grace, who so much admired our King for being such a comfort to me in the throes of my labor, will also love him for what he did in this instance, for he was the first one to reach me, looking as white as a sheet; and although I assured him that I had not hurt myself or fallen on my head, he would not rest until he had personally examined my head on all sides and finally decided that I had told him the truth; he also led me back to my room and even stayed with me for a while to see whether I might become dizzy. . . . I must say that even now the King still shows me his favor every day, for he speaks to me whenever he sees me and now calls for me every Saturday to have *medianoche*[1] with him and Madame de Montespan.[2] This is also the reason that I am now very much à la mode; whatever I say or do, whether it be good or awry, is greatly admired by the courtiers, to the point that when I decided to wear my old sable in this cold weather to keep my neck warm, everyone had one made from the same pattern, and sables have become quite the rage. This makes me laugh, for five years ago the very people who now admire and wear this fashion so laughed at me and made so much fun of me with my sable that I could no longer wear it. This is what happens at this court: if the courtiers imagine that someone is in favor, it does not matter what that person does, one can be certain that the courtiers approve of it; but if they imagine the contrary, they will think that person ridiculous, even if he has come straight from heaven. Oh how I wish it were possible for Your Grace to spend a few months here to observe this life: I am certain that Your Grace would have many a good laugh.

1. A nightly feast. 2. Mistress of the King.

To FRAU VON HARLING

Saint Germain, 31 January 1677

I had meant to answer your letter in Paris; however, all the visits I had to make while I was there did not leave me time, but now I thank you very much for your good wishes for the New Year. My own wish is that I might find the opportunity to show you my gratitude, for if there were to be a reckoning, you have done much more for me in my youth than I will ever be able to do for you; therefore I am embarrassed, my dear Frau von Harling, that you tell me that God should reward me for all my kindness toward you, which so far amounts only to good will, and that I continue to hold you dear is surely the least I can do. As for my somersault, I shall do my best not to let it happen again. It was not I who started this fashion, for two days earlier one of my ladies-in-waiting set the example. . . . I am eagerly looking forward to the pumpernickel and the smoked sausages, which I shall eat to your good health, and I thank you in advance. I imagine that the princesses of Wolfenbüttel resemble Duke Anton Ulrich, who also had white hair and eyelashes. This I do not find pretty at all, and would find it much prettier if you wrote me a long letter, for your letters amuse me very much.

In the spring of 1677, Elisabeth Charlotte's father had lost his morganatic wife, Raugräfin Luise, who died at the birth of her fourteenth child. Released from his vows to her, the Elector now considered marrying a princess of his own rank in order to produce an heir to his throne, since his son and successor seemed destined to remain childless and his sons by the morganatic marriage were ineligible. The only obstacle to another marriage was his repudiated wife, Elisabeth Charlotte's mother, who still refused to acknowledge the divorce. The Elector therefore threatened to blacken her name throughout Europe unless she agreed to the divorce. Such an action would have cast aspersions on the family background, possibly even the legitimacy, of Elisabeth Charlotte and her brother, and Madame was deeply concerned about its effect on Monsieur and the King. In the letter of 4 November 1677 she shares these fears with her aunt (who promptly passed them on to the Elector), and in the letter of 22 November she summons all her courage to demand an explanation from her father. We do not know whether or how he answered her, but in a letter to Duchess Sophie (24 November 1677) he expressed his irritation in the following terms: "I would like to know which ignorant or malicious person has persuaded Monsieur and Liselotte that it would be prejudicial to them or to the Electoral Prince if I married. You have answered her very well, and I shall give them, if the need arises, several examples showing that, in the French house itself, divorces and second marriages have not in any way jeopardized the legitimacy of the children of the first marriage. But I wish that Liselotte would stick to things that she understands better than this matter and that as long as she is unable to contribute anything to my tranquillity, she would at least abstain from causing me trouble, for those who make the laws believe that a child must have more respect for a father who has done more for her than a mother who has acted like a madwoman and a coquette." (E. Bodemann ed., Briefwechsel der Herzogin Sophie von Hannover mit ihrem Bruder, dem Kurfürsten Karl Ludwig von der Pfalz und des Letzteren mit seiner Schwägerin, der Pfalzgräfin Anna *[Leipzig, 1885].) In the end, the Elector did not remarry.*

To DUCHESS SOPHIE

Versailles, 4 November 1677

Every other day and quite often two and three days in a row I go hunting with the King, and we hunt here no less often than at Fontainebleau. Our King has suddenly taken a new pleasure in hunting the stag; this makes me very glad and I follow him as often as I can, for I am as fond of hunting as His Majesty is. It is a great pleasure for a merry little leaf-rustler like myself, since this is no time for dressing up and putting on rouge like at the balls. But speaking of balls: I am glad that Your Grace and her princess, my little godchild, were so well entertained at Amsterdam. . . .

God grant that we may be mistaken in our opinion concerning our princess at Heidelberg,[1] so that an end could be put to the things that are being said about the proposition that His Grace the Elector has made to Her Grace the Electress, my mother, things that I could not believe at first, not having heard a word about them from home, but which I can no longer doubt since it is Your Grace who writes to me about them. This serves His Grace very badly in this country and it is also being said that His Grace cannot divorce himself from Her Grace my mother without gravely wronging my brother and myself; for this reason I found Monsieur most exercised about it. The latter also told me that the King finds this matter very strange indeed, but I begged Monsieur to be patient until I have really found out where this matter stands, for I can scarcely believe that His Grace the Elector would wish to wrong my brother and myself, firstly because of the fatherly affection

I have always felt His Grace to have for both of us, and secondly I can believe even less that His Grace would wish to give us an affront, for after all we are so close to His Grace that this affront would be bound to fall back on his Grace. Moreover, Papa must be aware that I am now in a place where such things would hardly be tolerated. However that may be, I do wish with all my heart that His Grace the Elector might put such propositions out of his mind and place his trust in the Lord God. . . . I would much prefer to see our entire lineage extinct than to have His Grace the Elector accused of things that would serve him ill everywhere, and particularly in this country. . . .

As for the daughters of the Raugräfin, I should wish with all my heart to see them all established. Shortly before her death, the Raugräfin sent me a message through my old nurse, asking me to arrange a marriage for Karoline, my godchild, in this country. But here no one marries without money, and since I do not know whether they are rich or not, I have been unable to look for a match for her. If Papa were serious about this, I would have to be told what they can afford, and then it might be possible to find someone. But since, as Your Grace is telling me, a Count Wittgenstein is now asking for her hand, this marriage will no doubt come to pass.

1. The Elector's son's wife, who had not yet produced a child.

To ELECTOR KARL LUDWIG

Saint Germain, 22 November 1677

Considering that in three months I have not been favored with a single letter or any word from Your Grace, I have felt that respect forbade me to write and feared that my letters might importune Your Grace. Encouraged, however, by the filial trust I feel for Your Grace and by the memory of the past kindnesses and favors that Your Grace has always bestowed upon me, I have finally concluded that these sad times of war must be blamed and that nonetheless Your Grace has not seen fit to deprive me of his fatherly affection, for my conscience assures me every day that since the time when I was fortunate enough to pay my respects to Your Grace in person, I have done nothing that would make me unworthy of his good graces. These thoughts have caused me to content myself with being informed weekly by Breton that Your Grace is in perfect health, and meanwhile I have been wishing with all my heart that peace might return, in hopes that although even then it might not be possible to pay my respects to Your Grace in person, I would at least no longer be deprived of the comfort of being assured every week, or even every other week, by Your Grace's welcome letters of his continued good graces, without which I could never feel at ease. I was also willing not to write to Your Grace until the arrival of one of his welcome letters would, as it were, grant me permission to do so. But now I am forced to write by my most submissive filial attachment, for I believe that I would make myself unworthy of every favor I have ever received from Your Grace and of all the assurances of fatherly affection it has pleased Your Grace to bestow upon me if I failed to inform Your Grace of the prodigious rumors about Your Grace that have reached the ears of Monsieur and the King, rumors which, I fear, will at length greatly harm Your Grace in men's minds, for it is said that this case is unprecedented and altogether unheard of. It is claimed that Your Grace is, without cause, angry with my brother, keeping him a virtual prisoner and demanding that he persuade our mother, Her Grace the Electress, voluntarily to divorce Your Grace; it is also said that if she should refuse to do this, Your Grace would by fiat take another wife and disseminate wicked writings about our mother that would bring disgrace upon all of us. I confess that, having (as I said before) so often felt Your Grace's kindness toward my brother and myself, I am hard put to give credence to these tidings, however much I am assured that they are true; yet I do acknowledge that it pains me in my very soul to hear such things, and I do fear that if Monsieur and His Majesty were to be persuaded that Your Grace is embarked upon a course that would bring disgrace upon us, they would be most displeased and would seek to find means to cleanse me of any affront in order to keep me worthy of their alliance; this might well—and God protect us from this possibility—lead to worse misfortunes than if my brother were to die without heirs and the Palatinate fell into the hands of the Duke of Neuburg. But my brother and his wife are still young, so that there is still hope. Most submissively and on bended knees I therefore beg Your Grace to give most serious thought to this matter, and if there still be so much as a glimmer of Your Grace's fatherly affection for my brother and myself, I humbly beseech him to take pity upon us, considering that, if these rumors be true, nothing but evil can ensue from all this, for Your Grace's own person as well as for us. Your Grace may take umbrage that I am writing so freely, but I am counting on Your Grace's sense of justice, which will not permit him to condemn me, since in this matter I am much more concerned about Your Grace's reputation than about my own, and since this is the principal motive that has prompted me to write. For I still cannot give credence to the thing itself and therefore have not yet deemed it necessary to beseech Your Grace to spare me and my brother. I am looking forward to Your Grace's favorable reply, which will let me know how I am to answer questions of this kind in case His Majesty and Monsieur wish to speak to me further about this matter, as they have done before. Meanwhile I once again humbly beg Your Grace to believe that I would rather die a thousand times than be unfortunate enough to learn that either my brother or myself have lost Your Grace's fatherly affection and favor, believing as I do that I deserve this favor and affection by remaining until my last hour Your Grace's submissive, obedient, and most devoted daughter and servant Elisabeth Charlotte.

To DUCHESS SOPHIE

Saint Germain, 24 November 1677

Your Grace's valued letter of 26 October reached me at the end of last week in Paris. And since I see from it that Your Grace is pleased that Corneille's plays[1] are returning to favor, I will tell Your Grace that all the old ones are being played now, one after the other, and this is the best entertainment I have in Paris when I am there. Poor Corneille is very happy about it and assures me that this has made him feel so much younger that he wants to make another pretty comedy before his end. I wish that I might have the delight to take Your Grace to see it, but I am afraid that the war will last longer than dear old Corneille's life.

> 1. Pierre Corneille (1606–84), one of the great playwrights of the age. His plays had been eclipsed by those of Racine and Molière.

Saint Germain, 11 January 1678

Since this is the day when all of Germany celebrates New Year's Day,[1] I think it might not be too late to wish Your Grace, according to the excellent old German custom, a happy, healthy, and peaceful New Year, together with a long and healthy life. For myself, I wish for the blessed peace, so that I might once again have the happiness to pay my respects to Your Grace in person. For it seems altogether preposterous to me when I think that it has now been six years that I have not seen Your Grace. But when that blissful event comes to pass, I am certain that I should amuse Your Grace for at least an hour if I were to tell Your Grace about life here and the things that go on, which one cannot possibly imagine unless one sees and hears them and is in the midst of them, as I am now; indeed I believe that if I were to remain in Germany for several years . . . I would not soon . . . forget this court. . . .

I am being asked every day about this divorce story.[2] Your Grace and Oncle may make fun of me for being such a good Catholic and so eager to defend the sacrament of marriage, but this sacrament is agreeing well enough with me to make me wish it may be forever and that no means of divorce should be found, for if anyone wanted to divorce me from Monsieur he would not do me a favor; so Your Grace can imagine that I would be extremely displeased if such a thing should become the fashion. . . . I should wish with all my heart that His Grace the Elector shared my opinion, provided His Grace had as good a life as I do. I hope that my brother and our princess will soon get down to business and help us out of this predicament by producing a little child. . . .

There has been much talk here of the Prince of Orange's wedding;[3] among other things it is said that on the first night he went to bed with his wool breeches, and when the King of England asked him whether he did not want to take off this wool stuff, he replied that he and his wife would have to live together for a long enough time and that she would have to become used to his ways, and that since he was used to wearing his wool breeches he would not take them off now. And instead of supping with the King, the Queen, and the bride, he had supper in town and made the King wait till after midnight in the room of the bride, who had been put to bed; and when the King asked him where he had been all this time, he said that he had played cards after supper. Thereupon he threw himself into a chair, called for his valet, and had himself undressed right in the bridal chamber. With all of these manners I am not surprised that the bride was speechless; they almost remind me of the comedy of shrewish Kate and her husband.[4]

1. Germany still used the Julian calendar, whereas France had adopted the Gregorian calendar. 2. Her father's plans for a divorce. 3. The wedding of William and Mary. 4. Shakespeare's *Taming of the Shrew,* known in Germany from performances by troops of English comedians.

To RAUGRAF KARL LUDWIG

Saint Cloud, 13 May 1678

Dearest Carllutz, in earlier years I would have said, "There's a good boy," but now that you are so grown up, I say, "Splendid fellow, that was a jolly fine letter." Cantenac[1] will tell you how often I inquired about you. He told me that you have grown incredibly tall and even have a beard now; that makes me a little old lady, like Mutter Anneken, if you still remember that comedy. Adieu! Do write to me often if you have the time, especially when you are in Holland, and believe that you will always be as dear to me as I am to you! This you can count on, and be assured that I am your affectionate friend, Elisabeth Charlotte.

1. Cantenac, a minor French poet, served as Elector Karl Ludwig's secretary.

To DUCHESS SOPHIE

Saint Germain, 24 July 1678

I have properly received all Your Grace's letters; but even if the last one had fallen into other hands than mine, I can assure Your Grace that no one would have thought her silly because of the facetious parts that were in it. For Your Grace's reputation is well established here in every respect, and especially as regards her intelligence. Moreover, people are not particularly squeamish in this country and speak quite freely of all kinds of natural things. I know of one *galant,* whom I will not and may not name, who always goes to the nightstool with his mistress, and when one of them has finished, the other sits down on it, and so they converse with each other. And I know another couple who always confide in each other when they have had a clyster or are in need of one; this I have heard with my own ears when the lover said that he was in need of one because he had stuffed himself so much the night before that he had a great bellyache, therefore he wanted to have a clyster the better to eat at noon without feeling nauseated. How the French would laugh if Germans acted this way, but since they are doing it themselves it is considered good manners. I must tell Your Grace something else that at first seemed very peculiar to me; they talk very freely here of Mistress Catherine,[1] and the Queen, who is a most proper lady, talks about it with all the menfolks at public table. . . .

As for Your Grace's belief that as long as I have Monsieur I care nothing for heaven and earth, I must say that I am indeed very happy to be with him, but that even if it were true that I do not care about heaven and earth, I should be most distressed if Your Grace were to believe that she is included in heaven and earth and that I do not remember my dearest Ma Tante. Oh no! Never would Your Grace's Liselotte be so oblivious and so ungrateful, and if I do not answer immediately because a lot of riffraff here keeps me from writing, I am nonetheless thinking of Your Grace.

1. Menstruation.

To FRAU VON HARLING

Saint Cloud, 20 August 1678

I believe this letter will no doubt become very old [before it reaches you], but I did not want to let Mademoiselle de Montargis go without recommending her to you. . . . I herewith also send you the promised little box, using it as a cage for my bear-cat-monkeyface because I thought that you, my dear Mistress Uffel, would enjoy it. Here they always want to paint one prettier than one is, that is why they have made me fatter than I am, as you will see. It is not my fault if this is not a very good likeness, for just to please you I have sat here for a whole afternoon to have my picture painted, which is no fun at all; but then one sometimes does things that one would not otherwise do for one's friends, and especially friends to whom one owes as much as I owe to you. I am also sending a present from the Saint-Laurent fair to my little godchild, your pupil; it is a writing case with some pocket baubles in it, which have become quite the fashion, and which people carry around in their pockets. It is not much of a present, but then children are easily pleased and so I hoped that the writing case with these little things would have the same effect on the Princess.

To DUCHESS SOPHIE

I am proud indeed that Your Grace finds me prettier than the picture that I
sent to Frau von Harling. But it has been seven years now since Your Grace
saw me, and if Your Grace were to see me now, she might find that quite
the opposite is true. But it is not the hunting that makes me so old and ugly
but rather the cabals, which throughout these seven years have given me
so many wrinkles that my whole face is covered with them. . . .

This very moment Monsieur arrives from Versailles and tells me as the
latest news that next April we will travel to Flanders, from there to Lorraine, and from Lorraine to Alsace. I hope that at that time I can go to Strasbourg to see His Grace my father, my brother, and his wife. Your Grace
should plan a little trip there as well, that would be a fine rendezvous. I do
believe that if this were to come to pass I should die with happiness. What
I like best about it is that this is not a castle in the air but from all appearance
something that can and will be done. I beseech Your Grace most earnestly
to come to Strasbourg also at that time and to make my joy complete! Then
Your Grace will also see that all of us have the same coiffures as Mesdemoi-
selles de Valence and Montargis, for no one in France, except those who
always wear a piece of cloth, has any different hairdo. How Your Grace would
laugh if she saw me with this turkey-puff!

Paris, 3 February 1679

If it were too far for Your Grace to come to Alsace and Strasbourg, Your
Grace might give me rendezvous in Flanders, in whatever town would be most
convenient for Your Grace. I do not know why Oncle wishes Your Grace
to spend a great deal of money for such a journey, particularly since it would
be so much more convenient if Your Grace traveled incognito. That would
let Your Grace out of all the solemn ceremonies which I would curse from
the bottom of my heart if they deprived me of the happiness of paying my
respects to Your Grace, for it seems to me that if only I could see Your
Grace and Oncle once again I would gladly die afterward, but not without having continued all the way to Strasbourg and having seen Papa, my brother,
and my sister. To return to my text, however, I must tell Your Grace in plain
words that the haughtiness of this court stinks to high heaven, and that it
is well-nigh impossible to imagine or describe the high and mighty notions
and the stubbornness that prevail here. Therefore it is quite clear to me
that it would be impossible to see Your Grace in her proper rank, for my husband imagines that there is no comparison between him and any prince
elector; I have surreptitiously tried to find out whether Your Grace would
be given an armchair[1] . . . but they do not want to hear of it. So I will tell

Your Grace what my opinion is and what means I have found to see Your Grace. Your Grace would have to come incognito to a town in Flanders and let me know in which house Your Grace would be lodging . . . then I would pretend that I only wish to see that house, and then I would closet myself with Your Grace and Oncle in a room, where I would wish to be nothing but the Liselotte of former days, who will do anything Your Grace desires, for I am and will be to my dying day Your Grace's own bondswoman. And this would be the way to get out of all tiresome ceremonies. I would not have to be concerned about my retinue, for if I let Monsieur into the secret, I could send them off wherever I please and they could come back for me whenever Your Grace gets tired of me. And this I could do every day as long as we would remain in one particular place. I beg Your Grace to let me know very soon whether Your Grace likes this plan of mine; I also beg Your Grace not to be concerned about me, for I assure Your Grace that I can very well arrange to be by myself without a single person from my retinue. I beseech Your Grace for Heaven's sake to grant me this unutterable happiness! Indeed, I believe that I shall faint with joy if this comes to pass and when I set eyes on Your Grace and Oncle. I hope to do the same thing in Strasbourg to see His Grace the Elector, my brother, and his wife.

> 1. Armchairs in the presence of the King and the royal family were given only to reigning foreign monarchs. French dukes, peers, and cardinals were permitted *tabourets* (stools), and all others had to stand.

This visit did not materialize. However, in August of that year Duchess Sophie came to France. She was hoping to arrange the marriage of her ten-year-old daughter with the Dauphin, but in the end the latter decided to marry the Bavarian princess who had been proposed earlier.

To ELECTOR KARL LUDWIG

Saint Germain, 13 May 1679

To return to my black-curls who, thanks be to God, is now once again with me, the King received him most graciously when Monsieur presented him to His Majesty. Yesterday the King lent him some of his own horses for the stag hunt; this is a favor he rarely bestows on foreigners. His Majesty finds that Carllutz cuts a fine figure on horseback. Right now he is playing blind-man's buff with Mademoiselle.[1] . . . Now Your Grace will have to give orders as to when he wishes to have Carllutz back. But if I may make bold to express my opinion, it would not do him any harm to remain here for six weeks or two months; that would surely untie his tongue, and besides he will not get into any trouble, for Monsieur always lodges him in our house, here as well as at Paris and Saint Cloud.

1. Elisabeth Charlotte, Madame's daughter.

To DUCHESS SOPHIE

Saint Germain, 1 November 1679

This is a safe opportunity to send along the diamond buttons from the King.[1] Monsieur is very sorry that he cannot show Your Grace himself how they are to be worn on the dress or on the sleeves, and he has already deliberated about it with Madame de Mecklenburg, who is to send Your Grace a paper pattern. Then Oncle (I hope) will ask again what Your Grace wants with this crap. If I were allowed, I would often say the same thing to Monsieur.

1. A present on the occasion of the Duchess's visit.

Elisabeth Charlotte's father, Elector Karl Ludwig, had been in ill health for several years. His physical ailments were compounded by his frustration at occupying a position "between the anvil and the hammer," as he put it, that is, between his increasingly aggressive French neighbor and the impotent German Empire. After the Treaty of Nymwegen (1678), Louis XIV instituted a series of "reunion chambers," which established fictitious legal claims to areas he wished to annex. Karl Ludwig thus suffered the humiliation of seeing the arrival of French officials in his capital of Heidelberg. Madame's intercession with Louis XIV was unsuccessful, and the Elector was spared further chagrin only because he died (August 2, 1680). Elisabeth Charlotte's fears that her father was angry with her were indeed justified; his correspondence with his sister in the last years of his life is full of disparaging remarks about her failure to influence Louis XIV.

Saint Cloud, 24 September 1680

Although my eyes hurt so much from weeping that I can scarcely look out of them and therefore have great trouble writing, I did not wish to let our prince[1] leave here without giving him a letter for Your Grace, for despite my immense grief and sorrow about our dreadful loss, I believe that my heart will be somewhat lightened by writing to someone who is as sad as I am and shares this great misfortune with me. It would, of course, be impossible to describe to Your Grace what I feel and the pangs I suffer day and night, but Your Grace, alas, will be able to gauge this by her own sorrow. Now that I have a safe opportunity I can speak plainly, and I must therefore tell Your Grace that she is rather more fortunate than I am, for although her loss is as great as mine, she is at least not obliged to live with those who without any doubt have caused the death of His late Grace the Elector through all the anguish they have caused him, and this is hard for me to swallow. Your Grace says in her kind last letter that she rejoices with me that I am with the King whose company I enjoy so much. Yes, I admit that I was very fond of him and liked being with him before he began to persecute Papa so dreadfully, but since then I can assure Your Grace that it has been very hard for me and will be so as long as I live; indeed I would not have done it at all if he himself had not promised me at Fontainebleau to do better and to change his ways if only I would live in peace with him, and this is why during our journey I have done my best, though unfortunately without success, as Your Grace can see. If it should please God Almighty to let me follow Papa, nothing better could happen to me, for henceforth my entire life is bound to be wretched, as Your Grace must understand. I wish to God, too, that I could travel with the prince to Your Grace, for I would rather weep with Your Grace than be here with all these laughing faces, which would increase my sadness even further if that were possible. I also believe that His Grace the prince is not sorry to leave this country; and how right he is about that!

1. Georg Ludwig, Duchess Sophie's son.

To RAUGRÄFIN KAROLINE

Saint Cloud, 13 October 1680

As for you and your brothers and sisters, you may rest assured and also assure all of them in my name that I shall most gladly serve you to the best of my ability. And even though I am convinced that my brother's good character is such that he would never forsake you, His Grace our late father's children, I have nonetheless written to him about this matter and highly recommended your interests to him. I am totally ignorant of your affairs and therefore do not see for the moment in what ways I can be most helpful to you; therefore it would be advisable for Carllutz to come here to inform me about everything, so that we could plan together what steps must be taken. Ma Tante of Osnabrück also has very warm feelings for all of you, and I will frequently take council with her as to how I can best serve you. This you may firmly believe, and also that I shall always remain your affectionate friend.

To ELECTOR KARL

Saint Cloud, 13 October 1680

Karoline has written me a most pitiful letter on behalf of all the children, but I know your kind heart to be such that even without my intercession you would have compassion for these poor children and would not abandon them for they are, after all, the late Elector's children, and since they are now all alone in the world, the generous thing is to take care of them. For although you and I have suffered a dreadful loss as far as our tender love for His late Grace the Elector is concerned, it must be acknowledged that these poor young things have lost even more and that they would be altogether desperate if you did not take pity on them. But as I said before, knowing your kind heart as I do, I am not worried for them.

Saint Cloud, 27 November 1680

As for the children of the Raugräfin, I believe that our mother is entirely too reasonable to disapprove or to become alarmed that I speak up for these poor children. For I do not ask that they be paid in preference to Her Grace, God forbid! but only remind you not to abandon them, because they are our father's, the late Elector's, children and as such entitled more than others, and more than the servants, to your consideration. And this all the more since this will afford you a means of showing to the world the respect you had for His late Grace the Elector, which is bound to bring you nothing but praise. For it is always praiseworthy to take care of the unfortunate who are in need of help. Since your own interest thus coincides with theirs, I could not but point this out to you. Her Grace our mother is herself so generous that I have no doubt she will spur you on in this matter rather than hold you back, particularly since these children are not in a position to harm her own interests in any way. In short, I am glad to hear that you will treat them reasonably. For if you do that, they will be neither forsaken nor unhappy, and you, as I said before, will reap high praise from all and sundry and at the same time do your duty by her Grace the Electress who is near you and by His Grace the Elector who, alas, is in his grave, and all of this is bound to have God's blessing, which no one wishes you more cordially than I do.

To DUCHESS SOPHIE

Saint Germain, 11 December 1680

I fear that Papa has died of grief and sorrow and that if the great man and his ministers had not chagrined him so much we would have had him with us longer and I might even have seen him again. . . . I take some comfort from Your Grace's assurance that His Grace the Elector was not angry with me before his end. I am surprised, however, that he had not sent Your Grace the long dialogue I had with the great man. For I know for a fact that he received it two weeks before he fell ill, and since he did not answer it but only had Eck write that it had been received, I was afraid that he was not pleased with me. . . . Monsieur proposed to the Queen that she should make a vow . . . for her son's health; but I am telling Your Grace that he should rather advise the King to make a vow to practice justice henceforth, to return to everyone what he has taken and, in a word, not to covet what does not belong to him, this would be much better for his son's well-being.

To FRAU VON HARLING

Saint Cloud, 10 April 1681

Meanwhile I must . . . also tell you that I am now an old mother, for my son is wearing breeches and doublet, looking very smart. I wish that you could see him like this now, for he has become much more human and reasonable than he was when Ma Tante was here. And my little girl is now one of the funniest children you have ever seen and talks a blue streak about everything that comes into her head; she is a real tomboy, but I do not know how she will turn out in the end. She is not lacking in wit, but full of mischief, and although she is two years younger than her brother, she is much stronger and proportionally taller for her age.

To DUCHESS SOPHIE

Saint Cloud, 13 April 1681

In the last few days I have received three letters from Her Grace the Electress,[1] in which I am being reproached, albeit in a most polite manner, for taking so much interest in the children of the Raugräfin and writing so often on their behalf. My brother has not yet replied to my letter, but the Electress my mother goes into great detail about this matter. I do not write to the children themselves, for this does not help them and only irritates my brother and my mother. I shall advise Carllutz, considering that Oncle and Your Grace have extended him their gracious permission to call on them, to stay with them, for it appears to me from the Electress's letter that my brother hates him terribly, but she also says that he likes the girls and will eventually soften toward Carllutz. . . .

I know some fine stories, one of which I simply must tell Your Grace: I heard it three or four days ago, and it happened in a Jesuit college. The Chevalier de Lorraine claims that it is his son who did this trick and that he does this sort of thing all the time. One of the pupils at the college was full of mischief of all kinds, ran around all night long, and did not sleep in his room. So the reverend fathers threatened him with a tremendous beating if he did not stay in his room at night. The boy goes to a painter and asks him to paint two saints on his buttocks, on the right cheek Saint Ignatius of Loyola and on the left Saint François Xavier, which the painter did. With that the boy tidily pulls up his breeches, goes back to his college, and starts making all kinds of trouble. When the reverend fathers catch him at it, they tell him, "This time you'll be whipped." The boy begins to struggle and plead, but they say that pleading will not do him any good. So the boy gets down on his knees and says, "O Saint Ignatius, o Saint Xavier, have pity upon me and perform a miracle for me to prove my innocence." With that the fathers pull down his breeches, and, as they lift up his shirt to beat him, the boy calls out, "I am praying with such fervor that I am certain my invocation will be heard!" When the fathers see the two painted saints, they exclaim: "A miracle! the boy whom we thought a rogue is a saint!" And with that they fall on their knees to kiss the behind and then call together all the pupils and make them come in procession to kiss the holy behind, which all of them do.

1. Her mother.

To FRAU VON HARLING

Fontainebleau, 29 September 1681

It will be some time now before I can write again, for the King will be leaving from here tomorrow to hurry off to the siege of Strasbourg and the Queen, Madame la Dauphine, and I will follow more slowly as far as Nancy, where we will remain. . . . Adieu then, my dearest Frau von Harling, I must go to pack. At whatever corner in the world I may find myself, you can be sure that you have an affectionate friend there.

On 30 September Louis XIV succeeded in capturing and occupying the Free Imperial City of Strasbourg. Since no help was to be expected from the Emperor, the proud citizens were forced to swear the oath of loyalty.

To RAUGRAF KARL LUDWIG

Saint Germain, 1 January 1682

Dearest Carllutz, Ma Tante tells me in her letter that you wonder why you have not heard from me in such a long time. There are two reasons for this, the first being that I know that it is still hard for you to write with your hand and therefore wanted to spare you this trouble; the second is that I kept waiting for your reply to the letter I had sent you a few days before I sent Jasmin[1] back to you. This letter was dated 26 June 1681, but you do not mention it in answering the letter I sent through Jasmin. That is why I am beginning to worry that you might not have received it, for there was a lot of nonsense in it that would not be so good for others to read, stories about Cousin Fana[2] and tomfoolery of that kind; the whole letter was full of these, and I cannot imagine what must have happened to it. I have never lost a letter in the Hanover mail and would be quite unhappy if this were the first time. Please write me as soon as you can what you know about it, whether it was really lost or whether you forgot to answer it. God grant that it may be the latter. . . .

Since my return to Saint-Germain after our journey, I have received your kind letter of 11 November. I believe as you do that your business with my brother will eventually be straightened out. . . . Her Grace the Electress, my mother, does not have bitter feelings toward you at all, on the contrary, she tells me that she is fond of all of you children. Karoline also wrote to me when I was at Strasbourg and seems to be well pleased with Her Graces's attitude. I have done my best to recommend you to my mother and have told her that she could do me no greater favor than to be kind to you, that, knowing your good character, I am certain that you would be most appreciative of anything she would do for you, and that I am very fond of you. . . . How I would have wished that it had been possible for me to embrace you at Strasbourg. I do believe we would have bawled together; for as I was driving by the inn Zum Ochsen, I remembered that it was there that I had seen His Grace the Elector for the last time. This made me feel so dreadfully weepy that I simply could not hold back, and dear Coppenstein[3] and I wept together for more than an hour. It has made me quite fond of him. The poor man was so happy when he saw me that he turned as pale as a corpse. He is most devoted to you, and this is another reason why I think highly of him. . . .

For myself I do not know how the beginning new year will end for me, but the last one was certainly one of the most damnably bad years I have ever spent in my life, and it has made me feel so out of sorts and melancholy that people almost do not recognize me. Three weeks ago, when I was not feeling well, Wendt[4] thought that I would die because, he said, I was so changed; and so he cried all evening. I cannot tell you what upsets me so, but you are well enough acquainted with this country and this court to know that one can meet with a great deal of injustice, and that one can have plenty of reasons to become melancholy, however cheerful one may be by nature. But since I am beginning to feel that this is most harmful to my health, I am trying to put all of this out of my mind as much as ever I can. If you had been here, you would have been raving mad on my behalf. But what good does that do? One must be patient. But enough talk of all this! Adieu, dearest Carllutz!

1. Jeme. 2. Memories of Carllutz's escapades during his stay in Paris. 3. Master of the Horse at the court of Heidelberg. 4. Madame's *chevalier d'honneur*.

To DUCHESS SOPHIE

Paris, 23 January 1682

Your Grace is once again giving proof of her innate generosity in her treatment of dear Coppenstein and also Carllutz; but I am quite certain that neither of them will ever cause Your Grace to regret this generosity, for Carllutz's good character is already known to Your Grace, and Coppenstein too is most faithful and sincere; I therefore hope that your Grace will be pleased with his services. Carllutz, I imagine, will have had a merry time with the Holy Christ Child, for at his age he will not have been as frightened as I was when the Christ Child visited me at Hanover. I am happy to see that Your Grace still thinks of me often and also remembers all the things I did when I was a child. If Your Grace were to see my daughter now, she might make Your Grace remember even better, for she is just as wild as I was in every way, even to crapping in her skirt and not minding a bit being whipped; in a word, she is a real Liselotte. —Madame la Dauphine[1] is pregnant, but I am not, any more than I was when Your Grace was here; this is all I say, for as Your Grace will recall the mail is not to be trusted. . . . Your Grace is certainly correct in assuming that I would most willingly carry out Your Grace's assignment and help Cantenac.[2] However, as Your Grace adds herself right away, the great man does not always comply when I ask for something, especially when it comes to granting benefices, for there are so many who hope to snap them up. But I will try the Bishop of Strasbourg[3] and write to him on Cantenac's behalf to see if he might not use him for more than singing *pai pai* and *mai mai*, as Your Grace says, which made me laugh heartily.

1. The Bavarian Dauphine, Maria Anna Christine.   2. Secretary, librarian, and curator of Elector Karl Ludwig's art collections, he was out of favor with the new Elector and looking for a new position.   3. Egon Fürst von Fürstenberg.

Saint Germain, 19 February 1682

I am well aware that by being sad one only harms oneself and does one's enemies a great favor, but there are occasions when one cannot help but take things to heart. However much I seek to arm myself by reason, I often find myself caught, for I do not have as good a mind nor as much spunk as Your Grace and therefore cannot dismiss these things right away and accommodate to the ways of the world. I just go along as best I can, thinking that if I do not seek to harm others, I should be left in peace too. But then when I see that I am being set upon from all sides I become very cross, and as I am quite impatient to begin with, all these vexations make me lose what little patience I have left. And then I have to sort everything out in my own head in order to break out of this labyrinth, and there is no advice or help anywhere because everyone here is so calculating and false that one cannot trust anyone. That makes me preoccupied and cranky, and when I am cranky my spleen swells up, and when that is swollen it sends vapors into my head, which make me sad, and when I am sad, I get sick. These are some of the causes of my recent illness, but as for describing how they came about and what has upset me so much, that cannot be entrusted to paper, for I am quite certain that my letters are being read and opened. The post office is doing me the honor . . . of resealing my letters in the most careful fashion, but our dear Madame la Dauphine often receives hers in strange condition and ripped at the top; and when I see that I often think, as the Scripture says: "If they do these things in a green tree, what shall be done in the dry?" I assure Your Grace that I should by no means be bored at Hanover if I were so fortunate as to be there with Your Grace and Oncle; after all Your Grace knows that however much I hate convents I was never bored at Maubuisson as long as Your Grace was there. I also must confess one thing to Your Grace: all that glitters is not gold, and for all their boasting about the famous French liberty, all diversions here are unbelievably stiff and constrained. And besides, I have become accustomed to so many dreadful things since my arrival in this country that if I could ever return to a place where falseness does not rule everything and where lies are neither the daily fare nor approved of, I should think that I had come to a paradise. I therefore leave it to Your Grace to imagine whether I would (if I had the choice) be better off here or at Hanover. I have heard from others that Your Grace is having the entire château remodeled; I am only sorry that my room and my apartment are changed, for I flatter myself that if these remained as they were in my time, they would always remind Your Grace of her Liselotte, and that Your Grace would never have walked through my room without thinking of me. . . .

It seems that my credit with my brother is none too good these days, since he does not give Carllutz his due even though I had so earnestly begged him to do so; but I am not worried that he is angry with me for having become a Catholic, for if we were ever to see each other again, we would soon be good friends again, since I am convinced that he is fond of me in spite of himself.

Versailles, 10 July 1682

How I wish that I could have been at the ball at Herrenhausen; I would gladly have given Monsieur's jewels and finery for it, if they were mine to give. But if that had been the case, they would not soon see me again at the balls that are held here, and if Your Grace wanted to get rid of me she would have to chase me out of the house with sticks. . . . How I wish I were free to leave for Hanover this minute and to move there; I certainly would not lose any time nor wait until tomorrow.

The following letter, delivered by hand, contains the first veiled allusions to the cabal that spread the rumor that Madame was having a galanterie *with a minor courtier. Monsieur's favorites hoped to discredit her with her husband and with the King.*

Versailles, 21 July 1682

Comfort is what I need most, for I am again as gloomy as an old dog, and I believe that in the last year the devil has appeared here in human shape just to make me burst out of my skin and to teach me all about diabolical and human falseness. And in this science I have now become so perfectly learned that my teachers ought to leave me alone for a while, for I know only too well and find out every day about lies that do not contain a single word of truth, about broken promises, about acting in the most friendly manner while preparing terrible affronts and secretly cutting off one's honor, and even about pretending to believe awful things about one, knowing perfectly well that they are not true, and finally about those who wonder why one is sad and ask everyone else what could be the matter, knowing all the while in their conscience that they themselves are daily and hourly giving cause for this sadness. My bad humor would soon dissipate if I were permitted to call upon Your Grace for a time, but this joy I am not to have, and therefore I must not continue in this text lest the cobwebs in my head become even worse than they already are. What else is there to tell Your Grace. . . .

In an hour we shall go to an opera that will be played in the riding school. In a few days Madame la Dauphine will make a different music, for she is now five weeks into her ninth month and expects to be delivered any day.[1] I do not have such worries, for it is now four years and more that I am permitted to live in perfect chastity; this I can herewith tell Your Grace because I believe that this is a safe opportunity, and in the mail I should not dare put down such outrageous things as are written in this letter. Meanwhile the clock strikes seven, and since I want to write a few words to Carllutz, Your Grace will permit me to close.

1. On 6 August, the Dauphine gave birth to her first son, Louis, Duc de Bourgogne.

To RAUGRAF KARL LUDWIG

Versailles, 23 August 1682

Dearest Carllutz, [I write to you] even though I am in unspeakable melancholy and discontent because my enemies have persuaded Monsieur to chase away poor Théobon,[1] just as the Maréchale de Clérembeau[2] was chased away a few years ago when you were here. You know how painful such things are to me, and this latest affront involved even more to-do than the first, and this has upset me so much that I cannot even speak about it. I do believe they will end up squeezing the very life out of me. . . . These poor people committed no other crime than to be devoted to me. If you saw me now you would feel sorry for me, for I am grieved to the depth of my soul. I am not good for anything but bringing misery to those who love me. Therefore it would be best if God wanted to take me unto Himself, for I am thoroughly sick and tired of life.

1. A lady-in-waiting to Elisabeth Charlotte. She later married the Comte de Beuvron and was recalled to Madame's household after the death of Monsieur.   2. Another lady-in-waiting of whom Madame saw a great deal in later years.

To DUCHESS SOPHIE

Versailles, 12 September 1682

I would a thousand times rather live in a place ridden with ghosts and spirits, for to them Our Lord would not give power over me. But these confounded chevalier-ghosts[1] who, alas, have only too much flesh and blood, they are permitted by Monsieur and the King to perpetrate every evil deed, as I am finding out every day. And although the chevalier has debauched the great man's son, said nasty things about his daughter, and persecutes me every day, he is not taken to task for any of this and indeed is better off than others who only go along their straight path. Oh how I wish that Your Grace's wish came true and that Lucifer would take him into his kingdom soon; but since he might be frightened if he were all alone, I wish him a companion for his voyage, namely the Marquis d'Effiat,[2] who, I am sure, will know the way, for what with his horrendous vices and other wickedness too, I am bound to think that he must have been Lucifer's subject even before he assumed human form to betake himself here in order to make me burst right out of my skin. . . .

I am very fond of Mademoiselle de Théobon and would have been sorry under any circumstances to have her taken away from me, since I have always found her faithful to me and know that she is quite attached to me, and for this I shall thank her as long as I live; but this in itself would be no reason to become so terribly upset, and I would have taken it as I did when they sent away the Maréchale de Clérembeau and Beauvais,[3] who also had committed no other crime than to be faithful to me and devoted to my service, just like Théobon. But to give all the more punch to this latest trick they have played on me, my enemies have embroidered it with the following circumstances: three months earlier they spread the rumor that I was having an affair and that Théobon was carrying my letters, and then they saw to it that Monsieur chased her away without warning, ordering her not to have any more dealings with me as long as she lives, while the Chevalier de Beuvron[4] was dismissed only because it was feared that I might speak with him and give him messages for Théobon. I leave it to Your Grace to imagine what the world is bound to think of all this and whether it pains me to know my innocence and yet find myself in such dishonor, without ever being heard as to whether or not I can justify myself, even though I tearfully begged to be given this chance. . . .

As for Madame la Dauphine, I am extremely pleased with her, for she is very kind and shows her friendship for me whenever she can. The good princess cordially wept with me, which is another reason why I am so fond of her. I am well-nigh choking, for I cannot speak openly with anyone, and even now I must hold back, for I cannot entrust the mail with everything I would like to tell Your Grace. But I shall not make any bones with my faithful Wendt,[5] for in the six years that he has been with me I have found that he deserves this title, and so I have ordered him to tell Your Grace everything he has seen and heard here. . . . Your Grace can imagine how much I must be changed and how deeply all of this dishonor has touched my heart. I had made up my mind to spend the rest of my life at Maubuisson[6] and badgered the King about it for three whole days, to the point where he finally told me that he would absolutely refuse and that I should put the idea out of my mind since he would never give his consent, no matter what happened to me.

1. Allusion to the Chevalier de Lorraine. 2. One of her husband's favorites. 3. A squire in Madame's household. 4. Captain of Monsieur's guard. 5. Madame's *chevalier d'honneur,* who was about to travel to Hanover. 6. Convent near Pontoise, where Madame's aunt was abbess.

To FRAU VON HARLING

Saint Cloud, 15 September 1682

The bearer of this letter is certainly known to you, but I am also bound to say on his behalf that he is one of the most honest, faithful, and upstanding people I have ever known; I therefore hope that Oncle will not be sorry to have graciously accepted him as a squire at his court. If I were not so unfortunate that Monsieur believes my enemies more than he believes me and therefore will not let anyone who is faithful to me stay with me . . . I certainly would never have parted with Wendt.[1] For I can truthfully say about him that, however profitable it is here to be unfaithful to me and to betray me to my enemies, as many have done, I have never had the slightest doubt about his loyalty, and indeed he has risked everything by making it clear to the world that he is totally devoted to me. And since you, my dearest Frau von Harling, love me, I do not doubt that you will like Wendt for it, and I therefore beg you, as a favor to me, to assist him with your good advice at the new court that will be quite unfamiliar to him. . . . And since I am sending this by a safe opportunity, so that I can speak much more openly than in the mail, I shall also ask you please to tell Monsieur Harling from me that he must keep warning my little Harling not to fall into the vices that are current here. Happily, I have not yet noticed anything that would make me uneasy . . . but one cannot warn him enough. For even though I have a great deal to say to him about this, he may think that my own interest is involved; but if he hears the same thing from his uncle, he will realize that what I am telling him is for his own good. This I wish for two reasons: firstly so that Harling will turn out altogether perfect and you will not be sorry that you entrusted the child to me, but secondly also for my own sake.

1. Wendt returned to Madame's service after the death of Monsieur.

To ELECTRESS WILHEMINE-ERNESTINE[1]

Versailles, 6 December 1682

My dearest sister, I had meant to write Your Grace a great big letter through Count Schomberg,[2] but this has turned out as the proverb says, "Man proposes and God disposes." For he came here the day before yesterday and said that he would have to leave by Tuesday night, and that I would have to give him my letters on Monday. On that day I was unable to write because people kept coming in until six o'clock, and at six o'clock I had to go upstairs to the Queen's rooms, for it was *jour d'appartement.* Your Grace does not know what this means, but I will tell her as soon as I have done with what I am saying. Yesterday I wrote to my brother and to Karoline, and just as soon as I was about to start writing to Your Grace as well, my chambermaids came in to dress me, for at seven there was a confounded ball which I had to attend against my will and without pleasure, for of all entertainments I have come to hate dancing more than anything else. Today I gave an audience to an envoy of Parma, thereafter I had to write a long letter to the Queen of Spain,[3] and at eight I must go to see a new play with Madame la Dauphine. So I have only this hour to write, for tomorrow, right after the King's mass, I must go hunting with His Majesty and after the hunt it will be a bit late to write, for it is again *jour d'appartement.* And so that Your Grace can understand what this is, Your Grace must know that the King is having a great gallery built here, which goes all the way from his apartment to that of the Queen. But since this gallery is not quite completed yet, the King has had the part that is done and painted partitioned off and turned into a salon. Mondays, Wednesdays, and Fridays are *jours d'appartement.* Then all the men of the court assemble in the King's antechamber and all the women meet at six in the Queen's room. Thereupon everyone goes to the salon of which I spoke, and from there to a large room where there is music for those who want to dance. From there one goes to a room where the King's throne stands. There one finds various kinds of music, concerts and singing. From there one goes into the bedchamber, where three tables for playing at cards are set up, one for the King, one for the Queen, and one for Monsieur. From there one goes to a room that could be called a hall, where more than twenty tables, covered with green velvet cloth with a gold fringe, have been put up for all kinds of games. From there one goes to a large antechamber containing the King's billiard table, and then to another room with four large tables for the collation, all kinds of things like fruit cakes and preserves. This looks just like the children's table on Christmas eve. From there one goes into yet another room, where there are also four tables as long as those for the collation, and on these there are a great many carafes and glasses and all kinds of wines and liqueurs . . . so that those who want to eat or drink can make a stop in these two rooms. After one is done with the collation, which is taken standing up, one goes back to the room with the many tables; now everyone sits down to a different game, and it is unbelievable how many varieties of games are being played: lansquenet, trictrac, picquet, l'hombre, chess . . . summa summarum, every conceivable game. When the King and the Queen come into the room, no one gets up from the game. Those who do not play, like myself and a great many others, just stroll from room to room, now to the music and now to the game room, for one is allowed to go wherever one wishes; this lasts from six until ten, when one goes to supper, and this is called *jour d'appartement*. But if I should now tell Your Grace how magnificently these rooms are furnished and what great quantity of silver dishes are in them, I should never finish. It is certainly worth seeing. All of this would be delightful and most entertaining if one came to this apartment with a happy heart. Whether or not I have cause for that Your Grace will be able to hear from Count Mainhard, for he witnessed a fine example when he was here. But I do not wish to importune Your Grace further with such bothersome stories, being convinced that Your Grace herself is more in need of entertaining things to distract her than of reminders of the wretchedness of this world, for as I see from Your Grace's welcome last letter, Your Grace is only too familiar with that. Nonetheless Your Grace should not be so contemptuous of her own life and health. I can truthfully assure Your Grace that despite the many vexations that have been my daily lot, I have nonetheless been thinking about Your Grace's health and happiness and have wished many times that they might be as perfect as I would wish them to be with all my heart. For the rest, I beg Your Grace to have Carlchen show her the letter I have written him through this opportunity, for in it I tell him what I think of the married state; I believe Your Grace will share my opinion. . . .

But here they are calling me to go to the comedy with Madame la Dauphine, that is why I must close for this time. I commend Your Grace into the keeping of the Almighty and wish Your Grace everything that may bring her perfect joy, as Your Grace's faithful and most devoted sister and servant, Elisabeth Charlotte.

1. Electress of the Palatinate, Madame's sister-in-law.   2. Count Meinhard von Schomberg, later the husband of Raugräfin Karoline.   3. Her stepdaughter.

To RAUGRAF KARL LUDWIG

La-Ferté-sous-Jouarre, 18 July 1683

My dearest Carllutz, about two weeks ago I received your letter of 30 May at Bockenheim. But you can easily guess the reason why I was unable to answer it while there, since you have undoubtedly heard that I saw Her Grace my mother there; and since she stayed in a village three-quarters of an hour from Bockenheim, I went back and forth every day and therefore was too busy to write. . . .

Apropos of our court here, a certain person[1] asked me if you had completely forgotten her. I said that you had not but that, to your chagrin, you are not permitted to speak of her. She said I should give her a different name than her ordinary one. I said, "This has already been done and your name is Princesse Toutine." This made her laugh heartily and she said: "I beg you, Madame, when you write to the poor Raugraf, tell him that Toutine sends her greetings and that she loves him, not as the gossips have it but as a true friend, and that she hopes that he, too, will preserve the affection he has shown for her." This I promised and herewith keep my promise. When you write back to me, put your compliment in French so that I can show it to her! For you can see that the greeting she sends you deserves to be answered. That is all I will tell you for this time. Adieu, dearest Carllutz. Keep loving me and be assured that I shall be to my death your faithful and affectionate friend Elisabeth Charlotte. —All our young ladies often ask how you are and say that they would love to see you again; I believe that Toutine would also be pleased.

1. Probably Madame's second stepdaughter.

To DUCHESS SOPHIE

Saint Cloud, 1 August 1683

I am certain that Your Grace was dismayed by the dreadful news of the sudden and unexpected death of Her Majesty our Queen. I confess that this has deeply touched my heart, for in all of my troubles the good Queen had shown me every conceivable mark of friendship. Therefore Your Grace can easily imagine how painful it was for me to see her give up the ghost before my very eyes in the four days of her illness. On Monday night she was taken with a fever and on Friday last at three o'clock in the afternoon she expired. And that through the ignorance of the doctors, who killed her as surely as if they had thrust a dagger into her heart. She had an abscess under the left arm, which by repeated bleeding they pushed back into the body. And at the end, last Friday, they gave her an emetic, which caused the abscess to burst open inside the body. Thus she died a quick and gentle death. I was so affected by this scene that I cannot seem to recover. The King is terribly grief-stricken and cannot abide to stay here. So he will leave for Fontainebleau tomorrow, and so will the rest of us.

Fontainebleau, 19 August 1683

I too was deeply saddened that I could not have the joy of calling on Your Grace in Germany, but I saw no possibility of proposing a rendezvous to Your Grace because we are told every day that Oncle is preparing war against the King and is gathering his troops for that purpose. I therefore felt that this is not the time for a rendezvous. Yet I must not give up the hope of seeing Your Grace once more before my end; if I did that I could neither live nor die in peace. They are saying here that Count Starhemberg is putting up a valiant defense at Vienna;[1] he will gain more glory and honor from this war than the poor Emperor who so pitifully sued for peace; still, I feel sorry for him.

1. Against the Turks.

Fontainebleau, 29 August 1683

When Your Grace says that she hopes that my mind is above such things and that one does the greatest harm to one's enemies by despising them, this lesson would be easy to follow if the trouble came from people who are far away. But since it comes more from Monsieur than from anyone else, and since his friends (all of whom are precisely my enemies) have so taken command of him that he has more hate for me than any of the others, it is quite impossible for me not to be aggrieved from time to time. If one is hated and harmed by other enemies, one has the consolation to think that one will be able to pay them back some day; but there is no way to take revenge on this one, and even if there were a way, I would not want to do it, since whenever a bad thing happens to him, my husband, I myself am necessarily affected as well. For if he is aggrieved, I have to bear the brunt of his bad humor, and if some other misfortune befalls him, it is bound to fall on me as well. I must share all his troubles but am excluded from his good fortune. If he receives money, it is for his friends (my enemies); if he is in favor, he only uses it to harass me and to please them. . . . If I had some occupation, that might dispel some of my discontent, but in this respect my enemies have done such thorough work that I am never allowed to say anything, and if I so much as ask one of the servants what time it is in my husband's presence, he is afraid that it is an order and wants to know what it is. What sort of authority this gives me over the servants, I leave to Your Grace to imagine. If I speak two words with my children, they are examined for half an hour to find out what I said. . . . If there were still a single soul with me to whom I could open my heart and with whom I could weep or laugh about these things, I would be able to put up with it, but this is precisely why the good dark lady[1] was sent away.

1. Mademoiselle Théobon.

At the last hunt, which took place at Fontainebleau, I would have suffered a grave accident if I had not quickly remembered my old tricks and jumped off my horse. A doe that had been startled by the hunt bounded straight toward me so impetuously that although I reined in my horse with all my might I was unable to stop short enough, so that in coming at me the doe hit my horse's mouth so hard that the harness, the bit, and the reins were scattered all around. My horse was frightened out of its wits, snorted like a bear, and jumped to one side. When I saw that my horse had lost the bit, I quickly placed the reins into its mouth, jumped off, and held it until my men caught up with me. If I had not been very quick about it, my horse would without fail have broken my neck. I assure Your Grace that she would have lost a faithful servant in me. This adventure has caused such excitement at court that for two days no one talked of anything else. . . .

My daughter is a true little leaf-rustler; she will not learn anything, although her tongue is nimble enough and she is full of laughter and chatter. I am certain that if she were fortunate enough to converse with Your Grace and Oncle she would sometimes make them laugh, for she comes up with the funniest ideas. I must not be too familiar with her because she is not afraid of a single soul in the world except me, and without me no one can do anything with her. She is not a bit concerned about Monsieur, and if he wants to scold her when I am not present, she laughs right in his face. Her governess she deceives from morning till night. I do not know what will become of this girl, her vivacity is quite shocking. If she were to put it to proper use, everything might turn out well, but I do confess that I am worried about it, for we are living in a strange country. I wish that she and her brother could swap temperaments, for while he is also bright, he is as staid and proper as a girl should be, and she is as wild as a boy. I suppose it is the nature of all Liselottes to be so wild in their youth and just hope that in time some lead will be added to the mercury; in time she may well be cured of the desire to carry on, just as I have been cured of it since I came to France. . . .

They say here that the King of Poland[1] has found many boxes full of money in the grand vizir's tent and that he has received eight million worth of spoils for himself alone. A nice box full of ducats would not do any harm to our Raugraf[2] either. . . .

Some days ago as I was washing my hands, Madame de Durasfort told me that the late Prince de Tarente always had his hands washed, and his arms too, by two of his wife's ladies-in-waiting; one of them was called Maranville and the other d'Olbreuse. Then she asked me whether it is true that the latter is now a reigning princess and has risen so high; she said that she could scarcely believe it, having heard that German princes never make misalliances. I confess that this question really embarrassed me for Oncle and Godfather; therefore I quickly changed the subject.

1. John Sobieski, who had raised the siege of Vienna.   2. Karl Ludwig (Carllutz) had taken part in this campaign, as had two of Duchess Sophie's sons.

To FRAU VON HARLING

Versailles, 5 August 1684

Although I have not written to you in a very long time, I have received your letters with the greatest pleasure and am extremely obliged to you for your sympathy regarding all that has befallen me. Now, thank God, things have rather calmed down, God grant that it may last. It will not be my fault if it does not, for I shall do my very best to keep peace and quiet, and I shall always act so reasonably that you will not be ashamed to have brought me up. I should be very happy indeed if I could prove to you, my dearest Mistress Uffel, my gratitude for all the good things you have done for me; but since I am not fortunate enough to do that, I do at least beg you to accept my good intentions instead and to remain persuaded that I will be, until my end, your affectionate friend.

To DUCHESS SOPHIE

Versailles, 11 May 1685

. . . the King has sent his confessor to mine and this morning conveyed a horrendous scolding to me about three points. The first is that I am too free in my speech and have said to Monsieur le Dauphin that even if I were to see him naked from the soles of his feet to the top of his head I should not be tempted by him or anyone else.[1] The second is that I permit my young ladies to have *galants*. The third is that I laughed with the Princesse de Conti[2] at her lovers. These three things, I was told, have displeased the King so much that if he had not bethought himself that I am his sister-in-law, he would have banished me from the court. To this I replied that as far as Monsieur le Dauphin is concerned, I admit that I said this to him, never thinking that it is shameful not to have temptations, and also because I had never heard that this was a necessary part of being modest. As for the other things I had freely said to him about shitting and pissing, I said that this was more the King's fault than mine, since I had heard him say a hundred times that one could speak of everything within the family, and that he should have given me warning if he no longer thought this was proper, since it would have been the easiest thing in the world to correct. As for the second point, that my young ladies have *galants,* I said that I never meddle in anything that goes on in my household, and that I would certainly not start with the very thing that is most difficult to handle, but that this sort of thing is not without example, since such things have always been part of court life everywhere; in short, that as long as they do not do anything that soils their honor, I cannot believe that this can harm either them or me. As for the third point about his daughter, I said that I am not her governess and therefore in no position to restrain her if she wants to have lovers, and that I could not be expected to weep when she tells me her adventures. And since I had heard the King himself speak with her about this and had seen him laugh with her, I thought that this was permitted to me as well. I added that Madame la Duchesse is my witness that I had never involved myself in any of this, and that I am deeply hurt to see myself, though innocent, treated by the King as if I had committed some terrible crime and to hear words that I do not deserve and that I was not brought up to hear. I have not said a word about this to Monsieur, for I know how His Grace is, he would only make it worse; but I must confess that I am thoroughly angry with the King for treating me like a chambermaid, which would be more befitting for his Maintenon,[3] for she was born to it, but I was not. I do not know whether the King is sorry to have lectured me in this manner, but this morning when he went to mass he gave me a friendly laugh. But I did not feel like laughing, therefore I only made my usual deep curtsy, but with an extremely surly look on my face. What will happen further in this matter, I shall report to Your Grace as soon as I know more. If I had been innocently exiled, I think I would have run away and come straight to Your Grace.

1. It is curious that no one seems to have recognized this quip as an almost verbatim citation from Molière's *Tartuffe* (3.2).   2. Illegitimate daughter of Louis XIV, a famous beauty; see Cast of Principal Characters.   3. See Cast of Principal Characters.

On 26 May Madame's brother, the Elector Karl, died unexpectedly. He was the last of the house of Pfalz-Simmern.

To ELECTRESS WILHELMINE ERNESTINE

My dearest sister. On the day before yesterday I duly received Your Grace's valued letter. Your Grace certainly has no need to apologize that her last letter was not written throughout in her own hand. Indeed I was surprised that in her dreadful dismay my dearest sister was able to think of me, and I have taken it as a mark of Your Grace's warm feelings for me and have been exceedingly touched by them. I cannot express to Your Grace how much it pains me and how little I can accustom myself to the idea that my poor brother is in his grave. I know that he died happily and that he would not wish to be still among us. God grant me that I may leave the world as happily when my time comes. Yet for those of us who have loved him so dearly, Your Grace, our mother, and myself, it is indeed a terrible and unbearable calamity. But as Your Grace so wisely says, since such was the will of God, we shall at length have to accept it. God grant that we have lost him only through the ignorance of the doctors and not through human wickedness; for his illness was most peculiar, particularly the efforts that were made to keep him away from Your Grace and our mother. I am rather afraid that there was something untoward, for I know that you two were not permitted to see him until he was done for and beyond help. However, all of this is known to God, the impartial judge of every human heart. May he give those who have caused this disaster their just rewards, and may He grant Your Grace the strength, fortitude, and solace to endure all of this. And may He compensate Your Grace with a thousand joys for all the distress she has suffered through the death of her mother and that of my poor brother.

Saint Cloud, 30 June 1685

My dearest sister. I duly received Your Grace's valued letter of 11 June some days ago, but was unable to answer it before now, since I made a journey to Maubuisson, where I remained for three days. Given my present mood, I rather enjoyed this solitude, which at other times would have been abhorrent to me. Ma Tante, the Abbess,[1] and I spent a great deal of time moralizing together and we also contemplated what Your Grace says about the transcience and the vanity of the things of this world. The good princess is leading so austere, pious, and godly a life that she will without doubt also die a blessed death. I found her deeply affected by our loss, and although she is almost entirely detached from the things of this world, she does love her house and therefore grieves as much as if she had known my brother. And even though she is a nun, she does not have the monkish ways others have but is quite reasonable, very intelligent, and very similar to His Grace our late father in many of her manners. She asked me if Your Grace would go back to

Denmark, but since I did not receive Your Grace's letter until my return, I was unable to answer her question. I can easily imagine, dearest sister, how Your Grace will feel when all the new people arrive; and although the old Elector[2] is a meritorious lord, and quite generous too, it is very painful to see him in my brother's place; the very thought of it appalls me. Monsieur has written to Your Grace through Abbé de Morel, who was sent by the King to discuss my interests with the new Elector; I did not send a letter through this messenger because the abbé will not leave here before Wednesday and will no doubt take a long time, so that my letter would have become too old. I am most obliged to Your Grace for all of her good wishes; if all those I return to Your Grace were to come true, Your Grace would most surely receive comfort and joy from God Almighty. As for my brother's testament, I understand that it was drawn up in a most peculiar fashion by Langhans;[3] but if it was not done in the proper form, it might well be overturned. All of this we will see in due time.

1. Louise Hollandine, a sister of Madame's father. She had converted to Catholicism and had been abbess of Maubuisson since 1664. 2. Her brother's successor, Philip-Wilhelm von Pfalz-Neuburg. 3. Preacher at the Palatine court and favorite of Elector Karl.

To RAUGRÄFINNEN LUISE AND AMALIE ELISABETH

Versailles, 17 July 1685

Dearest Luise and Amalie. Two weeks ago Madame de Schomberg delivered your letter to me, and I see from it that my poor late brother's death has surprised and saddened you as much as it has saddened me. For my part, I confess that I never expected to see this unhappy time, for my brother seemed to be so very strong and healthy.[1] But however much this dreadful event may pain us, we will have to accept the will of the Almighty, which no one can change. I am most obliged to you for all your good wishes, and it would be a great joy to me if I could find ways to be of service to all of you, including your brothers, and to show my affection for you. Rest assured that in all matters under my control my feelings will never change. I also wish to tell you that since your letter is dated from Staufeneck, you must frequently see Count Ferdinand von Degenfeld;[2] I should therefore like to ask you to give him my regards and to tell him that since he used to give me many marks of his friendship when I was still at Heidelberg, I hope that he has not changed and will therefore be kind enough to do me a favor regarding a matter about which, I believe, he can give me more information than anyone else in the world. The favor I am asking of him is to tell me what actual claims I have to my brother's inheritance; for here they believe that all the allodial properties are mine, but it is not known which lands and properties fall into this category.[3] I would therefore like to ask Baron Ferdinand to

let me know what he knows about this. I would be greatly obliged to him, and
if it should turn out that the Raugrafschaft is part of my claim, I can assure you even now that all of you children will not be the losers. I have already
spoken about this to His Grace, Monsieur. In short, it seems to me that it
would be best for you if you came under my jurisdiction since, as I said before, I should never permit you to be disadvantaged in any way. But if the
Raugrafschaft should fall to the Duke of Neuburg, please write to me in what
other ways I can be of service to you, for I am always willing and ready to
do so. When you answer my letter and if Baron Ferdinand should have the information for which I asked, please do not make so many ceremonies and
write to me in all simplicity, as Carllutz does. This is all I can tell you for this
time. Adieu, dearest Luise and Amalia. Be assured that I shall always be
your affectionate friend. Elisabeth Charlotte.

> 1. Madame had been very poorly informed; the young Elector had been emotionally
> unstable and physically ill for some years. He died of consumption. 2. Uncle of
> the Raugräfinnen. 3. Allodial properties were lands and titles owned personally by
> the Elector and his family, as opposed to the State domain, which was attached
> to the electoral dignity.

To ELECTRESS WILHELMINE ERNESTINE

Chambord, 19 September 1685

His Grace the Elector, my late father, must have changed terribly and grown
very old after my departure from Heidelberg, since Your Grace reports that
he resembled the present Elector.[1] I saw His Grace twenty-one years ago, but
at that time he did not look at all like His late Grace the Elector; he had a
much longer, very red face, gray hair, and not many teeth in his mouth; also
he was much taller than His Grace my father. There may have been some
resemblance in their eyes, for both of them had dark blue and most intelligent eyes. Therefore I can imagine that since the late Elector had become
older and since the present one, as I hear, now wears a wig, there may indeed
be some resemblance. However, I can well imagine how Your Grace, and
also Her Grace my mother, must feel in all of these circumstances and when
they see the new court. The very thought of it makes even me shudder,
not to mention those who are there in person. The Elector is an upstanding,
extremely reasonable, and sagacious gentleman and his wife is an excellent
princess. The present Electoral Prince[2] also has a good character; yet all of
this notwithstanding, one is bound to detest the sight of others in our dear
Carlchen's place. But this, alas, is only to tell Your Grace what she already
knows only too well, and I do pity Your Grace with all my heart.

> 1. Philip-Wilhelm von Pfalz-Neuburg. 2. Johann Wilhelm, who was Palatine Elector
> between 1690 and 1716.

To DUCHESS SOPHIE

I humbly thank Your Grace and Oncle for their kind concern and for Oncle's opinion about my brother's testament. Here I am not told very much about what is being done in this matter, but I did learn from Breton that Abbé de Morel is bound and determined to overthrow my brother's testament and to base all claims on His Grace my late father's testament.[1] . . . As far as I understand all this, it will probably take so long that I will no doubt have long rotted in my grave before this matter is straightened out. The King here must think that I am still a Huguenot, for he has not breathed a word to me that he has placed my interests in the hands of the Pope,[2] and if Monsieur had not happened to mention it after it had already been done, I would not know it yet. However, it is best to keep quiet so that things do not get worse. The King has changed so frightfully in every way that I do not recognize him; and while I know very well where all this comes from, there is nothing that can be done about it, and so I must simply be patient. And since I do not wish those who wish me ill to be too pleased when they see me sad, I do not let on and act quite merry. But deep down it does pain me to be treated in this manner. But that is all I will say about this here, and it is only for Your Grace, and Oncle at most, but for no one else. As for those who might be curious enough to open my letter in the mail, they will see my opinion right here and thereby spare me the trouble of telling it to them later.

1. The latter was more favorable to Madame but did permit the French royal family to become involved in the affairs of the Palatinate. This may have been the reason why her brother was advised by his councillors to curtail Elisabeth Charlotte's claims.
2. The Pope was to arbitrate the litigation about the inheritance.

Versailles, 15 March 1686

In the last few months I have been very sad, and this has caused me to fail for so long in my duty of writing to my dearest Ma Tante. For I cannot tell all my stories, since all letters are being read in the mail. But to tell Your Grace the real reason now, Your Grace must know that one of my husband's favorites, namely his Master of the Horse,[1] has taken the trouble of getting my first maid-of-honor with child, which she wanted to abort; but since she was already three months pregnant, it could not be done in such a way that she did not become very ill, and so it all came out. In order to prevent me from dismissing her, this fine gentleman has stirred up all kinds of trouble for me with my husband, who is only too inclined to treat me badly to begin with. Nay, he has so set Monsieur against me that Monsieur in turn has spoken against me to His Majesty the King. All this skullduggery has been terribly upsetting to me, and recently this master of the horse even had the insolence to threaten me and to let me know that he would make life miserable for me if I said one word about the young lady.

1. Marquis d'Effiat.

I must tell Your Grace in all frankness that in my life I have too little hope for anything better and am usually too bored to muster the patience that would permit me to put up with the injustices and the constraints that are only too prevalent here. For if one has either some hope for better days or at least something with which to occupy or entertain oneself from day to day, then one can easily throw the bad things one encounters to the winds, since hope is a comfort for all ills, while diversions keep one from thinking about one's misfortunes. But when one has neither, grief is bitter hard to bear, and the least little thing that is added makes one altogether downcast; and that is what happened to me. As for all the things Your Grace is telling me, that it is a comfort to pray for one's loved ones when they are dead, I would have a great deal to say about them if I could do it in person, but it cannot be done in writing.

To ELECTRESS WILHELMINE ERNESTINE

Saint Cloud, 17 May 1686

My dearest sister. Some days ago His Grace the Electoral Prince of Saxony delivered Your Grace's valued letter of 8 April to me; I am exceedingly obliged to Your Grace for all the tender sentiments my dear sister expresses in it. This has given me very great comfort, but it has not surprised me, for Your Grace's good character, together with all her other virtues, is so well known to me that I could not doubt that the death of Her late Grace my mother would touch Your Grace's heart and that Your Grace would feel sympathy and pity for me. I humbly thank Your Grace for all her good wishes, and if Your Grace in turn were to encounter all the good things I wish for her, she would not only be entirely compensated for all her past misfortune and sadness, but Your Grace would also receive everything her heart desires and everything she could possibly imagine for her own pleasure. But I shall say nothing more about our losses, for this can only renew one's pain. I was so downcast by sadness that I was ill for two weeks, but the continual fever with minor *redoublements* at night lasted only for three days. With God's help and a good diet, I was finally able to pull myself out of all this. . . .

All winter long I have suffered so much grief that I thought I would perish and therefore was incapable of writing two lines, for I did not wish to burden Your Grace with my lamentations; indeed, I kept thinking that times would have to change sometime and that I would then be able to write Your Grace something that might amuse her. But even now I still do not know anything agreeable and must therefore close, though not without begging Your Grace not to forget poor old Liselotte and to keep a little place for me in her precious friendship, and also to believe firmly that I shall, to my grave, be most devoted to Your Grace, remaining Your Grace's faithful and devoted sister and servant, Elisabeth Charlotte.

To DUCHESS SOPHIE

Saint Cloud, 18 May 1686

Even though I am alone all day, I do not feel bored, for I have the consolation that as long as I am not in company my words will not be purposely misinterpreted and that I do not see any spies who look under one's nose to find out what one is thinking, according to the newest fashion.

Versailles, 4 June 1686

For all their boasting about *grandeur,* they are stingier here when it comes to ready money than anywhere else in the world; sometimes it is positively disgraceful. It does not surprise me that all the Germans find it peculiar that Monsieur alone is handling the matter of my inheritance, for they do not know about the French marriage contracts, which are drawn up in such a way that whatever comes to the wife during the husband's lifetime also belongs to the husband, and the husband, as *maître de la communauté, . . .* is lord and master over everything, can do with it and manage it as he sees fit, and the wife has no right to get upset. But if the husband dies, the wife can recover that part of her fortune which the husband has squandered from the man's inheritance; however, as long as both are living, the husband is master over everything, and this is frequently the reason why there are so many divorces in Paris. In the present inheritance case, it is also the reason why I cannot decide anything without Monsieur, even though everything must be executed in my name. If this were not the case, Your Grace can well believe that I would not have been so childish as not to look after my own interests and to leave everything to Monsieur. . . . Unfortunately I know very well where my inheritance will end up, but since nothing can be done about it, one must keep quiet.

Versailles, 11 June 1686

I do not know where Ma Tante of Maubisson can have picked up the idea that my daughter is beautiful, for her face is quite ugly, though her figure is not bad, so Ma Tante of Maubuisson must not have looked too carefully; but she is not lacking in wit and if she were fortunate enough to call on

Your Grace she might amuse Your Grace, for she is quite nimble of tongue. My son is better looking; he is a bit more serious than his little sister but not melancholy or timid for all that; he is a very good child, docile, and does everything he is asked to do. My daughter is not so docile but much more unruly, she rather lives up to her name of Liselotte and is as much of a tomboy as I used to be.

Saint Cloud, 26 June 1686

As for the rest, I should wish with all my heart that all those who are now so devout (I almost said bigoted) would heed Your Grace's sermon and seek to promote harmony and peace. Yet so far such have not been their maxims; on the contrary, they seek to stir up trouble wherever they can, setting husband against wife, father against son, servants against their masters, and doing other things of this kind, which certainly make people distressed and unhappy; seeing this, one is tempted to say as old Rabenhaupt used to say, "Bonjour Monsieur, you are making a devil of a mess." There also is an old German proverb that comes to mind now: "Where the devil cannot go, he sends an old woman"; this is something that all of us in the royal family have come to experience. But enough of this, more would not be prudent. There is one thing in Your Grace's sermon from which I take comfort, namely that I have more religion than all the great *dévôts,* for I live as righteous a life as I can without doing harm to anyone, and if I am not to be written up in the *Mercure galant*[1] until I harass my fellow-Christian and neighbor, it will be a long time before Your Grace reads about me.

1. A monthly magazine reporting the latest news and gossip about the court and about Parisian high society.

Versailles, 2 August 1686

It is quite certain that he[1] no longer wants to hear any banter and has become so earnest that it is altogether frightening. As to the person[2] to whom Your Grace applies the proverb that the snow falls as easily on a cow plop as on a rose leaf, emblematic epigrams have recently been made about her, but they sound quite different, and if one were to believe them she is wonderful. They say that the author has received a pension for making them. But enough of this, I am beginning to act like the preacher about whom Mistress Kolb used to tell me; his name was Herr Biermann and he used to say, "Enough and more than enough of all of this," after he had preached for three hours.

1. The King.   2. Madame de Maintenon.

Our King is not well right now, and they say it might turn into a quartan fever. If that were true, God help us, for this is bound to make him a hundred times crankier than he already is. Truly, anyone who has nothing to do with this court would laugh himself half to death to see what is going on here. The King imagines that he is pious because he no longer sleeps with young women, and all his piety consists of being cranky, of having spies everywhere who bear false tales about everyone, of flattering his brother's favorites, and in general making everyone miserable. The old woman, the Maintenon, gets her pleasure from making the King hate everyone in the royal house, except Monsieur; him she flatters with the King and sees to it that he is well liked and given whatever he desires. . . . Behind his back, however, this old woman worries that people might think that she esteems Monsieur, and therefore, whenever the courtiers speak to her, she says the very devil about him, calling him worthless, the most debauched person in the world, unable to keep a secret, false, and faithless. The Dauphine is quite unhappy, and although she does her best to please the King, she is treated very badly every day at the instigation of the old woman and must spend her life being bored and pregnant. Her husband, Monsieur le Dauphin, does not care about anything in the world, seeks his own amusements and pleasures wherever he can find them, and is becoming dreadfully debauched. So is Monsieur, and the only thing to which he applies himself is to make trouble for me with the King and to show contempt for me, to recommend his favorites, . . . and to get extra favors for them from the King. But when it comes to promoting his children, he could not care less. As for me, I must therefore be constantly on the defense, for they are causing me new troubles every day, even though I am trying my very best to avoid them by my conduct. Prince Carl[1] has seen me at all hours, and he can tell Your Grace how I spend my time and whether my conduct is anything but irreproachable; and yet something comes up every day. The old woman has already tried more than ten times to set Madame la Dauphine against me and told her that she would absolutely have to break off her friendship with me if she wanted her [Maintenon] to put her well with the King. But when Madame la Dauphine wanted to know what there is to say against me, she was unable to answer. Meanwhile I must suffer both the King's ill will through the woman's undeserved hatred and that of Monsieur, which comes from the hatred of my old enemies. That is my state, and I am certain that if I had the time to describe these things to Your Grace in more detail, Your Grace would find them well-nigh incredible. . . .

I could not, of course, have written all of this to Your Grace through the mail, but since this is a safe opportunity, I could not resist. If Your Grace desires to know further how things are at this court, I should add that all the ministers flatter the woman and seek to gain her favor through every kind of base behavior. All the others who are honorable men and of a reasonable age are sad; they have no money and are afraid of the countless spies; in short, they are malcontent and yet can do nothing about it. All the young people are dreadfully debauched and given to every vice, nor are they above lying and cheating and they think that it would be a disgrace to take pride in being honorable people; all they can do is guzzle, debauch others, and use filthy language, and whoever among them is the most unmannerly is admired and esteemed the most. All of this will easily permit Your Grace to judge how much pleasure there must be at this court for honorable people. But I am afraid that if I were to continue my account of this court any longer, I would bore Your Grace as much as I am often bored, and that boredom would at length become a contagious disease.

    1. Karl Philipp of Hanover, the Duchess's son, who carried the letter.

Saint Cloud, 13 May 1687

Your Grace is greatly mistaken to believe that the care and trouble I took during Monsieur's illness has done anything to soften His Grace. By no means, for as soon as he was well again, I was made to feel his hatred. . . . Your Grace desires to know whether it is true that the King has married Madame de Maintenon, but truly, I am not able to tell Your Grace. Not many people doubt it, but as long as this marriage is not made public, I find it difficult to believe. And because of what I know of marriage in this country, I do not believe that if they were married they would be as much in love as they are. But then, perhaps secrecy adds a special spice that other, publicly married people do not have.

Saint Cloud, 1 October 1687

I am also bound to tell Your Grace that court life is becoming so dull that one can hardly stand it any longer. For the King imagines that he is pious when he sees to it that everyone is properly bored and bothered. His son's wife is being harassed so much by the old women with whom she has been surrounded that it is almost unspeakable. Here is an example: her children are ill, and therefore the good princess wanted to stay here a few more days in order to be with them. For this she is scolded and told that she wants to stay here because she does not wish to be with the King. Then, when she says that she will go along, the women bruit it about that she does not care for her children and does not love them, summa summarum: whatever one does is wrong. I for my part cannot believe that loving old women and being cranky can be pleasing to Our Lord; if that is the way to heaven, it will be hard for me to get in. It is a wretched thing when a man does not want to follow his own reason and lets himself be guided by calculating priests and old courtesans; this makes life quite miserable for honest and sincere people. But what is the use of complaining; nothing can be done about it. Those of us who are caught in this tyranny, like the poor Dauphine and I, we can see that the thing is ridiculous, yet we do not feel like laughing at all.

To FRAU VON HARLING

Versailles, 18 November 1687

I was happy to hear that you are well again. One can never feel useless to the world if one has done as much good in it as you, my dear Mistress Uffel, have done. And also one should wish to stay alive so as not to sadden one's good friends with one's death. And why should you be afraid to live on? Given your resignation to the will of God, no misfortune can really touch you; and after all it is better to live than to die, for that will happen soon enough anyway. . . .

I am now treated neither well nor badly; God grant that this may continue, it will be good enough for me. My Harling is once again with me; he returned in fine fettle a week ago. My son and his men are full of praise for his good conduct in the battle. I had vigorously advocated his advancement in his regiment, but the favor of Madame de Maintenon and her recommendation have done more, I am sorry to report, than mine.

Versailles, 8 January 1688

Last Monday night in Paris my Harling met with a mishap about which I learned only last night; at first I was quite frightened and immediately sent someone out to find out about it, but today I hear, thanks be to God, that he is quite out of danger. I did not want to report this accident to you until I had found out exactly how he is and what had happened. Here is how the mishap occurred: Last Monday night he came from town and was on his way home, for in Paris he lodges with my master of the horse. Because of the cold he had wrapped himself in a brand new cloak; suddenly he feels someone grabbing his arm from behind and holding him. He turns around and sees two fellows who are taking his cloak and a third one who puts his hand into his pocket in order to take his purse. Thereupon he draws his sword and charges the three fellows, they too draw their swords, and while Harling wounds one of them, the two others stab at him; one of them wounds his arm but the other runs his sword through his body, and they would have altogether assassinated him if a coach had not happened to come by and made the scoundrels run away. My personal barber has dressed Harling's wounds and he earnestly assures me that he is in no danger and that he was very lucky; he has lost a great deal of blood and therefore is a bit weak. . . . Harling is so well liked here that everyone, from the greatest to the humblest, is full of sympathy for him; all evening yesterday no one spoke of anything else. That is all I can tell you for this time, for I must go to the chapel for the vespers that are held every Thursday and which the King also attends; I shall pray for my Harling.

Saint Cloud, 13 April 1688

Here then comes young Harling, as you wanted him to do. I have asked his officer to grant him two months' leave; but he must not stay away longer. I do not doubt that you will be pleased with him, for he is not lacking in wit and has a very good, honest, faithful, and sincere character. I am extremely fond of him and will miss him these two months of his absence; however, I am pleased to grant you the satisfaction of seeing him, for I am not at all ashamed to have brought him up, since he is known and liked by everyone here. He is particularly praiseworthy in these days when the young people here have fallen into every dreadful vice; it is certainly unusual that he has been able to stay out of them.

To DUCHESS SOPHIE

Saint Cloud, 14 April 1688

Dear Frau von Harling and her husband have asked me to send them their nephew so that he can divide his inheritance with his brothers, their father having died last year. I did not want to let this good and safe opportunity go by without unburdening my heart to Your Grace and telling her all the things that plague me and which I cannot entrust to the ordinary mail. And so I must confess to my dearest Ma Tante that I have been most distressed lately, although I try to show this as little as ever I can. I have been made privy to the reason why the King treats the Chevalier de Lorraine and the Marquis d'Effiat so well; it is because they have promised him that they would persuade Monsieur to ask the King most humbly to marry the Montespan's children[1] to mine, that is, the limping Duc du Maine to my daughter and Mademoiselle de Blois to my son. In this case the Maintenon is all for the Montespan, since she has brought up these bastards and loves the limping boy like her own child. . . . Now Your Grace can imagine how I would feel to see only my daughter so badly established, considering that her sisters[2] are so well married. Even if the Duc du Maine were not the child of a double adultery but a true prince, I would not like him for a son-in-law nor his sister for a daughter-in-law, for he is dreadfully ugly and lame and has other bad qualities to boot, stingy as the devil and without kindness. His sister, it is true, is rather kind, but extremely sickly, her eyes always look so dim that I fear she will go blind someday. But most of all, they are the children of a double adultery, as I said before, and the children of the most wicked

and desperate woman on earth. I leave it to Your Grace to think whether
I would wish this to happen. And the worst part of it is that I cannot properly
discuss this matter with Monsieur, for whenever I say a word to him, he has
the delightful habit of passing it right on to the King, to add to it, and to
make all kinds of trouble for me with the King. So I am in terrible straits and
do not know how I shall go about averting this disaster. Meanwhile I cannot help fretting inside myself, and whenever I see these bastards my blood
boils over. Also my dearest Ma Tante must know how much it pains me to
see my only son and my only daughter as victims of my worst enemies, who
seek and have sought to harm me every day and indeed have tried to impugn
my very honor by their false discourses. They say that d'Effiat was promised to be made a duke and that the Chevalier would receive a large sum of
money. Meanwhile they are being exalted to the skies by a hundred marks
of favor, while I am treated very badly, and probably should consider it a
favor that I am even permitted to live my life as I always have. . . .

Perhaps I will even be exiled over this matter, for if Monsieur ever seriously speaks about it, I shall not fail to let him know my exact opinion which,
as usual, he will report to the King and also to his favorites, who are sure to
twist the matter to my disadvantage when they speak to the King (whom they
are constantly badgering). And if the King himself, to intimidate me, should
speak to me about this matter, I shall tell him in plain words that I do not like
it at all; this will no doubt annoy him very much, however respectfully I
may word this refusal. So I might as well prepare for some difficult times. I
humbly beg Your Grace's forgiveness for entertaining Your Grace with such
tiresome and distressing discourses. Yet, my dearest Ma Tante, since Your
Grace is so full of kindness for me, and since there is not one person here in
whom I can have enough confidence to share my heartfelt grief, I had hoped
that Your Grace would not take it amiss if I unburdened my heart through
this safe opportunity. For Harling is most devoted to me and will certainly
not place this letter in any but Your Grace's hands. And may I ask Your Grace
not to say anything about this to anyone, except to Oncle and dear Frau
von Harling, and not to answer this letter through the mail, only through
Harling when he returns.

What else can I tell Your Grace; I know nothing good, for the pervasive
hypocrisy has made this court so dull that one can hardly stand it any more.
And at the very time when all others are being mortified to the very marrow of their bones in order (or so it is said) to teach them virtue and the fear
of God, the King chooses the most vice-ridden people in the world for his
constant companions, namely, the Lorrainers and d'Effiat. I have been unable to find out whether or not the King has married the Maintenon; many
say that she is his wife and that the archbishop of Paris married them in
the presence of the King's confessor and the Maintenon's brother; but others

say that it is not true, and it is impossible to find out what it is. What is certain, however, is that the King has never had the same passion for any of his mistresses that he has for this one, and it is amazing to see them together; when she is present he cannot last fifteen minutes without whispering in her ear and talking to her in secret, even though he has been with her all day long. She is a wicked devil, and although she is much sought after and feared, no one likes her very much. Dear Madame la Dauphine, who certainly is the best princess one can imagine and has a kind, sincere character, is suffering all kinds of trouble from her, even though Madame la Dauphine is doing her very best to gain her friendship. By contrast, the woman has altogether won over Monsieur le Dauphin, the better to make herself feared by everyone, and especially by the Dauphine. This is the present state of the court. . . . What will become of all this, time will tell.

1. The King's children by Madame de Montespan.   2. Her half-sisters, Monsieur's daughters from his first marriage. One was married to the King of Spain, the other to the Duke of Savoy.

To RAUGRAF KARL LUDWIG

Saint Cloud, 17 May 1688

My dearest Carllutz. It has been a few days since I received your welcome letter of 23 April, but it has been impossible for me to answer it before now. For I was at Versailles when I received it, and since we had not been there for a whole month, I received so many visits and also participated so assiduously in the hunting that I had no time to myself in which I could write. . . .

Since you will no doubt be again in Greece when you receive this letter (for you write that you will leave in four days) I hope, dearest Carllutz, that you will tell me all about the beautiful things you have seen and will see there, whether there is much left from antiquity and whether there are still buildings that might show how these cities were in the past. And since I know that much writing would be bad for you because of your hand, and also that you may not have the time because of your command duties, you should simply order one of your men to write an account and send it to me. For I confess that I am very curious to know what *Athene* and *Corintho* look like today. . . .

If I should receive what is my due from the Palatinate, I assure you that I will not rest until you, too, have benefited. . . . If there is anything I can do to serve you and your brothers and sisters, I shall not be slow about it, for I am fond of all of you, but most of all of you.

In 1685, Louis XIV revoked the Edict of Nantes, which had guaranteed freedom of religion to the French Protestants. Hundreds of thousands of Protestants felt compelled to emigrate. This hastened the formation of a coalition against Louis's aggression, which was joined not only by Protestant states (Sweden, Brandenburg, Saxony, Hanover, and the Netherlands), but also by the Emperor, Spain, and Savoy. Eventually England also joined the coalition.

To DUCHESS SOPHIE

Saint Cloud, 26 September 1688

Your Grace does not tell me what the young prince[1] is called and what names he was given. I wish that His Grace the Elector [of Brandenburg] would make peace between the two godfathers, namely, our King and the Emperor; that I would like better than all his fine diamonds and this would be a ceremony I would enjoy very much. Meanwhile, our Dauphin has now become a warrior and left for the army yesterday in order to besiege and conquer Philippsburg. He told me that after Philippsburg he would take Mannheim and Frankenthal and pursue the war on my behalf. But I told him, "If it were for me to decide, you would not go, for I confess to you that I can have only pain and no joy in seeing that my name is used to ruin my poor fatherland."[2] And so we said adieu to each other. . . .

Her Grace the Electress [of Brandenburg] is very right to send her prince to Hanover to be placed into the care of dear Frau von Harling; nowhere could he be brought up to become healthier and stronger, as we can see from the example of all of us who were raised by Frau von Harling.

> 1. Prince Friedrich Wilhelm, born 15 August, Sophie's grandson; her daughter had married the Elector of Brandenburg, later King Friedrich I of Prussia.   2. Philippsburg, Mannheim, and Frankenthal are towns of Elisabeth Charlotte's native land, the Palatinate.

Fontainebleau, 8 October 1688

On Saturday we went to hunt the boar with the King. But I was in great anxiety during this hunt, for we had received news from Paris that my daughter had had a relapse. I have asked Monsieur four times to let me go to Paris to look after the poor child, but so far he has not permitted it, and all because of a cabal, for the Grancey,[1] who meddles in everything, wants me to have a new doctor, and that is something I am not willing to take from her. In order to have this new doctor appointed by Monsieur anyway, he has been sent to my daughter; so now when my doctor says white, this one says black, and the poor child has to suffer for it. Yet if I were in Paris I could examine what is most useful and would abide by that without partiality. That is why they have put it into Monsieur's head not to let me go to Paris. And so I have to watch my only daughter being put to death for the sake of a cabal, which grieves me in my soul, and I just had to unburden my heart to my dearest Ma Tante. However, I was unable to abstain from saying a few words, which Monsieur has taken very much amiss. So all I can do is to recommend my poor child to God Almighty. . . . On Monday I received more bad news about my daughter, which again made me shed bitter tears . . . that evening I had to attend the *appartement* with red eyes. On Tuesday we again went hunting with the King and returned only at nightfall; on Wednesday we again chased the stag, but I did not chase away my discontent, as Your Grace can easily imagine. . . .

I wish with all my heart that I could serve the children of the Raugräfin. I would be so glad to do it, but what can I do? I am not even allowed to take care of my own children. They will be even more to be pitied now, for this wretched war will not be helpful to them, nor to me either. . . .

That my children are not afraid of anyone but me is only too true, for Monsieur never wants to take the trouble of saying a single word of reprimand to them, and both their governor and their governess are the silliest and most stupid people one could find anywhere. The children, thank God, are not lacking in wit and therefore cannot resist laughing at those who are in charge of them, and so it falls to me to tell them what they must and must not do. So they fear me, yet withal they love me too, for they are reasonable enough to see that what I tell them is for their own good. I do not scold often, but if it has to be, I really let them have it, that makes it all the more impressive. If they follow my advice, I will bring them up to be good people, notwithstanding all the bad examples these poor children constantly have before them.

But this, too, is a text that one had better bypass in silence, and I shall therefore turn to coiffures. I am certain that if Your Grace could see the great care and trouble that the women are now taking to make themselves repulsive, Your Grace would have a good laugh. For myself, I cannot go along with these masquerades, but the coiffures are getting higher every day. I think they will finally have to make the doors taller, for otherwise these ladies will no longer be able to go in and out of the rooms. When they are wearing wimples, they look just like Melusine, as I saw her painted in an old book that His Grace the late Elector had in his library at Heidelberg, and I believe that the train on their dresses will eventually turn into a snake, just as she did. If this happened to the Grancey I should not wonder, for she already has a snake's and adder's tongue with which she stings me only too often. But I think it is time now to end this long epistle.

1. A governess in the Orléans household and mistress of the Chevalier de Lorraine.

On 12 August Raugraf Karl Ludwig had died of a fever at the siege of Negroponte. Louis XIV had invaded the Palatinate under the pretext of conquering it for his sister-in-law. On the orders of Louvois, a zone of "scorched earth" was created, and the French troops committed untold atrocities. The war triggered by this invasion was to last until 1697.

On Friday I received the distressing news of my dear Carllutz's death which, as Your Grace can easily imagine, has put me in a dreadful state; for twice twenty-four hours I was unable to stop weeping, as Your Grace's two princes[1] may have reported to Your Grace, for both of them happened to be with me at the time. Although I now no longer weep as constantly as I did on the first days, I am so filled with melancholia and sadness that I know it will be a long time before I will get over the death of dear Carllutz. And my distress becomes even greater from being told every day about the preparations for burning and bombing the good town of Mannheim, which the Elector, my late father, had worked so hard to build;[2] this truly makes my heart bleed. And then they are outraged here that I am sad about it. . . .

During the ten days when I was ill in Paris, the King did not inquire about me; I wrote to him, but he did not reply. When I came back here, I was curious to find out what this meant and therefore asked friends to find out for me. Thus I learned that the King is angry with me because of something I said to the Duc de Montausier. This I will tell Your Grace: Monsieur de Montausier came to me in Madame la Dauphine's room and said, "Madame, Monsieur le Dauphin is your champion, he is off to conquer your fortune and your lands." At first I did not give an answer to this; thereupon he said, "It seems to me, Madame, that you receive what I say to you rather coldly." I replied, "Monsieur, it is true that you are speaking of the one thing in the world of which I least like to hear, for I do not see that it can be very profitable for me if my name serves to ruin my fatherland; and far from feeling joy, I am most distressed about it. I do not know how to dissimulate, but I do know how to keep quiet. Therefore, if I am not to say what I think, I must not be made to speak." This, I understand, the old man did not like at all and told it to others, who reported it to the King, who took it very much amiss. But I cannot help it; why am I being used in such a way! If his [the King's] brother does not want to open his eyes to see that we are being robbed, I cannot prevent mine from seeing the truth and from refusing to be tricked.

1. Christian and Ernst August von Hannover.   2. On 2 May 1663, Karl Ludwig had written to his second wife, "If we live another ten years and if there is no war and no mortality, we will make Mannheim into a second Rome, no matter how much we are envied." (W. L. Holland, ed., *Schreiben des Kurfürsten Karl Ludwig zu Pfalz und der Seinen* [Tübingen, 1884].)

Your Grace is well aware that there is nothing I like to do less than lament, and yet if one is as sad as I have been, alas, for a long time now, one cannot help lamenting, and the heart's grief easily spills over into speech. I am less given to sadness than others, for my dearest Ma Tante knows that I am not sad by temperament; but when one is beset by misfortune on all sides, as I have been, one is bound to have such feelings. I had barely begun to recover somewhat from poor Carllutz's death when the horrendous and piteous calamity was visited upon the poor Palatinate, and what pains me most is that my name is being used to cast these poor people into utter misery. And when I cry about it, I am treated to great annoyance and sulking. But to save my life I cannot stop lamenting and bemoaning the thought that I am, as it were, my fatherland's ruin, especially when I see all of the Elector's, my late father's, hard work and care suddenly reduced to rubble in poor Mannheim. I am so horrified by all the destruction that has been wrought that every night when I have finally dozed off, I imagine that I am in Mannheim or Heidelberg amidst all the destruction, and then I wake up with a dreadful start and cannot go back to sleep for two whole hours. Then I see in my mind how everything was in my day and in what state it is now, indeed in what state I am myself, and then I cannot hold back a flood of tears. It also grieves me deeply that the King waited to inflict the ultimate devastation precisely until I had begged him to spare Mannheim and Heidelberg. . . .

I was certain that the death of our good Queen of Spain[1] would touch Your Grace's heart; I cannot yet digest it either, and although, following the example of all of His Majesty's close and exalted family, I am again present at all *divertissements,* I return from them as sad as I went, and nothing can divert me from my discontent. . . .

But I must not keep Your Grace with my melancholy thoughts any longer and will therefore speak of other things. No doubt Your Grace will already know that the King of England[2] is no longer here. When I made my adieux to His Majesty, he asked me to send his greetings to Your Grace and to say that he would now be too busy to write to Your Grace. When seeing and speaking to this good King, one is bound to feel extremely sorry for him, for he seems to be kindness itself; yet one cannot wonder that the things we are seeing now have happened to him. The Queen, on the other hand, seems to be quite intelligent, and I rather like her. The Prince of Wales is a most well-mannered child; he very much resembles the portraits of the late King of England, is very vivacious, and has a pretty face. In order to tell the two kings apart, one can now say that the Prince of Orange is the King *of* England, while ours is the King *out of* England . . .

P.S. By Your Grace's kind leave I send my respects to Oncle. The Brandenburgian troops have given a bit of a drubbing to the French; what I think about that cannot be entrusted to paper, but Your Grace can easily imagine it.

1. Madame's oldest stepdaughter; she had died on 12 February, probably by poison.
2. King James II, who had been deposed by the English when they called his son-in-law, William of Orange, to the throne. Louis XIV received the ex-king in France.

I do not wish the present Palatine Elector any harm, nor do I blame him for the dreadful devastation that has been visited upon the poor Palatinate since it has come into his hands. What I cannot forgive is that the poor people of the Palatinate have been deceived in my name, for these poor, innocent people, out of affection for the late Elector our father, thought that the best thing they could do would be to surrender willingly, that this would make them my subjects, and that then they would live more happily than under the present Elector, since I am still of their rightful prince's blood. And yet they were not only deceived in their hope and most cruelly rewarded for their affection, but plunged into the utmost misery because of it. This pains me so much that I cannot swallow it. If there were anything here that could give me pleasure I might be able, notwithstanding all the misery one encounters, to enjoy myself now and then; but the very people who are responsible for the misfortune of my fatherland also persecute me personally here, and not a day passes without bringing me new troubles. And yet I shall have to spend the rest of my life with these people. If at least they would say what it is they want, one would know how to act, but one is not told anything and whatever one says or does is considered bad. I would be better off if I were beaten in secret and if that were the end of it than I am now, constantly set upon in this manner, for this squeezes the very marrow out of one's bones and makes life altogether unbearable. I have noticed something else, too, namely that whenever the King fears that Monsieur might get angry with him, as for example when he gives military governorships to his bastards but nothing to Monsieur, or when he is planning to refuse one of Monsieur's requests, or now, when he lets Monsieur sit around here without entrusting him with the command of a single army, or in other cases of this kind, the King will flatter the Lorrainers and all of my husband's favorites but treat me very badly and show contempt for me; and since Monsieur likes them and hates me, he is being paid in this manner. This satisfies Monsieur, and he stops asking for more. . . .

But I will not bother Your Grace with my lamentations any longer and speak of other things. Apropos of Your Grace's statement that she feels sorry for our King of England and that the priests will ruin everything if they have power, I must write Your Grace a fine ditty I learned today and which will surely be more entertaining to Your Grace than my lamentations: "The Prince of Orange rules everything, / Cardinal Fürstenberg sows trouble in everything, / the king of France wants everything, / the Pope refuses everything, / Spain loses everything, / Germany opposes everything, / the Jesuits meddle in everything, / if God does not straighten out everything, / the Devil will take everything." Whoever wrote this had as good an opinion of the reverend Jesuits as Your Grace, as Your Grace can see.

It would not be seemly for me not to agree with Your Grace that Monsieur is the best husband in the world, yet I hope that Your Grace will permit me to say only that Your Grace has not seen enough of him to form a perfect judgment and that I might know rather more about this, having by now, as the saying goes, eaten two kitchen boys or measures of salt with him and also having studied him so thoroughly that I have come to know him perfectly and therefore am only too aware, alas, of what I can expect. But these things are just too tiresome and I had therefore better be quiet about them and speak of something else.

If one could take comfort from not being the only one to be unhappy, one could find much comfort here. . . . Your Grace says that they can take away everything but a happy heart. As long as I was in Germany, I would have thought so, too, but since I have come to France I have learned, alas, that they can take that too. As long as those by whom one is chagrined are below oneself and if one is not dependent on them, one can save oneself by despising them, but when they are one's lord and master and when one cannot ever do one step without their permission, this is rather more difficult than one might imagine. If my children were in my power, they would give me great pleasure; but when I think that my daughter is already surrounded by such people that I cannot say a word in her presence from fear that I will get into trouble, and when I see that Monsieur is bound and determined to make the Marquis d'Effiat my son's governor, even though this man is my worst enemy and will set my son against me as much as he has set Monsieur against me, then I must confess that the children are giving me more chagrin than pleasure. The King has not permitted Béthune[1] to leave Poland in order to become my son's governor, so I am very much afraid that it will be the above-mentioned marquis, who is the most debauched fellow in the world, and particularly in the worst respect. If he becomes my son's governor, I can be quite sure that he will teach him all the worst vices, and this gives me little pleasure. As for my daughter, I fear, as does Your Grace, that this wretched war will prevent her from marrying the Electoral Prince of the Palatinate. Nonetheless I cannot give up this wish, for it would be a great comfort to me to think that the grandchild of His Grace the Elector, my late father, would once again rule the Palatinate and that my daughter would not have a limping bastard for a husband. Our young Raugrafen are unfortunate indeed to lose everything; if I had money I would love with all my heart to send them something, but Your Grace cannot image in what a miserable state I am myself: I only have a hundred *pistoles* a month, and since I can never give less than a pistole, my money is gone in a week for fruit, letters arriving in the mail, and flowers. Whenever the King gives me something, I must pay my old debts, and he never gives me anything except at New Year's, and Monsieur never gives me a single ducat; if I want the smallest trifle, I must borrow, so I simply cannot give presents. Even if I brought Karl Moritz[2] here and made him an abbot, he would not be given a benefice, which are becoming quite rare. Madame de Maintenon will certainly not give her protection to someone who is connected with me, that is quite out of the question; her hatred for me (which I have done nothing to deserve) is too great; and since she is so much in favor, the King has already roundly refused my request to take Raugraf Carllutz into his service, and I do not think that he will be more gracious to his brothers.

1. The Marquis de Béthune was the French ambassador to Poland.   2. Madame's half-brother.

Saint Cloud, 5 June 1689

Although I should be accustomed by now to the thought of my poor fatherland in flames, having heard nothing else for so long, I still cannot help being regretful and grieved every time I am told that yet another place has been put to the torch. It is most charitable of Your Grace to send alms to the poor people of the Palatinate. Recently Monsieur told me something that annoys me to the depth of my soul and which I had not known before, namely that the King has all taxes in the Palatinate levied in my name; now these poor people must think that I am profiting from their misery and that I am the cause of it, and that makes me deeply sad. I wish to God it were true that I received all the money that has been taken from the poor Palatinate and that I were free to do with it as I see fit, for then the poor young Raugrafen and the poor people of the Palatinate would be very much better off. But the truth is that I have not seen a red farthing of it. . . .

I must confess that since I see so many unchristian priests ordering nothing but barbarities everywhere, or at least doing nothing to stop them, I can no longer abide them and have come to loathe all of them so much that instead of seeing one of my kinsmen as a priest, I would prefer him to beg for his daily bread. But this is a text with which I must not stay too long, for if it should be read in the mail, it would no doubt be thought that I need dragoons to convert me,[1] therefore I had better speak of other things. Monsieur de Rebenac[2] has politely refused the Constantinople embassy. I have spoken to him about the death of the late good Queen of Spain; it is only too true that she was poisoned with raw oysters. Our Madame la Dauphine is not being poisoned, but she is becoming more run down all the time and I am deathly afraid that this cannot go on much longer. In the beginning the doctors, in order to pay their court to certain old women whom I will not name but whom Your Grace can easily guess, said that Madame la Dauphine is simply a hypochondriac and just imagines that she is ill. . . . In this manner they permitted the evil to eat so deeply into her that I fear not much can be done about it now. Now that she is completely bedridden, the doctors are forced to admit that there is a real disease, but they are quite ignorant and can do nothing but purge, bleed, and give clysters, and that is no help to Madame la Dauphine. Unless God gives us special help, I am afraid that a dreadful thing will befall us before very long; I shudder at the very thought of it, for the good Madame la Dauphine is very dear to my heart.

1. Allusion to the infamous *dragonnades* by which meetings of French Huguenots were broken up.   2. The French ambassador to Spain.

Versailles, 24 July 1689

When Your Grace says that all the maids of honor now want to be ladies-in-waiting, I am reminded of His late Grace my father who, seeing that all the maids at Neuburg wanted to be called ladies, said that they probably did not want to deceive anyone and that although they were called maids, this might not be true. The real ladies, namely the poor young Raugräfinnen, truly move my heart to pity, but I do not know what can be done for these poor children. When Your Grace and Oncle say that they are offended when I call myself old, I should reply that I might not feel so old if I were allowed to have some diversions; but boredom and continuous constraint age a person more in one year than ten years spent in freedom and happiness.

Versailles, 26 August 1689

I must tell Your Grace that my adversaries have put it into Monsieur's head to make his master of the horse my son's governor. But because I, along with all of France, know that this man is one of the most disreputable and debauched characters in the world, I have asked Monsieur to give my son another governor. This I have done because I think that it would not be to my son's honor if people thought that he is d'Effiat's mistress, for there is no doubt that there is no greater sodomist in France than he, and that it would be a bad beginning for a young prince to start his life with the worst debauchery imaginable. To this point Monsieur replied that he had to admit that d'Effiat used to be debauched and loved the boys, but that he had corrected himself of this vice many years ago. I said that it was not many years ago that a good-looking young German who was here made his excuses to me for not calling on me as often as he wished because he was bothered so much by d'Effiat whenever he came to the Palais Royal, and that this proves that he has not corrected himself as many years ago as his friends claim. But even supposing that he had not indulged in this vice for a few years, I told Monsieur, I do not believe that my only son should be used to find out whether or not the lord master of the horse can get along without his pages and thus be considered a depraved and dissolute person by those who do not know of d'Effiat's conversion; this, I said, was bound to ruin his reputation. I added that I find it strange indeed that a blackguard who only two years ago, without showing respect for either Monsieur or myself, had purposely gotten one of my maids of honor with child and insisted that she be delivered in this very house and who constantly keeps whores and knaves in the Palais Royal, should be my son's governor and therefore in a position to set a bad example for my son. I also pointed out to Monsieur that I had other reasons to ask him not to entrust my son to this man, namely that he is my worst enemy, that Monsieur should remember how before his own eyes I have convicted him of lying in everything he had said about me and that indeed he had asked my forgiveness on bended knees in Monsieur's presence, and that, in short, nothing could be more painful to me than to see this godless wretch rewarded with my only son for all the evil he has done me, for trying to cut off my honor with his lies, and for making me the target of Monsieur's unending hatred, so that I can expect nothing but hatred from my son as well if this man were to be his governor. I granted that Monsieur is the lord and master and that he can place my son in the hands of anybody he sees fit, but that d'Effiat would have neither my approval nor my consent as long as he lives. And that if it were to be my misfortune that my son be given this governor, no one should blame me for apologizing to the whole world and for letting everyone know that this had been done against my will. At first Monsieur said that Madame de Maintenon had been greatly in favor of this and had tried to gain the King's consent; to this I replied that that is a bad sign for Monsieur and my son, for if His Majesty allowed my son to fall into these hands it would be a sign that he no longer cared about him, since the King is so well aware of d'Effiat's many vices that he has often spoken to me about them, which is true; as for Madame de Maintenon's approval, I told Monsieur that this particular case should make him suspicious, for her love for Monsieur du Maine,[1] whom she has brought up and whom she loves as if he were her own child, is such that she must wish him to surpass my son in virtue; therefore she would be only too happy to approve d'Effiat as my son's governor, but that this very approval should open Monsieur's eyes and show him how unsuitable this governor would be for his son. When d'Effiat saw that I was so adamantly opposed, he said at first that he did not want the position, but later he changed his mind and sought it more eagerly than ever. Monsieur had already let me know, albeit with some annoyance, that d'Effiat did not want to become governor and had not been appointed for that reason, but that this had nothing to do with me. I answered laughingly that by this compliment Monsieur spared me the trouble of thanking him, but that I was so glad that I could not refrain from thanking not only Monsieur but d'Effiat himself. That night I was of good cheer and thought that everything was well; but later

Monsieur's confessor was sent to me, and when I went to Paris, Comtesse de Beuvron[2] told me that Monsieur had also sent his chancellor to her to transmit a proposition to me. Since both, alas, come to the same thing, I will report them to Your Grace together, and my reply as well; the only difference between the two was that the message brought by the confessor was not as frightfully harsh as the one to Comtesse de Beuvron. Whether the good Jesuit put the thing a little more gently for me, I do not know. Monsieur's message was this: that he had firmly decided to make d'Effiat governor whether I consented or not; that therefore I would be well advised to yield in this matter; and that if I did this in a gracious manner, he would send me a carte blanche on which I could write whatever I pleased; in addition he promised to receive the Comtesse de Beuvron again, to treat her well, and to seek to please me in every possible way. However, if I should remain stubborn and say that this is being done against my will, it would happen anyway, the only difference being that he would make life miserable for me, forbid the Comtesse de Beuvron ever to see me again, refuse every request I would ever make, distress me in every way, cause every kind of scandal that would upset me most, and thereby show that he was master in his own house. . . . Since then the King has chosen a governor for the Duc de Bourgogne, one of the most virtuous men in the world;[3] and therefore I wrote to His Majesty, begging him to make the choice for my son as well, but he neither wrote nor spoke to me in reply. What the end of all this will be, time will tell. Monsieur sulks a bit about it, but I act quite as usual and as if nothing had happened and try to be as polite as ever I can. Every day someone is sent to me to try to persuade me. I am surprised that Monsieur has not written to Your Grace to enlist her help as well, but I believe he feels that this will not do, since Your Grace may have heard that this d'Effiat is also suspected of having given the late Madame the poison which, they say, the Chevalier de Lorraine had sent from Rome through Morel; this accusation, whether it be false or true, makes another fine recommendation to entrust my son to him.

1. The King's son by Madame de Montespan.   2. Madame's good friend and former lady-in-waiting, née Théobon.   3. Fénelon, archbishop of Cambrai.

Saint Cloud, 21 September 1689

To let Your Grace know the sequel to this story, I have spoken to the King. His Majesty says that it is sheer lies that he wants d'Effiat as his nephew's governor. On the contrary, he said that he had kept Monsieur from making this appointment for a whole year. To which I answered that I very humbly beg His Majesty to do my son the added favor of choosing an honorable man and to propose him to Monsieur; and this the King promised me. Since then they wanted to threaten me again, but I said that I am not afraid and almost cited the proverb, "He who dies from threats shall be buried (by your leave) with farts." I let them know that I know quite well that they have lied. Since then everything has been quiet, and I have learned through the grapevine that the King is keeping his promise and that there is indeed hope that my son will have a different governor. God grant that we will be given an honorable man! Béthune is needed by the King, so he cannot be the one, which I regret very much. For if it had been he, I would have had no fears that he would stir up my son against me.

In the end, Philippe was given the Marquis d'Arcy as his governor. His preceptor was Abbé Dubois. Both were excellent educators. Dubois served as prime minister when Philippe became Regent during the minority of Louis XV.

Saint Cloud, 30 October 1689

Yesterday I was told something that touched my heart very deeply, and I could not hear it without tears: namely that the poor people of Mannheim have all returned and are living in their cellars as if they were houses and even hold a daily market as if the town were still in its previous state. And whenever a Frenchman comes to Heidelberg, droves of these poor people go to see him to ask about me, and they always bring up His Grace the Elector, my father, and my brother, weeping bitter tears when they speak of them; but the present Elector they do not like at all.

Versailles, 10 December 1689

I do not believe that a more wicked devil can be found in the whole world than she is,[1] for all of her piety and hypocrisy, and I find that she is a fine example of the old German proverb: "Where the devil cannot go, he sends an old woman." All the trouble comes from this slut; for my part I cannot boast of her favor, and she has no greater pleasure than to stir up trouble with the great man for me or for Madame la Dauphine. If Your Grace were to know everything that goes on, she would consider it quite unbelievable. But until I can tell Your Grace all about it it is better, I believe, not to go into this text, except to say that it would be nice if the woman stuck to taking care of her maidens in the convent.[2] . . . I seem destined to lose everything that I should get from my family: all the land the King has burned, and all the money Monsieur has taken unto himself without giving me a red farthing of it. But this I could easily do without, if only I were otherwise left in peace and not pestered the way I am day after day.

1. Madame de Maintenon.   2. Saint Cyr, the convent school for noble girls founded by Madame de Maintenon.

I am very much afraid that she will not be with us very much longer, and this would grieve me in the depth of my soul, for I am very fond of her, and the good Madame la Dauphine deserves to be in a happier state than she is. They are killing her with sadness. They are doing everything they can to reduce me to the same state, but then I am a tougher nut than Madame la Dauphine and before the old women have eaten me up, they may well have lost a few teeth. . . . I am taking very good care of my health, just to make them mad. The old woman is at least fifteen or perhaps even twenty years older than I, therefore I think that if only I am patient and take care of my health I shall have the pleasure of seeing her depart for the next world before me.

Versailles, 12 June 1690

Wednesday after that distressing ceremony[1] we went to Marly, where we stayed until Saturday. There I should have gotten over my sadness, since life went on as usual: all the rooms full of cardplayers, hunting in the afternoon, music at night; but if the truth be known, this made me only more sad. For since I found no one there who cares about me, and since I saw how soon the dead are forgotten here, I felt renewed pity for poor Madame la Dauphine. . . .

I was afraid that when Your Grace returned to Hanover, she would become sad again,[2] for all the things that remind us of our loss awaken our memories and renew our pain. And nothing brings up more memories than the places where we have often been with those who were dear to us. Would to God that Your Grace could have as hard a heart and as little love for her family as the great man, his son, and his brother have for theirs. For they never grieve for anyone, no matter who in their family has died. It is truly amazing how hard these people are. If this were a matter of strength of character one might perhaps appreciate it and admire them for it, but that is not the reason, for as long as they see the sad spectacle they cry, but as soon as they leave the room they laugh again and forget all about it. This makes me quite impatient, for I cannot follow their example, and even though it is considered a weakness to be sad, it is after all also a mark of a kind heart.

1. The funeral of the Dauphine, who had died on 20 April. Preparations for royal funerals were so elaborate that bodies had to be stored in a temporary crypt for weeks.
2. The son of Duchess Sophie, Karl Philipp, had died in January in the war against the Turks.

When the King of England[1] had returned to his coach and was about to drive off to Saint Germain, he found, a hundred paces from the gate, one of his valets who brought him news that all of Ireland is convinced that Marshal Schomberg has perished in the battle and that the Prince of Orange has died of his wounds. Since then it has been learned that what was said of poor Marshal Schomberg is indeed true, but that the Prince of Orange is only slightly wounded. But the joy that the news of his death has caused among the populace defies description, and although police constables were sent out to keep the frenzy in check, it was not possible. They carried on for twice twenty-four hours with great feasting and guzzling, forcing anyone who passed by to drink with them; they made bonfires, shot off their muskets, set off fireworks, and performed masquerades. Some prepared a funeral and invited all passers-by to help bury the Prince of Orange; others made a figure of straw and wax, called it the Prince of Orange, and shot at it all night long. The Cordelier monks also made a big bonfire in front of their monastery, came out and made a big circle around their fire, jumping, dancing, and singing. If I were to tell Your Grace of all the foolishness that went on in Paris, I would have to write a long book. Yet it is odd that our King's authority, however absolute it is, was unable to prevent this, for anyone who might have suggested that this is foolishness would have risked his neck.

1. James II had unsuccessfully attempted to reconquer England with the help of the French and the Catholic Irish.

Seeing that the foolishness that goes on here gives Your Grace some amusement, I herewith send Your Grace the songs that are being sung here, although they do not exactly celebrate our poor King of England. Your Grace will see that even though people in this country like the King [of England] and hate the Prince of Orange, they have more respect for the latter, as the songs indicate. Thursday last we had the poor King and the Queen here; the Queen was quite somber, but the King was as merry as ever. He again inquired about Your Grace. I do not know who the flatterers are who used to vaunt this king's intelligence so much, for as far as I can judge it, there is little evidence for it. . . . The more one sees of this king and hears about the Prince of Orange, the more one excuses the Prince of Orange and sees that he is worthy of esteem. Your Grace will perhaps think that old love never dies,[1] but it is certain that I prefer a bright mind like his to a fine face.

1. The Prince of Orange had been Liselotte's playmate at The Hague.

Saint Cloud, 23 August 1690

Although the great man is winning lots of battles, he is as cranky as he was before. The old women make him scared of the devil so that they can keep him to themselves and so that he will not look at younger ones. And yet this forced piety is completely against his nature. So he becomes cranky, and the price is paid by those who are not at fault; but this is just between us.

Saint Cloud, 13 September 1690

There is no question that religion and piety are being strangely twisted now in this country; this does not suit me at all, and I shall soon have to do like an Englishman by the name of Filding. Some years ago, Wendt asked him, "Are you a Huguenot, Monsieur?"—"No," he said. —"So you are a Catholic," said Wendt. —"Even less," replied the Englishman. —"Ah," said Wendt, "that's because you are Lutheran." —"Not at all," said Filding. —"Well, then, what are you?" said Wendt. —"I will tell you," said the Englishman, "I have a little religion all my own." And so I believe that I too will soon have "a little religion all my own." Good King James would have been better off if he had done the same, rather than lose three kingdoms through bigotry.

Fontainebleau, 20 October 1690

Now that I have come to know good King James better, I am quite fond of him; he really is the kindest man in the world. I feel terribly sorry for him, for sometimes he sighs so pitifully. Once he took me aside and earnestly wanted to know whether it is true that his daughter, the Princess of Orange, is so grieved at his misfortune that she did not want to dance when her Grace the Electress of Brandenburg visited the Hague and also whether it is true that she is glad that he did not die in Ireland. I assured him that this is perfectly true, and it seemed to me that this assurance gave some comfort to the poor, unhappy King.

Versailles, 2 February 1691

We are becoming more devout here every day; there is a rumor, although I do not know if it is true, that the King's old trollop has let all the ladies who wear rouge know that they should no longer wear it. I have saved her the trouble of sending this message to me. This is what they consider piety; but when it comes to giving the widower[1] a new wife, they can not be bothered.

1. The Dauphin, Louis; Madame had her daughter in mind.

It is a great good fortune that my dearest Ma Tante has not become ill after Your Grace suffered two such heavy blows.[1] I was mortally afraid. May God Almighty save Your Grace and make up for this great suffering with a thousand joys. The Princess of Ostfriesland must have a very kind heart, and I am most grateful to her for comforting Your Grace as best she could. I, who have already had a great deal of sadness in my life, know only too well how it is to lie in bed and to be too sad to sleep. And the worst part of it comes when one has dozed off a little and then wakes up with a start and again faces one's misery; that is altogether horrible. I am entirely of Your Grace's opinion (I almost said Your Grace's religion) that it is unchristian to pester one's fellow man; nonetheless this is precisely the beginning of all piety in this country, and I find it very difficult to get used to this. The widower[2] is a most unusual character, and I do not think that his insensitivity has ever been matched; unless one saw it with one's own eyes, one would not believe it. God alone knows who will have my daughter in the end, but it seems to me that no effort is being made to find a new wife for the widower; therefore I am sorry that the Roman King[3] will marry his aunt. In any case I would rather see my daughter remain Mademoiselle all her life than let her be put into an unbefitting marriage.[4] She is growing terribly tall, is almost taller than I; her figure is not too bad . . . she has nice skin but all of her features are ugly; an ugly nose, a large mouth, slanted eyes, and a flat face. . . .

1. After Karl Phillip, Sophie's second son, Friedrich August had also died in battle. 2. The Dauphin. 3. Subsequently Emperor Joseph I. 4. There was still talk of marrying Mademoiselle to the Duc du Maine, illegitimate son of Louis XIV and Madame de Montespan.

Taking the waters was very bad for Monsieur de Louvois,[1] but it is not known whether what did him in was sweet or sour water. All the doctors and barbers who opened him up say and have signed that he died of a horrible poison.[2] In the space of fifteen minutes he was well and dead. I had happened to meet him and speak to him half an hour before he died; he looked well and his color was so good that I told him that the water of Forches seemed to agree with him. Out of civility he wanted to see me to my room. However, I said that the King was waiting for him and so did not want him to do it. If I had let him go with me, he would have died on me in my room, which would have been an awful spectacle. . . . As long as he had to die, I wish it had happened three years ago, which would have been a good thing for the poor Palatinate.

1. The minister of war; see Cast of Principal Characters. 2. Present-day historians do not believe that this is true.

For my part, I would be happier if it had been an old trollop who had dropped dead rather than he. For now she will be more powerful than ever and in an even better position to give free rein to her viciousness. And since she hates me terribly, I will bear the brunt, along with everyone else. However, I am as cheerful as ever I can be, keeping in mind that I do not want to die of threats so that I will not have to be buried (by your leave) with farts, as the proverb puts it.

Saint Cloud, 23 August 1691

If it should be true that Monsieur de Louvois was poisoned, I do not believe that it is the work of his sons, vicious as they are.[1] Rather, I believe that a doctor has done the thing to please a certain old woman, who was very much annoyed at Monsieur de Louvois for speaking most freely of her, for they say that this happened when he went to Mons with His Majesty. The King did not seem particularly upset by Monsieur de Louvois's death; it had been a long time since I had seen him as merry as he was a few days after this man's death.

1. Louvois had seven sons; two of them, the Marquis de Barbézieux and the Marquis de Courtainvaux, held important government positions.

Fontainebleau, 18 September 1691

Monsieur de Louvois is so completely forgotten now that no one worries any longer whether he was poisoned or not. . . . Our great man here is incapable of undertaking such a thing. I know that there are people who have offered to assassinate the Prince of Orange. Yet he never wanted to permit it. But I do believe that there are plenty of others who can be carried away by their zeal. . . . I have always imagined that we are the Lord God's marionettes, for we are made to go hither and yon and to play various parts. And then we suddenly fall down and the play is over. Death is Punchinello, who hits each of the figures one by one and pushes them off the stage.

Fontainebleau, 14 October 1691

I am also glad that Your Grace agrees with me that we are Our Lord's marionettes. To love God with all our hearts and without seeing Him and to love our fellow man who persecutes us, these are two things that are not easy to do; it would be easier to admire and fear God; nor is it hard to love those who are good to us; but as long as we are here in the world we must do the best we can and leave the rest to God's mercy.

I must tell Your Grace a little story that happened here some two weeks ago, and which shows a new way of taking revenge for a slap in the face. A captain in the dragoons came to a house here in Paris where many ladies were playing cards. Two of these ladies were quarelling about some point in the game; one said the other had passed, the other denied it; the quarrel became heated, and all the ladies and the other cavaliers who were in the room came to their table. The captain in the dragoons also came, and one of the ladies asked him to be the judge in the matter. He condemned the one whom he thought in the wrong; she stands up and slaps his face good and hard. Without a moment's hesitation he says, "Gentlemen, this is the action of a man and not of a woman; I must find out about it," then jumps at the woman, lifts all her skirts over her head, and calls out, "Gentlemen, pay close attention. If it is a man, we will have to cut each other's throats, but if it is really a lady, I shall make a deep bow and kiss the hand that has struck me." Everyone in the room exclaimed, "It's a woman," whereupon he dropped the skirts, made a deep bow, and went away.

Although my eyes are so thick and swollen that I can barely look out of them, since I confess that I was foolish enough to bawl all night, I do not wish to let this Friday mail pass without telling Your Grace about the most upsetting thing that happened to me yesterday, when I was least expecting it. At half past three Monsieur came in and said to me, "Madame, I have a message from the King for you, which will not be too pleasing to you, and you are to give him your answer in person by tonight. The King wishes me to tell you that since he and I and my son are agreed on the marriage of Mademoiselle de Blois to my son, you will not be foolish enough to demur." I leave it to Your Grace to imagine how much this dismays and also grieves me. That night, shortly after eight, the King had me called into his study and asked me whether Monsieur had informed me of the proposition and what I had to say to it. "When your Majesty and Monsieur speak to me as my masters, as you are doing, I can only obey," I said, remembering what Your Grace once wrote to me about this text through Monsieur Harling, namely that if they really insisted on this marriage, I should give in. So now it has come to pass; this morning the King and all the courtiers called on me in my room to compliment me on this lovely affair, and I did not want to wait any longer to report this (I almost said misfortune) to Your Grace. My head hurts so much that I cannot say more than that I am and will be until death . . .

In the preceding letter, Madame had probably told her aunt less than the whole story. Under the same date, the Duc de Saint-Simon describes Elisabeth Charlotte's reaction to her son's projected marriage as follows: "Madame was walking in the gallery with Châteauthiers, her favorite and worthy of her favor. She was walking briskly, handkerchief in hand, weeping without restraint, speaking rather loudly, gesticulating, and giving a fine performance of Ceres after the abduction of her daughter Proserpina as she is searching for her in great wrath and demanding her back from Jupiter. Everyone respectfully kept out of her way. . . . [The next day Madame's] son approached her, as he did every day, in order to kiss her hand; at that moment Madame slapped his face so hard that the sound was heard several paces away, which, in the presence of the entire court, deeply embarrassed this poor prince. . . ." Duchess Sophie had no doubt heard of this scene and chided her niece for childish behavior. Hence Elisabeth Charlotte's reply:

Versailles, 21 February 1692

Your Grace was poorly informed if she was told that I acted childishly about this wedding. Unfortunately I am no longer of an age to be childish; to act childishly now would be sheer madness. . . . As far as my daughter-in-law is concerned, I will have no trouble getting used to her, for we will not see each other often enough to annoy each other; her years and mine are quite different, and so I will leave it to my daughter to entertain her. Saying bonjour and bonsoir morning and night won't take long.

Paris, 5 March 1692

Thanks be to God! Monsieur du Maine's marriage has been arranged,[1] so this weight is off my chest. I believe that the King's trollop must have been told what the populace of Paris is saying, and that must have frightened her. They said very loudly that it would be shameful for the King to give his bastard daughter to a legitimate prince of the house. However, since my son gives his rank to his spouse, they would let it pass, albeit regretfully. But if the old woman should have the gall to give my daughter to Monsieur du Maine, they would throttle him before the marriage was concluded. . . . I love the good Parisians for looking after my interest in this manner.

1. He married a granddaughter of the Grand Condé, thereby relieving Madame of the worry that he might be married to her daughter.

Paris, 11 May 1692

I appreciate the Germans' sincerity more than I appreciate magnificence, and I am most sorry to hear that this is being lost in the fatherland. It is easy to understand how luxury drives out good faith; one cannot be magnificent without money, and if money becomes so important, one becomes calculating, and once one has become calculating, one seeks every possible means of getting something, which opens the door to falseness, lying, and cheating, and this in turn altogether drives out good faith, loyalty, and sincerity.

Saint Cloud, 22 May 1692

In our day I believe that few know what is and is not holy. To my mind those are holiest who do the least harm to their fellow man and who are just in their ways. But this I do not find in the pious people here; on the contrary, no one in the world is more filled with bitter hatred, and it would be no worse to fall into the hands of the Turks than into those of these merciless people. I know the price one has to pay and have proof of it. I must confess to Your Grace that, although these pious people are my fellow men too, I cannot love them as I love myself, and if I examine myself I find that I love only those who love me, or at least do not hate me. So I find it difficult to follow the Scripture in this respect.

Saint Cloud, 31 May 1692

Why is it that Your Grace no longer sings? For it seems to me that Your Grace always used to sing when traveling by carriage. I have forgotten almost all the psalms, but I am still quite good at singing the Lutheran hymns and have forgotten very little. . . .

I am becoming a bit afraid for my boy, for they say that King William is on the march and wants to help out at Namur, and my son is in Monsieur de Luxembourg's army, which is supposed to stop him. But I hope that the siege will not be long, for people in the town are already frightened; more than fifty ladies of quality with their children and maids have walked on foot into the King's camp; they were treated as prisoners of war and whisked off to a convent. It seems to me that these ladies must either have a high opinion of the French soldiers' discretion or they must have been more afraid for their lives than for their honor or their jewels, for these poor ladies brought along all their diamonds. They were captured by soldiers who were after this loot, but when they promised each of them a *taler,* they were led into the King's encampment with all their belongings without a single penny being taken, and in this way they saved their pretty brocades and their diamonds. . . . Any executioner who would rid us of our old ragbag here I should consider an honorable man and would gladly recommend him for ennoblement.

I do not have enough vanity to believe that I am all that meritorious, yet the contempt with which the King treats me is so horrendous that there is no vanity in believing that I do not deserve it, especially since he permits me to be affronted by an old woman who all her life—and this is no title of glory for me—has led a more scandalous life than I have done. But I have made up my mind; henceforth I shall, whenever possible, take things as they come and only look after my health; for although I am no longer young, the old trollop is older than I, and so I hope that before my end I shall have the pleasure of seeing the old devil burst into bits.

Wednesday last we received the news of the surrender of the fortress of Namur. Later that day I happened to be driving to the arsenal, for I wanted to see a small house there where many fine Indian curiosities are kept. The ladies in my carriage called out to some tradesmen that Namur had surrendered, and so the populace fancied that I was driving around expressly to spread this news; they gathered around my carriage and shouted, "Vive le Roi et Madame." Others added to the rumor that I had driven to the Bastille and in my joy had set off the cannon myself, and that afterward in Notre Dame church I had presented to the Virgin a bouquet of mixed flowers so heavy I could not carry it myself. I am quite embarrassed that such foolishness is being told about me and am not looking forward to reading the *Lardon* or the *Quintessence des Nouvelles,*[1] for when this nonsense reaches Holland, I will be properly lampooned, although I certainly do not deserve it.

1. French-language newspapers containing extensive gossip columns, published in Holland. See also Madame's remarks about the gazetteer of Holland in the letter of 22 September 1720.

Before I begin to answer Your Grace's kind letter from Linsburg of 27 July, I must tell Your Grace of the great fright I suffered last Monday night, although by the grace of God that fright turned to joy in the end. I had already disrobed and was about to lie down in my bed at midnight, when I suddenly heard Monsieur's voice in my antechamber, and since I knew that he had already gone to bed in his room, I realized that something must be amiss and therefore jumped up and ran toward Monsieur to find out what it was. He held an opened letter in his hand and said: "Do not be alarmed, your son is wounded, but only slightly; there has been a raging battle in Flanders and the King's infantry has defeated that of the Prince of Orange. The King tells me that this is all we know so far and that there are no futher details." I leave it to Your Grace to imagine the anxiety that this news caused me; I stayed on my balcony and waited until almost three o'clock in the morning for a courier from my son. Every half-hour couriers arrived. One brought news of the death of Marquis de Bellefonds, another reported that Monsieur de Turenne was mortally wounded, for his mother was here; she and his mother-in-law, Madame de Vantadour, who loved him as if he were her own child, began to weep loudly, and since they lodge just below my room I could hear their crying; of course I pitied them with all my heart, but I kept thinking that I might soon hear the same thing about my son. In this anxiety I spent the whole night, but I did not find out much about my son until after dinner the next day, when a nobleman by the name of La Bertière, his former subtutor, arrived and told us that my son had been hit by two bullets, one tore his coat at the shoulder all to pieces without touching him, thank God, the other lodged in his left arm. He pulled the bullet out himself, then his arm was cut open and the wound dressed; whereupon he returned to the scene of the *melée* and did not leave until it was all over. At first our men had buckled, and the English and the Dutch advanced across hedges and ditches and took three of our cannon; at that point Monsieur de Luxembourg arrived with the regiment of the guard, Prince de Conti, Monsieur le Duc, and my son. They rallied the hussars, harangued them, and personally led the charge; this gave the soldiers so much courage that they broke through, driving the enemy so far back into the open field that they not only recaptured their own cannon but seven of the enemy's as well. But on both sides horrendous numbers of people have been killed, many of them men of quality. It lasted from nine o'clock in the morning until eight in the evening and was one of the most horrible battles ever to be seen.[1] . . .

As for my son's wife, she cannot complain about me, for I treat her well and politely, but I can never like her as long as I live, for she is the most disagreeable person in the world; her figure is all askew, her face is ugly, and she is unpleasant in everything she does, and yet she fancies that she is beautiful, primps herself all the time, and is full of *mouches*.[2] When I see all of this and think that she is nothing but mousedroppings,[3] I must admit that I find it a bit upsetting and that it takes considerable effort and trouble to do one's best. Your Grace's daughter-in-law[4] is only half as bad as ours, and moreover pleasant and kind as a person, which ours certainly is not. No wonder, then, that I find it more difficult to make the effort for ours than Your Grace for hers.

1. The battle of Steenkerke. 2. *Mouches* (literally, "flies") were artificial beauty marks and important items in the cosmetic arsenal of the *coquette*. 3. Here Madame refers to the proverb "Mousedroppings always want to mix with the pepper" to characterize this *mésalliance*. 4. Duchess Sophie's son Georg Ludwig had married

the daughter of her brother-in-law Duke Georg Wilhelm ("Godfather") and Eléanore d'Olbreuse. Following a scandalous adultery case that compromised the young princess, this marriage ended in divorce.

Saint Cloud, 14 August 1692

I have tried to find out how old the great man's trollop is. Some say that she is only fifty-six, and they think that they really know; others say that she is just sixty, but unfortunately she is no older than that. She was so frightfully scared to die, although there was no real danger, that she had prayers said for her in all the churches, though without naming her. It was only said that the prayers were for a person of rank "useful to the State"; of that I am not convinced.

Saint Cloud, 18 September 1692

I have just returned from Maubuisson where, I am happy to say, I left Ma Tante Luise in perfect health, but we were greatly startled to feel an earthquake while I was there. I was just speaking with Her Grace the Abbess when we heard all the doors slam; we thought that someone was hammering right below us, and at that moment I felt the room swaying under me. Ma Tante wanted to go and see what it was, but I said right away that it must be an earthquake. She laughed at me, but at that moment the nuns came, all frightened because they had seen the *reine blanche*[1] move in the church. They say that in Paris several houses have collapsed from the earthquake.

I must tell Your Grace a funny story of a woman who died the day before yesterday. She was in childbed and talking to her attendant; she told her how she had bought something cheaply that the other wanted to have, to which the latter replied, "The devil take you!" and then walked out of the room, happening to leave the door open. Living in the same house was a young person who was on a diet of goat's milk. The goat got loose and went to the woman's room; at the foot of the bed the curtain was not closed, so the goat with its horns opened it further and looked into the bed. The woman in labor fancied that it was the devil whom the attendant had conjured up, and this gave her such a fright that she died three hours later. This is a fine story for the nosy ones who open our letters; it will really teach them something.

1. A statue of the Virgin Mary.

Versailles, 1 January 1693

Yesterday before I left Paris the Comtesse de Beuvron sent me a letter that she had received from Monsieur de Balati. From it I see that the electoral dignity has finally been bestowed.[1] . . . I herewith wish to express my joy about this development to Your Grace, humbly begging her to convey my compliments to Oncle as well. It is a good beginning for this year; God grant that it may continue in the same manner. I received Your Grace's kind letter of 16 December from Berlin. I am delighted that my dearest Ma Tante is having a nice time now. I was extremely pleased to hear about the splendid entry that had been prepared for Your Graces, for this is still the proper German way. I told Monsieur about all the splendor at the court of Berlin; His Grace looked more and more serious as I was talking and, just between us, I think that there was a little bit of envy that the Elector of Brandenburg is more magnificent than he is. His Grace the young prince must have a good memory if he still knew Your Grace.[2] I believe that Your Grace must have been happy to see this little grandson, and it must have also been a joy to our dear Frau von Harling to see her dear prince again. It will stand him in good stead all his life to have received his first education from her hand, for none of those who have been brought up by her are delicate. . . .

I also beg Your Grace to convey my humble thanks to the Elector of Brandenburg for his compliments. . . . As my dearest Ma Tante knows very well, Liselotte means well but does not know how to turn a pretty compliment; as I have been all my life, so I still am. France has not polished me; got there too late.

P.S. I cannot resist telling Your Grace about a fine dialogue that I recently had with Monsieur, and I hope that it will make Your Grace laugh as heartily as it did my two children. One evening the four of us were alone here in this drawing room after supper, namely Monsieur, myself, my son, and my daughter. After a long silence, Monsieur, who did not consider us good enough company to talk to us, made a great loud fart, by your leave, turned toward me, and said, "What is that, Madame?" I turned my behind toward him, let out one of the selfsame tone, and said, "That's what it is, Monsieur." My son said, "If that's all it is, I can do it as well as Monsieur and Madame," and he also let go of a good one. With that, all of us began to laugh and went out of the room. These are princely conversations, as Your Grace can see, and if anyone should still be curious enough to break open my letters, I offer this incense as a New Year's present to the first person who might open this letter before Your Grace.

1. On 2 December 1692 the House of Hanover (Braunschweig-Lüneburg) had been raised to the electoral dignity. The Duke of Hanover thus joined the college of seven electors (the bishops of Mainz, Cologne, and Trier, and the princes of the Palatinate, Bavaria, Saxony, and Brandenburg) who elected the head of the Holy Roman Empire. It was said at the time that Duke Ernst August had spent more than a million louis d'or to obtain this dignity, which gave him great power within the empire. The philosopher Leibniz, who was employed as historiographer of the house of Braunschweig-Lüneburg, had been instrumental in these negotiations.   2. The son of the Elector of Brandenburg, later King Friedrich Wilhelm I, five years old at the time.

Never having had ambitions and desiring nothing but peace and quiet, I cannot understand why people do not want to keep to their station in life if it is good. This must be proof that no one can be happy in this world, and that those who are happy will not rest until they have lost their happiness. Another thing I cannot understand is why people worry about what will be said about them in the history books. If I had a life that pleased me, I should care very little what they will write about me, for during our lifetime we are sure to be flattered, and after we are dead there is nothing we can do if anyone wants to say bad things. Moreover, at that point no evil that is said about us can harm us, nor can good things benefit us; therefore I think that it is altogether vain to worry about it. I am glad that my opinion about preordained destiny coincides with Your Grace's. I do not understand how anyone who has lived a few years and has come to know the world can doubt this. If His Grace our late Papa had known the people here as I know them, he would not have doubted that once they were lords and masters of the poor Palatinate they would deal with it as they have done, for more ruthless people cannot be found in the world.

Saint Cloud, 19 March 1693

I can never hear a sermon without going to sleep; preaching is a true opium for me. Once here in France I had a bad cough and spent three nights without sleeping a wink. Then I remembered that I always sleep in church as soon as I hear preaching and nuns singing. Therefore I drove to a convent where there was to be a sermon. The nuns had barely begun to sing when I went to sleep, and I slept throughout the three-hour service; that made me feel much better. From this Your Grace can see that I am blessed with the ability to sleep in church no less than Your Grace and His late Grace my father.

Versailles, 28 June 1693

I do not know what has taken the King to Flanders, and even less what has brought him back. But I do know that he has returned. He is much friendlier than he was before his departure and now often speaks to me. However, I do not have the faintest idea of what has brought me this favor. Monsieur is suffering deadly boredom at Vitre. Monsieur is still the same as he was in his youth. This very winter he purchased 200,000 guilders' worth of charges in the regiment of the guards with which to reward some young fellows who have entertained him in not exactly an honorable fashion. When it comes to that, no expense is spared, and this is the most annoying part, for otherwise I should not care at all and would happily say to these fellows: "You are welcome to gobble the peas, for I don't like them."

I beg Your Grace to be kind enough to see to it that His Grace the Elector of Bavaria finds out that my son greatly appreciates his civility, for it is a fact that no one could have been more courteous than he has been toward my son and everything that concerns him. Nothing is being said here about the Duke of Berwick's[1] action; it seems quite appalling to me that the death of 1,200 people does not count and is considered a small loss; after all, each one of them had either a father, a mother, a brother, a wife, or friends who mourn him with bitter tears. My heart goes out to all those who have lost their loved ones, whoever they may be. War is an ugly thing, for those who are being praised today may be taken away by a cannon ball tomorrow, and nothing will be left of them. I am again in great anxiety because the two armies are so close together, and I am afraid there will soon be another battle. Your Grace is quite right in saying that if God wants to protect my son, no harm will come to him; however, our Lord has not given me a note or letter saying that He will protect my son, therefore I cannot help fretting. I humbly thank Your Grace for her interest in my son; he has led the cavalry of which he is general five times and lived through two hours of cannon fire before the real battle started; it is surely a great miracle that he was not killed. If my son, at his age, did not go to war every year, he would saddle himself with horrendous contempt and completely lose his reputation.

1. On 29 July, William of Orange had been defeated at the battle of Neerwinden. The Duke of Berwick, an illegitimate son of James II, had fought on the French side and was captured by the English.

The duchess[1] will be able to tell Your Grace what a wicked and devious devil the old trollop is and how it is not my fault that she hates me so dreadfully, since I have done my utmost to get along with her. She makes the King cruel, even though His Majesty is not cruel by nature. The King, who in the past seemed saddened when his troops committed disorderly acts, now admits publicly that the burning and ravaging takes place on his orders. She also makes him hard and tyrannical, so that nothing can move his heart to pity any longer. Your Grace cannot possibly believe or imagine the wickedness of this old woman. And all that under the mantle of piety and humility.

1. Benedicta of Hanover, daughter of the Princesse Palatine and Madame's cousin, who had been living in France for some time and was paying a visit to Hanover in 1693.

Smallpox has left a great many marks on me but has not changed me in the slightest, which has surprised everyone. The older I get, the more ugly I am bound to become, but my temperament and my character will always remain the same. . . . I am hated because it is thought that I do not approve of the ways in which the great man is being ruled and because it is imagined that my honesty makes me the only person capable of someday opening the great man's eyes and making him see how much he harms himself by his excessive love; that is why I must be kept away from the great man.

To FRAU VON HARLING

Versailles, 16 December 1693

I am very glad that my letter has been a little comfort to my dear Mistress Uffel; usually I am not very good at this art and always imagined that I am a poor comforter who is not much help, for wishing does not do any good, because otherwise my dear Frau von Harling would have been restored to perfect health long ago. Mine, thank God, is not too bad, but I do feel that I am beginning to get old and no longer have as much strength as in my younger years. Indeed, tomorrow or the next day I shall be a grandmother, since my son's wife is just beginning her labor. Since I am planning to write to Ma Tante tomorrow, my dear Frau von Harling will be able to find out, if she should be delivered today, whether it is a "he" or a "she" she has brought forth. It is all the same to me, whatever it may be, for I cannot possibly concern myself about it; but this is just between us. My dearest Frau von Harling is very right to believe that the widowed duchess[1] and her princesses are having a fine time at Hanover; they say that they think they are in paradise. If wishing had any effect, this duchess surely would not be in Hanover without me and I would be delighted to pay my respects to Ma Tante and Oncle, but alas, I do not think I shall ever be so fortunate. Anyone who has lived through tribulations as dreadful as those I have suffered is not accustomed to good fortune and considers himself happy as long as nothing bad happens. "Jan had no trouble getting into the doublet but tugged at one sleeve for fourteen years"; but I have been tugging at the sleeve for twenty-two years and still have not gotten into the doublet; therefore I believe that death will wear me as his doublet before I get into Jan's. As for my Harling, it is to be hoped that if God preserves his life and health, he will be promoted before long. In the enclosed note Monsieur Harling will find my answer; I think he will laugh that I still remember the old tale of Herr Öllerjahn. The things of the past I remember better than what happens from day to day.

1. Benedicta.

To HERR VON HARLING

Versailles, 16 December 1693

Pourquoi me parlez-vous français, Monsieur de Harling? Croyez-vous que je ne sache plus l'allemand?[1] No, I certainly have not forgotten it and therefore will thank you for your compliment in German, and so that you can see that my memory is better than you think, I will say, "Herr Öllerjan, frau Schrettlin Margrettlin, herut ihr dorchreckels, herut aus dem samschleger, treckt den därendecker an, nehmt den ermerlin, tut waterquatschen drin, den dat rattenstert hat die vielheit in profosshaus gebracht."[2] I do not believe that one word of this is wrong, although I do not rehearse it very often. I let you judge for yourself whether I have forgotten my German, mais pour que vos voyiez que je puis aussi parler français, je finirai en vous assurant de mon estime et de mon amitié.[3]

> 1. Why do you speak French to me, Monsieur von Harling? Do you think I no longer know German? 2. Untranslatable passage from an old farce. 3. But so that you see that I can also speak French, I shall end by assuring you of my esteem and friendship.

To ELECTRESS SOPHIE

Versailles, 30 May 1694

If peace does not come soon we will certainly be miserable, for the state of things here is unspeakable and must be seen to be believed. I truly believe that all the burning and ravaging has brought bad luck and that therefore winning battles and conquering cities cannot profit this country. Your Grace's comparison of the state of affairs here with the cancer is most apt indeed. . . .

I quite agree with Your Grace: I did not like the new play about Medea and find Corneille's incomparably better. Dogs are the best people I have found in France, and I always have four of them with and around me.

Versailles, 4 June 1694

A short while ago I found out that my coachman has accused me to Monsieur de la Reynie[1] of contempt for the State, of writing everything to Germany, and of planning to run away. At my bidding Wendt confronted him and asked him why he had done this. He replied that his confessor ordered him to do it because the feeling is that I am still a Huguenot. Right thereafter the fellow ran away. . . . What I do not understand, considering that they tried to harm me through the lowest of my servants, is that they did not have me poisoned outright. Perhaps it is because, knowing that I am not terribly attached to my life, they wanted to make my life harder for me by having me put in prison and because they thought that if I were accused by my own servants I would speedily come to a bad end.

1. Nicolas Gabriel de la Reynie (1625–1709), lieutenant general of the Paris police for thirty years.

Versailles, 28 November 1694

When I consider that Her Grace the Electress of Brandenburg[1] travels wherever she want to go, builds houses, keeps musicians, in a word, does what she pleases, I find that she is a thousand times better off being Electress of Brandenburg than she would have been if she had become Dauphine here, for then she would always have had to do what others want, could never have traveled without the King, been short of money, and never have seen her own family again.

1. Sophie Charlotte, Electress Sophie's daughter, whom Madame had earlier proposed as a bride for the Dauphin.

Versailles, 16 December 1694

If the rumors that are flying are true, the boredom here will soon get worse, for they say that all operas and plays are to be done away with and that the Sorbonne has orders to work on this. I am certain that this will be no more to Your Grace's taste than it is to mine, and what seems most peculiar is that they go after such innocent things and forbid them, even though the most dreadful vices are in vogue now, such as murder by poison, assassination, and abominable sodomy; but nobody objects to these and the preachers only preach against the poor plays, which do not hurt anyone and in which one sees vice punished and virtue rewarded. This makes me terribly angry. . . . It is certainly true that our King has very bad spies in Germany, for His Majesty is almost always wrongly informed of what is happening there. The best spies are being kept at court to gather a lot of useless information.

Paris, 23 December 1694

We almost had no more plays; the Sorbonne, in order to please the King, wanted to have them forbidden. But I understand that the Archbishop of Paris and Père de la Chaise[1] told the King that it was too dangerous to banish honorable entertainments because this would drive the young people even deeper into abominable vices. So, thank God, plays are here to stay, which, they say, has horribly annoyed the great man's old pruneface, because doing away with plays was her idea. . . . As long as plays are not completely done away with, I shall always go to see them, however loudly the preachers in their pulpits are made to howl against them. Two weeks ago during a sermon against plays, when the preacher said that the theater stirs the passions, the King turned to me and said, "He is not preaching against me, since I no longer go to see plays, but against all of you who love them and go to see them." I said, "Although I love plays and go to see them, Monsieur d'Agen is not preaching against me, for he speaks only of those who let their passions be aroused by plays, and that is not my case; I only let myself be entertained, and there is nothing wrong with that." The King did not say another word.

1. The King's confessor.

As soon as I have spent even two hours in Paris, my head begins to hurt and something sharp falls into my throat and makes me cough continuously. Also, I sleep poorly when I am there, for the kitchens are right below my room. And on top of that I cannot go hunting in Paris nor enjoy the plays. In the first place, one must drive to the theater; and once one is there one cannot enjoy the play, for the stage is always so crowded with spectators that they stand around among the actors, which is most annoying. Also, nothing is more boring than the way we spend the evenings in Paris: Monsieur plays lansquenet[1] at a large table; I am not allowed to come near or to be seen while he is playing, for Monsieur has the superstition that I bring him bad luck when he sees me. Yet he wants me to stay in the room. Therefore I am caught with all the old women who do not play and must make conversation with them. This goes on from seven to eleven and oh, how it makes me yawn. . . . Here, on the other hand, I have a nice, quiet life. Weather permitting, I go hunting; and if there is a play I only have to go down one flight of steps to reach the hall; no one is on the stage . . . and it does not cost me anything. If there is *appartement* I listen to the music, and after the music I am not obliged to make conversation with a lot of old women as I am in Paris. . . . Your Grace will see from my letter that I have the same idea as Your Grace and believe that the old trollop wanted to do away with plays so that those of her former husband[2] would no longer be performed.

1. A card game. 2. The playwright Scarron.

Two days ago I heard of another piece of dreadful spite wrought by the old trollop: two years ago Monsieur le Dauphin was willing to marry my daughter and said so to the old crone; she did not contradict him, lest he speak about it to the King earlier than he had meant to do. Instead, she called in the Prin-

cesse de Conti and her *confidante,* Mademoiselle Choin, and ordered them
to keep after Monsieur le Dauphin until he had promised to put this marriage
out of his mind. These two kept after the good Monsieur le Dauphin day
and night for two months until he promised them, and he has kept his promise, too. Thus Your Grace can see how greatly I am obliged to this old thing,
not only for luring my son into a bad marriage but also for blocking my
daughter's way to good fortune. In short, I have no reason to treat her gently,
and if she should open this letter, she will find a few home truths. Nor do
I care, for she cannot do me any worse harm than she has already done me
and I hope it will be enough to make her go to hell, where she may be led
by the Father, the Son, and the Holy Ghost—this is how a little Capuchine
monk here used to end his sermons: "You will go to hell, where you may
be led by" etc.—that is why I end my text for the old trollop with these words.

Versailles, 13 February 1695

Where in the world does one find a husband who loves only his spouse and
does not have someone, be it mistresses or boys, on the side? If for this
reason wives were to go in for the same behavior one could never be sure, as
Godfather so rightly says, that the children of the house are the rightful
heirs. Does the young duchess[1] not know that a woman's honor consists of
having commerce with no one but her husband, and that for a man it is
not shameful to have mistresses but shameful indeed to be a cuckold?. . . .

Your Grace would not believe how coarse and unmannerly French men
have become in the last twelve or thirteen years. One would be hard put
to find two young men of quality who know how to behave properly either
in what they say or in what they do. There are two very different causes
for this: namely, all the piety at court and the debauchery among men. Because of the first, men and women are not allowed to speak to each other
in public, which used to be a way to give young gentlemen polish. And secondly, because they love the boys, they no longer want to please anyone but
one another, and the most popular among them is the one who knows best
how to be debauched, coarse, and insolent. This habit has become so in-
grained that no one knows how to live properly any longer, and they are
worse than peasants behind the plough. . . .

It is a great honor to sit next to the King during the sermon, but I would
be happy to cede this honor to someone else, for His Majesty will not permit me to sleep. As soon as I go to sleep, the King nudges me with his elbow
and wakes me up; thus I can never really go to sleep nor really stay awake.
And that gives one a headache.

1. Electress Sophie's daughter-in-law, who was caught in a scandalous adultery with
Count Christoph von Koenigsmarck. About the long-term results of this affair, see
also the letter of 24 February 1718.

To RAUGRÄFIN LUISE

Paris, 14 May 1695

So dancing must be out of fashion everywhere. At every gathering here in France people do nothing but play *lansquenet*. This game is all the rage now, so the young people no longer want to dance. I do not do one or the other; I am much too old to dance and indeed have not danced since the death of His Grace our late father; and there are two excellent reasons why I do not gamble. One is that I do not have money, and the second is that I do not like gambling. The stakes are horrendously high here, and the people act like madmen when they are playing. One bawls, another hits the table with his fist so hard that the whole room shakes, and a third one blasphemes to make one's hair stand on end; in short, they show such despair that one is frightened even to look at them.

To ELECTRESS SOPHIE

Saint Cloud, 15 September 1695

The story of Saint Cyr is worse than it is written in the book,[1] and funnier, too. The young maids there fell in love with each other and were caught in committing indecencies together. They say that Madame de Maintenon wept bitter tears about this and had all the relics exposed in order to drive out the demon of lewdness. Also, a preacher was dispatched to preach against lewdness. But he himself said such filthy things that the good and modest girls could not stand it and walked out of the church, while the others, the guilty ones, were so taken by the giggles that they could not hold them in.

> 1. A book that had been sent to Madame by her aunt; among other things, it contained negative accounts of the convent school of Saint-Cyr, which had been founded by Madame de Maintenon.

To RAUGRÄFIN LUISE

Saint Cloud, 17 September 1695

I do not know in which newspaper you read about my son, but everything you read is true. It seems to me that lately the papers, all except the Parisian ones, have been more or less telling the truth. I confess that my son is very fond of war, and those who see him there say that he works very hard and knows his business; yet I often feel uneasy about it all, for in this business one can easily lose an arm and a leg, or indeed one's life. If the campaign had not been over, we would not have seen my son here. The fortress of Namur surrendered a long time ago; I am surprised that you did not hear about it until the fifth. I have also learned that there will not be another battle. No one can deny that war is an abominable thing.

It seems to me that the Palatine Elector would do better to spend his money on his poor, devastated subjects than on Mardi Gras entertainment; that would be more commendable before God and the world. . . .

You tell me about your face, which you call old-fashioned, never thinking that I am ten years older than you. It is not for me to speak of faces, nor will I ever hate or love anyone for their beauty or ugliness . . . just have to get through life the way it has pleased God to make us. But what I will always like about you, dear Luise, is your virtue and your kindness. That counts for more with me than beautiful faces, which will not stay beautiful for long anyway. Are the gowns that your brother-in-law, the Duke of Schomberg, has sent you real gowns or dressing gowns? From what you tell me about this subject, I can see that people in Germany are keener than ever on fashion. To my mind this is very foolish.

To ELECTRESS SOPHIE

Versailles, 30 October 1695

I continue in the Hanoverian tradition and am not at all devout. I feel that it is a wonderful thing if one can be truly devout, as I believe our duchess is, and if one is able not only to believe all manner of seemingly impossible things as if one saw them, but also to rejoice in and always speak to something that one never sees and that never answers back. Yet I also feel that it is a wretched thing to act as if one were devout when that is not true. For to force oneself year after year to put up with tiresome devotions without being convinced, that is a sordid way of spending one's life. I am not fortunate enough to have a faith strong enough to move mountains, and I am too honest to pretend that I am devout when I am not. Therefore I simply try not to sin too grossly against the Ten Commandments and not to harm my fellow man. I do admire God Almighty, though without understanding Him; I praise Him morning and night, know that He rules the world, and accept His will, for I know that nothing can come to pass without it: now Your Grace knows the long and short of my devoutness.

Paris, 15 January 1696

If Your Grace were Catholic and had to go to mass, she would find it even more boring, for not only is it always exactly the same, but one never hears anything but the singing of vowels, like "aaaa eeee oooo iiii"; it is enough to make one burst out of one's skin with sheer impatience. Stuffing themselves after the midnight mass is the custom of all Catholics. As for me, I am so tired from all the kneeling after the three midnight masses that I would rather go to bed than eat, since our services here last from ten o'clock in the evening until one in the morning. The ladies here think that they cannot be merry until they drink themselves under the table.

Yesterday Madame de Klenk[1] called on me to take her leave; she is to depart by Thursday, or Saturday at the latest. Therefore I will tell my dearest Ma Tante how everything is here, and I will begin with Monsieur. All he has in his head are his young fellows, with whom he wants to gorge and guzzle all night long, and he gives them huge sums of money; nothing is too much or too costly for these boys. Meanwhile, his children and I barely have what we need. Whenever I need shirts or sheets it means no end of begging, yet at the same time he gives 10,000 *talers* to La Carte[2] so that he can buy his linens in Flanders. And since he knows that I am bound to find out where all the money goes, he is wary of me, afraid that I might speak about it to the King, who might chase the boys away. Whatever I may do or say to show that I do not object to his life, he still does not trust me and makes trouble for me with the King every day; even says that I hate the King. If there is any bad gossip, Monsieur tells the King that I have started it and even adds a few stout lies of his own, and sometimes he himself tells me about the terrible things he has said about me. Thereby he so turns the King against me that I can never be in his good graces. Monsieur also continually stirs up my children against me; since he does not want my son to realize how little is being done for his future, he always indulges him in his debaucheries and encourages them. Then if I suggest to my son that he should try to please the King more and abstain from vice, Monsieur and my son laugh in my face, and in Paris both of them lead an absolutely shameful life. My son's inclinations are good, and he could make something of himself if he were not corrupted by Monsieur. My daughter, thank God, he does not drag into debauchery, and to tell the truth, the girl does not have the slightest propensity for *galanterie*. But Monsieur does not let me have control over her, always takes her places where I am not, and surrounds her with such rabble that it is a miracle that she has not been corrupted. Moreover, he is inculcating her with such hatred of the Germans that she can barely stand to be with me because I am German, and that makes me feel that she will end up like my son and one of these days will let herself be talked into taking the bastard.[3] It is true that in public Monsieur is polite to me, but in fact he cannot stand me. As soon as he sees that any of my servants, be they male or female, become attached to me, he conceives an utter dislike for them and does them harm whenever he can; those who despise me, on the other hand, have all his favor. Monsieur is doing everything he can to make me hated, not only by the King, but also by Monsieur Le Dauphin, and everyone else too. Then, if I say to him, "Why do you want people to hate me, Monsieur?" he does not reply but only shakes his head and laughs. And yet I am doing my best, treat him politely and with great respect, and do everything he wants me to do. Your Grace can well believe that this does not make for a happy or pleasant life for me. As for the Maintenon, she is so jealous of her authority that Monsieur does her a great favor by slandering me to the King; on several occasions she also would have liked to stir me up against Monsieur, for she often sees to it that I am told that Monsieur slanders me to the King. To that I reply that I hope that the King will be just enough to examine whether or not these allegations are true and that, knowing that I am doing my best to conduct myself in an irreproachable manner, I have no reason to be afraid, for when it turns out that these allegations are lies, those who spread them will reap nothing but shame. And if I were to be condemned out of hand, I would have to take comfort in the thought that I am unfortunate but not guilty. Your Grace would not believe what a wicked devil this old hag is, and how she seeks to stir people up against one another. Although she is now treating me more courteously, there is no reason to believe that she will ever do me a good turn, for in fact she hates me terribly, and the King blindly does everything she wants. My son's wife is a repulsive person, drinks herself under the table three or four times a week, and has no use whatsoever for me; when I am present it is impossible to get a word out of her. This suspicion has been planted by the Maintenon. Moreover, the King prefers all the bastards to me; if there is to be an outing, the Princesses' ladies-in-waiting have to go along . . . , and every night I must see with my own eyes that Madame de Chartres[4] enters the King's study while the door is shut in my face. I have told Monsieur what I think of that, but he is very pleased about it, and since the King sees that the less to-do he makes about me, the more Monsieur will be happy, I am bound to be treated badly at all times. Indeed, the King is so well aware that Monsieur likes me to be treated with contempt that whenever there is trouble between them, the reconciliation always amounts to extra favors for Monsieur's beloved boys and bad treatment for me. All the silverware that came from the Palatinate Monsieur has melted down and sold, and all the proceeds were given to the boys; every day new ones show up, and all of his jewelry is being sold, pawned, pledged, and given to the young men so that if—God forbid—Monsieur should die today, tomorrow I would be thrown upon the King's mercy and not know where to find my daily bread. Monsieur says quite loudly and does not conceal from his daughter and from me that since he is getting old now, he feels that there is no time to lose and that he means to spare no expense to have a merry time until his end; he also says that those who will live longer than he will just have to see how they can get along and that he loves himself more than he loves me and his children. And indeed he practices what he preaches. If I were to tell Your Grace all the details, I would have to write a whole book. Everything here is pure self-interest and deviousness, and that makes life most unpleasant. If one does not want to get involved in intrigues and *galanteries*, one must live by oneself, which is also quite boring. In order to clear my head of these dismal reflections, I go hunting as often as possible, but this will come to an end as soon as my poor horses can no longer walk, for Monsieur has never bought me any new ones and is not likely to do so now. In the past the King used to give them to me, but now times are bad. But I will not worry about it before it comes to that. One simply cannot enjoy anything here, for if one speaks freely, one gets into no end of trouble, and if one has to hold back, nothing is enjoyable. The young people are so brutal that one has to be afraid of them and does not feel like having anything to do with them; the old ones are full of politics and only seek one's company after they see that one has the King's good graces. From all of this Your Grace can see that things are in a bad way; but I do not torment myself and take the times as they come. I am living as honorably and as well as I can; if I find out something I keep quiet and do not let on. It is a lonely life, for as I said before, there is nothing here to give me pleasure.

1. The wife of the Hanoverian envoy.   2. One of Monsieur's favorites, a particularly greedy character.   3. The Comte de Toulouse, son of the Montespan.   4. Madame's daughter-in-law.

Marly, 11 May 1696

To my mind it is the greatest mark of friendship if a spouse is given a comfortable livelihood and if she is not pestered. It is a great error to believe that in this world one can have another person's entire heart, although I do admit that it would be wonderful if it were possible. But there is no example in the world to show that this can last for any length of time. So it is useless to want something that is not possible. What is perfectly possible, however, would be not to persecute one's wife, not to disparage her and to make her disliked by all and sundry, not to keep hatred for her in one's innermost heart while showing a friendly countenance, and not to let her suffer want while conspicuously giving plenty and then some to others and going through the wife's entire fortune to do it: these are tough morsels to digest. . . .

It is amazing how simple the great man is when it comes to religion, for otherwise he is not simple at all. The reason is that he has never read anything about religion, nor the Bible either, and just goes along believing whatever he is told about religion. That is why when he had a mistress who was not devout, neither was he, but since he has fallen in love with one who keeps talking about penitence, he believes everything she says, to the point that his confessor and the lady are often at loggerheads, for he believes her more than the confessor, but will not go to the trouble of finding out for himself what true religion is. One thing is undeniable, namely, that so far the great man has been exceedingly lucky, but whether this luck will hold out much longer, time will tell. . . .

The smoked sausages, I am afraid, will not arrive as safely as my inkwell, which does not tempt anybody, but I fear that the sausages will be gobbled up at the customs house, which I should greatly regret, for I would like to eat them myself to Your Grace's good health.

Saint Cloud, 24 June 1696

A French proverb says, "The days pass, and one is not like the other," and that is certainly true, for some are boring, others are jolly, some are good, and others are very bad. Yesterday I spent a very boring day, which seemed even more boring since I was ready for something better. I had arisen at half past five to hunt the wolf with Monsieur le Dauphin six miles from here, but we looked for a wolf for five hours without finding one, so I spent five hours sitting in the calash with Monsieur le Dauphin, who did not say a word because he never wants anyone to know what he thinks. Nor could I sleep, for he kept giving orders to his hunters, telling them where else they might search; so I must confess that it has been a very long time since I have suffered such excruciating boredom. However, I have sworn to myself that I will never again go to a wolf hunt without carrying a book in my pocket, so that I can read.

I am glad that Helmont[1] has returned to Your Grace, for his philosophy will amuse Your Grace and help pass the time. How can anyone understand something about which we cannot possible know anything? After all, no one has ever returned from the other world to tell us how it is there, and before we come into the world we are nothing; so I would certainly like to know how the good Helmont imagines these things to be. But that he knows how to be content at all times is a beautiful art, which I would love to learn. The selfsame book that Monsieur Helmont brought Your Grace from Sulzbach, of the *Consolation of Philosophy,* he gave to me at Heidelberg twenty-five years ago; I still have it and like it very much. It seems unusual to me that something is better written in German than in French.

1. Franz Mercurius Helmont (1618–99) was interested in the physiology of speech and in teaching the deaf and mute; he also espoused a philosophy of enthusiasm and believed in reincarnation.

Port Royal, 2 August 1696

I cannot quite get Monsieur Helmont's opinion through my head, for I cannot understand what the soul is and how it might come into a different body. Reasoning in my simple-minded way, I should be more inclined to believe that it is all over and that there is nothing left of us when we die, and that each of the elements that has contributed to making us takes back its share in order to make something else, be it a tree, a plant, or whatever else that can serve once again for the nourishment of living creatures. The grace of God alone, it seems to me, can make us believe in the immortality of the soul, for naturally this notion would never enter our heads, especially when we see what becomes of people once they are dead. God Almighty is so unfathomable that, it seems to me, we would espouse too petty a notion of His omnipotence if we were to enclose Him within the bounds of our own order. We humans, who have rules, can be good or evil, depending on whether we adhere to these rules or break them; but who can give laws to the Almighty? Another sign that it is not given to us to understand God's kindness is that our faith teaches us that He first created two humans and then proceeded, Himself, to contrive the impulse for their transgression, for why was it necessary to forbid one tree and afterward to place the curse on all of those who had not sinned since they were not yet born? By our reckoning, this is the exact opposite of kindness and justice, for it is to punish those who are not at fault and have not sinned. Further, we are also taught that God has sacrificed His only Son for us; by our reckoning this is not just either, for the Son had never sinned and indeed could not sin; therefore it seems to me that it is impossible to understand why God treats us as He does, so that we can only admire His omnipotence but cannot possibly reason about His kindness and justice. . . .

In my last letter I took the liberty of telling Your Grace my opinion about Christ's disciples' question concerning the blind-born man, but I would like to add that I do not think that this is proof that the soul goes into another body, for since all Jews and Christians believe that we are lost through the fault of Adam, our common father, the disciples could easily have believed that every man is tainted with his own forefathers' sins and that everyone is born sinful in this manner; yet our Lord Christ denies that the man had sinned before he was born, for He tells us that neither the blind-born man nor his father sinned and that it happened so that the works of God could be seen and His glory praised. Thus our Lord Christ's answer demolishes Monsieur Helmont's opinion. I quite agree with Your Grace that this opinion does not provide much comfort, for if one shared it one would still be aware only of one's death but know nothing about the next incarnation. I also find it unfortunate that one would know nothing about one's childhood, although I would be glad to forget how it was in the womb, for that must be offensive. Monsieur Helmont's contentment and calm, however, I would love to learn from him.

Political marriages sometimes involved children. When the Duke of Savoy obtained the prize of marrying his daughter Marie-Adélaïde to Louis XIV's grandson as part of the Treaty of Turin that ended the Dutch war, the bride-to-be was only eleven years old and the future groom was thirteen. In such cases, it was considered desirable to have the young princess educated at the court of her future husband. Pretty little Marie-Adélaïde thus arrived at Versailles when she was barely twelve years old, and the actual marriage was put off until she had turned fourteen. Having completely captured the hearts of Louis XIV and Madame de Maintenon, she was given the ceremonial rank of Duchesse de Bourgogne and First Lady of the Court, which cannot have pleased Madame, who had held that rank since the death of the Queen.

Paris, 8 November 1696

I must tell Your Grace a few things about the future Duchesse de Bourgogne,[1] who finally arrived at Fontainebleau on Monday last. When she arrived, I received her with peals of laughter, for I was absolutely in stitches: the crush and crowd was such that poor Madame de Nemours and the Maréchale de la Motte were pushed with their backs toward us all the way across the room and finally bumped into Madame de Maintenon. If I had not grabbed the latter by the arm, they all would have tumbled down like playing cards. It was quite funny. As for the princess, Her Grace is rather small for her age[2] but she has a very pretty and slender figure like a dainty doll; she has pretty blond hair, and a lot of it, black eyes and eyebrows, very long and beautiful eyelashes; her skin is smooth but fairly dark, her little nose neither pretty nor ugly, her mouth large and thick-lipped; in a word, a true Austrian mouth and chin. She walks well and has a fine and graceful demeanor; she is rather serious for a child of her age and frightfully political, makes little to-do about her grandfather,[3] and barely looks at my son and myself. But as soon as she sees Madame de Maintenon she gives her a big smile and goes to her with open arms; she does the same thing when she sees the Princesse de Conti. That shows Your Grace what a politician she already is.

1. Marie-Adélaïde of Savoy was the daughter of Monsieur's second daughter from his first marriage. 2. Twelve years old. 3. Monsieur.

Paris, 22 November 1696

The King no longer has anything in his head but this child; he cannot abide not seeing her and once even called her into the council. This girl is a real Italian and as political as if she were thirty years old. We have an envoy of her court here who served in her mother's household, so that she knows him very well; however, she acts as if she did not know him, barely looks at him, and does not speak to him for fear that the King might take it amiss and think that she is still attached to her fatherland. This I do not like, for a person of good nature and disposition should not hide her feelings in this manner and consider it a shame to love her parents and her fatherland. Indeed, those who do not love those who have borne and raised them are not likely to love strangers either.

Paris, 25 November 1696

Your Grace already knows how our little bride was received and that she was already[1] given the rank of Duchesse de Bourgogne after all, even though she is not yet to go by the name but is only called La Princesse. But since she will eventually rank above me anyway,[2] it cannot matter very much whether this happens a year earlier or later, and in any case I have derived very little advantage from being the first, except a place in the rank order . . . so I yield it without regret. . . .

The master's passion for that woman[3] is quite amazing; everyone in France says that as soon as the peace is concluded the marriage will be made public and the lady will assume her rank. That is another reason why I am glad not to be the first, for then at least I will come after a proper princess and will not be obliged to present the shirt and the gloves to the lady.[4] As long as it has to be, I wish it were already done, for then the court would once again have a proper form and would no longer be as divided as it is now. Time will tell what will become of this. . . .

I do not know whether the Duchesse de Bourgogne will be happier than Madame la Dauphine, Madame la Grande Duchesse, and myself, for when we arrived we were each in turn *merveilleuses,* but soon people grew tired of us. But then we did not have the advantage of being under the special care of those who enjoy the highest favor, as this little princess is; for this reason her favor may well last longer than ours did. No one could be more political than the little princess; they say that her father taught her this. She does not get it from her mother, who has a better and more sincere character. La Princesse is no beauty, but I do not find her as terribly ugly as some others do. But she is intelligent, there is no doubt about that, and one can see it in her eyes.

1. I.e., before her actual marriage.   2. The wife of the King's grandson ranked above his sister-in-law.   3. Madame de Maintenon.   4. This refers to the ceremony of the *lever,* in which the Queen of France was entitled to be handed her shirt and her gloves by the highest-ranking lady present.

Versailles, 2 January 1697

I very well remember the Duke of Wolfenbüttel, who was married to Princess Christine; his name was Albrecht Ferdinand, he had an odd way of rolling his eyes and he played little games with me when I visited Wolfenbüttel with Your Grace. If I recall correctly he is also the one who once picked that silly quarrel with his brother, Duke Anton Ulrich. I cannot understand how two people who were as foolish as this gentleman and his spouse have produced such well-mannered and sensible children. . . .

That Aurora Königsmarck[1] must be a strange creature and entirely without shame if she asked the mayor and syndic of a town to witness the birth of her bastard child.[2] I have a feeling that Germany is becoming very different than it was in my time, for I never heard of such shameless things. . . .

I think that in the past King James was considered courageous and firm but never particularly intelligent, for I remember that Madame de Fiene used to say about the late King of England and this one: "The King of England [Charles II] is very witty and extremely pleasant, but weak; the Duke of York [James II] is courageous and firm, but completely lacking in wit and deadly boring." Other people here who knew him when he was still on his throne have told me the same thing. But Your Grace twists her argument so cleverly in King William's favor that one might almost think that intelligence is attached to the English crown if one did not know that King William was just as intelligent when he was Prince of Orange as he is now as King of England. I believe that the histories that will be written about this court after we are gone will be better and more entertaining than any novel, and I am afraid that those who come after us will not be able to believe them and think that they are just fairytales. I do not recall where the Scripture says that one must not believe the tales of old women; but soon it will be in my interest not to cite this passage any longer, for I am no longer so young myself. Young Herr von Obdam must have a good memory if he remembers seeing me in Holland, for it has been thirty-six years since I was there with Your Grace. I wish this gentleman were here already, for it would be a sign that we have peace. I am much obliged to him for making this journey expressly in order to see me. Your Grace and I have the advantage that since we know nothing of affairs of State, we can say about them whatever comes into our heads, while others who do know about them cannot say anything for fear of betraying the State. It makes me laugh that Your Grace says that in this country the priests want to be the only actors. If I were to see the Schlosskirche in Hanover I would not recognize it, now that Oncle has had all the lovely gilding and painting put in. His Grace has done well to muzzle the priests; nothing is more tiresome than their bleating. I find it very agreeable to sing the Lutheran hymns; if I were allowed to sing them here I would not be half as bored in church.

1. The mistress of August the Strong of Saxony.   2. Maurice de Saxe, who became a famous general.

The King does only what his old trollop wants and will hate even those whom he loves most if she says so. Monsieur is only interested in his boyfriends' welfare and cares about nothing else. All the others are false too, and a bunch of stable grooms and petty valets are lords and masters over just about everything. A week ago he again gave 100,000 francs to a fellow by the name of Contades to buy Rubantel's company.[1] All his fine jewels and diamonds are being sold one by one. Meanwhile I am not given the bare necessities. My son is almost as bad as Monsieur, he spends everything on his mistress. . . . Monsieur le Dauphin does not concern himself about anything in the world and is at the Princesse de Conti's all the time; and although he makes fun of her, he is ruled by her as much as his father is ruled by the Maintenon. He is infatuated with an actress and has her brought to Meudon, where he keeps her all night. During the day he watches the people who work in his garden; he eats at four, for he does not eat at noon and only has breakfast. At four he eats with all the gentlemen of his household; he stays at table for two hours and drinks himself into a stupor. That is how he spends his life.

> 1. Military commissions, like court and government offices, were personal property and as such could be bought and sold. However, if the owner did not acquit himself of his duties to the satisfaction of the crown, he could be forced to sell his commission.

To RAUGRÄFIN LUISE

Versailles, 22 January 1697

It is perfectly true that some days one can bear one's misfortunes better than others; I have felt it myself. Yet in the end one learns not to take things to heart quite so much. It is most annoying that the priests keep stirring up the Christians against one another. If my advice were followed, the three Christian religions would consider themselves as one and would not worry about what people believe but only about whether they live up to the Gospel; they would preach against wicked ways but would let all Christians marry each other and allow them to go to whatever church they wanted without pestering them about it. If that were done, there would be more harmony among the Christians than there is now. I have so much esteem for King William that I would much rather have him for a son-in-law than the King of Rome. I can truthfully say about my daughter that she has no inclination whatsoever for coquetry and *galanterie;* on this point she gives me no trouble and I believe that whoever will have her will have nothing to fear in this respect. My daughter does not have a pretty face, but a good figure, a pleasant demeanor, nice skin, and a kind heart.

To ELECTRESS SOPHIE

Marly, 24 January 1697

My 1,100 *pistoles* all went to pay my debts and the little pensions I give every year. I would rather give my money to people who without it would lack their daily bread than gamble it away; Monsieur gambles away quite enough for both of us.

Versailles, 3 February 1697

Last week, on Wednesday morning and Tuesday night, two brothers died in Paris; they were twins and resembled each other like two drops of water. Their names were Messieurs de Bocquemar; one was president of the Parlement, the other, captain of the guards and governor of Bergen. These two brothers loved each other so dearly that they could never be without each other, always slept together, and could not be merry or content unless they were together. In fact, people say that when the president married, he could not at first sleep without his brother and took him into his bed on the first night. Whenever one of them was sick, the other was sick too. Last year when one was at his governor's post in Bergen and the other in Paris, the one in Paris suffered a stroke, and at that very moment the one in Bergen fainted and took a long time to come to, as long as it took his brother to recover (for the exact time was observed). Finally they both fell ill on the same day of the same disease and died within six hours of each other; surely a strong instance of sympathy. For between sixty-nine and seventy years they had lived in complete unanimity and with only one will. I have often seen them; they were a pair of homely fellows, but I understand that they were most honorable men.

Versailles, 2 May 1697

I certainly feel sorry for Your Grace for not having a better pastime than to reread my old letters. As long as my late Papa was alive, Your Grace will find my letters full of contentment about Monsieur, for I did not want His Grace to find out what really went on here, and so I did not put it into my letters. But when Your Grace came here in person I did not conceal anything from Your Grace. I concealed everything from His Grace the Elector because I was told that after I had left, His Grace worried so much about my coming here against my will, from pure obedience, and fully expecting to be unhappy here, that he became quite dismayed and sad. That is why I concealed everything as long as I could. In the end the Elector found out about it (though I do not know from whom) and gave me a good scolding for not writing about it. But when I explained the reasons, he forgave me. As for the King, I have been in his good or bad graces according to his mistresses' will.

At the time of the Montespan I was in disgrace, at the time of the Ludre[1] things went well for me, when the Montespan again had the upper hand they went badly again, when the Fontanges came they were better, and since the present woman holds sway they are always bad. But I assure Your Grace that I take the times as they come; after all, I know the people with whom I have to deal perfectly and know what to expect of them. So my mind is made up, and I only seek to have as much peace as I can. And since I realize that one cannot have peace here unless one is lonely, that is what I am. . . . It seems to me that we know both too little and too much to be happy. For one knows enough to want to know more and not enough to derive comfort from it.

1. Isabelle de Ludre (1638–1726), known as "La Belle de Ludre," had a brief affair with Louis XIV when the Montespan was official mistress. Like Mademoiselle de Fontanges, she was a lady-in-waiting in Madame's household.

To RAUGRÄFIN LUISE

Saint Cloud, 15 May 1697

Who would ever have thought that I would write to you from France and you to me from England? Strange things certainly go on in the world. I do not know if you remember Mistress Kolb, my former governess; she used to say: "There is no stranger place than this world," and how true that is. . . . I cannot understand that there are people who do not always love their good friends, for I can never change, and once I am someone's friend it is for life, unless that person totally changes toward me. . . . For Heaven's sake, dear Luise, do not ever tell me that you are afraid that your letters will be unwelcome to me! These are compliments for which I have no use at all. After all, you must know that I am quite artless. If your letters were not welcome, I would not say that they are, nor would I answer them as exactly as I do. Surely one does not write to one's good friends and relations in order to make a pretty and clever to-do? It seems to me that we do it to show them that we often think of them and that since we cannot talk to them face to face, this is a way to manifest our trust by putting down on paper what the lips cannot say. So when one is merry, the letters will be merry, and when one is sad, likewise; and in this way our friends can feel with us in everything that concerns us. If you knew how things are here, you would not be surprised that I am no longer cheerful. In my place a person of less cheerful disposition would probably have died of sorrow long ago; but I only get big and fat. I cannot help but believe that if I were fortunate enough to be with Ma Tante, there would be times when I could be quite cheerful again. But this, alas, seems quite out of the question. Here I have little company and keep to myself like a small Imperial town; I cannot say that I have more than four women friends in all of France. I was very fond of Ma Tante of Tarente,[1] but no one in the world is dearer to me than Ma Tante the Electress. . . .

My health is only too perfect now, I am becoming as big as a grenadier and have well-nigh lost my human shape. . . .

But here Monsieur sends for me to go for a ride, so that I cannot answer this letter as completely as the last one; but I would quickly like to add that what you wrote to me about the poor late Carl Eduard[2] has touched me deeply and has me made so sorry for him that it has brought tears to my eyes. And of Carllutz I must not even think, for I have still not gotten over his death. Adieu! I am being pressed to close, cannot read this letter over. Excuse the mistakes, dear Luise, and be assured that you will always be dear to my heart.

1. The Princesse de Tarente was a sister of Madame's mother. She was a friend of Madame de Sevigné's and a bit of a gossip herself. These two women enjoyed talking about how poor Madame, although unaware of her own feelings, was desperately in love with the King. 2. A brother of Raugräfin Luise and one of Madame's half-brothers.

To ELECTRESS SOPHIE

Saint Cloud, 16 May 1697

I went to Paris the day before yesterday because the poor child, Mademoiselle de Chartres,[1] lay close to death; her end is expected any moment. I felt very badly, but when I saw that her mother did not shed one tear, that her grandfather thought only of his gambling and therefore went off to Seissac's,[2] and that the mother called for a hearty collation of four big dishes, I thought that it would be foolish of me to be the only one to be distressed. But since the sight was hard to bear, I quietly got into my carriage and went home.[3]

1. Her granddaughter, daughter of her son. 2. An infamous gambler at the court.
3. The child did not die after all.

Saint Cloud, 6 June 1697

I prefer to live alone here and have become so accustomed to this life that I am never bored for a moment. I read, sometimes in French, sometimes in German, I write, I play with my little dogs, I look at engravings, I arrange my collection of seals; in short, I always find something to do. If that does not give me pleasure, at least it does not give me pain, and anyway, it makes for a quiet life. . . . If we do not find happiness in ourselves, there is no point looking for it elsewhere.

To RAUGRÄFIN LUISE

Saint Cloud, 19 July 1697

My dearest Luise, Sunday last in the evening I had the pleasure of receiving
two of your welcome letters, of 18 and 25 June, but I was quite unable to
answer them before now, for since my arm is still very painful I cannot write
many letters at one time. . . . The circumstances of my fall are quickly told:
We had spent two hours without finding a wolf and were ambling along
slowly to look for another one; suddenly a rider charges by, this excites my
horse, and it wants to follow; I rein it in, it wants to buck, I loosen the
reins and turn my hand to ride on. My horse had its hind legs on the wet
grass of a small rise, it slips and gently falls onto the right side, and I just
happen to hit the tip of my elbow on a stone, thereby wrenching the big bone
so that it sticks out of the middle of the arm. They call for the King's barber
to set the arm, but he cannot be found, having lost a horseshoe and ridden
off to a faraway village to have his horse shod. A peasant told me that
there was in his village a barber who was good at setting broken arms. I drove
there and indeed this peasant set my arm very well, and it would have
healed in two weeks if the court barbers had not practiced their art on me
afterward, which, I believe, will cripple me for good. My only consolation
is that I can move my fingers enough to hold the pen and to write, so at
least I do not have to use the other hand. . . .

I will be very eager to hear that you have safely arrived in Holland; the
sea is an element that I do not trust at all. To be seasick is not so bad,
for once one is back on land one is all the healthier for it; but to be caught
in a storm and to wonder whether one will escape with one's life, that
must be dreadful. That you still prefer Germany to all other countries, dear
Luise, is quite natural; one always likes the things to which one is accustomed better than strange ones. And the fatherland is always the best for us
Germans. . . .

It is a bad sign for a country when people want to know whether a
proper marriage prospect is rich, for it shows that true virtue counts for little.
I do not believe that England is the only place where bad marriages and peculiar men are found; if one wanted to avoid these, one would have to leave
this world altogether, and one who is eager to marry had better not consult
me, for I never advocate the married state.

To ELECTRESS SOPHIE

Port Royal, 18 September 1697

If he[1] should fall on hard times, he will never starve to death, for he knows
fourteen crafts. The great man here made fun of him for working with a
shipwright in Holland and helping to build ships. But when he finds out how

102   A WOMAN'S LIFE IN THE COURT OF THE SUN KING

well this gentleman has used the galleys he has built, he will forgive him and no longer think that this is trifling nonsense.

1. Peter the Great.

Prince Eugene of Savoy (1663–1736) had achieved great fame in Austria. He led the Imperial army against the advancing Turks and defeated them near Zenta.

Fontainebleau, 9 October 1697

Your Grace will have gathered from one of my earlier letters on what day we received the news of Prince Eugene's battle. How very true it is that "a prophet is never honored in his own country. . . ." If Prince Eugene had remained here, he would never have become such a great general, for here all the young people used to pester and laugh at him.

On 31 October 1697 the war that had begun in 1688 with the invasion of the Palatinate ended with the Peace of Ryswick. Louis XIV barely managed to keep his most important fortresses along the frontier and to maintain France's dominant position in Europe. He had to give up many of his earlier conquests in Flanders.

Paris, 10 November 1697

Of all the goods that came from the Palatinate earlier I never saw a red penny, and I believe that it will be the same this time. If I do get something, I should be all the more pleased; I certainly need it, for no one could be poorer in ready money than I am. When I asked whether the money from the Palatinate is not mine, I was told that yes, it is, but that Monsieur is *maître de la communauté,* who as long as he lives can dispose of it as he sees fit and that there is nothing I can do about it; but that if he should die these sums would have to be given to me from his estate. This did not seem particularly comforting to me, but since whatever I may say against it will do no good at all, I keep quiet and follow my own straight path. What annoys me most is that I see with my own eyes that my money is being spent so badly and on such despicable people.

To RAUGRÄFIN LUISE

Paris, 10 November 1697

My arm is now better to the extent that I can move and turn it like the other one, but in the place where the barbers have chilled it so much, namely high up at the shoulder, I still have a weather calendar; especially when it is about to rain I still feel some pain, but otherwise it no longer hurts. I hope that the Florentine oil that has helped me so much all along will altogether cure me. Now that there is peace everywhere, it just might happen that we might meet again. One must never give up hope. If it should come to pass, as rumor had it some months ago, that my daughter will become Duchesse de Lorraine, we could easily arrange a meeting at Nancy, and I do not doubt, dear Luise, that you and I and Amelise would get along splendidly.

You will by now have learned that the peace treaty with the Empire and the Emperor has also been concluded and signed. There must be a strange curse on the general peace, for almost no one is happy with it, even though everyone has wished for it for so long; the people of Paris were not willing to rejoice, they almost had to be forced to it. I do not think that war will start again soon. In Poland, I believe, it will only be a small war, for they say that things are not going well there for our Prince de Conti.[1] His Grace may well be back soon, and in this I would consider His Grace more fortunate than if he were King of Poland, for it is a wild and dirty country, and the great lords there are just too self-interested. The Elector of Saxony was here for two years, so I am well aware of his strength, but it seems odd for the newspapers to speak about it. The same thing cannot be said of the Prince de Conti, for although he is of taller stature than the Elector, he is quite weak.

1. The Prince de Conti and August the Strong were competing for the throne of Poland.

Versailles, 5 December 1697

Dearest Luise, yesterday I found your letter . . . in Ma Tante's packet, but what Ma Tante reports about Oncle's utterly miserable condition makes me fear that His Grace is not yet out of all danger, and that troubles me very much.[1] To your wish for Oncle and Ma Tante I can only say amen with all my heart. From the looks of things, the peace will not cause much joy anywhere. If wishing could help, things would be different than they are now. I do not know whether it would not be better for me and for my son if he had to participate in a few more campaigns, for this country is too full of dreadful temptations for young people, and they gain more honor from war than from just hanging around here and going in for debaucheries, for which —just between us—my son has only too much inclination. He thinks that since he only loves women and is not interested in the other debauchery, which is now more common here than in Italy, he should even be praised and thanked; but I do not like his life at all.

As soon as I received your letter yesterday I consulted Monsieur to find out whether anything might be gotten from His Majesty the King. Unfortunately Monsieur told me in plain terms that the King would not do it, for he does not want to hear anything about reparations and has also given orders to his ambassadors that they should rather break the peace than grant demands for reparations, so I must not say anything about it for now. However, do send me a French *mémoire* about your claims with more details than the German one I have received. I will keep it, and some time when I see the King in good humor I will tell him in jest that he should make restitution to me for the damage he has caused my poor Raugräfinnen and show him the *mémoire*. Who knows, it might be helpful. As for Monsieur, I have told him in plain terms that he still owes you money. He asked me to give him a memorandum and said that he would study it, so I will make an extract from your note, give it to His Grace and also strongly recommend the matter to the chancellor and to my husband's advisers. That is all, dear Luise, I can do in this matter. I wish to God that it were up to me, then you would soon have perfect satisfaction, for you can be assured that I would never place my interest above your friendship. Those who have occupied our poor fatherland these many years have done well for themselves, therefore they do not want to give back any of the sums they have drawn. I was never given a penny of it.

1. The Elector of Hanover died in January of the following year.

To ELECTRESS SOPHIE

Versailles, 12 January 1698

All we hear about now is of thieves and thievery. On Saint Genevieve's Day the thieves of Paris thought of a particularly clever trick: one of these fellows disguised himself as a father of Saint Genevieve, put up a table and writing materials right in front of the church door, and said to all the people who wanted to go in, "There is too much of a crowd in the sacristy to collect the money for masses, so our abbot has ordered me to collect the money here." Everyone paid his money, and the false priest neatly wrote it all down; but one man who did not agree with the price called the sacristan and asked why the masses had become so costly. The sacristan replied that they were no more costly than usual. The man pointed to the thief in priest's garb; the sacristan thought that some roguish prank must be afoot and wanted to arrest the fellow in disguise; the latter whistled for his companions, who came in great numbers, helped him get away, and they all ran off. They could not be caught. When the list of what he had received was read, it turned out that they made off with eight hundred francs.

I firmly believe that the wild life that my son leads, carousing all night long
and not going to bed until eight in the morning, will do him in before long.
He often looks as if he had been pulled out of the grave; this is sure to kill him,
but his father never wants to reprimand him. But since nothing I could say
would do any good I will be quiet, although I do want to add that it is truly
a shame that my son is being dragged into this profligate life, for if he had
been accustomed to better and more honorable ways, he would have become
a better person. He is not lacking in wit, nor is he ignorant, and from his
youth he had every inclination for that which is good, commendable and
befitting his rank; but ever since he has become his own master, a lot of
contemptible wretches have attached themselves to him, making him keep
company with, begging your leave, the vilest kinds of common whores, and
he has changed so much that one does not recognize either his face or his
temperament, and since he leads this life he no longer takes pleasure in anything; his pleasure in music, which used to be a passion, is gone too. In
short, he has become quite insufferable, and I fear that in the end he will
lose his very life over it.

Monsieur is keener than ever on the boys and now takes lackeys out of the
antechambers; every last penny he has is squandered in this way, and some
day his children will be complete beggars, but he does not care about anything but providing for these pleasures of his. He opposes me in everything
and avoids me at all times; he lets himself be ruled completely by these
rakes and everything in his and my house is being sold for the benefit of these
fellows. It is shameful what goes on here. My son has been completely captivated by Monsieur's favorites; since he loves women, they act as his pimps,
sponge off him, gorge and guzzle with him, and drag him so deeply into
debauchery that he cannot seem to get out of it; and since he knows that I
do not approve of his ways, he avoids me and does not like me at all. Monsieur is glad that my son likes his favorites and not me and therefore puts
up with everything from him. My son's wife does not love her husband; just
as long as he is away from her, she is content, and in this respect they are
well matched; all she cares about is her brothers' and sisters' grandeur. That
is how things are here; so Your Grace can imagine what a pleasant life it
is for me.

It happens to a lot of people here that piety addles their brains. But one can see very well that the reverend fathers only have their fun with religion and think of it as a lot of fables, for that is how they talk about it. If one man can be another's devil, the priests surely are the worst. The proverb used to say: "Where the devil cannot go, he sends an old woman," but here in France one might say: "Where the old woman cannot go, she sends a priest," because I have been told for a fact that in every Parisian parish the old woman has placed priests who are to report to her everything that goes on in all of Paris. Some parishes have rebelled and refused to accept these spies. The King is set against the Reformed worse than ever; as long as the old woman rules, this is bound to continue, for this is her only way to prove the zeal of her high piety. If the Reformed had made up their minds right away to go to the woman with a few million, scaring her at the same time by saying that they would make life miserable for her if she did anything against them, I am convinced that they would have been left alone, for the woman is faint-hearted. If I were to frown every time I saw something here that displeased me, my brow would already be covered with wrinkles as thick as my finger. As for laughter, I must still have some of the laughter of my youth within me, but now I do not laugh much. . . .

Your Grace must have heard of a famous courtesan here, who used to be called Ninon, but now they call her Mademoiselle de Lenclos. I am told that she has a great deal of wit, all the old seigneurs of the court spend much time at her house because of her pleasant conversation. . . .

It is remarkable how my daughter is already accustomed to being betrothed; she thinks about how she will have things done at Nancy as if she had been married all her life. From this Your Grace can see that my children's temperament is different from mine, for as Your Grace knows, holy wedlock never seemed so agreeable to me that I expected much joy from it. God grant that her joy may not turn to ashes. Your Grace is so right, Madame de Maintenon does deserve the name of *Pantocrate,* for she is indeed all-powerful in this country. I cannot believe that her marriage will ever be made public and would have to see it with my own eyes. They cannot do it, even if they want to; the Parisians are too much against it, and the woman would not be safe if it happened. Last year when we went to Fontainebleau they put up big placards against it at the Pont Neuf and made threats; that quickly put an end to all rumors of publication.

Now that Mademoiselle de Lenclos is old, she leads an extremely virtuous life. . . . My son is quite good friends with her, and she is very fond of him. I wish he went to see her more often; she would give him better and more noble sentiments than those with which his good friends inspire him. . . .

At court one does not hear a word about the Reformed. If this persecution had occurred twenty-six years ago when I was still at Heidelberg, Your Grace would never have persuaded me to become a Catholic. All these bad things are done because certain persons here never use their own minds and only believe whatever they are told by monks and wicked old women, and because they are quite ignorant in these matters. That has been most unfortunate for a lot of honest people here. . . .

The Pantocrate is so afraid of the Parisians that she will not go around in Paris in her own coach. Yesterday we met her; the coach in which she rode was surrounded by bodyguards in disguise, and it was the King's coach. If the market women could get hold of her, she would be torn to pieces, that is how much they hate her.

To RAUGRÄFIN LUISE

Saint Cloud, 17 June 1698

I do not wish for death, nor do I fear it; even without the Heidelberg Catechism one can learn not to be too attached to the world, especially in this country, where everything is filled with falseness, envy, and wickedness, and where all the vices are thriving. Yet because dying is completely against nature, one cannot wish for it either, even though one does not love the world. Here at this great court I have well-nigh turned myself into a hermit, and there are not many people in the country with whom I keep steady company, and I spend long days all alone in my sitting room, where I occupy myself with reading and writing. If someone calls on me, I see them for a short while, talk of the weather or the latest news, then it's back to my solitude. Four days every week I spend writing: on Monday to Savoy,[1] on Wednesday to Modena,[2] and on Thursday and Sunday I write great big letters to Ma Tante in Hanover, and between six and eight I go for a ride with Monsieur and our ladies. Three times a week I drive to Paris and write to my women friends there; once or twice a week I go hunting. That is how my time passes. . . .

Is it possible that the pastors at Frankfurt are silly enough to consider theater plays sinful? Their ambition to lord it over people is a much greater sin than watching an innocent spectacle that makes us laugh for a moment; for this kind of nonsense I cannot forgive priests of any stripe. Adieu, dearest

Luise! I still have three more letters to write and therefore must close, but not without assuring you that you are very dear to my heart.

1. To her stepdaughter Anne Marie d'Orléans, the wife of Victor Amadeus of Savoy and the mother of the Duchesse de Bourgogne. 2. To Charlotte Felicitas, daughter of the widowed Duchess of Hanover. Charlotte Felicitas had married the Duke of Modena in 1695.

Marly, 4 July 1698

Those who cannot imagine that things here are as bad as they really are think the King and the court are still as they used to be, but the sad fact is that everything is changed so much that if a person who had left the court since the Queen's death were to return now, he would think that he had come to an altogether different world. A great deal more could be said about this, but it cannot be entrusted to paper, since all letters are read and then re-sealed. Ma Tante always says, "One man is the other's devil in this world," and how true that is. We do know that everything comes from God and that in His all-powerful way He has decided from all eternity how things are to be; but just as the Almighty has not consulted us beforehand, so He also does not let us know why things happen as they do; so we can only acquiesce in His holy will. I do not doubt that Karl Moritz[1] will have many a dispute with Monsieur Helmont at Hanover. I wish Karl Moritz every good thing and a long life, but I doubt that for all his learnedness he can ever become as dear to me as my dear departed Carllutz was. . . .

It does not behoove me to look at other people's beauty or ugliness, considering that it has pleased God to make me so very ugly; however, I have now reached an age where one more easily finds consolation, for even if I had been beautiful, I would have become ugly by now, so it all comes to the same thing. But then I set greater store by inner than by outward beauty anyway. I already wrote to you what I think of parsons and priests who forbid comedies, so I will say nothing more about it, except to add that if these reverend gentlemen were able to see a little further than their noses, they would understand that the common people's money is not wasted on comedies. In the first place, actors are poor devils who make their living from the theater, and furthermore, comedies give pleasure, pleasure gives health, health gives strength, and strength makes people work better; so in fact they should order rather than forbid them.

1. The last of the Raugrafen.

To RAUGRÄFIN AMALIE ELISABETH

Port Royal, 22 August 1698

On Monday last at Versailles, one of my very good friends died suddenly of a stroke, her name was Princesse d'Espinoi. She was a lady of great merit who had a fine mind, exceedingly good manners, and the best heart in the world; she thought of nothing but how she could be of service to her friends and relations; she was excellent company. . . . Even if one is beautiful, it does not last, and a beautiful face is soon changed, but a good character is good at all times. You must not remember me very well if you do not count me among the ugly ones; I was ugly all my life and have become even worse here because of smallpox. Moreover, my shape is monstrously fat, and I am as square as a cube; my skin is reddish mixed with yellow, I am beginning to get gray and my hair is already all pepper and salt, my brow and eyes are full of wrinkles, my nose is as askew as it always was, but embroidered by smallpox, as are both cheeks. My cheeks are flat, I have big jowls, my teeth are worn down, and my mouth too is changed a bit, having become larger and more wrinkled. So much for my beautiful looks.

To ELECTRESS SOPHIE

Fontainebleau, 22 October 1698

My God, how terribly badly, to my mind, they are bringing up the Duchesse de Bourgogne; I really feel sorry for the child. They let her get away with everything; right at the table she starts singing, dances in her chair, pretends to be greeting people, makes awful grimaces, pulls chickens and partridges apart on the platters with her fist, sticks her fingers into the sauces; in short, she could not be more unmannerly. And those who stand behind Her Grace exclaim, "Oh how graceful she is, how pretty!" Her father-in-law[1] she treats without respect and calls him *tu;* that makes him think that she likes him, and he is as pleased as he can be. They say that she is even more familiar with the King.

1. The Dauphin.

Paris, 16 November 1698

My daughter has had to learn quickly about her strange new state.[1] I am told from Nancy that the duke is horribly keen on his pleasure; after their ceremonial entry my daughter had to change her clothes, for her skirt was so heavy that she could not walk in it. Just as she was undressed, the duke came in and left the room with her. She is already quite used to the thing and does not dislike it as much as I did. If I had had my way, my daughter would have been brought up even better than she was, but Monsieur often made a shambles of everything I had worked on for years on end; still, the roughest edges have been planed off. The Duc de Lorraine must not be so extraordinary after all . . . if he always lies with my daughter and it does not do her any harm. On this side I will be more pleased to become a grandmother than on my son's side, for his children seem like bastards to me. That Monsieur has had the silver toilet table melted down is not so upsetting, for it was his. But one day he came in and, despite my urgent pleading, gathered up all the silver dishes from Heidelberg and some other silverware that decorated my room and looked quite pretty, had them melted down, and pocketed all the money himself; he did not even leave me one poor little box in which to put my kerchiefs.

1. I.e., marriage.

"In dulci jubilo-ho-ho, sing, Christians, and rejoy-hoy-hoyce, our hearts' deli-hi-hight lies in praesepio-ho-ho, and sparkles like the su-hu-hun, matris in gremio-ho-ho, alpha es et o-ho-ho, alpha es et o." If Your Grace has not sung this herself today, I am certain at least that the kettle drums and trumpets have played it for her, since today is New Year's Day for Your Grace; so I wish Your Grace every happiness and joy that Your Grace may wish and desire for herself.

Yesterday at table we talked about the Duchesse de Lesdiguières, who certainly has a strange temperament. All day long she does nothing but drink coffee or tea; she never reads or writes, nor does she do needlework or play cards. When she takes coffee, her chambermaids and herself must be dressed in the Turkish manner; when she takes tea, the servants who bring it must be dressed in the Indian manner. The chambermaids often weep bitter tears that they must change their clothes two or three times a day. If anyone comes to call on the lady, her antechamber is full of pages, lackeys, and noblemen; then one comes to a locked door, and when one knocks, a great big moor wearing a silver turban and a big sabre comes to open up and lets the lady or gentleman, whoever it may be, enter, but all alone. He leads the caller to a second door, which is also locked, and it is opened by another Moor who bolts it after the people have gone through, just as the first one had done. The same thing happens in the third room. In the fourth one there are two valets who lead the caller to the fifth room, where one finds the Duchess all by herself. All the portraits in her room are of her coach horses, which she had painted. These she has led one by one into the courtyard every morning and watches them from the window wearing spectacles, for she does not see well. In her room she also has a painting of the conclave, done in an unusual manner: the Pope and all the cardinals are depicted as Moors, and she also has a piece of yellow silk embroidered with a whole lot of Moors. In her garden, which is very beautiful, there is a marble column with an epitaph to one of her deceased cats which she had loved very much. If her son wants to see her, he must ask for an audience, and so must his wife; after they have inquired six or seven times whether they might be permitted to see her, she receives them, but with the same ceremonies as if they were strangers.

Saint Cloud, 14 June 1699

Nothing more is being said about the Archbishop of Cambrai.[1] I am sorry that he will not publish the novel of *Télémaque,* for it is a very well written and beautiful book, I have read it in manuscript; some think that it will be printed in Holland.[2] It was to be printed here, and one volume had already appeared, but when this archbishop[3] found out about it, he bought up every copy and forbade the printing. . . . God grant that the instructions given in this book will make their impression on the Duc de Bourgogne, for if he follows them he will become a great king when the time comes. If the King of Spain were to die, there would certainly be a war. But I can truthfully tell Your Grace that no one here would be pleased about it, for everyone is exceedingly tired of war. . . .

Most of the Huguenots who have left France are poorly educated people from the provinces. I think people here are ashamed to talk about the treatment meted out to the poor Reformed, for we never hear anything about it; the intendants are often harsher than they are ordered to be.

1. François de la Mothe de Salignac Fénelon (1651–1715), tutor of the Duc de Bourgogne and originally a protegé of Madame de Maintenon. He lost the King's favor in the controversy over Quietism, a mystical form of religious enthusiasm that had been brought to Madame de Maintenon's school of Saint Cyr by Madame Guyon and subsequently captured the imagination of many members of the *dévôt* set at court. As soon as Bishop Bossuet, whom the King respected as a pillar of orthodoxy and a moral preceptor to the monarchy, attacked Quietism as heresy, Madame de Maintenon dropped Madame Guyon; but Fénelon came to her defense. A protracted duel of pamphlets between Bossuet and Fénelon was finally submitted to the arbitration of the Pope, who ruled against Fénelon. Fénelon lost his position as tutor to the Duc de Bourgogne and was obliged to acknowledge his error publicly in his own cathedral. 2. *Télémaque,* the novel from which the Duc de Bourgogne was to learn by example how to be a virtuous prince, was indeed printed in Holland, through the indiscretion, it was said, of one of Fénelon's associates. Louis XIV did not like this book even before Fénelon's disgrace, because the description of the fictitious kingdom ruined by an arbitrary monarch bore too many traits of his own France. 3. Fénelon.

The following letter furnishes a concrete example of the function of etiquette as a battle for rank. In this case, Madame lost but was able to save face. In the situation described in the letter of 11 October 1699, a battle is avoided but at great personal cost.

Marly, 2 July 1699

Yesterday I visited all the ladies who are in favor; first I called on the Duchesse de Bourgogne, and from there I went to the Maintenon. I found her in a royal state: she sat at table in a big armchair, Mademoiselle de Charolais, Monsieur le Duc's second daughter, and Madame de Montchevreuil were eating with her, sitting on stools; she was kind enough to have another stool brought in for me, but I assured here that I was not tired.[1] I had to bite my tongue and almost laughed out loud. How things have changed since the time when the King came to me to ask me if I would allow Madame Scarron to eat with me just once so that she could cut Monsieur du Maine's meat for him, since he was still a child. Such reflections call forth a lot of thought about the ways of the world. . . . When the King walks in the garden, the lady sits in a sedan chair fitted with four wheels and four fellows are pulling her. The King walks alongside like her lackey, and everyone else follows on foot. . . . Everything here looks to me like the world upside-down; the only thing I like is the scenery.

1. It would have been most humiliating for Elisabeth Charlotte to sit on a stool when Madame de Maintenon occupied an armchair, reserved for persons of royal rank.

Port Royal, 23 July 1699

What I find unfortunate about Monseigneur[1] is that he does not take real pleasure in anything. He goes hunting all the time, but is just as content to ride along slowly for three hours without saying a word to anyone as he is to participate in the most exciting hunt. If this gentleman should come to rule, things would not go as Your Grace thinks, for he is capable of forming a bad impression of people if his steady companions speak evil of them; and his best friends are not kind. Moreover, this Dauphin is rather fearful, so the hypocrites are sure to get to him once he is King. . . . I cannot believe that one will be happier under his rule than under his father's, for I do not see that he has more esteem for honest and sincere people than for false and mendacious ones, which are the majority. . . .

The Duchesse de Bourgogne cannot possibly get tired of the life she is leading, for she is allowed to do whatever she pleases; sometimes she drives around in a little cart, sometimes she rides a donkey, and she runs around in the garden by herself all night long; in short, she does whatever comes into her head. There is no doubt that she is intelligent; she is afraid of me and that is why she is so polite to me, for I have spoken quite sternly to her a few times when she wanted to make fun of me, so now she no longer dares to do it in my presence.

1. The Dauphin Louis (1661–1711).

There is no doubt that if Monsieur were not so weak and did not permit himself to be bamboozled by the wicked characters whom he likes so much, he would be the best husband in the world; therefore he is to be pitied more than to be hated when he does one a bad turn. My son is extremely intelligent, and I am certain that his conversation would not displease Your Grace; he knows a great deal, has a good memory, and can speak about the things he knows without pedantry. He is quite able to express himself in the grand manner, but his character is not elevated enough, and he prefers the company of lowly people, of painters and musicians, to that of people of rank and thinks that he must do what he sees other young people doing, even if it is contrary to his nature and his temperament; also, he thinks that he is ten times stronger than he is. This, I am afraid, will kill him some day; he never follows good advice, only bad; and although he knows perfectly well what virtue is, he thinks it is smart to despise it and to approve of vice. He is kind and will never willingly harm anyone, but he is unsure of himself. ... Right now he is working hard for Your Grace, painting a fable, for everything he paints must have to do with history. He says he must go to Paris early in the morning to paint but, just between us, there is a young girl of sixteen, very sweet, an actress; our cavalier is quite smitten with her and has her brought to him. If he paints her little face into his Antigone, she will be pretty indeed. I have not yet seen the picture, but if he uses her face in the painting, I will let Your Grace know.

I confess that I would be happier if reincarnation were true than if I had to believe in hell or the extinction of our soul; this last idea I dislike most of all, but unfortunately it seems more likely than the other two. I think that the person who wrote the book proving that hell does not exist has done so out of compassion, in order to comfort the sinners. It is quite certain that there cannot be two eternities; the Scripture may well have said "from eternity to eternity" to express the idea of eternity more forcefully. I have great trouble believing in ghosts, for if there were something that is quite unknown to us and yet can manifest itself, one would know about it from better sources; yet ordinarily ghosts appear only to superstitious people, drunkards, or sad people troubled by their spleen, and what they say cannot be trusted. If one looks into the matter, one usually finds trickery, thievery, or amorous intrigues.

To RAUGRÄFIN AMALIE ELISABETH

Marly, 7 August 1699

Yesterday I went with the King to review his guards, and today I have to steal, as it were, an hour to write, for I have already been to Saint-Germain to take leave of the English royal family; it seems that my journey to Bar, which has been planned and put off so many times, will finally take place, unless some unforeseen obstacle arises between now and a week from Sunday. . . .

My goodness, dear Amelise, you must no longer look like yourself as a child if you resemble the Queen our grandmother. I remember her as if I had just seen her, but her face was very different from yours when you were a child, for then you had blond hair, a broad face, and lovely color; but the Queen of Bohemia had black hair, a thin face, and a straight nose; in short, a completely different face. The Elector our late father resembled the Queen his mother in many ways. By *gezwungenheit* I mean *contrainte* and not *affectation,* but I do not know the proper German word for it. Don't you know someone in the Fruchtbringende Gesellschaft[1] of Frankfurt whom you might ask? It cannot be "stiffness" either, because many affected people do not carry themselves stiffly but constantly twist and wiggle their whole bodies. It is beyond me how anyone can speak and remember more than one language aside from his mother tongue. . . .

Drunkenness is very common among French women; Madame de Mazarin has left a daughter who is quite an expert in this; it is the Marquise de Richelieu. Now I have replied to everything in your letter, and since I have already written four long letters in addition to this one, my hand is a bit tired, and so I must close. Please embrace Luise for me and be assured that both of you are dear to my heart.

1. A literary society.

To ELECTRESS SOPHIE

Fontainebleau, 23 September 1699

The poor Reformed are to be pitied that they are not safe in Copenhagen after they thought they had found a refuge there. Those who have settled in Germany will spread the use of the French language. Monsieur Colbert is supposed to have said that many subjects constitute the wealth of kings and princes and therefore wanted to make everyone marry and have children: so now these new subjects will become the German electors' and princes' wealth.

To RAUGRÄFIN AMALIE ELISABETH

Fontainebleau, 1 October 1699

It would be fortunate for all of Europe if the Queen of Spain could have a
child; boy or girl, it does not matter, if only there were a child and if it
stayed alive. One does not have to be a prophet to see that war is inevitable
if the King of Spain should die without heirs. After all, everyone knows
that none of the exalted princes who lay claim to this succession will yield to
another, so that the matter must needs be decided by war.

*Madame and Monsieur had planned to visit their daughter, the Duchesse de
Lorraine, who was expecting her first child.*

To RAUGRÄFIN LUISE

Fontainebleau, 11 October 1699

Dearest Luise, here I am in the place where I have the least opportunity for
writing because of the many hunts, comedies and *appartements.* . . .
 Of the sad story of my planned journey to Bar, which was called off, I
will say no more, except to thank you, dear Luise, for your sympathy. It
all happened because the King did not want us to circumvent a point of ceremonial; the difficulty is that the Duc de Lorraine claims that he is entitled
to sit in an armchair in the presence of Monsieur and myself because the Emperor gives him an armchair. To this the King replied that the Emperor's
ceremonial is one thing and the King's another, and that, for example, the
Emperor gives the cardinals armchairs, whereas here they may never sit at
all in the King's presence. The King cited the precedent of the duke's ancestors who came here and yet never claimed that they were entitled to an
armchair; although the old Duc de Lorraine was the late Monsieur's[1] own
brother-in-law, he never had more than a stool in the presence of either
Monsieur or his own sister. Monsieur would be willing to give him a high-
backed chair without arms, and to this the King agreed, but the duke
feels that he should be treated in the same manner as a prince elector, and
this the King will not admit. Monsieur proposed that we should do as the
King of England does: He claims that we are not entitled to a chair, but we
claim that we are, therefore he himself only sits on a stool when we call
on him. That is what we wanted to do, but the King absolutely did not want
to have it, and we did not want to go to Bar to force a confrontation with
our duke, and so the journey was called off. Now you know the real reason
for all of this.
 I would have been glad to see Karl Moritz. But if he had behaved as I hear
he now behaves in Berlin we would not have remained friends for long and
I would have gotten quite irate. For I am told that he drinks himself into a

stupor every day and then bothers Her Grace the Electress of Brandenburg with a lot of incoherent talk; I really think that is a disgrace. If I could believe that an earnest reprimand could correct him, I would write to him. This makes me feel the loss of my dear Carllutz all the more keenly, for he did not go in for unseemly behavior. From whom does he get this drinking? Our late Papa surely was never given to drink. It is annoying that the only son who is left of my late father should be a drunkard. For Heaven's sake, do try your best to correct Karl Moritz![2] . . .

My daughter is very happy with her Duke; he anticipates her every wish and they love each other with all their hearts. . . .

I cannot understand that people are foolish enough to make the journey to Rome. What pleasure can they get out of seeing a lot of priests running around in the churches? For that I would not go from my table to the window, let alone to Rome.

1. Gaston d'Orléans, brother of Louis XIII.   2. Madame was more naïve than her aunt Sophie, who seems to have realized that alcoholism is a physical disease. "He [Karl Moritz] cannot help it," she wrote to Raugräfin Luise. "He has become so accustomed to it that he gets sick when he does not drink." (E. Bodemann, ed., *Briefe der Kurfürstin Sophie von Hannover an die Raugrafen und Raugräfinnen von der Pfalz* [Leipzig, 1888], letter of November 1701.)

To ELECTRESS SOPHIE

Fontainebleau, 10 October 1699

Your Grace is right to think that nothing is said here about the torment that is being inflicted on the poor Reformed; one does not hear a single word about it. As for Your Grace's further remarks on this subject, Your Grace can imagine that I am not allowed to respond to them; but thoughts pass toll-free. . . . I do believe that if King William had pressed this matter a little harder during the peace negotiations, things would not have come to this extremity, for his opponents were bound and determined to make peace, and if he had made it a condition that the persecution of the Reformed must stop, it would have stopped. . . .

Not one of my portraits resembles me very much; my fat is in all the wrong places, which is bound to be unbecoming; I have a horrendous, begging your leave, behind, big belly and hips, and very broad shoulders; my neck and breasts are quite flat, so that, if the truth be known, I am hideously ugly, but fortunately for me I do not care one whit. For I do not desire anyone to be in love with me and know that those who love me as friends are interested in my character and not in my appearance. . . .

It is certainly true that Monsieur Leibniz writes a perfect French; I wonder if his accent is as perfect as his way of expressing himself. . . .

I rather like the new fashion, for I never could stand the terribly high hair-

dos. It is quite rare for as beautiful a person as our dear Electress of Brandenburg[1] to care so little for fancy clothes and to dress so quickly. . . .

Fond as I am of our Duc de Lorraine,[2] I must admit that I rather sided
with the King and it seems to me that our Duke would do better not to
worry so much about his rank and to seek to please the King; for rank is a
chimera, but gaining the King's favor so that nothing untoward will happen
to him in his dukedom is a solid and much more important matter. After
all, it is likely that he will always be more dependent on the King than on the
Emperor . . .

1. Electress Sophie's daughter.   2. Her son-in-law, who had just had a quarrel over a
matter of precedence with the French court.

Paris, 16 December 1699

What has become of the hymns that used to be sung in Hanover during
Advent? In my day, no Advent passed without the hymn "Now Comes the
Heathens' Savior"; what always intrigued me most was the stanza "Not
through man's flesh and blood / through the Holy Ghost alone / has God's
Word become a man / has a woman's flesh borne fruit." That makes me
remember the whole hymn. I remember things I saw and heard in my childhood better than things that happened ten years ago. . . . It seems to me
that the Lutherans rarely have musical instruments in their churches; in my
day we did not have any and everyone sang together, just as Your Grace
does in her church. It seems to me that singing along is much more entertaining than the finest instrumental music. If the angels in heaven can assume
human shape and human voices, they must sing beautifully, but I doubt that
Our Lord is all that amused by instruments.

To RAUGRAF KARL MORITZ

Versailles, 12 January 1700

Dearest Karl Moritz, you will think that I am a bit late in answering your
letter of 11 November 1699, and you can truthfully complain, as one usually
does only as a manner of speaking, that a century has passed since I wrote
to you. But it is not my fault, and it is as if the devil had played a trick on me
by sending me one interruption after the other, and it has been like in the
comedy *Les Facheux,* where just as one obstacle disappears another one turns
up. Today I am writing to you even though I have already spent three good
hours at a wolf hunt; so, if I wanted to, I would have another good excuse.
But I do not want to put off my reply to you any longer. As long as I know
that you, dear Karl Moritz, no longer disdain our dear German tongue, and
as long as you know that I do not disdain it either, you may write to me
in the way that is most comfortable to you, and it is true that French is

shorter than German. I am glad, dear Karl Moritz, that my friendly admonitions have been so well received by you. No one is asking you to be as pure as an angel or to do the impossible, all I ask is that as far as your own actions are concerned you use the fine mind that God has given you to gain a good rather than a bad reputation; this I hope you will do and this I will always be happy to hear. For after all we are close enough kin so that whatever happens to you must be of concern to me. Be assured, dear Karl Moritz, that although I have not seen you since you were a child, I am still fond of you!

To RAUGRÄFIN AMALIE ELISABETH

Marly 21 January 1700

Dearest Amelise, although there is not much time to write here, I will answer your letter of 20 December 1699–10 January 1700 today, for once one has started putting it off, one never does find time and something always comes up. Soon you will no longer date your letters in the old style, for I am told that all of Germany will adopt the new one on 1 March.[1] . . .

It is not a tale that the King of Morocco wants to have the Princesse de Conti for his queen, but the King has flatly refused him. The Princesse de Conti was very beautiful before she had smallpox but has changed since then; however, she still has a perfectly beautiful figure and a noble countenance, and she dances exceedingly well. I have never seen an engraving of the Princesse de Conti that resembles her. That people go to Rome to see the antiquities, as my cousin the Landgraf of Kassel did, I can understand, but not that they want to see all that to-do of priests; nothing is more boring. Many probably also went to take a look at the thirty thousand ladies of easy virtue; but anyone who is curious about this sort of thing might just as well come to France, where he will find quite as much of it. Anyone who wants to repent his sins has no need to run off to Rome; repentance is just as good in his own room. In France people do not set much store by Rome or the Pope; they feel, and rightly so, that one can go to heaven without him.

1. In 1700 Protestant Germany also adopted the Gregorian calendar.

To ELECTRESS SOPHIE

Versailles, 24 January 1700

Madame de Maintenon has so little reluctance to show that she hates me that she once publicly said to a lady, "There is only one thing wrong with you, and that is that you like Madame." But I assure Your Grace that this woman's hatred does not torment me; if the King wants to hate and despise me because of her, that is a weakness on his part . . . for I have never done anything against the King that would make him hate me. If he dislikes me as a person, that is a misfortune but not a crime; so I must cheer up and hope that the day will come when he sees me with different eyes than those of his old lady. After all, at the time of the Fontanges[1] and in the one year when I was in the Montespan's favor the King did not find me as disagreeable as he finds me now and enjoyed my company. So I will not despair and continue to go my own straight path. . . .

Hanover must be exceedingly changed since I was there, for in my time plays were performed in the small hall near Ma Tante Lisbeth's room and near the chapel; the theatre was not very large. But now the château must be magnificent, if Your Grace now has two separate halls for plays and operas. . . .

Now I must tell Your Grace how it was at Marly. On Thursday right after supper the King sat down in the salon that had been readied for the ball. Soon the Duchesse de Bourgogne came in, costumed very prettily as Flora in a dress covered with silk flowers, which was most becoming to her. She had a great many ladies with her, but, to tell the truth, the costumes were not quite as becoming to some of them. . . . The Duchesse de Sully, for example, is a bit short and stout. . . . When all the masks had taken up their places . . . the sound of a big drum was heard, and in came a Sarmathian, followed by a camel with a Moor who beat the drum, and after him came a group of Amazons. The King's pages are very nimble in vaulting and fencing. After this pageant had left the room, a great many minuets were danced. After a while the three princes also put on costumes and danced a dance like "Willst du mit nach Rompelskirchen / willst du mit, so komm," etc.[2] On the next day, that is, Friday, I drove to Paris at half past nine, arrived at half past eleven, and attended mass with Monsieur. From there we drove to Saint Eustache, where we were to stand godparents to a bell. I almost burst out laughing, for they had wound a wreath of flowers around the bell and had covered the top with a piece of brocade. I said to Monsieur, "I see that the bell is also costumed as Flora," because it looked exactly like the Duchesse de Sully. To the clapper were fastened golden ropes with golden tassels; these were placed in our hands and we had to pull three times to make the bell ring. Just between us: this ceremony is really funny. The church was packed with people who had come to see the solemn ceremony; and when it was over all the populace went to ring the bell; they think it protects them from thunderclaps. One thief was caught as he tried to steal an officer's sabre; that made a tremendous commotion in the church.

1. Mademoiselle de Fontanges was Madame's lady-in-waiting when she became the mistress of the King.   2. A kind of "musical chairs" dance.

I also have a very big book of songs. It was given to me by the good Grande Mademoiselle[1] before she died, and it amuses me very much. At the late Monsieur's court there were many clever people who made up the funniest songs. There are people in Paris who have ten or twelve big volumes of these old songs and take very good care of them. In France one can find out about every period from songs, because songs are written about everything. They are a much better way to learn about the court than the history books; for these are full of flattery, but in the songs they sing what is really going on. And just as medals teach us about the history of Rome, so one can find out the truth about occurrences in this country through songs. So they are not as useless as one might think.

1. The niece of Louis XIII and the daugher of Gaston d'Orléans, the first Monsieur.

Monsieur, thank God, has gotten over his fever, but His Grace is still quite languid and melancholy and does not take pleasure in anything. I think I know what makes him so dejected: His Grace realizes that his past life cannot go on any longer; yet all his plans and actions used to turn only on his pleasures, which are all that he cares about. Of course, he does not want to die either, yet he realizes that his wild life and his activities must come to an end. That makes His Grace very sad, and this sadness prevents him from regaining his strength; so I am quite worried about Monsieur.

My son has such a great talent for all aspects of painting that he never uses any expedients for designing and sketches everything from nature and living models. Coypel, his former teacher, says that all the painters should be glad that my son is a great lord, because if he were an ordinary fellow he would surpass them all. He can draw anything that comes into his head, his conceptions are strong, and he knows how to make the most difficult postures look easy. . . .

I cannot understand how anyone could imagine that the Song of Solomon has anything to do with God or with piety. One only has to read it to see that this is a lover carrying on. It must have gladdened the hearts of the reverend Jesuits of Regensburg to see two boys playing the lovers. I am now reading Ecclesiastes, and find it a beautiful book, but I am surprised that it was included among the books of the Bible, for it clearly shows that Solomon did not believe in an afterlife. . . .

In my youth I often deceived the good Mistress Kolb by eating at night, but we did not eat such dainty things as chocolate, tea, or coffee, but stuffed ourselves with a good cabbage salad with bacon. I remember that once at Heidelberg, while a door was being changed in my room, my bed and that of the Kolbin were moved to the room next to that of my maids. The Kolbin had forbidden me to go ito the girls' room at night; I promised that I would not cross the threshold and told her that she might as well go to bed, because I was not yet sleepy and would like to look at the stars for awhile. The Kolbin did not trust me and did not want to budge from her night table; finally I told her that I felt sorry for her and suggested that she go to bed leaving the curtains open so that she could see me. This she did. As soon as she was in bed, the girls opened the door and placed the plate of cabbage salad on the threshold. I pretended to drop my handkerchief, picked up the plate with it, and went straight to the window. I had just swallowed three good mouthfuls when suddenly the cannon that stood on the terrace under my window was set off because a fire had broken out in the town. The Kolbin, who was dreadfully scared of fire, jumps out of bed; I, not wanting to be caught, toss my napkin out of the window along with the silver plate and the bacon salad, so that I had nothing to wipe my mouth with. Right then I heard someone come up the wooden stairs; it was the Elector our late father, who had come to see where the fire was. Seeing me with my greasy mouth and chin, he started to swear, "*Sacrement,* Liselotte, don't tell me you smear stuff on your face!" I said, "It is just some lip balm that I have put on because my lips are chapped." Papa said, "You look dirty." Suddenly I was seized with a fit of laughter; Papa and all those who were with him thought that I had gone mad to laugh so hard. The Raugräfin had also come up and passed through the girls' room; she came in saying: "What an odd smell of bacon salad in the girls' room." Then the Elector saw what the joke was and said: "So that is your mouth balm, Liselotte." When I saw that the Elector was in good humor, I confessed the whole thing and explained how I had gone about deceiving the governess. The Elector only laughed about it, but the Kolbin did not forgive me for a long time. This is an old story, and I only tell it to show Your Grace that I know how much fun it is for young people to eat at night against the governess's will.

Saint Cloud, 20 May 1700

I must tell Your Grace something pretty that my son told us at table; they found it on a Flemish church window where the sacrifice of Isaac is depicted. Isaac is tied down on an altar. Abraham has a musket at his cheek and is about to shoot his son. God the Father is painted in the clouds; he gives a signal to a little angel that sits on Abraham's head. The little angel pisses on the musket pan of Abraham's musket, so that the gun cannot go off. That is how Isaac is saved. I do not think that Your Grace has ever seen it painted in this way.

I am happy to see that Your Grace asked for the mail right after her arrival at Wesel. . . . They say here that His Grace the Electoral Prince of Branden-burg[1] is to become Stadthouder of Holland in King William's place and that the Elector his father has sent him to see King William about it. I can easily understand that Your Grace is fonder of this grandson than of the others, whose pepper is so mixed in with mousedroppings. Dear God, as long as Your Grace is traveling incognito anyway, with the coats-of-arms on the carriages removed, might it not be possible to add a little excursion to Maubuisson? For it is quite impossible for me to come to the frontier. Truly, my life is alto-gether too full of constraint, but I have never felt this as painfully as just now. Sometimes I think I must escape and run all the way to Your Grace, as heavy as I am. Even Fontainebleau will seem a sad place to me when I think that I must always be with people who hate me and that I am not allowed to see those whom I know to be kindly disposed toward me, even though they are close by. My eyes are not dry as I write this to my dearest Ma Tante. Being Madame is a miserable job, and if I could sell it as they sell offices in this country, I would have put it up for sale long ago. . . .

Not much is new here. The King has had the Duc d'Estrées put into the Bastille by *lettre de cachet.*[2] Some weeks ago d'Estrées wrote a long letter to the King, promising to give up his debaucheries and to lead a decent life; nonetheless he again went on a wild drinking spree with his own lackeys, and they ended up by setting fire to several houses in Paris. Drinking them-selves into a stupor and committing insolences of all kinds is considered nice by the young people of quality these days, but they do not know how to exchange two words with reasonable people. Nothing could be more brutal than the youth of today.

1. Electress Sophie's grandson.   2. A royal order to imprison or exile a person with-out formal accusation or trial. Private individuals could also obtain *lettres de cachet* if they felt the need to send an unruly member of their family to prison or, in the case of a woman, to a convent. Very influential persons could even obtain blank *lettres de cachet* and fill in the name of the offender themselves. Prisoners of this kind often disappeared without a trace.

To RAUGRÄFIN AMALIE ELISABETH

Fontainebleau, 7 November 1700

Dearest Amalise, please read what I have written to Luise. There you will find the reason for my long silence, so I will not repeat it here and only say how happy I am that you are well again and that you liked my present from the vil-lage fair. But I am embarrassed that you make so much to-do about it, for it was only a little thing and more a joke than a real present; I just wanted to show you the kind of work that is done here and also send along my bear-cat-monkeyface to find out whether you would still know it. Now you can carry me in your pocket, and that will make both of you think of me more often. Karl Moritz has written to me, thanking me profusely for inquiring and worrying about him. I have written him back, but I shall send the letter to Monsieur Spanheim; in this manner it will reach Berlin sooner than if I had sent it to you in Frankfurt.

Madame's letter of 1 October 1699 had contained her first comment on the Spanish succession, a topic of conversation and debate that was to displace all others at every court and chancery in Europe when the sickly Charles II of Spain died childless on 1 November 1700. The inheritance of the Spanish crowns was an enormous prize, since the kingdom included not only Spain but parts of Italy, the Netherlands, and vast possessions in the Americas as well.

With Charles II, the male line of the Spanish Hapsburgs came to an end; the question was whether the succession should go to the Austrian Hapsburgs, whose claim went back to Philip III, or to the French Bourbons, who had a claim through Philip IV's daughter Marie-Thérèse, the wife of Louis XIV. Marie-Thérèse, it is true, had waived her rights to the inheritance in her marriage contract, but the renunciation was conditioned upon the delivery of a dowry that was never paid, and the French therefore insisted that it was not valid. Both the Hapsburg Emperor and Louis XIV knew that the other European powers would not permit them to unite the Spanish crowns to their own and therefore claimed them for younger sons of their houses. The two principal claimants were thus Archduke Charles of Austria and Philippe, Duc d'Anjou, Louis XIV's second grandson.

For several years before Charles II's death, no one knew whom he would designate as his successor. Since all the powers feared the enormous increase in influence that an undivided inheritance would afford the sponsor of the eventual successor, France, England, the Netherlands, and Austria had conducted negotiations with a view to partitioning the Spanish Empire after the death of Charles II. This prospect, however, was so abhorrent to the princes of Church and State in Spain that they persuaded their dying king to name the Bourbon prince as successor to his entire realm. They assumed that France was in a better position to defend the integrity of all the Spanish possessions than was the Austrian Empire, which was occupied with problems in faraway Eastern Europe and furthermore had no navy. Reports of the means by which Charles II was made to sign his last will reached Madame, who passed them on to her aunt in the letter of 20 December 1700. Louis XIV and his advisers—and, indeed, even Madame—knew perfectly well that accepting the Spanish crowns for the Duc d'Anjou would mean that the Empire, England, and the Netherlands would go to war to claim their share of the projected partition and also to defend the existing balance of power in Europe. Yet dynastic considerations—a great crown for a prince of the

French royal house—were more powerful than the desire for peace. During the ensuing war, Madame proved herself a loyal Frenchwoman who rejoiced in French victories and bemoaned French defeats. When her German aunt suggested that the archduke might make a better king of Spain than would Philip V, she coolly cited the proverb, "He who has the bride is the groom." (Based on John B. Wolf, Louis XIV *[New York, 1968], chap. 29.)*

To ELECTRESS SOPHIE

Fontainebleau, 10 November 1700

Today I can tell Your Grace a piece of big news that arrived here yesterday morning, although it was expected for some time, namely, that the King of Spain[1] has died. The Queen is said to be ill with grief. The King died on the first of this month at three o'clock in the afternoon. Our King was sent a copy of his will. The Duc d'Anjou[2] was chosen to be the heir; they say that a grandee of Spain immediately took the post-chaise carrying the original of the will in order to bring it to the Duc d'Anjou and to ask him to be King. And in case our King should refuse the request for the Duc d'Anjou, that same Spanish grandee has orders to betake himself right away to Vienna to offer the Spanish crown to the Emperor.

1. Charles II.   2. Louis XIV's second grandson, sixteen years old at the time.

Fontainebleau, 13 November 1700

Yesterday people kept whispering into each other's ears, "Do not say anything about it, but the King has accepted the Spanish crown for Monsieur le Duc d'Anjou." I kept quiet, but at the hunt, when I heard the Duc d'Anjou behind me in a narrow path, I stopped and said, "After you, great King; please pass, Your Majesty." I wish Your Grace had seen how surprised the dear child was that I knew it; his little brother, the Duc de Berry,[1] almost died laughing. He, the Duc d'Anjou, looks every bit like a king of Spain, laughs rarely, and is always solemn and dignified. They say that two days ago the King had him secretly informed that he is King, but that he should not let on. He happened to be playing *l'hombre*[2] in his room, and although he did not say a word, he could not quite contain himself, jumped up, but immediately sat down again, looking as solemn as before. While this king does not have as much vivacity as the youngest of his brothers, nor as much intelligence, he has other, exceedingly good qualities; a kind heart, generosity (which does not run in his house), and truthfulness, for he would not tell a lie for anything in the world, and no one loathes lying more than he does. Also, he will keep his word and is compassionate and courageous; in short, he is a truly virtuous lord, and there is no evil in him. If he were an ordinary nobleman, one could say that he is a good, honest man, and I believe that those who are with him will be fortunate. I believe he will be as strong as the King of Poland,[3] for even a year ago the strongest man here was unable to bend his arm. He looks quite Austrian and always keeps his mouth open; I have told him a hundred times to close it, and when one tells him he does it, as he is very docile; but as soon as he forgets, his mouth is open again. He does not speak much, except with me, for I keep after him all the time and tease him a lot; sometimes I can even make him laugh. I like him better than the Duc de Bourgogne[4] because he is kinder and not as disdainful as the Duc de Bourgogne, also better looking. But the one I dearly love as if he were my own child is the Duc de Berry; he is a delightful child, always merry, and full of laughter and funny chatter.

1. Fourteen years old. 2. A card game. 3. August the Strong of Saxony. 4. His eighteen-year-old brother, the "second Dauphin."

Paris, 18 November 1700

On Tuesday morning the King called the good Duc d'Anjou into his cabinet and told him, "You are King of Spain!" and thereupon bade the Spanish ambassador and all the Spaniards who are in this country come in. They knelt down before their king, kissed his hand one by one, and lined up behind their king. Thereafter our King led the young King of Spain into the salon where the whole court was assembled and said, "Gentlemen, greet the King of Spain!" This gave rise to shouts of joy, and everyone drew near to kiss the young King's hand. Then our King said, "Let us give thanks to God; please come to mass, Your Majesty," holding out his right hand to the young King, and so they went to mass together, where the King made him kneel to his right on his own prie-dieu. After mass our King saw him to his apartment, the large one; afterward his brothers came to call on him; my Duc de Berry was so happy that he kissed his brother's hand from sheer joy. In the afternoon the young King drove to Meudon to call on his father,[1] who was there. The latter came out to the antechamber to receive him. He had just been in the garden, not expecting his son the King of Spain to arrive so early; therefore he was out of breath when he came and said, "I can see that one must never swear to anything, for I would have sworn that I would never lose my breath going to meet my son the Duc d'Anjou; yet here I am out of breath!" The good young King was completely bewildered to see himself treated like a foreign king by his own father who, when he left, accompanied him all the way to his coach. Yesterday morning Monseigneur returned the call to his son the King.

1. The Dauphin, Louis.

This morning Herr von Loo came to see me. . . . He told me a detail about Helmont's death and said that not long before his death, Helmont helped a Fräulein von Merode[1] get out of a convent, made her marry a government official in a village, and then proceeded to instruct her in his philosophy. When he felt that his death was near, he sent for this lady in order to impart his spirit to her. It seems that he told her to place her mouth on his, breathed into it, and said: "I herewith bequeath to you my spirit," whereupon he turned away and died. The lady, I am told, is firmly convinced that Helmont's spirit now dwells within her. It seems to me that, if thoughts are any indication, our spirit is lodged in the head rather than in the body, and therefore I should think that when it comes to receiving a spirit it would be better to hold out an ear than the mouth. For if the spirit goes down into the stomach, one is liable to expel it with the natural winds; therefore it is to be feared that the good Helmont's spirit may have ended up in a secret haunt instead of staying with Madame Merode. . . .

His Imperial Majesty[2] had not wasted his time and had won over the late King of Spain's confessor, who made this King sign a will in favor of the archduke.[3] He therefore thought his cause was secure, and so it would have been if the confessor had not left the King of Spain. For this monk, in order to show off his good work, went to Cardinal de Portocarrero and told him that he, as Archbishop of Toledo, could now give the King his absolution, since he, the confessor, had prepared His Majesty's soul for a blessed end. The cardinal replied that this being the case, the confessor was no longer needed by the King and that he, the cardinal, would take care of everything. So he went to the King and told him in plain words that he could not give him absolution. The King wanted to know why not. The cardinal said: because Your Majesty is wronging his rightful heirs and has chosen an heir for the kingdom who does not have a proper claim to it, namely, the Archduke. Your Majesty's empire rightfully belongs to the Dauphin and his sons.[4] The King said: "It is true that I have signed a will in favor of the archduke. But I cannot change it now, for I am not in a state to make a new one." The cardinal said that he had one ready in his pocket. All he had to do, he told the King, was to sign it after it was read to him. So he read it right then and there, and the King signed it. Then the cardinal gave him absolution and did not let the confessor enter the King's room again. That is how it went. Therefore Your Grace can see that it was not the Emperor's fault, for he could not foresee that the confessor would be fool enough to let himself be hoodwinked by Cardinal de Portocarrero. It was a Dominican. I think if it had been a Jesuit, he would not have been hoodwinked as easily. . . .

Since dinner I keep standing by the window to watch people sliding around on skates. There have been some pretty good somersaults; I don't know why they do not break their necks.

1. His niece. 2. Leopold I. 3. Charles, who later became Emperor. 4. Actually, this was a controversial point; Louis XIV had signed a renunciation when he married the Spanish infanta. (See John B. Wolf, *Louis XIV* [New York, 1968], p. 493.)

Versailles, 2 January 1701

I keep thinking (but I may be flattering myself) that the King does not hate me and would see more of me if the old woman did not prevent it. Yet he does not like me enough not to sacrifice me to her hatred. Still, he has sent me 1,000 *pistoles* for the New Year, which I would have put to good use if I had not been so short in the last few years that I had to borrow gold. But I have already paid off more than 1,000 *pistoles*. This year, God willing, I shall clear up everything. . . .

I do not know if Your Grace knows that the Pope has admonished the Emperor not to start a war in Christendom. If this prevents the Emperor from going to war, it would be an honorable pretext for everyone to settle this matter peacefully. The Emperor called on the Pope not to recognize the King of Spain as king and to refuse him the investiture of Naples and Sicily. But the Pope replied that the King of Spain is the rightful heir to the crown, recognized as such by all the Spanish kingdoms and appointed by the people, and that he is therefore bound to recognize him as the rightful King of Spain. . . . Here everyone is firmly convinced that war will break out, and everyone is preparing for it. I think that King William will not be sorry to occupy his Englishmen, so that they will not give him any trouble.

Versailles, 23 January 1701

Yesterday I was told something new in strict confidence; I have trouble believing it, but would give a great deal to know that it is true. There is a rumor in Paris that the Pantocrate is selling her wedded husband for money and that she takes money from the Emperor. It would be just too pretty if it were true. That the same person draws millions from Alsace and fleeces the nobility there is quite certain, and also that she is paid by people here. The prettiest part of it is that she carries on as if she had nothing, and when her husband wants to give her money, she says: "Oh no, please keep it, you need it more, and I can get along." This makes him think that no one cares less about money than his wife and he admires her moderation, when in fact no one in the world is more greedy. I think it is quite funny. . . . I cannot understand what this old woman, who does not even have any children, wants to do with all the millions she has accumulated. But that is none of my business. She has made a real show of her hatred for me during my illness: all of France, from the King to the lowliest, has come to me or has inquired about me; she alone stood apart and did not even send to find out how I was. But her disfavor has not prevented me from getting well and agrees quite well with me; I can stand the old pruneface's hatred rather better than the fever, which is much more harmful to me. . . .

We too hear nothing now but talk of war and soldiering, so I am much afraid that there will be war. Breton[1] writes to me from Berlin that the Prussian coronation cannot take place right away because the baggage carts have been held up by ice. I feel strongly that an elector[2] who is richer than all royal highnesses, and has more land and subjects too, could well be satisfied with his title and dismiss mere words as chimeras, especially if these words bring with them more constraint than freedom. But as Your Grace describes this king to me, he loves *éclat* and constraint because he loves ceremonies; so I am not surprised that he wanted to be king. And as Your Grace so rightly says, everyone will soon be used to it.

1. French ambassador to the court of Brandenburg. 2. Elector Friedrich III of Brandenburg, who had himself crowned King of Prussia on 18 January, assuming the name Friedrich I.

Marly, 10 February 1701

Yesterday I had the joy of receiving Your Grace's letter of 31 January upon my return from church, where they had smeared ashes on my brow. I said that I did not need this because it is only for those whose amusements during carnival might make them forget that they are mortal. But since I had spent the first days of my carnival being sick and the last days being bored by watching poorly danced minuets, I said that the pleasures of carnival had by no means prevented me from being mindful of my mortality. I added that I also have a spleen that reminds me of it enough and more than enough. But since it is the custom, I had to put up with this smearing of ashes. . . .

It seems to me that to have someone canonized is an unnecessary expense, for if people are in heaven, I believe that neither they nor Our Lord care very much whether there is a ceremony to certify them as saints, and if they are in hell, they will not be treated as saints anyway. So, however one takes it, canonization is a perfectly useless expense.

Saint Cloud, 24 March 1701

Your Grace put the matter very poetically and eloquently in saying that the sun here lets itself be darkened by the shadow of an old woman. Of this sun it can be said that it is not without spots. Sometimes one profits from the weakness of the great, but the great man's weakness is my misfortune. The *éclat* and renown of great kings are like the machines at the opera: seen from afar, nothing is grander and more beautiful, but if one goes backstage and takes a close look at all the ropes and wooden slats that make the machines move, they are often most ungainly and ugly. It is only equitable, as Your Grace says, that as human beings we must put up with one another's faults, and I assure Your Grace that I do put up with quite a few. Only, one would hope that those whose weaknesses I tolerate would also tolerate mine, but Your Grace is the only person to do me that kindness.

Versailles, 17 April 1701

Now Your Grace can see that I was not mistaken when I assured Your Grace that she, along with her sons, would be called to the crown of England.[1] They say that the Princess of Denmark[2] is terribly given to drink and has burnt her insides so badly that she will never be able to have children; consequently, she will probably die soon. King William also is so sickly that he will not live long. Thus Your Grace will soon come to her grandfather's throne. That will make me very happy, for I would rather see Your Grace in this place than myself or my children because I love my dearest Ma Tante more. When the time comes, I shall make Your Grace a great, long compliment, sprinkling it throughout with "Your Majesty." But for now I do not have to make compliments, since Your Grace is as yet only what she was before, namely, the worthiest person in the world to become a great queen. . . . Now I am glad that I am here and a Catholic, because it means that I cannot be an obstacle to the crown for Your Grace.

> 1. Electress Sophie and Madame's father were grandchildren of James I of England. Madame was excluded from the English succession only because she had converted to Catholicism. 2. Princess Anne, James II's second daughter.

In May 1701 Prince Eugene with the Imperial army invaded Italy and defeated the French in a first battle. Louis XIV's many political and military pretensions resulted in a war that soon involved almost all of Europe, the War of the Spanish Succession.

Saint Cloud, 9 June 1701

This comes to Your Grace from the most unfortunate of creatures; Monsieur has suffered a stroke last evening at ten o'clock. He is in the throes of death and I, though in the most wretched state in the world, will remain unto death Your Grace's faithful kinswoman and servant Elisabeth Charlotte.

1701–1715:

Widowhood

To ELECTRESS SOPHIE

Versailles, 12 June 1701

Now that I have recovered somewhat from my first shock, I can turn for comfort in my misfortune only to Your Grace, whom I love more than anyone in the world. So I will tell my dearest Ma Tante everything. Wednesday last in the morning Monsieur was still hale and hearty and drove to Marly, where he ate an excellent dinner with the King. After dinner, His Grace drove to Saint-Germain, returning toward six full of good cheer and telling us how many stools he had counted at the Queen of England's. Toward nine I was to go to supper, but could not eat because I had just had a four-hour bout of fever. Monsieur said to me, "I am off to supper because, unlike you, I am hungry," and with that he goes to the table. A half hour later I hear a noise and see Madame de Vantadour, white as a sheet, come into my room, saying, "Monsieur is not well." I ran over to Monsieur's room; His Grace was conscious but could not speak intelligibly; all I heard was, "You are ill, go back to your room." His Grace was bled three times and given eleven ounces of emetic and three whole bottles of *gouttes d'Angleterre,* all to no avail. Toward six in the morning he took a turn for the worse. At that point I was forcibly dragged out of the room; I was in a near-swoon. I was put to bed but could not stay in bed, arose, and since in joy and sorrow Your Grace is always in my thoughts, my first impulse was to write to Your Grace; but I do not remember what I wrote. After I had sent off Your Grace's letter, the King came to me; he too was very moved but nonetheless did his utmost to console me and was extremely kind to me. Madame de Maintenon was much moved also and spoke to me. The King left. At twelve Monsieur expired. I got into my coach right away and came here. The King sent Monsieur le Premier to inquire how I was. The shock had driven away my fever. Madame de Maintenon asked my son to tell me that this would be the time for me to make my peace with the King. I seriously thought about it and remembered how often Your Grace had advised me to make peace with

131

the lady herself; therefore I asked the Duc de Noailles to tell his lady on my behalf that I was so touched by all the friendship she had shown me in my misfortune that I should like to request her to be good enough to come to see me, since I was unable to go out. This she did yesterday at six. I immediately told her how very pleased I was and that I desired her friendship, and I also confessed that I had not liked her in the past, thinking that she had deprived me of the King's favor and hated me, that I had heard this from Madame la Dauphine also, but that I would be happy to forget all of this if only she would be my friend. To this she replied with many beautiful and eloquent words, promised me her friendship, and we embraced. Later I said to her that it was not enough that she had informed me of the King's displeasure, and that she should also tell me how I might recover the King's good graces. She advised me to speak very frankly about everything with the King, to admit voluntarily that I had hated her because I had thought that she was disparaging me with the King, and also to say why I had been angry with the King. This advice I followed, and since Monsieur had told me that the King was angry that I write too freely to Your Grace, I also brought up this point and said that His Majesty should not find anything strange in this, considering that Your Grace is the person in the world to whom I am most attached, . . . that I have always opened my heart to Your Grace and that as long as I was in His Majesty's good graces I had proudly reported it to Your Grace, but that I had lamented to Your Grace when the King had treated me badly and could never act differently toward Your Grace. The King said that he knew nothing of my letters, had never seen one, and that Monsieur had only imagined this. He said that he saw nothing wrong with my loving and honoring Your Grace as a mother, but that Your Grace hates him. I said that Your Grace has always admired his great qualities and would also love him if His Majesty wished it. After I had explained everything to His Majesty and made it clear that however badly he had treated me I had always respected and loved him, indeed that I had always delighted in being merely tolerated in his presence, the King embraced me, begged me to let bygones be bygones, and promised me his favor; he even laughed when I said to him quite naively, "If I had not loved you, I would not have hated Madame de Maintenon so much, thinking that she deprived me of your good graces." So everything turned out very well in the end.[1] I said to His Majesty that since this is the only comfort in my misfortune, I cannot keep from telling Your Grace all about it today, and the King approved. Today I shall have another sad day, for at three the King will return for the opening of the late Monsieur's testament, which will cause me horrendous pity and grief.

1. Actually, the meeting with Madame de Maintenon may have been one of the worst moments of Madame's entire life. If we are to believe Saint-Simon, who claims to have his information from Madame de Ventadour, the only witness to this scene, Ma-

dame de Maintenon listened to Madame's expressions of gratitude for her gracious sympathy and then pulled a letter from her pocket: "Do you recognize this, Madame?" It was one of Elisabeth Charlotte's letters to her aunt, castigating the machinations of "the old trollop" and, almost worse, describing the miserable conditions in the kingdom. Speechless confusion, tears, apologies on the part of Madame, generous forgiveness on the part of Madame de Maintenon! The conversation then proceeded as described above, but the experience was so humiliating that Madame simply could not bring herself to report it.

Versailles, 26 June 1701

After much worrying and fretting that I had not received a letter from Your Grace, I was finally gladdened by three of Your Grace's kind letters the day before yesterday at eleven o'clock at night, and this has given me the only good night I have had since my great misfortune. For the horrendous shock into which I was cast by Monsieur's attack and his extremely rapid demise has made such a strong impression upon me that as soon as I am about to go to sleep this spectacle reappears before my eyes, so that I sit up in my bed with a dreadful start and cannot find two hours of uninterrupted sleep. But the joy of receiving Your Grace's kind letters and of learning that she is well, thank God, and still kindly disposed toward me has filled me with such peace that I slept between one and six in the morning. And that I needed to give me a little strength to live through the day yesterday. I had to receive the King and Queen of England in ceremony, in an outlandish costume: a white linen band over my forehead and over that a bonnet tied under the chin, over the bonnet a wimple, and over the wimple a veil-like linen cloth that is attached to both shoulders like a light mantle and hangs down seven ells. With that I wore a gown of black cloth with sleeves down to the fists; on the sleeves was a strip of ermine as wide as two hands and on the gown also ermine of the same width from the neck down to the feet. A black crepe belt tied in front reached down to the floor, and the train of the ermine skirt was also seven ells long.[1] In this getup I was led to a completely black room (even the parquet was covered and the windows draped in black) and laid on a black bed with the train arranged in such a way that the ermine showed. A big candelabra with twelve tapers was lit in the room, and ten or twelve were burning on the mantelpiece. All my servants, big and little, were there in long mourning cloaks, and some forty or fifty ladies in crepe mantles. All of this looked perfectly awful.

1. Thirty-three feet.

Versailles, 30 June 1701

By now Your Grace already knows that the King will take care of me. Monsieur has left seven million and a half in debts. I do not think that I shall ever be rich; God grant that I can even make ends meet. . . . I believe that I would be better off if I had died myself than to have lived through this. Monsieur was indeed aware that he was dying; for twelve hours His Grace was most unnecessarily martyrized with emetics, bleeding, cupping . . . and a hundred other things, various clysters too. He only lost his mind very shortly before he died and knew everyone, but had great trouble speaking because His Grace's lower lip was hanging down limp and swollen. Just before His Grace suffered this dreadful attack he was hale, hearty, and in high spirits, ate at table with great appetite, laughed and chattered, so that when his speech first became blurred the ladies thought he was joking, but alas, it was no joke at all. If those who are in the next world could know what is happening in this one, I think His Grace the late Monsieur would be most pleased with me, for I have gone through his boxes to find all the letters written to him by his boyfriends and have burnt them unread, so that they will not fall into other people's hands.

Versailles, 7 July 1701

That Monsieur has not remembered me in his will is not surprising, it cannot be. In this country the husband cannot bequeath anything to the wife, nor the wife to the husband; but what he gives her during his lifetime is hers to keep. But Monsieur preferred to give it to those who amused him, for it turns out that three young fellows alone were given incomes of a hundred thousand *talers* each. Nor would Monsieur have recommended me to the King's good grace, for he did not wish me to have it. Your Grace can well imagine that I will do my best to keep the King's favor and Madame de Maintenon's friendship. But who can be sure that this will last? After all, Your Grace must be aware that my son and I will encounter more and more envy as the King continues to grant us favors and that at great courts like this one the art of setting people against each other is known only too well. All things considered, then, the prospects for my future do not look too bright. . . .

I do confess that Monsieur often plagued and chagrined me, but this was only because he was weak and captivated by those who provided for his revels and pleasures. The King himself told me that recently His late Grace was no longer disparaging me as much as he had done some years ago, indeed that he seemed to like me, which makes me grieve all the more. I was also touched that although he could barely speak after his attack, when I said to him, "How are you feeling now, Monsieur?" he said, "a little better," and then, with great difficulty, "and you?" I said, "Never mind about me, think of yourself, I will be fine." He said, "You have there," pointing to his pulse in order to say "a fever," which he could not pronounce; and then he said fairly clearly, "go away!" And when they wanted to give him something he did not want to take, they said, "Madame has ordered this," and he took it. That showed me that he trusted me after all, and I am really heartsick about it. All this keeps rising before my eyes, for as I have often written and said to Your Grace, I have never hated the poor gentleman but loved him, however unjust he often was to me. . . .

My tertian fever is gone. I think I cured myself by eating cherries. I was told I could not have cherries, but then I received a basket of beautiful cherries from Saint Cloud, which I gobbled up in secret, and since then my fever has not returned. . . .

Those who can go to the theater are lucky; this will now be forbidden to me for two years. . . .

The King of Prussia leads a strange life. It is unheard of that anyone arises at two o'clock in the morning; if the monks do this, they have other times when they can sleep. His servants will not be able to stand it, for they can only go to bed one hour after the King and must arise a good hour before His Majesty, so they will only have three hours of sleep. No one can live on that. His whole court will go mad if this goes on for any length of time. The King's letters to Your Grace are as short as his sleep.

To RAUGRÄFIN LUISE

Versailles, 15 July 1701

Dearest Luise, today it is only a week since the fever left me; after my misfortune I suffered another eighteen bouts of fever and was beginning to hope that my wretched life would finally come to an end. But such was not God's will, and I recovered without remedies. Yet I still feel exceedingly languid and my thighs are quite weak, which seems very odd to me because nobody at court used to walk better than I. But I suppose that is the end of that, for at my age one rarely regains one's strength. . . .

The King has been most gracious to me since my misfortune; henceforth I shall have to depend on his grace alone, and Amelise was poorly informed when she heard that I am so well provided for. But since lamenting is not at all my affair, I will not go into this matter and only say that every year I will be short 80,000 francs for the necessary expenses of my household, to say nothing of any surplus for my pleasure or entertainment. This will show you how fortunate I will henceforth be. But enough of these tiresome matters, for to speak of them only makes one sad and does not do any good.

To ELECTRESS SOPHIE

Versailles, 21 July 1701

Madame de Maintenon continues to be most friendly to me, I am very pleased with her; and if she continues in this manner I shall certainly remain her friend. I am not of an age to become bored in her and the King's company,

like the Duchesse de Bourgogne, who can only think of fun and games. . . .
I am fairly racking my brains to figure out why it is that the Maintenon
has decided to turn toward me in this way. For there is no doubt that shortly
before my husband's death she still bore me dreadful hatred, and all of a
sudden she changed without my doing anything about it. But when I saw that
she had turned toward me, I did not let the matter go by and immediately
made friends with her. Yet the more I think about what might have caused
her to do it, the less I can understand it. Because one thing is certain: this
woman does not do anything without thinking about it or for nothing. Sometimes I imagine that since she has such a great passion for the Duchesse de
Bourgogne, and since the latter, as rumor has it, has grown quite tired of her
and can no longer stand to be with the King because she is bored in the company of these elderly people, that the lady has chosen to make the Duchesse
de Bourgogne jealous—for she is of a jealous temperament—and hopes to
bring her back to her by this means. Or perhaps she was afraid that since Monsieur can no longer disparage me with the King, the King might once again get
used to me and that, unless she were my friend, I might be capable of opening
the King's eyes. So she might have thought that it would be best if she were
my friend and could keep me in check before it came to that; or perhaps she
has something else in mind and thinks she can bring me down more easily
once she has me in her claws, or whatever else it might be, for it is quite certain that something must be behind this. It simply is not natural for a person to change her ways overnight, as she has done. So I must be very careful
at all times of what I do and say and cannot be sure of what will happen. . . .

What will become of my financial affairs I do not know, but there is no
doubt that I will not have enough to live according to my rank unless the
King helps me. . . . The poor late Monsieur left things in a complete shambles
and has not provided for me at all, for he could have done this during his lifetime, though not in his will; but he has preferred to distribute everything
among his boyfriends, who loved him much less than I did.

Marly, 28 July 1701

I cannot possibly be really cheerful, but I am doing my best not to be altogether melancholy. The Palatine Elector does not want to give me any
more money; this diminishes my income by another 200,000 francs. Things
will be pretty meager for me, for what with the present war, the King is not
likely to give me very large sums. How I wish that lots of people made demands on me and that I had lots of money to give; in that case I would not be
importuned by their demands. It would have suited me much better if I had
enough to live without the King, for then I would not have been a burden to
the King, and if he had given me extra favors and presents, I would have spent

them with pleasure. As it is, I am like a beggar-woman and the King has me on his hands; it is most unfortunate. . . .

Once, a long time ago, I asked Herr Salmond[1] why it is that although the Scripture says that man is created in God's image, we are so very imperfect. He replied that God created man perfect, but that he has lost his perfection by his fall. I said, Since man was so perfect, how could he sin and fall? Herr Salmond said, this happened by the instigation of Satan. I said, Surely it was not a mark of perfection to do the devil's bidding. All he said to this was: One must not brood too deeply about these things. That was the end of it.

1. Her former teacher.

Versailles, 4 September 1701

This good king[1] will end up killing himself by his excessive piety. Only the day before yesterday he knelt and prayed for so long that His Majesty fainted dead away and remained senseless for so long that it looked as if he were going to die.

1. James II; he died on 16 September at Saint Germain.

Fontainebleau, 15 October 1701

If my marriage contract had simply been like all others that are made here, everything would be fine for me. But they purposely put in special clauses that prevent me from getting anything. Therefore I have come to the conclusion that my late Papa must not have understood this matter correctly if he made me sign such a thing. But then Papa had me on his hands and was afraid that I would become a little old maid, and so he got rid of me as quickly as he could. This was foreordained as my destiny, and I shall simply have to carry through what was ordained. . . .

I am sorry with all my heart that dear Frau von Harling is so very ill . . . I am most distressed about it, for I love her very much and am deeply indebted to this good woman for all the care and trouble she took for me in my childhood.

To RAUGRÄFIN AMALIE ELISABETH

Fontainebleau, 4 November 1701

Do you really think, dear Amelise, that I no longer read the Bible, just because I am here? I read three chapters every morning. You must not think that the French Catholics are as silly as the German Catholics; this is all very different here, almost as if it were a different religion. Here the Bible is read by anyone who wants to read it; nor is one obliged to believe in trifles and absurd miracles. People here do not consider the Pope infallible; when he excommunicated Monsieur de Lavardin[1] at Rome, people here just laughed. He is not being worshipped, nor is anyone keen on pilgrimages and that sort of thing, and in this all the French are different from the German Catholics, as well as from the Spaniards and the Italians.

But to return to what you say about melancholia. It is certainly true that sadness does not serve any purpose, but then it is not always up to us whether we are cheerful or sad, and it is hard to be cheerful if one must spend one's life in solitude, if one has nothing to be happy about, and indeed a lot of sad things on one's hands. Pleasure gives as many wrinkles as chagrin, and if one spends much time in sun and wind, one is bound to get wrinkles. Laughing gives as many wrinkles as crying. . . . I assure you, dear Amelise, that I have no ambition whatsoever and that there is nothing I wish less than to be a queen. The higher one's station the more constrained one's life, and if the position of Madame were an office that one could sell, I would have gotten rid of it long ago, and cheaply, too; so there is no question of my wanting to be a queen. The Princess of Savoy was not called to the kingdom for nothing;[2] after all she is made of the genuine stuff that queens are made of, and she is of irreproachable stock both on her father's and on her mother's side. She is the late Monsieur's grandchild but not mine, as you know; but the dear child writes to me with such warmth as if she were indeed my grandchild. The reason is that her mother[3] was barely two years old when I came to France; since she did not know her own mother, she came to love me as if she were my own child. I also love the good Duchess with all my heart and do not make much difference between my own children and Her Grace. She has impressed it on her daughter the Queen that she should love me.

1. In 1687, the Marquis de Lavardin, French ambassador to the papal court (and, by extension, Louis XIV and his government) had been excommunicated by Innocent XI for refusing to give up the right to grant asylum to anyone who applied for it in the French embassy at Rome.   2. Philip V of Spain, grandson of Louis XIV, had married Marie-Louise-Gabrielle of Savoy, Madame's step-granddaughter.   3. The youngest of Madame's stepdaughters.

To ELECTRESS SOPHIE

Versailles, 17 November 1701

That dear child, the Queen,[1] was not warned that all her people would be sent back; when the poor child got up in the morning, she found a lot of horrid, ugly old women instead of her own people. She began to cry and wanted to go back with her people. The good King, who is already very fond of her, thought that this would be possible, and since he is still a bit childish himself he too wept and thought that his wife would leave him. But they consoled him by pointing out that this could not happen because the marriage is consumated. As it was described to me, the Queen felt just as I felt when I was given Madame Trelon instead of my dear Frau von Harling. This was greatly taken amiss here; but I told the King that one should rather just laugh at it and be glad that the Queen has such a faithful character. The dames du palais by whom this queen is surrounded are wicked old things. The Queen requested to be given French food, since Spanish cooking does not agree with her, so the King ordered the Queen's food to be prepared by his French chefs. When the ladies saw that, they had Spanish food prepared for the Queen anyway, served only these plates, and did not bring in the French ones. This made the King angry and he forbade the Spanish cooks to cook anything and had everything prepared in the French manner. When the ladies saw that, they took the French soups and poured all the broth off; they said it might spoil their dresses and brought the Queen the soup without the broth. The same thing they did with the *ragouts*. They refused to touch the big platters of roasts, such as leg of mutton or loin roast, saying that their hands are too delicate to carry such platters. So they just pulled three chickens out of another platter of roast meat with their hands, put them on a plate, and served that to the Queen. It would be hard to find more wicked people than these, and on top of that they are horribly ugly.

1. Marie-Louise-Gabrielle of Savoy.

Versailles, 4 December 1701

I never heard of such a thing as a goosedown blanket; what keeps me nice and warm in my bed are six little dogs that lie around me; no blanket is as warm as the good little dogs. . . .

The little Queen of Spain has now gotten used to things and has resigned herself to them. I feel sorry for the dear child. She writes to me often and so lovingly that she has quite won my heart. Madame de Bracciano, who is now called the Princesse des Ursins, will continue to be *camarera majore;* they say that the King of Spain thinks exceedingly highly of her. She has a rather strange duty: when the King comes to sleep with the Queen, she must take off and put on his dressing gown at night and in the morning and also carry his sword and his chamber pot from room to room. This amuses the young Queen, and she has given me a very funny description of the palace etiquette.

To RAUGRÄFIN LUISE

Versailles, 10 December 1701

As for your wish that God may send me everything I need for my temporal and eternal well-being, I am much obliged to you for it, but in this world I no longer expect any well-being; I am much too old to enjoy anything. As for the eternal one, I do hope that since I faithfully pray to God, do my best to live according to His commandments and to serve Him without superstition, I will, after the many tribulations He has visited upon me in this life, have done enough penance for my sins and will, through my trust in the redemption by our Lord Jesus Christ, go to heaven after this life has ended. In short, I do not worry about this world or the next. . . .

My household is so large that even though the King gives me a 250,000-franc pension, and even including my dowry property and everything, I am still short a sum equal to the royal pension if I am to live according to my rank. The reason is that all court offices carry an income, and since all of them are purchased, I cannot abolish any of them; in addition everything has become so expensive as to be out of reach. So it is by no means true that the monies from the Palatinate are an extra, and play money, as it were; I must have them to keep up my rank, and there will be nothing left to put aside. . . . The doctors of law, I can see, are just like those of medicine. I can easily imagine how much you would wish to be rid of these people.

To ELECTRESS SOPHIE

Marly, 15 December 1701

I once asked a reasonable person why our King is always praised in all writings. I was told that the printers have been given express orders not to print any book that does not contain the King's praise, and that this was done to impress the King's subjects. For the French read a great deal, and in the provinces they read everything that comes from Paris; to read the praise of the King therefore gives them the proper veneration and respect for him. That is why it is done, and not for the King, who never hears or sees any of this, now that His Majesty no longer goes to the opera.

To RAUGRÄFIN AMALIE ELISABETH

Versailles, 23 December 1701

Not much is new at court right now, but some extraordinary stories are heard in Paris. A young burgher's daughter, fairly well-to-do and fourteen years old, was taken advantage of by a young fellow and became pregnant. She was clever enough to conceal the thing and to be delivered in secret, giving birth to a son. She immediately took him to the *enfants trouvés*[1] as if he were not her child, but marked him, so that in time she would be able to recognize him. For a few years she took very good care of the child and gave him everything he needed. Eventually a rich merchant of Paris fell in love with this young woman and married her. Being, as I said before, a clever girl, she thought that if she continued to go to the *enfants trouvés* her husband would become suspicious, especially if she were to take money; so she made up her mind at once not to go there any more. Thus she lived for twenty years with her husband, who made all his property over to her and then died.

She had a great inclination for her husband's first clerk; he was fond of her too, and she married him this summer. When her husband was with her without clothes, she suddenly noticed that his body bore the mark she had put on her son. This gave her a start, but she did not let on and went straight to the *enfants trouvés* to ask what had happened to the boy she had left there. They said that as he was growing up he had shown an inclination for business, had therefore learned that trade, and gone to work in the business of a rich merchant, and then they named her first husband. Now the woman could no longer doubt that her second husband was her son. She went straight to her confessor and told him the whole story. The confessor said that she should keep it all secret and not sleep with her husband until the matter has been placed before the Sorbonne. It is not yet known what the Sorbonne has decided; if I hear about it, I will let you know.

1. The Foundlings' Home.

To ELECTRESS SOPHIE

Versailles, 29 December 1701

I am quite certain that Your Grace does not have as many wrinkles as I do. I have them because for many years I have often been burned by the sun while hunting. But this does not bother me in the slightest; I was never beautiful and therefore have not lost much. Moreover I see that those whom I used to see when they were so beautiful are now as ugly as I am: Madame de la Vallière no one in the world would know any more, and Madame de Montespan's skin looks like paper when children do tricks with it, seeing who can fold it into the smallest piece, for her whole face is closely covered with tiny little wrinkles, quite amazing. Her lovely hair is all white, and her face is red, so her beauty is quite gone. Therefore I do not feel badly that I never had what fades so quickly. Your Grace has a beauty that can never fade, namely great intelligence and vivacity, generosity and kindness, and constancy toward those who have once gained Your Grace's good will; and this is also the reason that all and sundry are so attached to Your Grace and that I, for one, remain until death utterly devoted to Your Grace as her own bondswoman.

Versailles, 8 January 1702

I am doing my best not to become melancholy and try to keep busy in order not to think of the past and the future. . . . Your Grace is very right in saying that the world is like a garden full of different herbs, good and bad; it is true that weeds wither as early as the good plants, but they are quicker to spring up again. Mistress Kolb used to say, "Something new every day, but rarely anything good." . . .

Why would Your Grace want to hold back anything that flows into her pen? After all, Your Grace is only speaking to her Liselotte who takes great pleasure in reading everything Your Grace writes. If I stopped writing in German I would completely forget my German, and that I should regret very much, therefore I always write to Your Grace in our mother tongue. If Ma Tante the Abbess of Maubuisson had written in German more often, Her Grace would not have forgotten her German so soon. She writes a very good hand in French, but her spelling is faulty and she often forgets words. Still, she has not lost her vivacity, and her letters are quite funny.

Versailles, 12 January 1702

The reason that I have not forgotten the Lutheran hymns is that I sing them every year with Frau von Ratsamhausen[1] when she is here; so unfortunately my memory is not as good as Your Grace imagines. I do not think that the King of Spain will be able to abolish the Inquisition; the monks, especially the Dominicans, are just too dangerous. The King's life would not be safe if he attacked them.

> 1. Eleanore von Ratsamhausen, a friend of Madame's youth, whom she also called "the Rotzenhäuserin."

Marly, 9 February 1702

If my advice had been followed, the authorities here would have sought to make better Christians rather than more Catholics and to change peoples' morals rather than their faith, which can never be forced; and I believe that if this had been done things would now be better than they are, and there would be more money in the country. Although there are no slaves here, the King is so absolute that none of his subjects, whoever they may be, may leave this country without His Majesty's permission.

To RAUGRÄFIN LUISE

Versailles, 12 March 1702

Dear Frau von Harling's death has deeply touched my heart; I am very sad about it, and while it was best for the poor woman, since she could never have been well again and would only have suffered, one always grieves to lose a good friend. I believe that the good Queen of Prussia will also be sorry, for she too was brought up by the good woman.[1] I do not know the circumstances of the good woman's death. Please tell me about it! . . .

The confounded priests in Rome have caused me to lose my court case,[2] but fortunately the sentence is put together in such an outlandish way that I am assured it can be contested, so my advisers here do not think the matter is settled yet. I do not think that I shall see the end of this litigation in my lifetime. So be it! If only my children benefit, I do not care.

1. The Electress's daughter, Sophie Charlotte, and her son, later King Friedrich Wilhelm I, had also been raised by Frau von Harling. 2. The litigation about Elisabeth Charlotte's property rights in the Palatinate, which had been submitted to the arbitration of the Pope in 1685. Cf. letter of 1 November 1685.

To RAUGRÄFIN AMALIE ELISABETH

Meudon, 8 April 1702

In my time the nobility of Hanover were not so proud; they were willing to give the Imperial counts all the honors to which they are entitled. Since when has this changed? Does one now say *hoffenherzig* in German, as you write? In my time one said *offenherzig*. It makes me feel very good that you say that I have not completely forgotten my German. I now speak it so rarely that I shall soon have forgotten it; however, I now put my hopes in Frau von Rotzenhausen who will come here soon, and with whom I always speak German.

To ELECTRESS SOPHIE

Versailles, 20 April 1702

Yesterday I gave Madame de Châteauthiers a beautiful parrot, which talks amazingly well. I wanted to hear what it can say and let it into my room; my dogs became jealous and one of them, by the name of Mione, started to bark at it; the parrot kept saying: "Give me your paw." I wish Your Grace could have seen how surprised Mione was to hear the bird talk: she stopped barking, stared at it, then looked at me; and when it continued to talk, she took fright like a human being, ran away and hid under the day bed, and at that point the parrot screamed with laughter. That made me think of Herr Leibniz, since Your Grace tells me that he maintains that animals are endowed with reason, are not machines as Descartes has claimed, and that their souls are immortal.[1] In the next world I will be delighted to find not only my family and good friends but also my dear little animals. But the joke would be on me if it should mean that my soul will become as mortal as theirs and that all of us will be nothing together; therefore I would rather believe the other notion, which is much more comforting.

1. Leibniz later wrote an article titled *Commentatio de anima brutorum* (*Commentary on the Souls of Animals*).

To RAUGRÄFIN LUISE

Dearest Luise, a number of days have gone by since I duly received your letter of 6 April, but I did not have a chance to answer it before now because of the celebration of Easter, when one has to spend the entire day in church here; and I must confess that on the days after the holy days, in order to make up for the boredom I had to endure in the churches, listening to the (just between us) eternal bawling of Latin, I decided to take advantage of the lovely weather and to take some rides to Trianon, which is the most beautiful garden one can ever hope to see. . . .

I was most sorry to hear of King William's death.[1] Last autumn Lenor[2] sent me an Augsburg Almanac for this year; it clearly foretold this king's death with the following words: "NB♂♄☉, 20 March 1702. A potentate goes to his grave / and others will be glad; / so now there is a vacancy / and room for something new."[3] I can easily imagine all the allies' grief about King William's death. . . .

All we hear is talk of war and soldiering. The Duc de Bourgogne will be off to the army on Tuesday next. Everywhere one sees people who are taking their leave. The court will soon be quite empty; but that is the least of my worries, for it does not deprive me of any company, since I am alone in my sitting room all day long and not bored; indeed I find the days too short. I have many flowers outside my window, many dogs of which I am very fond, engraved stones, and lots of books; these things are enough to amuse me, and they do not offend God or the world. One of my prettiest bitches just had puppies in my room.

1. William of Orange had died on 19 March; his sister-in-law Anne became Queen of England. The further succession designated the house of Hanover. 2. Eleanore von Ratsamhausen. 3. The signs stand for Mars, Saturn, and Sun.

To ELECTRESS SOPHIE

On Friday last the King led me to the stag hunt in his calash; I greatly needed some distraction, for my heart was still dreadfully heavy because I had lost my poor Mione. Yesterday when I returned from Marly, it gave me another pang to see all her sisters coming to greet me without her. I miss her everywhere, in bed and on the promenade; at the toilet table in the morning she always lay on my lap, and when I was writing she sat behind me on the easy chair. She was always with me, and the most beautiful little creature in the world, with a short little face and big, beautiful eyes full of fire and intelligence. But Your Grace will think Liselotte has gone out of her mind with her dog, but my dearest Ma Tante, I cannot help it, I must tell Your Grace all my joys and sorrows, and so I had to let Your Grace know about the loss of my poor Mione and how much I have taken it to heart. . . .

Today I received a letter from my brother's wife; she is very pious and gave me a long sermon about how we must not be afraid of death. . . . I am far from such perfection, I must admit it, and unfortunately a strong faith is not at all in my nature. I say "unfortunately" because I can see that it makes people happy, and I do think that, since we must die anyway, it is a wonderful thing to be convinced that one will be much happier after death and therefore look forward to dying. I am so coarse that I must confess I cannot conceive of anything agreeable without my senses, and I cannot get it through my head how I could see anything agreeable without my eyes, hear anything agreeable without my ears, or think without my head; and that rather keeps me from looking forward to dying. I cannot deny it, in this respect I am quite unlike my late brother who did experience a foretaste of life eternal. This is a grace that Our Lord grants to very few people; but I am too unworthy to reason about these things and will therefore speak of something else. . . . To comfort myself about my poor Mione I thought about Herr Leibniz's opinion right away. It is quite certain that Our Lord will arrange everything for the best, and that we must leave everything to Him, for whether we leave it to Him or not, things will happen according to His will anyway. . . .

Oh how I wish that I could help Your Grace count her paces on her promenade; even if it were to make me sweat to follow Your Grace with my fat belly and my, begging your leave, fat behind, I should be ever so happy to toddle after Your Grace and cannot think of anything in the world that would give me more pleasure than to wait on my dearest Ma Tante.

To RAUGRÄFIN LUISE

Versailles, 12 May 1702

I have to laugh that you are glad that I am not taken in by the bawling of Latin. Except for a few real simpletons, no one here is taken in by it; one only goes to these places in order not to scandalize the populace, but otherwise no one sets much store by it. But as for getting out of this nonsense altogether, that is quite out of the question; my calling and filial obedience have brought me here, and here I must live and die and fulfill what was foreordained for me. I serve my God as best I know and understand, and for the rest trust in His Ways. . . .

Here we always hear the good news but rarely the bad, and yet I would like to know everything. . . .

The commissioners in Rome who handled my case were paid 50,000 *talers* each. Abbé de Thessut has seen the original receipts. When he told this to the Pope, the Pope replied: "I am to be pitied that I must deal with such godless, false, and wicked people who twist justice for money!" But of righting this wrong he did not say a word. Abbé de Thessut is much more distressed about this than I am, for I gave this case up for lost as soon as Monsieur sent it to Rome, had made up my mind about it, and therefore was not upset when the news arrived. . . .

I thank you very much for the verses you sent me. I find them quite clever and not as scandalous as you do; on the contrary, they are quite funny. If you should receive more lampoons of this kind, please send them to me. Here we have absolutely nothing new; to quote the Hinderson[1] one might say that things are *schlappjes*. Tomorrow I hope to have Lenor with me; I am sure she will bring me some news.

1. Lady-in-waiting at Hanover; she accompanied Elisabeth Charlotte to France and married the Marquis de Foix.

To ELECTRESS SOPHIE

Marly, 6 July 1702

We are told that there will soon be a battle in Flanders, for the two armies are facing each other, separated only by a small marsh; in Italy too something is liable to happen soon. It certainly is a dreadful thing that we poor humans, whose lifetime is so short to begin with, are going to such trouble to shorten one another's lives even further and do each other in as if it were so many mosquitoes. Speaking of mosquitoes: the confounded gnats here do not let me have an hour's sleep; they have chewed me up so much that I look as if I had smallpox again. We are also plagued with wasps; not a day goes by that someone is not stung. A few days ago there was tremendous laughter: one of these wasps had flown under a lady's skirt; the lady ran around like mad because the wasp was stinging her high up on the thigh, she pulled up her skirt, ran around, and cried, "Help! Close your eyes and take it off!" It sounded just too funny. . . .

I do not know anything new, and even if I knew something, I would not be allowed to say it, because I have been warned that the people who read my letters are making rather strange comments about them in order to get me in trouble with the King. . . . If the King were to do me the kindness to ask me about this, I should certainly be able to answer for myself, and I wish I had a chance to confront the little minister with the perpetual grin on his face;[1] I am certain that he would not wish to face me with his false interpretations. Will the gentleman who translates from the German please translate this carefully, so that the minister knows exactly how I feel; and if I should hear anything more about this, I shall spare him the trouble of speaking further to the King, for I shall apply for an audience myself and ask His Majesty whether he has ordered all my letters to be opened and commented upon. What I write can be read by everyone, as long as it is reported without lies and falsification. I do not know why this little man is so keen to hurt me; I have never done him any harm and should think that, given the important matters of State at hand, he would have better things to do than to puzzle over my letters to my closest kin in order to make trouble for me.

1. Torcy, who was in charge of the mail.

To RAUGRÄFIN AMALIE ELISABETH

Versailles, 22 July 1702

Dearest Amelise, about my recent illness I will say nothing more; I am now, thanks be to God, in perfect health and on the day before yesterday duly received your welcome letter of the thirteenth of this month. That I keenly feel and regret Karl Moritz's death and also that I have conveyed my heartfelt sympathy to you and Luise does not deserve any thanks, it is no more than I owe you. You are doing the right and Christian thing to resign yourself to God's will, for to fight it would serve no purpose other than to make yourself ill. That women, who are usually not too happy, do not care if they die does not surprise me, but I am surprised that Karl Moritz was so glad to die. If Karl Moritz had not loved wine so much, he would have been a perfect philosopher. But for this he paid dearly, because I am convinced that drink shortened his life. That he could not be without drinking is shown by his overheated and burnt liver. I wish he could have bequeathed his good memory to me, I could certainly use it here. I know very well why no one liked Karl Eduard[1] as much as Karl Moritz. He was too sly and never ever wanted to say his opinion; I was never able to get out of him what he hated or loved, liked or disliked. I used to ask him a thousand times, "Tell me what you like to do, what you enjoy." Then he would only make a deep bow, give an embarrassed little laugh, but aside from that I could not get anything out of him; that is tiresome and makes one impatient in the long run, and so I did not like him nearly as much as Carllutz. As for Carllutz, I still cannot think of him without getting tears in my eyes. Whatever one may do to prepare for misfortune, when it comes one is still bound to feel it; and especially when one loses a close relative, the blood is bound to stir. . . .

When the French court was as it used to be, one could really learn manners here! But now that no one, except the King and Monseigneur, knows what *politesse* is, when all the young people think of nothing but sheer and disgusting debauchery, and when the most unmannerly are considered to be the cleverest of all, I would not adivse anyone to let his children get into that, for instead of learning good manners they would learn nothing but bad habits here. So you are quite right in disapproving of the many Germans who now want to send their children to France. One must always have respect for those who give their blood and property for their fatherland, I certainly agree with you there. I wish you and I were men and in the war; this is a useless wish to make, but sometimes one cannot help it.

1. Another half-brother.

It is no wonder that people who rarely speak French sometimes mix up a letter. I am keeping my promise to correct your French for you, but you and Luise do not correct my German sentences, even though I think they are often in need of correction. For I rarely speak German and realize that it no longer comes as easily as it used to; so if I do not have help I am sure to forget it. Even though I read every day in my German Bible, a psalm and a chapter in the Old Testament and one in the New Testament, this is not the same as speaking every day. Nor can I learn to speak properly from the Rotzenhäuserin, for she speaks a terrible German herself; I am teaching her more than she teaches me. There is nothing shameful about not speaking a foreign language properly; one must simply speak up in order to be corrected, that is the best way to learn. Since everyone in Germany now wants to speak and write French, I am surprised that they do not watch their spelling better. Why is it that you have a French lady of honor? For they are usually of very bad nobility, and not even comparable to our German nobility; any commoner here who buys an office of *secrétaire du roi* is immediately considered a *gentilhomme,* and moreover they never have any qualms about misalliances and marry all kinds of commoners' daughters, even peasant girls, just so long as they have money, and therefore are often kin to all kinds of artisans. Ordinary nobility commands very little respect here.

To ELECTRESS SOPHIE

Meudon, 14 December 1702

The proverb says, "The days go by and each one is different"; that is what has happened to the King's armies this year. The French troops are as good as their leaders; if they have chiefs whom they trust, they fight like lions, but if their generals are faint-hearted and lack daring in the first heat of battle, they give up right away.

Versailles, 22 December 1702

We keep hearing about the entertainments at the court of Wolfenbüttel; I think they are quite right to be always merry there. When one is always occupied with agreeable things, one does not feel the approach of old age. Here they still do not want to believe that the Dutch want war; I also hear that the Palatine Elector is very ill-disposed toward France. I know the

French; they may be angry at their King, but their anger goes no further than the singing of songs against his Majesty, and for all that, every one of them would rather starve to death than leave their King without money, so the resources of this country are greater than one might think.

When Monsieur de Créqui returned from his embassy in Rome he brought back the body of a saint, which he wanted to present to a church or a monastery. Such relics, if they consist of a saint's whole body, are received with great ceremony, for a bishop in full regalia lifts the body out of the crate in order to place it into the church's reliquary. When everything was in readiness, the crate was brought and opened with the usual ceremonies. But when the bishop pulled out its contents, there was nothing in the crate but big sausages and Bologna salamies, for the crates had been mixed up by mistake. There was much laughter when the sausages were brought out with such solemnity, and the bishop left in great embarrassment.

I have never had a miscarriage, but it seems obvious that there must be less pain when something small comes out of the body than when it is large. It has been some time since I have been safe from such trouble, and ever since I was delivered of my daughter I have not been in any such danger, for very soon thereafter Monsieur began to sleep in a different bed, and I did not enjoy the business enough to ask the late Monsieur to return to my bed. When His Grace slept in my bed I had to lie so close to the edge that I sometimes fell out of bed in my sleep, for His Grace did not like to be touched, and if perchance I happened to stretch a foot in my sleep and to touch him, he would wake me up and scold me for half an hour. Consequently I was well content when His Grace decided on his own accord to sleep in his own room and to let me lie in peace in my own bed, without having to worry about being scolded in the middle of the night or falling out of bed.

Once the excitement caused by Monsieur's sudden death had abated, Madame's life became easier. It is true that she was, much to her chagrin, usually excluded from the King's private circle, but at least she did not have to worry about Monsieur's erratic behavior, which had upset her so often in the past. Many of her letters during the years 1701–5 are concerned with religious questions; her interest was undoubtedly stimulated by the intense preoccupation with religious matters on the part of many of the most important personalities at court: the dévôt *circle around Madame de Maintenon had completely captivated the King; his former mistresses were doing penance for their sins in convents; the young Duc de Bourgogne preferred prayer and meditation to court functions; Jansenism continued to attract some of the best minds in the French Church and in the judiciary; the persecution of the Huguenots was at its height; and the Calvinists in the Cevennes were actually rebelling against the government. In Germany, meanwhile, Madame's half-sisters were increasingly influenced by the* Schwärmerei *of "born-again" Protestant preachers, whose narrow-mindedness contrasted sharply with the latitudinarian attitude that had pervaded her father's court in her youth. In thinking and reading about these matters, Elisabeth Charlotte truly developed "a little religion all her own."*

Versailles, 1 February 1703

The populace here is still very superstitious; the *dévôts*[1] act as if they were pious but are not; the others keep still about it. . . . They say that there is amazing wealth at Loretto. But I do not see what this is good for, since Mary, the Mother of Our Lord Christ, does not need anything in heaven and also got along quite well in this world without riches, for she lived and died a poor woman. Why, then, do they want to tell us that she has become greedy in that world where she does not need anything and that she does not do anything unless she is given presents? That is a heavy and unnecessary expense for great lords and to my mind a bad idea. . . .

Nothing in the world can give me more pleasure than Your Grace's kind letters; what else could Your Grace tell me but day-to-day occurrences? Philosophy I do not understand; theology even less; and affairs of State I do not know anything about either; so Your Grace is bound to conform to my weakness and must tell me things that I can know and understand. God forbid that Your Grace should ply me with high-flown discourses, for in that case I could no longer write to Your Grace and would have to live in fear that Your Grace might say, Silly old Liselotte, what is this foolish and tiresome babble of hers, she had better keep quiet.

1. Religious zealots, especially at the court.

Versailles, 28 February 1703

Monsieur Goertz[1] just came in to tell me that he has his passport and is about to return to Hanover. I shall use this opportunity to give him this letter, so that for once the confounded Torcy cannot steal it. I am sending Your Grace a song . . . expressing discontent with the King and the Prince de Conti, which I could not send through the mail. Otherwise I have little news to tell Your Grace through this good opportunity. Things are going along in the usual way.

1. Freiherr Friedrich Wilhelm von Goertz, a court official at Hanover.

To RAUGRÄFIN LUISE

Versailles, 8 April 1703

The war must have altered the air in the Palatinate, what with all the burning; for in my time there were all kinds of people at Heidelberg, Mannheim, and also in the mountains behind the Neuburg monastery who were over a hundred years old. Near the Neuburg monastery I met a man who still worked in the forest at one hundred and ten; at Mannheim there was a man of a hundred and two, and his wife was a hundred years old, and my brother told me that near Meisenheim he saw a peasant who was a hundred-and-twenty-four years old. So you see that there used to be many examples of this.

To ELECTRESS SOPHIE

15 April 1703

In my day bride and groom did not sit on any benches but stood up straight before the parson. Marriages that begin with laughter are not always the happiest ones. But we all nearly died laughing when Monsieur le Dauphin was married to Madame la Dauphine at Châlons: the Grande Mademoiselle stood on the highest step, her foot slipped, and she fell on the Cardinal de Bouillon, who was about to unite the couple; the Cardinal fell on Monsieur le Dauphin and Madame la Dauphine, and they too would have fallen down if the King had not stretched out his arm to catch them. They fell like a deck of cards. In those days I was still thin and light; I realized that Mademoiselle was about to fall on me and jumped down four steps at once, that is why she fell on the cardinal. That the bridegroom slept through the wedding sermon I can forgive him, it is difficult to avoid. And in any case it was good for the bride that he did not need any more rest, having slept before he went to bed.

17 May 1703

My little dogs are more eager to please me than Your Grace might think, for they are jealous of one another, and so each of them thinks of something to outdo the others. Rachille usually sits down behind me on my chair, and Titti lies down next to me on my writing table; Mademoiselle Minette lies on my feet under my skirt; Charmion, her mother, whines until someone places a chair next to mine, where she lies down; Charmante lies on my skirt on the other side; Stabdille sits on a chair across from me and ogles me, and Charmille lies under my arm, and so they spend almost the whole day. I have to laugh that Your Grace considers my little dogs more reasonable than the pietists.[1] I doubt that one can feel an inner joy that does not appear outwardly; it seems to me that the eyes betray it right away. But if it should be true that many blows make them happy, they can easily be happier than other people, for blows are easier to come by than good things. . . .

Your Grace is too kind to believe that I am intelligent, but I fear that Your Grace's kind affection for me makes her judge me rather too favorably. Even if I had had some intelligence, it would have been worn down by the many vexations and all the constraints I have endured here and also by my immense solitude, which causes one to become rusty. But as long as I shall have enough intelligence to please Your Grace, I will be quite content.

1. Electress Sophie took a very dim view of the preacher August Hermann Francke (1663–1727) and his followers, who practiced a most austere Christianity that condemned all earthly pleasures as vain and indeed sinful and considered suffering in this world as the prerequisite of eternal bliss in the next. First elaborated at the University of Halle, the Pietist movement had a wide following among all classes of German society; in 1700, for example, Electress Sophie reported to Raugräfin Luise that the Duchess of Eisenach had been converted by Pastor Francke and now went in for "Pietist nonsense," such as refusing to drive with six horses, eating out of wooden bowls, and leading her servants in prayer. (E. Bodemann, ed. *Briefe der Kurfürstin Sophie von Hannover an die Raugrafen und Raugräfinnen von der Pfalz* [Leipzig 1888].)

Versailles, 11 November 1703

After dinner I spoke to a merchant who has traveled a great deal and has visited all of Egypt, Persia, and Judea, and the stories he told were so interesting that if I had not planned to write to Your Grace I think I would have listened to him all day long. He says that in the Nile there are four-footed animals that prey on the crocodiles; but if, as is the custom there, the men swim across the Nile, these creatures chase after them and bite off their private parts, although otherwise they do not eat human flesh. He also said that in Egypt he has seen flying animals with human faces, and that he once shot one; an Arab who was with him at the time told him that he must not touch the creature because it was very poisonous and dangerous. He also ate a fruit between Jerusalem and Damascus that prevents him from swallowing any other fruit now; he can chew it but not swallow it. Also, he saw a crowned snake, which in that country they think is a devil, namely Asmodeus, the devil that was banished to Egypt by the angel who was Tobias's companion. He has many other fine stories of that kind, and they will all be in his book, which he wants to dedicate to me.

Versailles, 18 December 1703

I predicted right away that my marriage would not serve any useful purpose, but Your Grace and the Elector my father did not want to believe me. Someone must have given the King a horrendous aversion to my company, for he will not spend one moment with me. At Marly His Majesty permits me to follow his hunt, for there each person goes in his own calash; but here the King has gone hunting twice without taking me along because from here I would have to ride with him in his coach. At first, I must admit, I was a bit hurt by this contempt, but now I have made up my mind that I will no longer fret about these things. . . .

I am too fond of our King and Queen of Spain to call another man King of Spain; and as the Scripture says: he who has the bride is the groom; therefore, since our prince is King of Spain and recognized as such by the peoples there, he must be the true king, and not the archduke. Aside from that, I do not deny the archduke's good qualities; I believe that he is intelligent, well-mannered, and handsome; I hope that he will chase away the Turks and become Emperor over all of Asia, but I want all of Spain to remain in the hands of our young King.

To RAUGRÄFIN AMALIE ELISABETH

Versailles, 30 March 1704

I have not performed the good work of keeping the fast; fish does not agree with me and I feel strongly that one can do better works than to upset one's stomach with too much fish. . . .

Since I have the honor to know the King of Poland, I am sorry for him; yet no one can deny that he was very foolish to make himself King of Poland. Here one could truthfully say, "Pride goeth before a fall." . . . To speak quite frankly, it seems to me that what is going on in Germany is so outlandish that it looks as if the Germans were no longer Germans; what I hear about it makes me think that I would not recognize anything and that everything must be amazingly changed.

You speak well about the pains suffered by women given to coquetry, but not about their joys. One suffers more for the sake of human beings than for the sake of eternal salvation, because to love human beings befits our weakness, whereas eternal salvation is so inconceivable a notion that it does not easily find a place in the human heart. I am not given to coquetry by nature, as everyone will attest; yet I do understand what human weakness can do and pity those who fall into such calamities more than I condemn them. The preachers in their pulpits say what they are supposed to say, and not always what they think or know. I agree that temporal happiness is not worth much, but eternal and heavenly bliss is hard to understand, and I think that it is a pure grace of God if the Almighty illuminates a human being enough to understand the divine and eternal salvation. I do believe that as long as we keep asking God to grant us this grace, we should not fret too much about what others do. In this world everyone has his troubles. God alone knows why He has ordained everything and how He has set the day and the hour for each of us; to Him I resign myself in everything.

To ELECTRESS SOPHIE

I had thought that Herrenhausen was Your Grace's widow's seat and that
nothing could be changed there without Your Grace's orders. I have no house
now except my widow's seat, the old château of Montargis, but that is a
three or four days' journey from here. If I went there I would get stuck in
that château and lead a most boring life like a lady of the gentry, without any
honors or anything. That does not befit me, so I prefer to keep going along
here, even though I am not admitted to the inner sanctum and am not among
the chosen few. . . .

I had an interesting time watching one of my bitches having puppies;
in a half hour she has already had two; now Monsieur Titti, who is not even
twenty-five months old, already has thirty-two children, and all without
being united with the words "Be fruitful and multiply."

Marly, 26 April 1704

This morning we already caught a stag. The weather is perfectly beautiful,
and one cannot think of a more agreeable place than the preserve where we
hunt. This morning it was not too warm because there was a cool breeze;
the forest is full of cowslips and violets; together with the young foliage this
gives a wonderful smell to the air. The woods are full of nightingales; if one
follows a false lead, as happened to me today, and does not hear the hounds
and bugles, one still has this lovely music, which sounds all the sweeter
after the great noise of hounds and bugles.

To RAUGRÄFIN AMALIE ELISABETH

Versailles, 29 April 1704

Are you really so simple-minded that you think the Catholics do not know
the fundamentals of Christianity? Believe me, dear Amelise, the fundamental
tenets of Christianity are the same in all Christian religions. The differences
are only a matter of priests' squabbles, which are never the business of gentle-
folk. Our only business is to lead a good and Christian life, to be merciful,
and to practice charity and virtue. The reverend preachers should endeavor
to preach this to the Christians rather than worry about how every little
point is to be understood, but that would diminish these gentlemen's authority. That is why they are only interested in this and not in the most important and most necessary matters. . . . Lenor is here with me and has asked
me to tell you, dear Amelise, that she begs you not to become too devout,
because she wants to go to heaven in the same chariot with you. These words
will tell you that her temperament is still the same.

To ELECTRESS SOPHIE

Versailles, 1 May 1704

Today we are celebrating a religious holiday[1] like Your Grace and will have
to go to Vespers this afternoon, which is tiresome indeed. Today Your Grace
will sing, "To God on high alone / be praise and thanks for his gra-ha-hace /
that henceforth and forever / no ha-ha-harm can co-ho-home to us" (that is
how it was sung in my time). "God does rejoice in us / peace reigns forever
now" (I do not know where it has gone), "all strife is at an e-he-hend" (although it seems to me that there is still plenty of strife everywhere). The
holy days of the Reformed and the Lutherans are not as tiresome as those of
the Catholics; in the first place the services of the former are not as long,
and in the second place one can understand what is being sung and sing along,
that passes the time; but the bawling of Latin is hopeless, and besides it goes
on and on. The laws of the Almighty are badly kept, for it seems to me that
there has never been more hatred among men than now. It is surely a pity that
since life is so short, human beings, instead of using what reason they have
to live happily and joyfully, should be so intent on making life miserable for
themselves and others. That is ill-considered and altogether contrary to
God's command; however, since all things are foreordained, Our Lord must
want it to be this way, for otherwise it would be different. . . .

If I had to read novels all the time and in one sitting, I would get bored
with them, but I read only three or four pages when I am sitting, begging your
leave, on the pot in the morning and at night, and in this way I am amused
and neither fatigued nor bored.

1. Ascension Day.

Marly, 10 July 1704

The people in the Cévennes must not be really Reformed, for the Reformed
do not hold with inspirations as these people do. A few days ago I spoke
to a nobleman who comes from there and used to be Reformed himself; from
his description the insurrectionists sounded more like Quakers. He was with
them trying to persuade them to surrender to the King. They were all ready to
do it when all of a sudden a girl of eleven or twelve came running along, crying out, "I have an inspiration, do not trust him or you will be deceived."
Hearing that, they immediately changed their minds and wanted to kill this
gentleman; he barely escaped from their hands. The young girl was a parson's daughter. Yet they do not have real parsons either; one of the artisans
simply steps forward and begins to preach.

I can see that Your Grace is of my late Papa's opinion and also believes that things would be better in the world if we could get rid of the three kinds of charlatans: priests, doctors, and lawyers. I believe that it is not the fault of the true religion that things are going so badly but that it is the fault of those who use religion as a pretext for their own politics. I have to laugh about Your Grace's litany of all the evils that have been wrought by religion, which is almost as long as Saint Paul's litany of those who have been justified by their faith. The end of Your Grace's letter is a paraphrase of Our Lord Christ's own words, for He says that to love God with all our souls and all our hearts is to follow the law and the prophets; so it must be the true religion. . . .

I can drink neither tea, nor chocolate, nor coffee; all this foreign stuff is repugnant to me: I find chocolate too sweet, coffee tastes like soot to me, and tea more like a medicine, in short, in this respect as in many others I cannot be à la mode.

Versailles, 26 October 1704

I feel sorry for the Princess of Ansbach because I know what it is to be in that situation.[1] If one wants to convince someone, one must stick to true things and not utter such foolishness as that the pope is the Antichrist; he may not be a good Christian, but he is not the Antichrist. I am sure that Your Grace will dispel all the scruples of this princess. . . .

It would scarcely have behooved me to worry about my finery; having been ugly all my life, I never enjoyed looking at my bear-cat-monkeyface in the mirror, so it is no wonder that I did not do it very often. But to be young and beautiful and yet not enjoy looking into the mirror like the Princess of Ansbach, that is unusual indeed.

> 1. At the time Karoline of Ansbach was receiving instruction in the Catholic faith because she was to marry Archduke Charles. In the end, however, she decided against the conversion and broke the engagement. In 1705 she was married to the heir to the electorate of Hanover, Georg August, who later became King George II of England. As Karoline of Wales, the princess was to correspond with Madame for many years.

Versailles, 16 November 1704

Your Grace says that Our Lord God loves variety in everything, and this is the very answer that the King of Siam gave to our King's emissaries. When they pressed the aforesaid King to become a Christian and a Catholic, he said: "I believe that your King's religion is good, but if God wanted to be served by only *one* religion he would have put only *one* into the world, but since there are so many, it is a sign that he wants to be served in as many ways. So your King is right to stay in his religion and I in mine. And to prove that God loves variety, one only has to look at the many different things in nature." To this they did not exactly know how to respond. One thing I keep wondering about is that Our Lord Jesus Christ, when speaking of the Last Judgment, only says, "I was naked and you have not clothed me, I was thirsty and you have not given me drink, I was hungry and you have not fed me," but that he does not ever say, "You have not believed in me in the right way." So it appears that to do good is the foremost prescription for salvation; the rest is priests' squabbles.

Marly, 14 December 1704

Beauties have become exceedingly rare here; to be beautiful has gone quite out of fashion. The ladies are doing their bit too, for what with painting their ears white and pulling their hair tightly back from the temples, they all look like white rabbits when one holds them up by the ears so that they cannot get away and to my mind make themselves look quite ugly. And since they have also become so lazy that they go around unlaced all day long, their bodies are becoming thick so that they no longer have a waist. In short, one no longer sees beautiful bodies or faces.

Marly, 19 February 1705

This dear deceased Queen's[1] end as well as its cause prove once again that the time and manner of death are foreordained for everyone, otherwise so sensible a queen would not have refused to be bled or at least to take a potion after so severe a fall. Our dear Queen must have had a premonition of her death, as has happened to many others before her. . . . Since this calamity had to be, it must be considered a special grace of God that this dear queen was not touched by any fear of dying and moved on to the next world with such great courage.

1. On 1 February the Electress's daughter, Sophie Charlotte of Prussia, had died at Herrenhausen, near Hanover.

To RAUGRÄFIN LUISE

Marly, 19 February 1705

It is a shame what they are doing to the mail. In Monsieur de Louvois's day the letters were read just as they are now, but at least they were punctually delivered. But now since that little toad, Torcy, is in charge, one has to fret and worry terribly about the mail, and yet I have never been more impatient to receive news from Hanover because I am dreadfully afraid for Ma Tante the Electress in the disaster that has befallen her.

To ELECTRESS SOPHIE

Versailles, 9 April 1705

These are the days when one has to spend an awful lot of time in church; today I have already done a good five hours and was supposed to go to the *salute* too, but I could not have answered Your Grace's kind letter if I had gone there as well. When I returned from the high mass I was gladdened with two of Your Grace's kind letters; so God Almighty has already repaid me for the boredom I suffered in His service. . . . These days Your Grace will also be singing, "O Man Repent Your Grievous Sins." I still know the melody and at least six stanzas of this very long hymn. It is really much more agreeable when one can sing along instead of having to listen to some bawling in a language that one does not even understand; that is most distressing, especially if it goes on for three hours.

To RAUGRÄFIN AMALIE ELISABETH

Marly, 18 April 1705

When I hear that you cannot dissimulate, dear Amelise, I want to say, "I recognize my blood." I have never learned it either, although it would have stood me in excellent stead in this country where one finds so little sincerity. What keeps me from making friends here is that whenever one is friends with someone, people will immediately say that this person is in love with you or that you are in love with this person. That has made me break off all commerce, and I no longer have any friends at all, spending my life in solitude, rather boringly but at least in peace.

Marly, 16 May 1705

No Carthusian monk leads a quieter and more solitary life than I do. I think I shall end up by forgetting how to speak. However, I shall soon speak a little more; Frau von Rotzenhausen will arrive tonight or tomorrow; she and I often go through the old stories of our youth. Let me tell you about my life here: Every day except on Sunday and Thursday I arise at nine, then I kneel down to say my prayers and read my psalm and Bible chapter. After that I wash myself as clean as I can; thereafter I ring for my chambermaids who come in to dress me; at a quarter to eleven I am dressed; then I read or write. At twelve I go to mass, which lasts less than a half hour. After mass I talk to my ladies or others. At one o'clock sharp one goes to table. Right after dinner I walk up and down in my room for fifteen minutes, then I sit down at my table to write. By half past six I send for my ladies and we walk for an hour or an hour and a half, then it's back to my room until supper. Isn't this a real hermit's life? Sometimes I go along on the hunt, which lasts an hour, two at most, then it's back to my room. At the hunt I am all alone in a calash and often go to sleep if the hunt is not going well. Supper is at ten, and over at a quarter to eleven. Then I wind my clocks, put the things from my pocket in a basket, and undress. At twelve I go again where I go in the morning, read there, and then to bed. Such is my life, and it is not too much fun. As long as it lasts, you will always be dear to my heart.

To ELECTRESS SOPHIE

Versailles, 24 May 1705

One might say about Count Rappach's[1] drops what we hear in the Lutheran hymn, "For death there is no remedy, / good Christian man, prepare thy soul / for all that lives must die." Here they say that the Emperor, having received the sacraments, asked the doctors whether they knew of anything else that might help him. When they answered this question with "No," he called for all his musicians, sang hymns to their accompaniment, and thus died singing.[2] I do not believe that the priests will have as much credit with the new Emperor[3] as with his predecessor. . . .

It must be admitted that the King of Prussia[4] is most generous to provide so well for all his late wife's entourage; one does not see this very often. Since Berlin and Charlottenburg are so close, they may some day become a single town.

1. The Imperial ambassador at Wolfenbüttel. 2. Emperor Leopold had died on 5 May. 3. Joseph I. 4. Friedrich I.

Versailles, 7 June 1705

As for their concern that I might tell Your Grace what certain persons are saying, all it would take is the word "Do not write this," for the King cannot say that I have ever done anything against his orders, nor will I ever. But that is not the trouble; this concern is expressed to please those who dislike me, there's the rub . . . I assure Your Grace that my solitude is not at all annoying to me.

To RAUGRÄFIN AMALIE ELISABETH

Versailles, 18 June 1705

Dearest Amelise, you are quite right to keep your letters coming. It is not always necessary to tell me new or clever things; if that happens, so much the better, but as long as I know that you are well and what you are doing, I am quite content. I was never scolded for sleeping in church, which is why this has become such a habit that I cannot seem to break it. If there is a sermon in the morning I do not sleep, but in the afternoon I simply cannot help it. I never sleep in the theater, but quite often in the opera. I do not think the devil cares whether or not I sleep in church, for sleeping is an indifferent thing, not a sin but only a human weakness. There are not many preachers who know how to dampen the passions; if the passions are strong, they overpower us, if they are weak, we overpower them. But the reverend preachers do nothing for or against it; they are human beings just like ourselves and have enough to worry about themselves. If you want to preach, I promise not to sleep through your sermon, and since you are a joyful Christian I should hope that you will string garlands along the path to heaven. It is a good command to keep up a happy spirit. But since in this country one sees as much cheerful as sad wickedness, happiness is not a sign to be trusted. Our Lord gives us the temperament to be cheerful or sad, but then time and age do things to us. I was much more cheerful when I was young than I am now. Now I am tired of just about everything.

To ELECTRESS SOPHIE

Marly, 2 August 1705

Madame la Duchesse de Bourgogne must be better, for she went hunting with the King yesterday. I see her every day, but in two weeks she barely says a word to me, only makes her bows and looks down her nose at me; but I have made up my mind about this and do not care at all, for this does her more harm than it does me, since it only shows that she is an ill-mannered child. . . . One no longer knows who one is; when the King goes walking, everyone wears a hat, and when the Duchesse de Bourgogne goes walking, she always goes arm in arm with one of the ladies and the others walk beside her, so one cannot see who she is. In the salon here and in the gallery at Trianon all the men sit in the presence of Monsieur le Dauphin and the Duchesse de Bourgogne; some of them are even sprawled on the settees. I am having a hard time getting used to the way things are now, which is not at all like a court; but truly, it is hard to say what it is. All of this is supposed to be fun, and yet one does not see anyone having fun and senses that there is more spite than pleasure.

Versailles, 29 October 1705

The first year of the young newlyweds[1] is not yet over, and we shall see whether they can win the Archbishop of Paris's vineyard, which no one has claimed yet. I do not know whether Your Grace knows that if a pair of newlyweds can spend the entire first year after their marriage without one of them regretting that they were married and without ceasing to love each other for a moment, they can ask for the vineyard of the Archbishop of Paris and will receive it; only so far, this has not happened. God grant that Your

Grace's grandchildren will earn it and that their happiness will last for many years to come . . .

1. Georg August and Karoline von Ansbach, the Electress's grandson and his wife.

To RAUGRÄFIN LUISE

Marly, 5 November 1705

Princesses rarely marry for love, but only for practical reasons. Beauty has nothing to do with that; virtue and intelligence are enough. These last longer than beauty, which is a passing thing and wears down soon enough. . . . I know Ma Tante, she is as stout-hearted as a man of courage. She is not easily frightened. At Clopenburg I once saw her escape from a fire in her night-gown as the flames were engulfing her room on all sides; she was very pregnant but not frightened at all and only laughed. Another time we had new horses on a calash; they bolted while we were in it and ran over the coachman; Oncle jumped down and held the horses, but Ma Tante was not frightened that time either, even though it was a very dangerous situation.

To RAUGRÄFIN AMALIE ELISABETH

Versailles, 26 November 1705

Not much more is new here than at Hanover; I have never seen this court so quiet. . . .

Few people are altogether without religion, but each one practices it in his own way as best he can believe or understand it. The Good Lord has caused people to be born with such different temperaments that one person cannot possibly think like another. To be blessed with a pure piety without hypocrisy I consider a great grace of God that cannot be attained by human power, for we are not capable of doing what we want to do or ought to do unless God gives us His special grace; all we can do is desire it. But, my dear Amelise, I cannot get over it that you and Luise are so shocked when someone makes fun of religion and does not act pious. Our court of Heidelberg must have changed a great deal after my departure; after all, our late Papa always made fun of all religions, only in jest and to amuse himself, just as our dear Electress still does.

Versailles, 3 December 1705

Where have you and Luise been that you know so little of the world? It seems to me that one does not have to live at court very long to know all about it; but if one were to hate all those who love young fellows, one could not like—or at least not hate—six persons here. There are various kinds of such people; some of them hate women like the plague and can only love other men, others love both men and women . . . some only go for children of ten or eleven, others want young fellows between seventeen and twenty-five, and these are the most numerous; some of the debauched characters love neither men nor women and have their pleasure by themselves, but there are fewer of them than of the others. Some also engage in debaucheries of various kinds, with animals or people, whatever comes their way. I know one man here who boasts that he has done it with everything, even down to toads. Ever since I learned this, I loathe the sight of this fellow. He was in my late husband's service and is a really wicked person, without any brains at all. So there you see, dear Amelise, that the world is even worse than you ever thought. . . . I really had a good laugh when I read that you, dear Amelise, would rather get married than commit the sin of something-or-other. In the sight of God this is indeed much more commendable, but to look at it in human terms, as many people do, marriage is more burdensome, for a husband one takes for life. But if a *coquette* is tired of one lover, she takes another, that is ever so much easier.

Versailles, 17 December 1705

Dearest Amelise, I received your sister's letter a week after yours and am answering both of them today. In the things that concern Our Lord God there is nothing to be made fun of; but when it comes to His servants, who are human beings like ourselves and often have even more foibles than others, I do believe that one is allowed to laugh about them, if only to make them mend their ways. . . . The reverend preachers are usually not very entertaining. I think one loses one's respect for clergymen if one sees them from close by and often; but they are certainly people like everyone else.

Versailles, 25 February 1706

Our carnival is over now. On the last day even I, old lady that I am, had to put on a costume. All that my disguise consisted of was a piece of green taffeta, which I had tied to a forked pole topped by a big rosetta of pink ribbon. The taffeta had a slit from the head to below the stomach. I slipped into this taffeta with my clothes on, tied it at the neck, and carried the pole in my hand. The face was hidden, and because of the height I looked thin, so no one could possibly recognize me. I made the King quite impatient, for whenever he looked at me I dipped the pole, which looked as if someone was bowing. Finally the King became really impatient and said to the Duchesse de Bourgogne, "Just who is that tall mask who keeps greeting me?" She laughed and finally said: "It's Madame." I thought the King would burst with laughter about my disguise.

Don't they dance any more German dances now, that people make fun of them? I do not think that it is foolish to make merry, for it is healthy. What is foolish is to be sad, for that makes one ill and serves no purpose. My foot is not yet completely better, I can still feel the pain. I do not like French dancing, and I cannot stand those eternal minuets, which is why I have spent carnival like Good Friday, with reading, writing, and basket weaving. But I love the theater and have not missed a single play; some were good, some were bad. . . .

On all sides one hears of cases of people dying suddenly. Until my turn comes, you, dear Amelise, will always remain dear to my heart.

To ELECTRESS SOPHIE

Versailles, 30 May 1706

One truly needs some consolation now, for I have never experienced a more unhappy time than this in the thirty-five years I have now spent in France. Not a day passes without bringing more bad news. . . . Prince Louis[1] has no need to bestir himself, Mylord Marlborough stirs around quite enough— more than enough, alas—for both of them. . . . Those who believe in witch- craft will think that he has made a pact with the devil to make him so amazingly lucky. . . . What a pitiful and unhappy turn things have taken for our King of Spain at Barcelona[2] Your Grace knows already, so I will say nothing more about it. I do not know with what kinds of holy medals they have covered the archduke, but he is lucky, for to all appearances the affair should not have gone in his favor. His best relics are the English and the Dutch.[3]

1. Ludwig von Baden, a general of the Empire.   2. At that point Philip V was de- feated and had to flee from Barcelona; however, he later regained his control. 3. They were the archduke's allies.

Versailles, 10 June 1706

Such reversals as have happened in the last twenty years are unheard of; the kingdoms of England and Spain have changed as swiftly as the situation in a play. I think that when future generations read the history of our time, it will look to them like a novel, and they will be unable to believe it.

Versailles, 1 August 1706

It has become the fashion here to complain about the air; the Princesse de Conti does not want to go out at all and never takes a walk, and neither does Madame d'Orléans; they are forever having purges, bleedings, acidulous water, and baths; and what is really exquisite is that they all keep oohing and aahing about my good health. I tell them every day that if I were to live as they do, I would be even sicker than they are, and also that I am healthy because I do not use any medicines and get a lot of fresh air and exercise. But they simply do not want to believe it.

In the battle of Turin on 7 September Prince Eugene of Savoy defeated the young Duc d'Orléans, whose army was annihilated.

Versailles, 16 September 1706

I am sad to the depth of my soul, for the very day when Your Grace wrote her last letter to me was a most unfortunate one for me, and all because Marshal de Marsin and the other generals did not want to believe my son, who wanted to attack the enemy with his army from his own lines; but neither Marshal de Marsin nor any of the other generals agreed, and so the order was given that this must not be done. So my son, unfortunately, was obliged to go along with their confounded bad advice. The enemy attacked the retrenchment in the place where Monsieur de la Feuillade had neglected to fortify it, relying on two rivers that flow there, but failing to consider that the streams would dry out in the heat. The enemy came through the water, 35,000 men against our 8,000; in other words, they made a breakthrough and have freed Turin. My son defended himself as long as he could and is wounded in two places; he has a bullet wound from a musket in his hip and another at the right arm between the elbow and the hand. His barber-surgeon has written to me, assuring me that there is no danger. Marshal de Marsin has paid for his bad advice with his life; he was killed in the battle. Today it is clearer than ever that things would have gone better if my son had had his way.

Versailles, 29 September 1706

. . . will report on my son's condition tomorrow and only say here what I cannot say in the regular mail, namely how wretched things are here. Half of the money one receives is in *billets de monnaie;* if one wants to exchange these for real money, one loses one fifth. That adds up in the long run, and so one hears nothing but complaints and lamentations, which is tiresome indeed. Still, I have to praise the King in two respects; for one thing, he bears his misfortune with great fortitude. Spain and France are going to rack and ruin because of the greed of two old women: in Spain it is that of the Princesse des Ursins who, in order to get everything, has stirred up all the Spanish grandees against their King; here it is the Maintenon, who, because of her greed, deprives the King of good servants by recommending only those who give her money, and she makes money out of everything. However much she hates me and keeps me away from the King, he treats me politely, which is surprising, but he does say a few words to me every night at the table, and this astonishes all those who know how much this old woman and her pupil, the Duchesse de Bourgogne, hate me.

Versailles, 1 November 1706

The old Maintenon is dreadfully hated; when, a few months ago during our stay at Meudon, she drove to Notre-Dame and Sainte-Geneviève, the old women of Paris abused her and loudly called her all kinds of filthy names. It is said that she blames all of France's misfortunes on the fact that the King has not made her marriage public, and that she is putting on strong pressure to be recognized as Queen. If it should be true, as some people think, that the smelly Choin was married,[1] this marriage will no doubt be made public at the same time. That will make for a fine royal court; it is just as if everyone had gone stark mad here. The reason that the old woman is becoming more and more set against me is that she thinks I would laugh at her and prevent the King from being foolish enough to declare her Queen, and that fear of hers I cannot allay. They say that she promised the Duc de Bourgogne a share in the government of the country and also that he would get his beloved Archbishop of Cambrai[2] back. How all of this will end, time will tell.

1. To the Dauphin, her lover.   2. His former teacher, Fénelon.

To RAUGRÄFIN AMALIE ELISABETH

Versailles, 3 February 1707

All year long I eat at noon all by myself and hurry as much as possible, for it is annoying to eat alone and to have twenty fellows stand around, looking into one's mouth and counting every bite; therefore I am done in less than a half hour. At night I eat with the King; there we are five or six at table. Everyone just eats away as in a monastery, without saying anything, except perhaps a whispered word to a neighbor.

To ELECTRESS SOPHIE

Versailles, 10 February 1707

Your Grace is respected and loved by everyone and still knows what a proper court is, which everyone else seems to have forgotten; grandeur comes naturally to Your Grace, for there is no mishmash in her and her court is regulated to perfection. Here no one seems to remember who he is, all ranks are confused, and one barely knows oneself who one is. —God grant that Your Grace may receive much satisfaction from the prince,[1] and more than Your Grace receives from his father, for from all I hear about him, he seems to be an odd bird. I hope that Your Grace will be here to see the marriage and the children of this prince, then she will be able to say, "My son, tell your son that his son's son is crying." On the Berlin side, Your Grace will perhaps become a great-grandmother by the end of the year, for since the crown prince and the crown princess are so fond of each other, the princess is sure to become pregnant before long. I cannot get over it that His Grace the Elector of Braunschweig, whose birth and childhood I remember as if it were today, should be a grandfather now. I am exactly eight years older than His Grace, for I was born on 27 May 1652 and the Elector on 28 May 1660. I remember seeing everyone terribly worried about Your Grace, and running to Your Grace's room . . . I lay down flat before the door in order to hear what was being said inside. Soon Frau von Harling found me there and led me into the room where Your Grace was. The prince was being bathed behind a screen; I looked all around and still seem to see him before my eyes. —King Augustus must be very fickle in love, although I am not surprised that he has become tired of so brazen a creature as Countess Cosel. I think that King Augustus's brain is a bit addled from all his drinking. I know all about his strange temper, for C. A. Haxthausen[2] has often tearfully told me that he was afraid this pupil would not bring him any honor; he complained that his prince has the strangest and maddest temper he had ever encountered, and that he was a dissembler to boot, and perfectly able to behave himself and to hide his temper, which is the worst part of it.

1. Her great-grandson. 2. Former governor of August the Strong, King of Poland.

Versailles, 17 April 1707, five o'clock in the evening

We are just returning from church, where we have been since half past two, and this morning's service already went on for an hour and a half. They tell me that there was a thunderstorm during the sermon, but I did not hear anything, even two very strong thunderclaps, for a sweet slumber prevented me from hearing it. Seeing that everything has turned green now and the weather warm one can sing what the little boys used to sing on the hill at Heidelberg: "Strew, strew, straw / it's summer time, hurrah: / Lean days are here again / the farmers scrape the barrel / and when they scrape the barrel / may God send us a fruitful year / Strew, strew, straw / it's summer time, hurrah." These are pretty verses, which will teach the nosy ones who read our letters a lot and make them wise and learned.

Marly, 22 May 1707

I have had strenuous exercise, which always agrees with me. We hunt in a most beautiful place, for the preserve here is like a lovely park; there are ten or twelve avenues, which are like a real vault; six or eight of the avenues form stars. The many hedges, in full bloom now, perfume the air, and the

nightingales and other birds are singing so beautifully that it is a pure joy
to be in this place. . . .

I do not know what Princess Elisabeth[1] was made to read at her abjuration
in Bamberg; to me they only read things to which I had to answer yes or
no, which I did quite according to my own mind, and a few times I said no
when I was supposed to say yes, but it went through just the same; I had
to chuckle to myself. Against the condemnation of the parents I protested so
vehemently that in my case nothing was said about this. I listened carefully and replied according to my own mind, but Princess Elisabeth could
not do this because she had to read something. No one could go through
such a spectacle without some palpitations. Queen Christina[2] was brazen,
that is why she considered the whole thing a farce. . . .

I know some clergymen here who share Herr Leibniz's opinion and believe that the souls of animals will go to the next world. I would like that,
for I should be happy to find all my little dogs in that world; if I could believe
it, their death would grieve me less.

1. Elisabeth Christine of Braunschweig-Wolfenbüttel, who married Archduke Karl
(later, Emperor Charles VI) in 1708. She became the mother of Empress Maria
Theresa. 2. Christina of Sweden, the daughter and successor of Gustavus Adolphus,
who resigned her throne in favor of her cousin, converted to Catholicism, and spent
her last years in Italy.

Marly, 21 July 1707, five o'clock in the morning

Here I sit in my shirt writing to Your Grace; at this hour one does not have
to fear an invasion of unwelcome callers. The heat here is so great that the oldest people cannot say that they have ever experienced anything like it. One
keeps hearing of dogs and horses that have dropped dead; workmen faint and
well-nigh suffocate in the fields, and hunters also faint and drop like flies.
Yesterday everyone kept to his room in his shirt until seven at night; one constantly had to change shirts; I changed mine eight times in one day, and it
was as if they had been dipped into water. At table too people keep mopping
their faces; it is really awful. If it should be even warmer in Spain, my son
and his army will melt away and suffocate. On all sides one hears of illnesses.
Otherwise there is nothing new here.

Versailles, 28 January 1708, eight o'clock in the evening

Since three o'clock I have been back here; before dinner I walked for an hour,
for today we had the most beautiful weather in the world. The sun was so
warm that all the flower beds in Marly have buds; the honeysuckle is all green
already, and in the orchards the almond and peach trees are in full bloom.
Yesterday the King ate a pancake filled with the small mushrooms that are
called *mousserons* here, and which no one had ever seen before the end of

March or even April; they come out at the same time as the morelles. . . .

To be queen would not please me as much as it pleases Queen Anne;[1] the life of royalty is too full of constraints to give pleasure. To live a pleasant life one must, for one thing, have enough money to help one's good friends and, for another, be able to go wherever one wants without ceremonies and constraints, that is what makes for a pleasant life. I believe that Monsieur de Louvois is burning in the other world because of the Palatinate; he was horribly cruel and unable to feel pity for anything. . . .

It seems to me that Villars[2] might well be satisfied with what he has already gotten out of Germany, for no one in France is wealthier than he. It is a great flaw in a hero to be greedy; it seems to me that this is bound to lead to trouble sooner or later, because it usually makes for injustices that do not bring good luck. I therefore do not believe that Mylord Marlborough will come to a good end.

1. Of England; sister-in-law and successor of William of Orange.   2. French marshal.

Versailles, 5 April 1708

If I were still at Heidelberg, I would now sing, "Rejoice dear Christians all / And let us sing with glee / That one and all in happiness / We jump for love and joy," . . . for I have just returned from the Lord's Supper. However, I am afraid that if I were to jump the room would cave in, because I am a heavy package. . . .

We still do not know what has happened to our young King of England.[1] I should be heartily distressed if anything unfortunate should happen to him. . . . I had to laugh that Your Grace calls the King of England king *in partibus* like the bishops; yet the fact is that he is the rightful heir. I should be very sorry if he were to be captured; it would be a dreadful thing if Queen Anne were to have her own brother executed. . . .

Unless Prince Eugene has changed, Your Grace will see a little snub nose, a rather long chin, and an upper lip so short that he always keeps his mouth partly open, showing two big white teeth; he is not very tall, has a slender waist, and, in the days when I knew him here, straight black hair. But I believe that he now wears a wig. He is intelligent and was not greatly respected at the time; he was very young then and everyone thought that he would never be more than an abbot. This cornerstone has already fallen onto quite a few people and has crushed them to bits. I am glad that my son will not run into him this year.

1. In the spring of 1708 James Stuart, son of the deceased King James II, attempted to regain his crown with the help of a French fleet. He was hoping for a popular uprising in his favor, but this did not materialize.

Marly, 29 April 1708

I am now so sure where our King of England is that yesterday I spent a half-hour with His Majesty. I have never understood why there was so much public talk about the surprise attack in Scotland. Of course I may not say what I think through the mail, but I was not really surprised, since everything here has become incomprehensible, both at court and in the council. The reasons for all this are easy to surmise. This reminds me of the old German proverb: When soldiers live off the fat of the land / and warlike clerics are out of hand / and when to boot women hold sway / the end must surely bring dismay.

Fontainebleau, 27 June 1708

I often think that it is odd that in Our Lord Christ's day people had so little curiosity. I can see that they would not question Our Lord Christ very much; it would not have been respectful. But Lazarus, to whom they did not owe any respect, he should have been thoroughly examined about the next world. If my brother had risen from the dead, I surely would not have failed to question him, and that for the sole purpose of better serving God Almighty. But I am getting very sleepy and must take a little snooze.

I am awake now and will not fall asleep again, my nap only lasted a half-hour. I was thirsty and had a good drink of beer to Your Grace's health.

Versailles, 20 September 1708

Unfortunately I cannot report to Your Grace anything nicer than that the old woman is more malicious than ever and brings up her pupil, the Duchesse de Bourgogne, to be just as malicious and false. She keeps sending the Duchesse de Bourgogne to every high mass wearing big hoods that make her look mournful and pious. And at the evening service she always looks as if she were weeping and fasting, yet at night we have seen her through her windows holding *medianoche* with her ladies and having a merry old time. She can guzzle down two bottles of pure wine without showing it and is so coquettish that she even runs after her own *écuyers.* There Your Grace sees how falseness holds sway everywhere. The old woman has humbugged the King into believing that there was never anything like her in piety and virtue, and the good King believes it like the Gospel truth. Every day she offends me in some way; at the King's table she has the plates from which I want to eat pulled out from right under my nose; when I call on her she gives me the cold shoulder and does not speak to me or laughs at me with her ladies. All this the old thing does on purpose, hoping that I will get mad and make a scene, so that one could say that I am impossible to live with and pack me off to Montargis. But I am on to this trick and therefore only laugh at everything they are trying; I do not complain and never say a word about it.

169   1701–1715: WIDOWHOOD

The cold here is so fierce that it fairly defies description. I am sitting by a roaring fire, have a screen before the door, which is closed, so that I can sit here with a sable fur piece around my neck and my feet in a bearskin sack, and still I am shivering with cold and can barely hold the pen. Never in my life have I seen as rough a winter as this one; the wine freezes in the bottles. In Germany I never saw such a winter. . . .

I certainly have cause to express my gratitude for the beautiful medals, for Your Grace cannot imagine the wonderful entertainment they provide me; I spend days on end with them and also with my antique medals. Only last Monday I bought another 150 of these with the King's New Year's gift. I now have a whole cabinet full of gold medals, the whole set of all the emperors from Julius Caesar to Heraclius, and not one is missing. Some of these are very rare items that even the King does not have. All of this I was able to buy quite cheaply; 260 of these medals I bought by weight alone, and all in all I now have 410 gold medals.

To RAUGRÄFIN AMALIE ELISABETH

Versailles, 19 January 1709

In your letter you act, dear Amelise, like the *coquettes* who always deprecate their prettiest features as ugly in order to be complimented. That is what you do when you say you are afraid that I will soon grow tired of your letters. You know perfectly well that this is not the case, for in the first place you write very well, and in the second place I am too fond of you not to be glad whenever I hear from you and Luise, even if it were only to hear about the fatherland and to keep up my mother tongue; but when all these reasons come together I am bound to be pleased to receive your letters. Therefore please do not have any more scruples on this point! It is certainly true that the good honest Monsieur Polier[1] is a wonder; he just turned eighty-nine this month and still reasons as well as he did forty years ago. His piety is not a late development, it must be forty years now that he is so pious, and moreover he has always lived a good, Christian life. I do not believe that Our Lord requires Christians to think of nothing but spiritual matters, otherwise He would not have enjoined us so strongly to love our neighbor. Since the Almighty has placed us into the world to honor Him and serve our fellow man, it is necessary to pay attention to everything and thereby be spurred on in both these duties; in this manner anyone who wants to hear only of spiritual things would fall into useless bigotry. Monsieur Polier is not at court; he lives in solitude in Paris and only goes out to attend the services at the Swedish envoy's, and when I am in Paris he comes to see me. But he writes to me every day, and always something edifying.

1. Director of Liselotte's education at Heidelberg; he followed her to France.

To ELECTRESS SOPHIE

Versailles, 20 January 1709

Every day people die of the cold here; some eighteen or twenty are buried in a day. No one, no matter how old he may be, can remember having lived through such icy cold. In Paris all spectacles have ceased, and all litigation has stopped because no one can get to the courts and the presidents and councillors are staying at home. No one can ride in coaches, everyone goes on foot, and every day one hears of people who have broken their bones; in every house someone is sick. Well-nigh all of my people are sick; those who are healthier than the rest are coughing and sneezing.

Marly, 7 February 1709

We came here yesterday even though it is still dreadfully cold. A week ago we had a slight thaw, but last Sunday the cold weather returned worse than ever. . . . I am sitting by the fireside and can barely hold my pen. Last night we had a concert, but it was not very good because half of the musicians could not make their way up the hill in their hackney coach, for all the streets are icy and people keep falling down and breaking their bones. . . .

In order to enjoy this life to the fullest, one would have to be one's own master and not dependent on others. In my Bible I am now reading the first book of Moses, for I started over on New Year's Day. I find it most entertaining reading. . . .

The Duc de Bourgogne and the Duc de Berry were brought up together and in the same manner, yet they are of entirely different temperaments. The Duc de Berry is not pious at all, has no respect for anything in the world, neither God nor man, and no principles; he does not worry about anything as long as he can amuse himself with whatever it may be: shooting, playing cards, talking with young women who have no common sense whatsoever, stuffing himself with food, these are the things that keep him happy, and ice skating is another. My son is an altogether different kind of person; he loves war and is an expert at it; he does not care for hunting, shooting, or card playing, but he loves all the liberal arts and above all painting and paintings about which, the painters say, he knows a great deal. He enjoys distilling[1] and conversation and is a good conversationalist, for he has studied seriously and knows many things because his memory is good. He loves music and he loves women; I wish he did not love the latter quite so much, for this is something that ruins him and his children and also often drags him into the most profligate company that keeps him from his better pursuits. . . .

I am not saying that the King is married, but supposing he were married, no one would object with one word if the King wanted to make the marriage public. The Dauphin is reputed to be mismarried himself,[2] and the Duc de Bourgogne is too much afraid of the King and the lady to open his mouth. Moreover this lady and the Duchesse de Bourgogne are but one soul in two bodies. The Duc de Berry does not know himself who he is; he does not know anything, and everything is fine with him. So Your Grace can be quite sure that it is not the princes who have prevented this declaration. Some people who think that they are very well informed say that until now the King's confessor, Père de la Chaise, has prevented it; how it will continue, time will tell.

1. Experimenting with chemicals.   2. I.e., married to Mademoiselle de Choin.

Versailles, 23 March 1709

The King would always be kind if he were allowed to follow his own inclination. But he is often made to change his mind. No one at this court has more courtly manners than he himself. Of the almighty lady I will only say that she is desperately looking for ways to make me angry and to make me say something unpleasant to her, so that she will have cause to complain about me to the King. But all her efforts are in vain: I will never get angry . . . nor will I give up and go to my widow's seat. Of this I herewith give her notice, since she always wants to know what is in my letters to Your Grace; so now she knows what to expect.

Marly, 18 April 1709

This new confessor of mine is reasonable in all things, except when it comes to religion; on this point he is just too simple-minded, even though he has a good mind; it must be his upbringing. He is very different from my other two confessors . . . they admitted that there are trifles and bad things in this religion, while this one does not want to do that and wants me to admire everything. That I cannot do, nor do I want to be talked into anything. He also said that I am not docile enough, but I told him quite plainly that I am too old to believe simple-minded things. He would like me to believe a lot of trifling things about miracles. On Maundy Thursday something funny happened, which gave me a good laugh: After I returned from church where I had partaken of the Lord's Supper, we talked of miracles and someone said . . . that Madame la Princesse Palatine had been converted because she had held a piece of wood from Our Lord's Cross in a candle flame and it had not burned. I said, "That is not a miracle, because there is a

kind of wood in Mesopotamia that does not burn." Père Lignières said that
I simply do not want to believe in miracles. I answered that I had proof in
hand, and this was true, because Paul Lucas had sold me a large piece of the
wood that becomes red hot and does not burn. I rose from my seat, fetched
the wood, and gave it to Père Lignières, asking him to examine it thoroughly
to make sure it was wood. He cut off a piece of it and then threw the rest
of it into the fire, where it became red hot like a piece of iron but did not
burn up. Well, that was one embarrassed and flustered confessor, for I could
not keep myself from laughing. But after a while he recovered and said that
since it was not written anywhere that the wood of the Holy Cross does not
burn, it was an impious act to throw it into the fire. I said that if I had not
shown him proof about this wood, it would have been very wrong of me not
to believe this great miracle. In the end he had to laugh himself and admit
that he would not have believed this about the wood if he had not seen it himself. . . . When Frau von Rotzenhausen hears me argue like this with my confessor, she always says mischievously, "I hope to God that one of these
days Your Royal Highness will succeed in educating her confessor properly."
. . . My son, I am happy to say, reasons extremely well and knows all religions thoroughly; he is not a pedant, but the way he walks would shock
Your Grace, for he walks very badly, keeps his head down and swings one
arm and one leg, although he can do better if he wants to. When he dances
he becomes a different person, for then he holds himself straight.

Versailles, 30 April 1709

Since the Prince of Wolfenbüttel's valet will leave from here on Friday next,
I shall once again answer Your Grace's welcome letter through him. Here
I shall speak up more plainly than I do in the mail because this man will deliver my letter into Your Grace's own hands. Therefore I will say that I
now lead a very quiet life, although the old trollop is doing her utmost to
annoy me and to make others despise me. But I just let her carry on and
pretend that I do not notice anything. All day long I amuse myself with writing, with my coin collection, chiseled stones, copper engravings, and such
things; if the weather is fine I go for walks and rides and act as if I loved solitude, for if I wanted to have company no one would come to see me, because everyone knows very well that the lady does not like me. I do not enjoy
gambling, and in fact would not last anyway, for no one wants to play for
small stakes and high stakes would be too dear for my purse. My life is rather
like what they say about limbo: without pleasure and without pain; my
greatest pleasures are Your Grace's kind letters, which I frequently reread. My
son is good company, but I do not get much consolation from him; in two
weeks I barely see him for half an hour, he is much too stuck in his profligate

doings in Paris to be seen much elsewhere. I get along well enough with his wife and she with me, but there certainly is no real sympathy between us, so we cannot keep company with each other. The King is not allowed to have me around him; I only see His Majesty at table and after the meal in his study for a moment. Sometimes he asks me if I have been for a walk and where, but that is all; if I want to say anything further, he bows and turns his back on me. The old woman must have a scheme that I cannot grasp at all, for we are sure and certain that she has forty million in cash. I have been made hateful to the Dauphin and to the Duc de Berry, whom I have loved as if he were my own child. In the beginning all of this pained me very much, but now—thanks be to God—I have gotten over it and no longer care a fig. I have read the passage in Procopius[1] that Your Grace quoted but found that there is one big difference, for Justinian did not amount to much to begin with, whereas our King here is after all of high birth and therefore should not have wasted himself in this manner, nor his son either, if indeed it is true that he has married that foul-smelling Choin. The woman is frightfully malicious, I mean the old one; no one at court has any doubt that she has poisoned Louvois and Mansard, the former because he advised the King to make a journey without her, and the latter because he was about to advise the King to give the postal administration to the bankers, who in return would have liquidated promissory notes, which would have been a good thing for the country as a whole. It is this wicked trollop who opens all my letters, twists them so badly and gives me such trouble about them; she is capable of anything one can think of and yet carries on as if she were the most God-fearing person in the world. The King is dreadfully afraid of the devil, he is ignorant in religious matters and only believes what the woman wants to make him believe, for he never ever reads anything, gives everything to read to the lady, to his ministers, and to his confessor and lets them inform him of what is in it. Thus they can tell him whatever they like, and they can easily do harm if they want to. It is quite certain that the woman believes neither in God nor in the devil, else she would not be so malicious to do harm to everyone and to poison people.

1. Roman historian of the sixth century.

Marly, 2 May 1709

I know the King of Denmark quite well and have often seen His Majesty here. He pretended to be in love with my daughter, but he carried on so that we fairly died laughing about it; I am quite certain that Your Grace would have been most amused to see it. He would approach her, look at her, then look up in the air, not utter a word, and just stay that way. This, I believe, was supposed to mean being in ecstasy. He loves to dance but has no ear at all and dances very badly, in the minuet he hops around in a very odd way . . . wears his hat too far back and starts the minuet at one end of the room, ending up at the other. One cannot describe it as comically as he does it, and even a very sad person would be unable to watch this king dance without having to laugh. Speaking of laughing: On Saturday a lady will show up here who is always given to hearty laughter, namely Frau von Ratsamhausen. I hope she will bring me some funny stories that I can tell Your Grace, for here we hear of nothing but sad things, such as that the price of bread is rising every day, that people starve to death, and such.

Versailles, 30 May 1709

Our King could force his grandson to become king, but he cannot force him to leave his kingdom if his subjects want to keep him. I hope that, God willing, things will go so well this year that I will be able to report more than one victory to Your Grace, for as the proverb says, "The devil does not come only to the poor man's door," and the odd years are lucky for us; therefore I hope that this year the Dutch and the English will have to "put water in their wine." If I cite any more proverbs, Your Grace will mistake me for Sancho Panza; I already have his shape and perhaps his simplicity as well, for if one speaks as little as I can speak here, it would be no wonder if I were to become simple-minded.

One of the peace conditions imposed on the defeated King of France was that he himself must drive his grandson Philip V out of Spain. This unreasonable demand caused the French nobility to fight with renewed dedication and bravery. Nonetheless, the French cause would have been lost if Archduke Charles had not become Emperor through the death of his brother, and thereby unsuited for the Spanish succession in the eyes of his allies. In England, moreover, the peace party had come to power, with the result that the great general Marlborough was recalled from the theater of war.

To RAUGRÄFIN LUISE

Marly, 15 June 1709

The allies' propositions are simply too barbaric; it would be better to go to death and perdition than to consider them. I do not know how they could think of such a thing and how they could believe that our King would even consider it. They say that "pride goeth before a fall," therefore I hope that Mylord Marlborough and Prince Eugene will be punished for their insolence. The latter should remember that this country is his fatherland and that he was born the King's subject. I am quite provoked with him for having prevented the peace. . . .

I am reflecting on the strange ways in which God distributes His blessings. You two have your freedom but are in poor health, while I live in slavery and am hale and hearty. This goes to show that in this world one cannot have all the good things.

To ELECTRESS SOPHIE

Marly, 20 June 1709

My son has one of these burning glasses or burning mirrors. It cost him 2,000 *talers* and he and his doctor, a German by the name of Homberg, are using it for many experiments. I do not know if this glass was made by Herr Hartsoeker,[1] but if he sells his microscopes, I shall ask Luise to buy one for me, of the kind that makes a louse look so big. . . .

One often treats people as enemies who in fact are not enemies at all, while mistaking those who have caused all one's misfortunes for friends; others can see this and are not allowed to say anything; but hush, lest I am carried too far in this text. Still, I cannot refrain from saying that anyone who has any intelligence at all realizes and says publicly that all the misfortunes we are suffering now were caused solely by the persecution of the Reformed. Père de la Chaise may be suffering for this in the next world, but unfortunately not all those who helped in this pursuit are dead yet, and they are sure to contrive a great deal more mischief. The French weep about the King's misfortune because they are in Hanover; if they were here they would make songs and malicious verses about him. That is how they are; if you've seen one Frenchman, you've seen them all; they are all cut from the same cloth. Your Grace is fortunate not to have to worry about this; it will not make her suffer. But I, poor devil that I am, was not allowed to enjoy the good times when there was plenty and then some of everything, and yet I now have to share the bad times, which are none of my fault, for if they had asked for my advice, the Reformed would still be living here in perfect tranquillity and our King would have many more millions of money and subjects than he has now. —My confessor does not forbid me to go to the opera or to the theater, except on the day before confession; he would be pleased if I did not go at all, but since I know that what I do there is not sinful I have no scruples whatsoever about it. In the old days the clerics talked the laypeople into believing that the Last Judgment was at hand, therefore the latter gave all their goods to the clerics in return for their prayers, so that they would not be damned. They had not learned that one must wash off one's sins by one's own contrition and not by the prayers of others. Human beings do not find anything strange, however outlandish it may be, if they are accustomed to it from childhood; I wish it were permitted in our religion to believe in reincarnation, for it would be comforting to be firmly convinced that those whom one has loved will live again and also have the hope of returning to this world oneself.

1. Dutch mathematician and optician.

To RAUGRÄFIN LUISE

Marly, 22 June 1709

I thank you very much . . . for all the printed matter you have sent me. One only has to read it to see that this is no way to make peace. This is what is called here a *partage de Montgomery:* All for one side and nothing for the other. This cannot lead to peace, for the proposals are simply too barbaric. To set a grandfather against his own grandson who has always been submissive and obedient is altogether barbarous and unchristian; I hate it and am quite certain that those who have thought this up will be punished for it by God Almighty.

To ELECTRESS SOPHIE

Versailles, 15 August 1709

In the thirty-eight years since I came to France I have changed coaches and had new ones built only four times. But the linens are renewed every three years; the old ones go to the first chambermaid. One does not really own anything here; all the linens, nightgowns, and petticoats belong to the first chambermaid, all dresses from one year to the next belong to the first lady-in-waiting, as does the lace; the coaches belong to the first *écuyer;* and if I die my silver plate belongs to the first *maître d'hôtel,* unless he is given an equivalent sum of money.

Versailles, 22 August 1709

As I was driving through the Porte Saint-Honoré in Paris, I saw people running about, looking all upset, and some of them were saying, "Ah mon Dieu"; all the windows were full of people, and some of them had climbed on the roof. Down below, stores were being closed up and house doors locked. Even the Palais Royal was closed. I did not understand what the meaning of all this was, but when I came into the inner courtyard and alighted, a townswoman whom I do not know came to me and said, "Do you know, Madame, that there is a revolt in Paris that has been going on since four o'clock this morning?" I thought the woman had gone mad and began to laugh, but she said, "I am not crazy, Madame, what I am telling you is true, so true that forty people have already been killed." I asked some of my people whether this was true. They said that it was true indeed and that it was why they had closed the gates of the Palais Royal. I asked about the causes of the revolt; it was because of the work on the Saint Martin gate and wall, where each worker is paid three sols and a loaf of bread. There are two thousand workmen on this job, but that morning four thousand had appeared unexpectedly; they loudly clamored for bread and money, but the authorities did not have it, and when one woman was particularly insolent, she was seized and tied to the pillory. That is when the uproar started, and instead of four thousand, suddenly there were six thousand who pulled the woman off the pillory. Many retired lackeys had joined the crowd; they shouted that they should loot and ran right to the bakeries to loot. The guard soldiers were called in to fire on the rabble, but the mob realized that this was only to scare them and that there was no shot in the muskets. So they called out, "Attack them, they have no bullets!" Therefore the soldiers were forced to shoot down a few of them. This went on from four in the morning until noon, when Marshall de Boufflers and the Duc de Grammont happened to be driving through the section where the revolt was taking place and where the stones were flying. They alighted from their coach, talked to the populace, threw out some money and promised to tell the King how they had been promised bread and money and had failed to receive anything. They calmed down the uproar right away; the people tossed their caps into the air, shouting, "Long live the King; we want bread." They are good people, the Parisians, after all, to calm down so quickly. Yesterday they all went to the market and were perfectly peaceful; but as much as they love their King and the royal house, they hate Madame de Maintenon. I wanted to get a breath of fresh air because it was warm in my rooms, which are small and have low ceilings; but I had only just set foot outside when a great crowd of people gathered. They asked God's blessing for me, but then they started to say such nasty things about the lady that I was obliged to go inside and close the windows; they said in plain words that if they could get hold of her they would tear her to pieces or burn her as a witch.

To RAUGRÄFIN LUISE

Marly, 31 August 1709

How I wish, dear Luise, that I could think of something that would comfort you. How gladly I would do it for you! Poor Amelise[1] has often given me pleasure through her letters, for what she wrote was funny and written in an unaffected style. I was very fond of her, and her death has touched me deeply. Having mourned for Carllutz, Karoline, and all your brothers, I am bound to mourn for Amelise too. I confess that when it comes to those who have been dear to my heart, I always want to know how they have lived until their end, what they have thought and said. It seems to me that this helps us to come grips with death. It does not surprise me that she died full of piety and resignation. . . . I think you were quite right not to have Amelise opened, for one only dies when the appointed hour has come, and not before. Also, it does not seem that the fact that so many people are opened now has saved a single person's life. Here bodies are not opened until twenty-four hours after death, so they are no longer warm. In my will I have forbidden the opening of my body. . . . The best means to have a long life is to do like Frau von Wehlen, namely, to try to keep entertained and not to worry about anything. Of all the little games Mistress Charlotte or Frau von Wehlen used to make us play, I remember only one: "Here he comes and turns and turns, with a friendly tack-tack-tack, and turns around again with a friendly tick-tick-tick, and turns yet once again."

1. Amalie Elisabeth had died on 13 July.

Versailles, 14 September 1709

Now you will have many companions in sadness; four days ago our army lost a battle near Mons,[1] but since this time our soldiers fought back terribly hard, both sides suffered great losses. One sees nothing but mourning and tears. The only son of Madame Dangeau, who was born Fräulein von Löwenstein, has been dreadfully wounded. One of his legs was amputated near the belly, and it is not yet known whether he can survive. . . .

My son does not even pay me what he is supposed to give me, let alone any advances. His Spanish campaigns, in which he was not provided with anything so that he had to purchase everything with his own money, have just about ruined him. It is horrendous how much money my son has spent. The King did not give my son a farthing, and the entire cost of traveling, campaigning, sieges, and everything was borne by him. A more wretched and unhappy time than the present I have never seen. God grant that a good peace will bring a change!

1. The battle of Malplaquet on 11 September, in which 33,000 men died.

To ELECTRESS SOPHIE

Versailles, 22 September 1709

I find that the Czar[1] is most intelligent and speaks much to the point. I believe that he has his prince[2] travel for such a long time in order to tame him, just as birds of prey are tamed by being carried around on a man's fist for nights on end. The citadel of Tourney is taken; Monsieur de Surville has just called on me; he has gone half deaf from all the cannon fire. Monsieur Schulenburg has kept up his reputation, as always. Another person who has gained much honor in this battle is Harling, who first made a sortie from his retrenchment to help another brigade, and when he wanted to return to his retrenchment, he found enemy troops there, so he just simply chased them out again and did his best to get through. I think his uncle will be pleased.

1. Peter the Great.   2. The czarevitch.

Versailles, 28 September 1709

Since this is a safe opportunity and my letter will not go through the mail, I want to send some songs which, I believe, Your Grace does not have yet. It is quite true that everyone is short of funds because of this lady; but to me the funniest part of it is that in order to make sure that the King approves of her doings, she gives him a share of her lucre, and to the Duchesse de Bourgogne as well. Meanwhile no one receives any money; we are paid only in assignations, that is, nothing but paper, and at that one has to scramble to get it. If for example one were to receive a sum today, it would be in the form of an assignation to be paid three, four, or even five months from now, and even then it would not be easy to get it. The wretched misery of these times defies description. The famine is so horrendous that on all sides one sees people collapsing and dying of hunger; everyone is full of sorrow and lamentation, from the greatest to the most lowly. The court is full of cliques; some want to curry favor with the powerful lady, some with Monsieur le Dauphin, and some with the Duc de Bourgogne. . . . That is a crazy, mixed-up clockwork, and I could say, as the song has it, "If one were not dying of hunger, one might die of laughter." The old crone sets all these cabals against one another, the better to rule herself. I do not belong to any of them, continue to walk my straight path, and let them go on as they please. I treat everyone as politely as I can and do not trust anyone, for all these people hate me, particularly the Duchesse de Bourgogne. I believe, and it seems to be true, that the person who hates me least is our King, and the one who hates me most is Madame de Maintenon. About my son I will say nothing here since I already told Your Grace about him on Thursday last. The King has a good deal of affection for him; if he were willing to force himself to stay with the King, he would enjoy greater favor than any of the King's children. But he will not force himself to spend so much as one week here and haunts nothing but bad company.

To RAUGRÄFIN LUISE

Versailles, 26 October 1709

These are certainly sad times. Whenever one goes out one is followed by crowds of poor people who are half dead with hunger. Everything is paid in promissory notes, money is not to be found. Everyone is dejected, there is no joy anywhere. . . .

If your and my wishes were to be fulfilled, dear Luise, Ma Tante will surely live for more than a hundred years. In January the good, honest Monsieur Polier will turn ninety. His mind is still as good and as clear as if he were only forty, his memory is good, he reads without spectacles, but his legs have become stiff and his face a little paler than it used to be; aside from that he is unchanged. I consider him a real saint. He lives with great piety and does as much good as is in his power; at the same time he is perfectly calm and serene, does not fear death, and accepts the will of God in all things.

Versailles, 7 December 1709

The almighty woman does not trust me, for she has always worked against me. In my husband's days his favorites had won her over because they were afraid that I might complain to the King about how they were fleecing my late husband, about the dreadful things they were doing to me, and about their outrageous life in general. That is why they won this woman over by threats and by scaring her, saying that they knew all about her life and would tell everything to the King unless she took their side; I heard about these threats from the lady herself, although she did not say what they threatened her with; but this I learned from the friends of the Chevalier de Lorraine. Therefore she has persecuted me all her life and does not trust me one whit because she thinks that I am as vindictive as she is, which is not true; but these are the reasons why she keeps me away from the King. And now there is another reason, namely her great love for the Duchesse de Bourgogne, and her fear that since the King has no aversion for me and since my unaffected temperament has never displeased His Majesty, so now she is afraid that because, as she is well aware, I have great respect and love for the King, he might more easily become attached to a person of my age than to a young princess like the Duchesse de Bourgogne, and that in this manner I might supplant the latter in the King's favor. That is why she must keep me away, and so she does; nor is there anything to be done about it.[1]

1. In writing this letter, Elisabeth Charlotte was so carried away by strong feelings that her syntax fell apart. The attentive reader may have noticed other instances of this throughout the correspondence.

To ELECTRESS SOPHIE

Versailles, 5 January 1710

I must tell Your Grace something that moves me to pity in a way, although I am glad that it has happened, namely that my son has finally, and of his own accord, broken off with his brown sweetheart[1] and will no longer see her. This is very hard for him, because he still loves her, but he has every reason in the world to break off with her, for in the first place she was dreadfully greedy and he could never give her enough, and in the second place she treated him like a slave, scolded him by calling him the grossest names that one would not call the lowest stable boy; she used to kick him with her feet and he had to be so submissive that whenever she beckoned he had to drop everything and wait on her; he was not allowed to do anything without her leave. If he had promised one of his household something without clearing it with her, she forced my son to give it to one of her creatures. She was brazen in everything; her son had to be provided for more sumptuously than the Duc de Chartres,[2] otherwise my son was given a tremendous tongue-lashing. She dragged him into the worst company imaginable, nothing but whores and knaves, by your leave, and he was not permitted to keep any other company. All of Paris was scandalized by it. Because of this outrageous life my son was in very bad odor with the King; so in order to regain the King's favor he has broken off and will not see her any more. I am of the opinion that my son deserves more praise for gaining mastery over himself than for winning a battle, for no one wins a battle by himself, and others can be as responsible for the victory as the commanding general; but if a man moderates his passions, all the honor is his, and it is a harder thing to do than anything else in the world. . . . My son's brown and cranky sweetheart left yesterday for her father's house, where she will be able to live very well indeed, as my son let her keep the 42,000 livres a year that he had given her. All the men approve of my son, all the ladies disapprove. Setting the example of leaving one's mistress voluntarily greatly displeases the ladies.

1. Comtesse Parabère.   2. The Duke's legitimate son.

Versailles, 5 March 1710

I once had a funny dialogue with the poor Archbishop of Reims. As Your Grace knows, he is the First Duke and Peer of France. Once, as we were walking together in the valley of Saint-Germain, he said to me, "It seems to me Madame, that you are not too impressed with us, the dukes of France, and that you think much more highly of your German princes." I answered quite drily, "That is true." He said, "If you do not want us to compare ourselves with them, then to whom do you want us to compare ourselves?" I replied, "To Turkish pashas and vizirs." He said, "How so?" I said, "Like these men you have all the dignities but no birth to go with them, for the King makes you what you are, just as the Grand Turk makes pashas and vizirs; but in the case of the German princes, they are made only by God and by their parents, and thus you cannot be compared to them. Moreover, you are subjects, and they are free." I thought the poor man would burst out of his skin; still, he was unable to refute me.

New medals are rarer here than the antique ones; of those I can find more
than enough in Paris. If that rogue, my treasurer d'Avous, had not robbed me
blind and caused me to lose 50,000 *talers,* I could buy plenty of gold medals;
as it is I can get only five or six at a time, but still this permits me to aug-
ment my collection every month. I started out with 160, now I have 511, and
so in time I hope to build up a fine collection of rare medals. . . .

I do not think that there is another country in the world where people revolt as often and as easily as in England. The Germans love their masters
more than other nations; the French are given to saying and singing all kinds
of slanderous things about their kings but nonetheless let them rule as
they see fit.

To RAUGRÄFIN LUISE

Marly, 6 November 1710

Before anything else I must tell you that two days ago I had the most dreadful fright I ever experienced in my life. In brief, let me tell you, dear Luise,
that on Tuesday last, when we all celebrated Saint Hubert's Day, had already
caught one stag, and were hunting a second one, I saw a rider galloping by
and fall with his horse. At first I thought it was a groom, and I could see that
he was badly hurt, because he had trouble getting up. When he was helped
to his feet and I could see his face, it was my son. You can imagine how I felt.
I took him in my calash and brought him here. He was in horrible pain, but
we had no way of knowing whether the arm was broken or only dislocated; it
turned out, however, that it was only dislocated. But since it happened to
the shoulder where my son had already been wounded twice and where some
nerves were cut off, the pain was so horrendous that he was like a person
in the throes of death. As soon as the shoulder was set, the pain ceased; he is
quite well again and has been bled. He does not keep to his room, carries
the arm in a sling, and walks all around.

To ELECTRESS SOPHIE

Marly, 13 November 1710

The French women have this foolish craving for hiding away in dark places.
Madame de Maintenon has had several niches built for her, where she goes
to lie down; they are something like a small daybed, enclosed in a kind of
little house of tight-fitting boards, which are like curtains. The Duchesse de
Bourgogne also has a niche, and so does the Princesse de Conti. I would
suffocate if I had to sit or lie in one of these; I love to see the dear bright sun.
. . . What they do not realize is that this is precisely why the air becomes
unhealthy for them, for they are no longer accustomed to it. I am the very

opposite; as soon as there is a moment of good weather, I open all my windows.

To RAUGRÄFIN LUISE

Versailles, 14 December 1710

All of a sudden the Duchesse de Berry[1] fainted dead away; we thought it was a stroke, but after Her Grace the Duchesse de Bourgogne had poured vinegar into her face she came to again. Then she had a horrendous fit of vomiting; nor is this surprising, for in the theater she had continually stuffed herself for two hours with all kinds of filth, caramel peaches, chestnuts, a paste of gooseberries and currants, dried cherries, and lots of lemonade with it, then at supper she ate fish and drank on top of that. So she felt sick, and when she wanted to hold it in, she fainted. Today she is hale and hearty again, but one of these days she will make herself really ill with these eating binges, for she will not listen to any admonitions.

    1. Madame's granddaughter.

To ELECTRESS SOPHIE

Marly, 11 January 1711

How I would have liked to see the Christ Child! Here this is quite unknown. I wanted to introduce it, but Monsieur said, "You want to bring us your German customs to spend more money; I kiss your hands!" I love to see the children's joy, but my son's children do not enjoy anything in the world; I never saw such children.

To RAUGRÄFIN LUISE

Versailles, 28 February 1711

I know many ladies here who smear their faces with this white balm after it has been prepared with spirits of wine. The late Monsieur once wanted to smear it on my face, but I could never stand it and would rather keep my wrinkles than smear white stuff on my face. For I hate all makeup and do not want rouge for myself. . . .

    The pain in my foot is almost gone, but my knees are no good at all and hurt day and night. There are strong reasons to keep me from going to a warm-water spa; in the first place I do not have the money for it, secondly I am not permitted to travel incognito, and thirdly I would not be allowed to leave the kingdom. I am not even allowed to travel to Lorraine, let alone to Aachen. No slaves are more subject to their master than the royal house is to the King. I am so distressed that such a proposal is impossible that I do not even permit myself to think about it. Much as it grieves my heart, we will never see each other again in this life. But let us stop speaking of such sad things!

To ELECTRESS SOPHIE

Marly, 16 April 1711

I must tell Your Grace about the great sadness all of France and all of us here are feeling owing to the totally unexpected death of Monsieur le Dauphin.[1] I saw the King yesterday at eleven; his sadness would have melted a heart of stone, and yet he is not cranky for all that but speaks most gently to everyone and makes all the sad arrangements with great firmness, although tears keep coming to his eyes and he sighs to himself. I am deadly afraid that he will fall ill himself, for he looks awful. . . . I bear the misfortune with patience and only worry for the King. While I do feel sorry for Monsieur le Dauphin, I cannot grieve as much for someone who had no love and no use for me as for someone who has always remained my friend. . . .

The art of saying much in a few words is not my forte, that is why my letters are so long. . . . Considering that when writing one has time to think about what one wants to say and therefore can compose it better, I think that people of intelligence who write badly are simply too passionate and want to express all their thoughts at once, which makes their style hard to understand.

1. Louis, the son of Louis XIV.

To RAUGRÄFIN LUISE

Marly, 14 May 1711

I have been weeping bitter tears all day long, and not without cause, for today I received the sad news that my daughter has also lost her oldest son and her youngest daughter, and that the two younger princes are not yet out of danger, so that there is reason to fear that within a week my daughter will have lost all of her beautiful and dear children.[1] I am afraid she will die with grief or go out of her mind, for the lovely children were my daughter's only pride and joy. Everyone who saw them praised their intelligence and beauty. I am quite undone. The dear children, the three who have died, wrote to me every week; now I will have time to spare for writing. . . . So many terrible things are happening that it looks as if the vessels of the Book of Revelations were being poured out.

1. Four of the Duchesse de Lorraine's children reached adulthood. She had fourteen pregnancies.

I cannot understand how Ma Tante has enough patience to read my letters
more than once and can only ascribe it to her kind affection for me. For
I myself could not possibly reread my own letters; this would be more trouble
for me than to write twenty pages in the first place. If you, dear Luise, like
completely unaffected speech, I am not surprised that you like to read my
letters. I will never learn to speak differently than I think, that is why I am
doing so poorly in this country.

Marly, 9 July 1711

Dearest Luise, I am writing even though my heart is sad and heavy today because I learned yesterday from Monsieur de Polier's nephew that the good,
honest man died the day before yesterday. . . . He died like a young man, in
a fever fit, and happily too, having lived for ninety-one years, six months,
and two days. His mind did not give way for a single moment. In the last ten
or more years he had been extremely pious, given almost all of his meager
resources to the poor, and lived like a real saint. His death touches me deeply.
. . . What the dying say is not the Gospel. The Duchess of Wolfenbüttel for
example told her husband that he would follow her within the year, but it did
not happen.

To ELECTRESS SOPHIE

Fontainebleau, 12 August 1711

I imagine that Herr von Leibniz's book will be for sale in Frankfurt; I shall
ask Luise to have someone find it for me and send it. My son is very keen on
reading new books, and Herr von Leibniz will do him a great favor to send
him his book. I herewith send Your Grace something that will interest Monsieur Leibniz. When they were digging to make a new altar at Notre-Dame,
they found a lot of carved stones that were made at the time of Tiberius in
his honor by the boatmen of Paris. All the *curieux* are flocking to see this,
and the members of the *Académie* are writing about it.

Marly, 10 October 1711

I see that Your Grace is not like myself when I was still at Heidelberg
and Mannheim, where I much rather went to the German than to the French
church, because our German psalms are incomparably more beautiful than
Marot's.[1] Hearing the French psalms is like reading Amadis de Gaule; this old
French is used here only in jest, but there is nothing funny about the German psalms, they are in good German. Another thing that used to shock me
in the French church was the different intonations in which the children
recited the Ten Commandments: "Thou shalt not kill, thou shalt not steal,

etc." but said in such different intonations that it was quite funny; this was not done in the German church either. If one were allowed to talk back to the preachers, the one whom Your Grace heard might have been told: the storks know the country for which they are headed, but we poor humans know only where we are and not where we are going, therefore it is no wonder that we are not as eager and ready to leave as the storks. I also believe that if someone had taken the preacher by his word and offered to send him to the next world, he would have declined with thanks. Nonetheless it is true that some people are happy to die. . . .

If someone is sent to the Bastille, no one finds out about it, neither at court nor in town. Even stranger things have happened: one man was in the Bastille for many years, and died there with a mask on; he was always flanked by two musketeers who had orders to shoot him down immediately if he should ever remove his mask. He ate and slept in his mask. He must have been somebody important, for he was very well treated in every other way, lodged well, and given everything he desired. He took communion wearing his mask, was very pious, and read all the time. No one was ever able to find out who this person was.[2]

1. Clement Marot had translated the psalms into French.   2. The so-called Man in the Iron Mask, a mysterious prisoner of State.

The following series of letters, in which Madame reports the deaths of the Dauphine, the Dauphin, and their son, as well as the manner in which the only heir to the crown was saved, is famous in medical history.

Marly, 14 February 1712

We are full of sadness here, for on the day before yesterday at a quarter before nine the poor Madame la Dauphine[1] expired. I am convinced that the doctors have killed this poor princess as surely as what I am writing to Your Grace here is true. They had given her a little Mylady Kent powder, only a few grains, when she began to sweat profusely, but they did not have the patience to wait out the sweating: right in the midst of it, when she had already broken out into an angry red rash, she was placed into a warm bath and bled for the fourth time, and this caused the rash to draw back into the body. . . . Now it is all over. I cannot look at the King without getting tears in my eyes; his grief would melt a heart of stone.

I congratulate Your Grace on the safe delivery of her granddaughter, the Crown Princess of Prussia. May God grant a long life to this prince.[2] The King of Prussia must be doubly pleased, firstly about having a grandson, and secondly about the occasion for a ceremony, which will surely be provided by the christening. I am full of wonder about the differences that exist in this world: while happiness reigns at Berlin, all of us here are in sadness and loneliness. . . . Monsieur le Dauphin is deeply sad, but he is young and can remarry to replace what he has lost; but Madame de Savoie's[3] loss is forever, as is our King's, for she [the Dauphine] was brought up to his entire satisfaction and was his only comfort and joy; she was of such a cheerful temperament that she could always find some way to cheer him up.

1. Marie Adelaide of Savoy, Duchesse de Bourgogne, and Dauphine after the death of the first Dauphin, her father-in-law, in 1711. 2. The prince born on 24 January was to become Frederick the Great. 3. Mother of the Dauphine.

Marly, 18 February 1712

I had thought that today I would only have to write to Your Grace about the sad ceremony in which I had to participate at Versailles yesterday,[1] but a new disaster has befallen us, for the good Monsieur le Dauphin[2] has followed his wife and died this morning at nine o'clock. Your Grace can easily imagine the dreadful sadness that this loss has brought to all of us. The King's grief is so great that I tremble for His Majesty's health. It is a horrible loss for the entire kingdom, for Monsieur le Dauphin was a virtuous and just lord, and sensible too; France could not suffer a greater loss, and everyone here will be the poorer for it; I am moved to the depth of my soul. Next to God, I can turn only to Your Grace for comfort. Since the King is suffering from a cold, he was not awakened but learned the dreadful news soon enough. The King loses an important councillor in this lord, for since his father's death the King had brought him into all the royal councils and the ministers were working with His Grace; he relieved the King of as many burdens as he could, was charitable, and gave alms liberally; in fact he sold all of his late mother's jewels and gave the money to impoverished wounded officers. He did as much good as was in his power and has never harmed anyone. I do not think that what we shall see here has ever happened before, namely that a husband and wife are taken to Saint-Denis[3] in the same hearse. I am still in such a shock that I cannot seem to recover. The sadness here is indescribable, it fairly looks as if all of us here will die one by one.

1. The requiem for the Dauphine. 2. Louis, Duc de Bourgogne, the second Dauphin.
3. The burial place for the kings of France.

Marly, 20 February 1712

This is not a mail day, but when my heart is as fearful and sorely troubled as it is now, I have no other comfort but to pour out my grief to Your Grace. . . . Wicked people have spread the rumor in Paris that my son has poisoned the Dauphin and the Dauphine. I, who would place my hand in the fire for his innocence, at first thought that this was only foolish talk and that no one could possibly say such a thing in all seriousness. . . . Some say that this wicked rumor was brought in from Spain. If this were true, the Princesse des Ursins would be a true devil and carry her revenge against my poor son very far indeed;[1] he is paying a high price for having made fun of this lady.

1. Philippe had given military help to the Spanish king but had probably involved himself in the domestic affairs of Spain and also made his own plans for a possible succession; this had caused him to be recalled from Spain by Louis XIV and accounts for the hostility of the Spanish court mentioned here.

Versailles, 5 March 1712

My heart is filled with pity for the King. Even though he forces himself to appear cheerful, one can see that he is suffering inside. May God preserve the King for us, otherwise we will have utter confusion. Some people already fear that my son wants to be part of the future government, that is why they try to turn the court and the Parisians against him and spread rumors of poison, as I already wrote to Your Grace. Whenever anyone dies at court, he is blamed for it . . . there is no wickedness of which he is not accused.

Versailles, 10 March 1712

I have no doubt that Your Grace will be shocked to read how the disasters here continue. The doctors repeated the same mistake they made with Madame la Dauphine, for when the little Dauphin was already covered with the red rash and sweating, they bled him and then gave him an emetic, and during that operation the poor child expired. And here is proof that the doctors have killed this Dauphin too: his little brother[1] has the same disease; yet since the nine doctors were occupied with the older prince, the nursemaids of the younger one locked themselves into a room with the younger one and gave him a little wine and bisquit; yesterday, when the child had a high fever, the doctors wanted to bleed him too, but Madame de Vantadour and the prince's subgoverness, Madame de Villefort, fought off the doctors and absolutely refused to permit it; they simply kept him nice and warm. This one, thanks be to God, was saved, to the shame of the doctors, for he would surely have died if the doctors had had their way. It is quite beyond me why the doctors themselves did not change their ways after they saw the dire consequences of their bleedings and emetics with Madame la Dauphine, and how they had the nerve to kill that poor child in the same way; and what frightens me is the King's blindness when it comes to these people; he does not believe that Madame la Dauphine died through their fault. . . . The King bears his misfortune with such constancy and firmness that I cannot admire His Majesty enough. One can say truthfully that except for Madame de Maintenon the King has lost everything he has loved most in the world, and in Madame la Dauphine his only pride and joy.

1. Who grew up to be Louis XV.

Versailles, 13 March 1712

I am certain that more than a hundred saints were canonized who deserved it less than our late second Dauphin. For in eleven months we have lost three Dauphins, which is appalling, forty-nine, twenty-six, and five years. . . . May God preserve the King; this is extremely important for the whole kingdom and for all of us here. When speaking to him in his study, I am doing my best not to make the King think of anything sad, laugh and chatter about all kinds of trifles; but it is hard to come up with something entertaining when the calamities are piling up as they are doing here. The King was often prevented from being friendly with me, but deep down he must not have conceived too much aversion for me, because despite all the bad things he was told even by Monsieur himself and several others, His Majesty still likes me and now permits me to see him as much as others who are loved more than I am.

Marly, 14 April 1712

The arts and sciences, these are properly befitting to my son and come naturally to him, but when he wants to play the buffoon, one feels like throwing up because it becomes him so very poorly, and the young people, even his own daughter, make fun of him when he does it. But nothing can be done about it; my son is like the child in the tale of the fairies who are invited to the christening: one makes the wish that the child will become handsome, the other that he will become eloquent, the third that he will learn all the arts, the fourth that he will learn all the sports, such as fencing, riding, and dancing, the fifth that he will become proficient in the art of warfare, the sixth that he will be more courageous than others. But the seventh was not invited to the christening, and she says: I cannot take away from the child what my sisters have given him, but I will set my face against him as long as he lives so that the good gifts he was given will not profit him. I will give him such an ugly gait that he will look like a limping hunchback; I will cause him to have a heavy black beard and with that . . . I will give him grimaces that will distort his features; I will give him a dislike of exercise and will fill him with such boredom that he will abandon all his arts, music, painting, and drawing, and will give him love of solitude and loathing for honorable people. I will often give him bad luck in war; I will make him believe that debauchery is becoming to him, and I will give him loathing for his best friends' advice; and in this way all the good things my sisters have given him will be spoiled. And this is precisely what has happened, and it is the reason why he would rather sit around with his daughter and her chambermaids, listening to a lot of foolish cackle, than to have commerce with upright people or to manage his own household in keeping with his rank. So now Your Grace knows how this came about. . . . The King treats my son well, which gives me hope that the lies have not made any impression upon His Majesty. On his own, my son is not given to drink, but he often keeps very bad company and thinks it is the friendly thing to do to act the good-natured fool with them. Then he gets roaring drunk with them, and once he is drunk he no longer knows what in the world he says or does. I have begged him a thousand times not to have anything to do with these drunkards, but the more I forbade it, the more he did it; so I made up my mind not to say anything more about it, until now; and now I only said: If you had followed rather than scorned my good advice you would not be in this kind of trouble. He admits it, but it is a bit late for that, he should have thought about it earlier.

Marly, 24 April 1712

The nightingales are singing and yet Your Grace is still at Hanover rather than at Herrenhausen! There she could go for better walks than at Hanover. I am writing to Your Grace here by my window, looking out on lovely beds of narcissus, tulips, and imperial crowns; the beds are enclosed by two avenues and a horseshoe of white, red, and brown marble. In the middle is a wide stone staircase and on the two sides are also steps decorated with statues and white marble flowerpots. Right in front of the staircase is a hill from which the cascade called *la rivière* tumbles down; the cascade is also decorated at the top and at the bottom with white marble statues, but along the sides there are only two broad beds of lawn; it is flanked on either side by an avenue so that one can drive up by calash. So Your Grace can see that I have a fine view, but unfortunately it does not give me any clever inspirations.

Versailles, 21 May 1712

Although the old woman is our worst enemy, I wish her a long life for the King's sake. For everything would be ten times worse if the King should die now. He loves this woman so terribly that he would be sure to follow her to the grave.

To RAUGRÄFIN LUISE

Marly, 7 July 1712

I am far from writing as beautifully as you do, dear Luise. Karoline's French hand resembled mine a great deal. What has happened to our good writing master with his burned hand? He was extraordinarily short-sighted, and I often scared him, but he was a good, pious, honest man. I do not use spectacles; although my eyes are no longer what they used to be, I still see well enough to get along without spectacles. Both in summer and in winter I write by light.

To ELECTRESS SOPHIE

Versailles, 10 December 1712

I well remember having seen the play of Wallenstein at Hanover; in the end a man by the name of Leslie stabs Wallenstein, who is in bed with a camp follower. I also remember that when we saw the play of Doctor Faustus and when the devil carried off Doctor Faustus, the news came that the Bishop of Osnabrück had died, which made everyone laugh. . . .

When Your Grace last saw her Liselotte who could run and jump so well, she was young and light; now I am old and heavy, that has made for a big change. I am certain that if I should be fortunate enough to see Your Grace in a place where she would not expect to see me, Your Grace would not recognize me, unless I spoke. My wrinkly eyes, my big hanging cheeks, my snow-white hair, the sunken place between my ears and my cheeks, and my large double chin would not remind Your Grace of Liselotte at all. . . .

Knowing that the joys of the next world are of a kind "that no ear has heard, no eye has seen, no human heart has ever felt," I do not try to imagine them and only think that since God is all-powerful and truthful, and since He has promised me joy, He will surely find a way to make me feel it, even though I cannot know yet how and when it will be. In this I place my trust. . . . The King also graciously asks me about my health, and I give him an accounting of it. Sometimes I put it in a way that makes His Majesty laugh.

The Peace of Utrecht, concluded in 1713, made it clear that France's hegemony in Europe was broken and that England had become a world power. Although France did not lose any territory in Europe, it had to relinquish large parts of its colonial empire. Internally, the country was weakened, and major outbreaks of popular unrest were prevented only by the well-functioning machinery of the centralized State. The treasury was empty.

To RAUGRÄFIN LUISE

Versailles, 18 June 1713

I shall send my portrait to Ma Tante at the first opportunity. I shall have it painted from life, so that it will be an original; nothing will ever be as true to life as my portrait by Rigaud. The little dog is still alive and more intelligent than ever; I am very fond of it. It will be no hardship for me to send you a present from the country fair like this last one every year; that cannot ruin me and I am happy to have found something that you like and enjoy. But, dear Luise, have you not inherited any jewelry from your mother? Diamonds have become rare here, but not the colored gems, especially the small ones.

Versailles, 2 July 1713

If it were not for the pain in my right knee and foot, I could say now that I am, thanks be to God, in perfect health, for I do not sleep more than I should and am not too short of breath. My knee and foot, however, are getting worse every day, but I suppose we must be patient if God sends us something and realize that He is indeed merciful, because we deserve even worse. . . . To keep quiet is excellent for the chest, but old women are always being accused of being unable to keep quiet. Dear Luise, I cannot answer some of your questions by mail, for I am not allowed to write about matters of religion; but as soon as I have a safe opportunity I shall carefully answer all your questions about the communion.

To ELECTRESS SOPHIE

Marly, 24 November 1713

I did know about the book by Père Quesnel that made so much noise here and was condemned by the Pope.[1] The Jansenists are hated here quite as much as the Reformed. . . . The Jesuits were able to have Père Quesnel chased away. I do not meddle in these things and am neither of the one nor the other party, but I could not resist telling my confessor that it annoys me when people of the same religion persecute one another in this way. Because of the Pope's declaration there is a great gathering of bishops in Paris; what they will do about it will not rob me of any sleep. . . . My son and his daughter[2] who, as Your Grace knows, used to love each other so much that unfortunate rumors[3] were spread about them, are now beginning to hate each other like the devil, quarrel every day, and, worst of all, the daughter creates trouble between the father and her husband; the father left for Paris in a huff. The father keeps all of this secret from me, but I find out about it just the same; his wife tells me everything.

1. This was *Le nouveau testament en Français avec des réflections morales,* published in 1692 by the Oratorian priest Pasquier Quesnel (1634–1719). Pervaded by the spirit of Jansenism, an austere doctrinal movement within the French Church, this book preached a return to the discipline and simplicity of early Christianity and recommended frequent reading of the Scripture in the vernacular. Jansenism had a wide following within the French Church as well as in the highest circles of the judiciary, and since many Jansenists had also been *Frondeurs* during the early years of Louis XIV's reign, the movement was considered not only a threat to the unity of the French Church but an actual political danger. Louis XIV therefore put pressure on the Pope to condemn certain propositions of Quesnel's book as heretical, which

was finally done by Clement XI's bull *Unigenitus* of 1713. This was a triumph for the Jesuit order, whose worldly and pragmatic attitude (the Jansenist Pascal said that they "placed cushions under the sinners' elbows") had long been castigated by the Jansenists as one of the principal reasons for the moral decay of modern Christianity. 2. The Duchesse de Berry; her husband was a grandson of the King.   3. The "unfortunate rumors" concerned an incestuous relationship between the Duc d'Orléans and his daughter.

Rambouillet, 15 June 1714

I humbly thank Your Grace for her kind wishes. If every year one could shed a year, one would eventually become a child again. As long as Your Grace lives and enjoys good health, I shall not become tired of my life.

On 8 June Electress Sophie had died; she had suffered a stroke while walking in the garden. Elisabeth Charlotte was devastated.

To RAUGRÄFIN LUISE

Marly, 24 June 1714

Dearest Luise, having learned from a letter from Hanover describing the course of the woeful misfortune that has befallen us that you were recalled there, I am certain that you are once again in Hanover, and so I write to you, not in order to find comfort for both of us but to mix my tears, which are flowing so freely now, with yours. Our loss is eternal; my weeping may cease but never my grief. This dear departed Princess was my only comfort in all the adversities I have so often suffered here; whenever I poured out my grief to Her Grace and received a letter from her in return I was comforted. Now I feel all alone in the world. I believe that Our Lord has sent me this calamity in order to dispel my fear of death, and it is true indeed that I will now see my end approach without sorrow and without regret about leaving anything in this world. My children are provided for and have enough consolation in this world to forget me soon enough; so there is nothing to keep me here whenever it shall please God to call me away. . . . I should dearly love to continue speaking to you, for it eases one's sorrow to speak to those who share it; but, dearest Luise, my head and my eyes hurt so much from constant weeping that I barely know what I am saying. Against my will I must therefore close and only tell you that you will remain dear to my heart as long as my wretched life shall last.

Marly, 1 July 1714

I do not recall, dear Luise, whether I told you in my last letter how I heard about this calamity and how my confessor was charged with breaking the news to me. I was seized by trembling like a person who has a shaking fit in

a high fever; at the same time I turned white as a sheet and did not weep
for a good fifteen minutes but gasped for breath and felt as if I were choking
to death. After that the tears came often, flowing day and night, then I
would dry up and choke until the next flow of tears, and this has been going
on until now. What I do not understand is how I nonetheless stay so healthy,
for I am not ill at all. Twice I was invited to go hunting, but I could not make
up my mind to go, for I cannot take pleasure in anything. You are so right
to say that this dreadful news has pierced my heart and soul. You are so pious,
dear Luise, that if God Almighty should send me comfort and ease my sorrow, I would ascribe it to your prayer. . . . It must have been a stroke that
caused our dreadful calamity, but as you so rightly say, it was God's will to
call our beloved Princess. Those who go to God are not to be pitied, unlike
those who must stay behind in this wicked, unbearable world. Oh Lord,
how often did Ma Tante tell me in her letters that she considered a sudden
death to be the best kind, and that she thought it a bad thing to be dying
in bed, with the pastor or the priest on one side and the doctor on the other,
even though neither can help. She said that she did not want to give this
spectacle, and alas, she spoke only too truly. . . . Once misfortune gets started,
there is no end to it, as you and I are now experiencing. But I did not need
all of this to learn about the vanity of this world: great courts are the best
schools to learn it. Oh my dear Luise, how far I am from having Ma Tante's
virtues and intelligence! No indeed, there is nothing in this world to compare with Her late Grace. Oh Lord, dear Luise, how can I ever get over this
misfortune! Ma Tante was my only comfort in all the adversities I have
suffered here; her cheerful letters made even the seemingly saddest situations
easier for me; until now they have surely kept me alive. Besides, for what
should I conserve myself now? I am of no use to anyone and a burden to myself. . . . You are the only one left of all those who were near and dear to
me in Germany. Adieu, dear Luise! I know how much you are to be pitied,
for I am certain that your feelings are the same as mine. But in whatever
state I am, my attachment for you will remain unchanged as long as my
wretched life shall last, and you will always be dear to my heart.

Marly, 10 July 1714

I cannot possibly describe to you what I am going through day and night, and
in addition I suffer the torment of having to hold in my feelings, for the
King will not tolerate sad faces. I must also participate in the hunts against
my will; at the last one I wept bitter tears when the Elector of Bavaria came
to my coach to express his condolences about my loss. This broke my composure and the tears burst forth, and this lasted throughout the entire hunt. I
could see that people were laughing at me, but I could not help it. Yet though
I am sad to the depth of my soul I do not fall ill; my body is healthy but

my soul is ill, as it were, for it is deep inside that I suffer most. . . . I am living at this court like a *solitaire;* I never go to the salon where all those who are at court assemble, and I never gamble. I am always in my room, where I read or write, for to tell the truth, I am no longer interested in anything. My only joy, pleasure, and comfort were the letters of Ma Tante, our dear departed Princess, and these too, alas, are gone now.

Fontainebleau, 14 October 1714

For the sake of God, my dear, do seek some distractions to keep yourself from falling into melancholia! Nothing is more dangerous to the health, and it is dangerous for the head too. You are no more alone in the world than I am; for as you have seen from my letters I am not only in a foreign land but all alone in the world, I have powerful enemies and nowhere to go for comfort. Yet I am not melancholy, because I think it is bad enough to be tormented by others without distressing myself. I firmly trust in my God; He knows why He has called me here and what He plans to do with me, and I have often felt His help when I thought all was lost; therefore I place myself entirely into His providence and do not count on human help. . . .

I am not given to fright, dear Luise, and four years ago when my coach tipped over pretty dramatically, I was not the least bit frightened or afraid. One of my ladies broke a window in the coach with her shoulder, which gave her two cuts in the shoulder, otherwise no one was hurt. I had a good laugh about it. . . .

Just between us, I believe that the King of England[1] would have a better time at his *Göhrde*[2] than in all his splendor in England. For my good cousin the Lord King is no more taken with ceremonies than his old cousin, my Excellency. . . .

I am very sorry, dear Luise, that I will not see you again at your present age, having seen you when you were so very young. Do you remember the good cry we had together when I took you to the convent of Neuburg to meet Countess Labach?

1. George I of England; he had succeeded Queen Anne after she had died childless on 1 August.   2. Hunting lodge near Lüneburg.

Fontainebleau, 20 October 1714

Dearest Luise, this, unfortunately, is the last letter I shall write from my dear Fontainebleau, for on Wednesday we will leave here, and on Monday we will have the last hunt in this beautiful forest. There is nothing around Marly and Versailles that comes even close to it. Another thing I like about this place is that all the halls and galleries look so German; when one enters the Swiss's hall, it looks just like an old German hall with bay windows, wains-

cotting, and benches. I clearly feel that the air here and the hunting agree
with me and give me good health; they drive away and dissipate sad thoughts,
and nothing is worse for my health than sadness. So far, thank God, all our
hunts have ended very well. Last Thursday they captured a stag that was a bit
angry. A gentleman climbed onto a rock behind the stag and wounded it
in the thigh, in this way the stag could not lower its head and therefore was
not dangerous. Behind my calash was a calash bearing three clergymen, the
Archbishop of Lyon and two abbots, who are not accustomed to hunting; as
soon as they caught sight of the stag two of them jumped out of the calash
and hid behind it, lying down flat on the ground. I am sorry that I did not see
this scene; I would have had a good laugh, for we old hunters are not so
afraid of stags. —At the hunt I conveyed your greetings to the Electoral Prince[1]
telling His Grace that you, dear Luise, send him your respects. He only bowed
deeply to me but did not make any reply. I am not in his favor. I think he is
afraid that I might speak to him about religion, wanting to persuade him to
change, for he has not done it yet. But the good gentleman is much mistaken;
I am no apostle and am all in favor of everyone's believing what his conscience
tells him. If my advice were followed, there would never be any squabbles
about religion, and the priests would go after vice rather than faith and would
try to improve and correct. . . . Perhaps he also does not like me because I
am an old woman; but that cannot be helped and in fact will get worse every
day.

1. Friedrich August von Sachsen.

Versailles, 22 January 1715

I can easily understand that you like the dear fatherland better than England,
and I think that your brother-in-law[1] and your nieces should be much obliged
to you for crossing the sea to be with them. It would certainly be the greatest
mark of friendship if I ever crossed the sea to pay a visit to someone. . . .
Everything I hear about the Princess of Wales makes me esteem and like her;
she has noble and beautiful sentiments and I feel much affection for her.

1. The Duke of Schomberg.

Versailles, 10 May 1715

The old rancor will end only with death, and as long as the old trollop is able
to think up more things that can harm and upset me, she will do it. Now
she has a new grievance, namely that I have refused to see her bosom friend[1]
who was chased away by the present Queen of Spain.[2] The reason that I
did not want to see this woman is that my son requested it; she is his worst
enemy and has publicly called him a poisoner. My son, not satisfied with
proving his innocence, has had all the records deposited at the Parlement,[3]

where they are to be kept. The other cannot forgive me for refusing to receive such a woman, but then, as the proverb has it, "Birds of a feather flock together." I must always be prepared for trouble and have patience. . . . If sorrow is the way to salvation, I cannot doubt that I will be saved, for I have had more of that in this country than pleasure and joy, as God is my witness. If it is a sign that one is loved by God when one is weary of the world, then God Almighty loves me very much, for no one in the world could be wearier of the world than I am. . . .

Here I am back in my drawing room. I was unable to call on the Princesse de Conti, for her first lady-in-waiting, the Marquise d'Urfée, told me that her stairs are hard to climb, and I cannot even climb easy stairs, let alone hard ones; so I sent my excuses and came back here, and I cannot use my time better than by talking to you, dear Luise, until my dinner is brought. It is indeed true that one must have patience here, but, as the German proverb says, "Patience will get the better of buttermilk."[4] Whenever something upsets me, I try to find all kinds of things to distract me, and so I get over it in a few days, continue in my straight path and trust in the ways of God.

1. The Princesse des Ursins. 2. Elisabeth Farnese of Parma. 3. The Parlement of Paris was the foremost of the kingdom's courts of law. By submitting all the records clearing him of false accusations to the Parlement, the future Regent meant to demonstrate the legality of his defense and perhaps also to win the goodwill of this powerful political body. For his further relations with the Parlement, see the headnote before the letter of 26 September 1715. 4. See the discussion of this translation in the Preface.

Marly, 30 May 1715

This afternoon we spent a long time in church, because today is Ascension Day. My goodness, how time does pass! Fifty-two years ago I was at Cleve on Ascension Day, on my way back to my beloved Palatinate; but I must not think back to those happy times. . . .

Oh my dear Luise, you are almost the only one in Germany who cares about me, now that death has taken all the others away from me. When I think about all this, I sometimes feel as if I had dropped out of the sky. Adieu, dear Luise, I embrace you with all my heart, wishing you a good night and that you may wake up with a happy heart in the morning.

Marly, 31 May, ten o'clock in the morning

Good morning, dear Luise. Now I hope to finish answering your letter while it is still cool. . . . I have a real weather-spy in my knees and feet, which gave me a hard time yesterday; I went walking but had to come back in after only three or four turns in the flower garden in front of my room because my knees and feet hurt so much that I could not stand it any longer. I think there must have been a storm somewhere and that the rain we had here was only part of it. . . .

I had a good laugh about the stargazer who wants to figure out and calculate the Day of Judgment. He must not have read the Bible, where Our Lord Christ speaks of the Day of Judgment and says that His heavenly Father alone knows the time and that the angels in heaven do not know the time and the hour, which will come like a thief in the night. How smart of him that he wants to know more than the angels in heaven.

Marly, 8 August 1715

Madame d'Orléans[1] is of a very different temperament than I, and would like all her daughters to become nuns. She is not so simple-minded as to think that this would make it easier for her daughters to get to heaven; it is sheer laziness, for she is the laziest person in the world. She is afraid that if her daughters stay with her, she will have to take care of their education, and that is too much trouble for her; she told me so herself. There is nothing in the world I find more disgusting than snuff; it deforms people's noses, causes them to speak through their noses and to smell awful. I have known people here who had the sweetest breath in the world, yet once they began to use snuff it took only six months to make them as stinking as he-goats. . . . Our King— not to compare myself to him—does not like it any more than I do, yet his children and grandchildren keep taking it, regardless of the King's displeasure.

1. Françoise Marie, Madame's daughter-in-law.

The following is a classic description of "The Good Death."

Versailles, 27 August 1715

Our good King, having prepared himself for death and, as is the custom here, having received his last sacraments on the day before yesterday at eight o'clock in the evening, and also having given all the orders concerning the arrangements to be made after his death, sent for the young Dauphin[1] in order to give him his blessing and to speak to him. Thereafter he sent for the Duchesse de Berry, myself, and all of his other daughters and grandchildren; to me he said adieu with such tender words that I am still amazed that I did not faint dead away. He assured me that he had always loved me, and more than I had known myself, and that he was sorry that he had ever caused me chagrin; he begged me to remember him sometimes and said that he believed I would do this, being convinced that I had always been fond of him; he also said that in dying he wished me all the best and God's blessing and hoped that I would be happy all my life. I threw myself on my knees, took his hand, and kissed

it; he embraced me. Then he spoke to the others and advised them to stay
united. I thought he was speaking to me and I said, "In this I shall be obedient
to Your Majesty as long as I live"; he turned around, smiled, and said, "I
am not saying this to you, knowing that you are too reasonable to need it; I
am saying it to the other princesses." You can easily imagine the state in
which I found myself after all of this. The King's composure defies description, he keeps giving orders as if he were only going on a journey. He has
spoken to all his servants and said farewell to them. He has given thorough
instructions to my son and has appointed him Regent with such loving
kindness that one is moved to the depths of one's soul. I believe that I shall
be the first one of the royal house to follow the King when he dies; for he
is still alive but he is steadily weakening and there is no hope, alas. . . . It is
not true that Madame de Maintenon is dead; she is in good health in the
King's room and stays with him day and night. . . . The King has a good,
strong constitution, and I believe that he could have been saved if the proper
steps had been taken earlier. If the master dies, as cannot be doubted, it
will be a greater calamity for me than you can ever imagine, for many reasons
which cannot be written down.

    1. His great-grandson, Louis XV, born 1710.

*Louis XIV died on 1 September. The Duc d'Orléans, Elisabeth Charlotte's
son, became Regent for Louis XV, five years old at the time.*

1715-1722:

Mother of the Regent

As soon as Louis XIV died, the court abandoned Versailles, which would not be inhabited again until Louis XV reached maturity. Indeed, there was no proper court during the Regency, since the royal family no longer lived under one roof. The young King, following the wishes of his great-grandfather, was brought up at the château of Vincennes, "where the air was good" (and, as one historian has put it, the walls strong). The Regent took up permanent residence at the Palais Royal in Paris, which also became the seat of government. Madame divided her time between Saint Cloud and Paris. The Duc and Duchesse du Maine lived at the splendid château of Sceaux, and the Princes of the Blood scattered to their various properties in the vicinity of Paris. Madame de Maintenon retired to her school of Saint Cyr.

In the beginning of this period, much of Madame's interest was absorbed by her son's regency. A brief commentary about his struggle to establish his position is in order: Under the terms of Louis XIV's will, Philippe d'Orléans was to share power with a regency council composed of the Prince de Condé (as soon as he reached the age of twenty-four), the Duc du Maine, the Comte de Toulouse, three marshals of France, the four secretaries of State, and the comptroller-general of finance. Immediately following the King's death, his will, like every royal edict, had to be submitted to the Parlement of Paris, the foremost of the kingdom's courts of law, which claimed the right to examine all legal matters as to their compatibility with the traditions and customs of the realm before registering them. Since there was no fixed law concerning the organization of a regency during the minority of a king and since, indeed, there were two recent precedents (the regencies of Marie de Médicis and Anne d'Autriche) for abolishing regency councils and placing all power into the hands of one regent, the Parlement of Paris decided to break the late King's will and to grant full powers to the Regent. In a special session in 1718, the Parlement also granted the Regent's request to nullify Louis XIV's earlier edict conferring the status of "true Princes of the Blood" and potential heirs to the crown on his legitimized sons, the Duc du Maine and the Comte de Toulouse.

201

To GOTTFRIED WILHELM VON LEIBNIZ[1]

Paris, 26 September 1715

I thank you very much for sharing my sadness about the loss of our King as
well as the joy you imagine me to feel about my son's position as Regent.
But this matter is no different from almost all the things of this world, in
which our sadness is always more perfect than our joy. For while my son's
position has great splendor and *éclat,* it also causes me a great deal of anxiety.
The kingdom that is entrusted to his care is not in a good state, and his
worries and troubles are already such that he does not have time to eat or
sleep, which makes me fear that he will end up by falling seriously ill. I
am also afraid that his regency will—without carrying the comparison too far—
follow the pattern of the great wine barrels at Heidelberg: these were built
by the electors who did not drink, while those who were given to drink did
not leave any. The late King was not learned and yet made learning and
scholars flourish; but my son, though not ignorant and most interested in
scholars, will not, I fear, be able to foster them because the disarray here
is so great that it will be very difficult for my son to do the things he most
wants to do. He will also make a great many enemies for himself, for fifty
people lay claim to something that only one can have; that makes forty-nine
malcontents, not counting those who only envy my son. All of this, I must
confess, has robbed me of my joy about my son's present glory.

1. The philosopher (1646–1716) friend of Electress Sophie.

To RAUGRÄFIN LUISE

Paris, 27 September 1715

I do not know if my son will become King; that is in God's hands. But even
if this should come to pass, he would not be able to do anything without
the consent of the regency council,[1] to which I was not appointed, as you
can well imagine. One thing is certain, namely, that if he could follow his
own inclination, no one in the world would be harassed for his religion; but
priests are hard to deal with. I often tell my confessor that the reverend
fathers of his order[2] are too zealous and hot-headed, but he says that they
are accused of many things they have not done because people hate them.
Here is what I do: I only worry about myself and let all others believe and
act as best they know.

1. In this council Dubois, the Regent's former tutor, had the greatest influence.
2. The Jesuits.

I simply want to find out what might be done for the poor galley-convicts and will plead for them in general. If this has results, I shall be happy indeed; if not, I shall at least have done my duty and will not have to reproach myself. I am afraid that the regency council will not allow my son to do anything for the poor fugitives, for priests will always be priests.

Paris, 15 October 1715

This very moment I am returning from my walk. We are having the most beautiful weather one can ever see, just like in May. I went to the little woods called the Bois de Boulogne; in it there is an old château built by François I; it is called Madrid because it is modeled on the château in Madrid where this king spent some time as a prisoner. In the courtyard a lady who used to be my maid of honor (I should say lady-in-waiting) by the name of Chausseraye has a pretty little country house; I visited her there and walked around in her little garden.

Some members of the royal family were conspiring—in league with elements of the Spanish Bourbon court—against the Regent. The latter was energetic and diplomatic enough to hold his own.

To GOTTFRIED WILHELM LEIBNIZ

Paris, 21 November 1715

My son is so beset with troublesome affairs that I see him only for a moment every day. He has distributed all the directorships of the academies but has kept that of the liberal arts for himself in order to refresh his mind there after his troublesome workday. If science is indeed the heavenly manna, there must be many hungry souls. In fact I fear that if this were the case I would go hungry myself, for no one could be less learned and more ignorant than I am, even though I daily seek to find within myself means to achieve serenity, but this is much more difficult for those of us afflicted with a troublesome spleen, which acts like a microscope in human beings, enlarging all of our troubles and prolonging our sadness. It seems to me that it will be difficult to find ways to keep everyone healthy, unless it is possible to find as many remedies as there are people in the world; for what cures one person will kill another, since people's insides are as varied as their faces. . . . It seems to me that so far no one has yet found the art of living longer or more happily, and I fear that we shall have to wait in the outer court for some time. . . .

You, Herr Leibniz, will never need anyone but your own name to announce yourself to my son; he knows you better than you think, for your reputation in Paris is very great. My son must believe that one can do everything at once since, as I said before, he wants to direct the *académie des sciences* himself. . . .

The nation here is hard to satisfy; people often go along with the first person who tells them something, and in the provinces with what is written to them from Paris, especially when the vermin of priests has a hand in it. What is really happening I do not know, for I am extremely concerned that it might be thought that my son is ruled by women and therefore, in order to set an example to his wife and his daughters, I have announced loudly that I will not meddle in any of his affairs. My son has also told me that he has requested his wife and his oldest daughter to follow my example. So far I have not been sorry to have taken this resolution.

Madame's correspondence with the Princess of Wales, which began at this time, was encouraged by the Regent as part of his policy of rapprochement with England. Since the two women had never met, it is not surprising that many of Madame's letters evoke events of her childhood and her early life at the French court; after all, she had to acquaint her new correspondent with the circumstances of her early, as well as her present, life. Moreover, Elisabeth Charlotte was now in her sixties, a natural time for retrospection. Much of her correspondence from this period therefore takes on the character of memoirs; it is also understandable that health—her own and that of her contemporaries—becomes a major topic.

To KAROLINE OF WALES[1]

Paris, 9 January 1716

More different brothers than His Majesty the late King and the late Monsieur cannot be imagined, and yet they were very fond of each other. The King was tall and *cendré,* or light brown, his looks were virile, and he had an extraordinarily noble mien. Monsieur's looks were not ignoble, but he was quite short, had pitch-black hair, eyebrows and eyelashes, a very long and narrow face, large nose, a tiny mouth, and poor teeth; his manners were more feminine than masculine, and he was not interested in horses and hunting but only in gambling, receptions, good food, dancing, and dressing up, in a word in all the things that the ladies love. The King on the other hand loved hunting, music, and the theater, but my husband was only interested in large gatherings and masquerades. The King loved *galanteries* with ladies; I do not believe that my husband was ever in love.

1. Born Princess of Ansbach, she married the Prince of Wales (son of George I).

To RAUGRÄFIN LUISE

Paris, 21 January 1716

The year when your brother Carllutz came here, I was on very bad terms
with the Chevalier de Lorraine, and the false rumor was going around that I
had sent for Carllutz in order to take vengeance on the Chevalier de Lorraine. Many gentlemen of the court, upstanding people, came to me and
begged me, for the love of God, to accept them as the Raugraf's second. I
had a good laugh about this and said that I had no intention of starting a
brawl. I do not know if the Chevalier de Lorraine had heard about this, but
once when Carllutz and I and many other Germans were in my room, the
Chevalier de Lorraine came in; when he saw all of us Germans together he
turned on his heels and ran away as if he had seen the devil.

To KAROLINE OF WALES

Paris, 19 March 1716

Once jealousy is permitted to take root, one cannot get rid of it; one must
make up one's mind right away. My daughter does not show her feelings,
but she is often distressed inside, nor can it be otherwise, because she loves
her children very much and that jade[1] whom the duke loves so much, along
with her husband, do not leave her a farthing; they are ruining the duke
completely. That man Craon surely is a confounded, conniving cuckold. The
Duc de Lorraine is aware that my daughter knows everything, but I think
he is thankful that she does not give him any trouble about it but bears it all
patiently, for he treats her well, and she loves her husband so dearly that
as long as he gives her a few kind words she is quite content and of good cheer.

1. Madame de Craon, mistress of the Duc de Lorraine.

Saint Cloud, 22 September 1716

Why I do not want to meddle in anything I can explain quite frankly: I am
old and need rest more than I need trouble. I do not want to start anything
that I cannot bring to a good conclusion. I have never learned to govern; I
do not understand politics or affairs of State and am much too old to learn
such difficult subjects. Fortunately, my son has enough intelligence to
handle these things without me. Besides, my meddling would give rise to too
much jealousy in his wife and his oldest daughter, whom he likes more than
he likes me; there would be constant bickering, and that is something I dislike
intensely. I have certainly been pestered about this enough, but I have stood
firm because I wanted to set a good example for my son's wife and daughter.
After all, this kingdom has long been ruled to its detriment by old and young
women; the time has come to let the menfolks have their way. That is why
I have made up my mind not to meddle in anything. In England women have

the right to rule, but according to the law men alone should govern in France. What good would it do me to torment myself day and night? All I want is peace and quiet. All the members of my family are dead; for whom should I worry my head? My time is over, now I must see to it that I live in such a way that I can die in peace; and in the great affairs of the world it is not easy to keep a clear conscience.

To RAUGRÄFIN LUISE

Saint Cloud, 19 November 1716

It would mean nothing to me if people dressed up in pretty clothes for my birthday, for that is of no interest to me, and I never notice how people are dressed. If someone stole my own clothes and wore them in my presence, I would not even realize it, for I never pay attention to people's dress, unless it is completely ridiculous. To speak foreign languages is important for all children. My grandchildren in Lorraine are fluent in both German and French.

To HERR VON HARLING

Saint Cloud, 26 November 1716

I confess that the sudden death of poor Herr von Leibniz has surprised me. It is too bad that such a learned man did not get any further than this . . . although he must have had a peaceful death, since it was so quick. When someone has lived like this man and as Monsieur Harling describes it to me, I cannot believe that he needed to have priests around him, for they had nothing to teach him, he knew more than any of them.[1] Saint Paul says that good works are the sign of true faith, being its fruits; habit is not piety, and one must know what one does out of piety. To partake of the Lord's Supper from habit cannot be pleasing to God; it must follow from true faith. And such faith we show by being grateful to God, by loving Him and trusting in the merit of His redemption, and also by our earnest endeavor to love our neighbor and to help him as God has commanded us to do. I do not believe that otherwise taking communion can serve any purpose. I have no doubts whatsoever about the salvation of Herr Leibniz and think that he was fortunate not to have suffered for long. May God grant all of us a blessed end.

1. Harling had told Madame that no minister was present at Leibniz's deathbed or at his funeral.

To RAUGRÄFIN LUISE

Paris, 15 December 1716

I wonder why Her Grace the Princess of Wales has not received my letters, for although I could not expect to hear from Her Grace, I have not missed a single mail. I hope they will eventually be given to her; I think that man

Torcy[1] is doing it on purpose to set the Princess against me and to make Her Grace believe that I do not care about her. He came to see me, and I told him politely what I thought about this. He turned all red in the face and said that it was not his fault if the letters are late. I laughed and said, "You just told me yourself that the letters of the 7th have arrived, yet I do not have my letters, even though I am sure that the Raugräfin has not failed to write; therefore someone must be holding up my package.". . .

If I could not stand perfumes I would have died long ago, for in all my confinements my husband sat with me in perfumed Spanish gloves. . . .

I have never liked balls where there was French dancing, for there is nothing I dislike more than watching a minuet. But I do like to see plays, whether they are acted by children or by adults.

1. Jean Baptiste Colbert, Marquis de Torcy, secretary of State for foreign affairs, also superintendent of the mail. Toward the end of the Regency he was dismissed by the Regent, who replaced him with his former tutor, Abbé Dubois.

To KAROLINE OF WALES

Paris, 18 February 1717

After my husband's death, when it looked as if I might win my case in Rome and receive some money, the old trollop had me informed on behalf of the King that if I should win my case I should promise to make over half of the money to my son right away and that, failing this, I would incur the King's disfavor. I laughed and replied that I did not see why I had to be threatened, considering that I had no other heirs but my son, but that in case I should receive anything, it would be no more than equitable to make him wait until my death. Moreover I said that the King is too just to be angry with me for doing nothing more than what is right and proper. Later the news came that I had lost my case, which, for the aforementioned reasons, did not displease me.

Paris, 19 March 1717

No one in the world could have uglier hands than mine. The King often reproached me for it, which always made me laugh heartily; for since I never had reason to pride myself on anything pretty, I had made up my mind to be the first one to laugh about my ugliness. This has stood me in good stead; I have had many a good laugh.

To RAUGRÄFIN LUISE

Paris, 14 May 1717

Dearest Luise, today I had an important visitor, namely my hero, the Czar.[1] I find him a very good man, in the way we used to call someone good, namely, when he was completely unaffected and informal in his manners. He is most intelligent, and although he speaks in broken German, he speaks intelligently and makes himself very well understood. He is polite with everyone and extremely well liked here.

1. Peter the Great.

The King contracted heavy debts because he did not want to retrench any of his royal splendor; so he borrowed money, eagerly encouraged by his ministers. For whenever the King drew a farthing, they and their creatures received several *pistoles,* and by their swindling and thievery they made the King and the kingdom poor and themselves immensely rich. My son is toiling and worrying day and night to straighten all of this out, and no one thanks him for it; he has many enemies who purposely twist everything he does and have gone to great length to hire people who will stir up the people against him, which is not hard to do, especially since he is not bigoted. My son is so disinterested that he never takes the sums to which he is entitled as Regent; he has not taken a farthing of this money, although he needs it very badly because of his many children.

I am glad that my letters have reached you in good order. Monsieur de Torcy is by no means my friend; if he could find something to harm me, he would be sure to do it. But this is one thing I do not have to worry about, my son knows me too well and realizes that I love him dearly, so it would be hard to set him against me. That the letters are properly sealed does not mean anything; they have a material made of mercury and other stuff that can be pressed onto the seal, where it takes on the shape of the seal. After it is taken off and permitted to dry in the air, it becomes very hard, so that it can be used as a seal. They take off all the original sealing wax, making sure to note whether it is black or red. After they have read and copied the letters, they neatly reseal them and no one can see that they have been opened. My son knows how to make the *gama* (that is the name of the material); I use it only to amuse myself.

I certainly have never seen noble, let alone princely children brought up as miserably as these children here are being brought up. They have the same governess whom my daughter had, but she, thank God, was not brought up in this manner. I once asked this governess why she was not raising my grandchildren as she had raised my daughter, and she replied: "With Mademoiselle

I had your support, but when I first came to these children, their mother laughed at me along with them when I made a complaint. When I saw that, I decided to let things go their own way." Hence the fine results. Since I had nothing to do with this marriage, I have never taken care of the children either and leave them to their father and mother.

Paris, 11 December 1717

There is only one service and comfort, alas, I can provide for those who are near and dear to me, and that is to encourage them to take hold of themselves and to reawaken their own reason when it has been lulled to sleep by melancholia, so that they will recognize and make use of the common sense which, after all, was given to us by the good Lord for that very purpose. It is true enough that each one of us has his own weakness and that all of us need constant encouragement. As long as the good, honest Polier was alive, I did not lack this comfort, but now I have to find it within myself, which is hard work indeed and demands a great deal of praying. To trust God entirely is comforting at all times. God's wisdom, like the Almighty Himself, is infinite, and He alone knows why everything happens as it does. We must make use of the reason God has given us, but for the rest we must let Him rule and submit to His will. And since He has so loved the world that He has sent his only begotten Son to the end that all who believe in Him will not be lost but will have Life eternal, there is no reason why we should not be calm and contented. . . . Dr. Luther was like all the clerics in the world, who always want to be the master and rule over others. But if he had thought about the general welfare of Christendom, he would not have broken away. He and Calvinus would have accomplished a thousand times more if they had not broken away and if they had gone about their teaching without making a lot of noise; for then the most foolish of the Roman instructions would gradually have disappeared on their own. Few clerics listen to anything that goes against their interests, so there was no hope that Lutherus could be heard, considering that he attacked them so strongly, but if he had left Rome alone and gradually shown the French and the Germans their errors, he would have accomplished a lot more.

Paris, 20 January 1718

It has always been something of a misfortune for us that Germany not only apes France but even exaggerates all the things that are done here. Therefore I am not surprised that in order to copy the French the Germans have fallen into such outrageous ways. . . . If the Prince of Nassau-Siegen has no other resources than what I give him, he will soon starve to death. I have only what I need for myself and certainly not the means to provide for the upkeep of a prince; for my rank I am poor rather than rich. What is this lord doing here anyway, and why does he not go to Germany? Here he is nothing but everybody's laughing-stock. They are a pair of strange birds, he and his brother. His brother . . . kept badgering me to tell him why his wife cannot stand him. He has a disgusting, foul breath, so I told him that I believe this to be the reason.

To HERR VON HARLING

Paris, 24 February 1718

I pity the princess[1] with all my heart; on the seventeenth of this month her newborn little prince died of convulsions and cough at Kensington. The princess is said to be dreadfully distressed about this loss. In her last letter Her Grace tells me that she and her husband have begged the King's forgiveness three times, but to no avail. I do not understand anything about this matter, but I am afraid that the prince shares in his mother's misfortune[2] and therefore cannot ever be loved, and that is a hopeless situation. However, it seems to me that since the King has acknowledged this prince as his son, he should also treat him as his son; nor should he be so severe with the princess, who has never done anything against him and has always honored, respected, and indeed loved him as if he were her own father. As I see it, I do not think anything good will ever come of this, the bitterness has grown too great; yet the King would be well advised to put an end to this matter, for it only gives rise to a lot of impertinent talk and brings up ugly old stories that had much better be entirely forgotten.

1. Karoline of Wales.   2. The wife of George I had been repudiated for marital infidelity by her husband and had been a virtual prisoner for many years.

In the spring of 1718 Madame's daughter and the Duc de Lorraine, her husband, paid their first official visit to the French court. Lavish entertainment and presents were provided for the Regent's sister and her entourage. Madame enjoyed herself. The next four letters are probably a reflection of the discussions of family matters between Madame and her daughter.

To RAUGRÄFIN LUISE

Paris, 13 March 1718

I believe the time has come in which the Scripture says that seven women will run after one man's breeches. Never have women behaved as we see them now: they carry on as if they were finding heavenly bliss in sleeping with men. Those who think of marriage are still the most honorable. What one can hear and see every day defies description, and that in the highest circles. This was not usual in my daughter's time. She is positively dumbfounded and cannot get over all the things she sees and hears. Her amazement often makes me laugh. In particular she cannot get used to the sight of ladies, many of them bearers of great names, who right in the opera lie down in the laps of men whom supposedly they do not hate. My daughter keeps calling out to me, "Madame, Madame!" I say, "What do you want me to do about it, child? These are the mores of the time." "But they are nasty," says my daughter, and so they are. When they find out in Germany, where they are so keen to ape all things French, how the princesses are living here, everything will go to rack and ruin. . . . It is certainly true that my own children are on very good terms with me and continue to fear me as if I could still spank them. I am very fond of them, too.

To DUKE AUGUST WILHEM VON BRAUNSCHWEIG

Paris, 23 March 1718

Your Grace will forgive me, I hope, for letting a few days pass before answering his welcome letter of 15 February. The reason is that this past month my daughter and her husband, His Grace the Duc de Lorraine, have been with me; and since in view of my advanced age this may well be the last time that we will see one another, I am spending as much time with them as I possibly can. In the last few days a more serious reason has prevented me from writing, namely that for two days my son's spouse was at death's door; the danger abated only yesterday. She very nearly died of a severe colic. This ailment is extremely common in Paris this year.

To RAUGRÄFIN LUISE

Paris, 31 March 1718

My children of Lorraine are pleased with me and I with them. I am also very pleased with my eldest granddaughter,[1] and I am hopeful that she will become an excellent person. For she is changed for the better in every respect; she is intelligent and has a kind heart, and she is beginning to have the desire to pray to God Almighty for the will to hate vice and love virtue—and all of this without falling into superstition. That is why I hope that God will have mercy upon her and change her heart altogether. Of her third sister[2] I do not have as good an opinion; for one thing it would not occur to her to pray, and for another she does not have a kind character, cares nothing for her mother and little for her father, except that she wants to rule him. Me she hates like the devil and also hates all of her sisters. She is deceitful in all things, often contemptuous of the truth, and dreadfully coquettish withal. In short, this girl is sure to bring us a lot of grief. I wish she were already married and living in a faraway country, so that we would not have to hear more about her. I am afraid that we will also have grief and sorrow about the second

one, who is bound and determined to become a nun,[3] although the dear girl
is deceiving herself, for she does not have nun's flesh at all, and I fear that
the thing will no sooner be done than she will fall into deep despair, and
then she would be capable of doing away with herself, for she is courageous
and has no fear of death. It is a pity for this girl; she has many good traits,
is most pleasing in appearance, tall, well-built, with a pretty and pleasant face,
a beautiful mouth, and teeth like pearls; she dances well, has a lovely voice
and is a fine musician who can sing from sight anything she likes, without
grimacing and very prettily; she is naturally eloquent, has a kind heart, and
likes all the things she should like. She tells everyone that I am the only
person she will miss. So I am very fond of her. It is not hard to like this one,
she is very pleasant, and so I am quite distressed that she wants to become
a nun. My fourth granddaughter is a good child, but very ugly and contrary.[4]
The fifth one, by contrast, is a beautiful and pleasant child, well mannered,
cheerful, and funny; I like her too. She is called Mademoiselle de Beaujolais,[5]
and she will be quite intelligent some day. The sixth one, whose name is
Mademoiselle de Chartres,[6] is not too bad-looking, but a horrid child; for as
soon as one so much as looks at her, she starts to bawl. The Duc de Chartres[7]
is a nice boy and has intelligence; yet he is a bit too serious for his age and
so dreadfully delicate that I cannot look at him without worrying. He must
not drink a drop of iced beverage, or else he immediately gets a fever, nor
must he eat fruit or anything but the things to which he is accustomed. I keep
fretting that he will not last very long, and that would be a dreadful calamity
for all of us and also a pity for the child who is so smart and kind-hearted
and who learns everything he is taught. He is not beautiful but more on the
pretty than on the ugly side and resembles his mother more than his father.
The child has a natural disposition to all the virtues and is not given to any
vice. This makes me very fond of him. But this is enough talk of my children
and grandchildren. . . .

Histories are lies, too. . . . Why, if such lies can be told about things that
have happened right under our noses, how can we believe anything that
happened in faraway places and many, many years ago? I therefore believe
that histories (except those in the Scriptures) are no more true than novels,
the difference being that the latter are longer and more fun to read.

1. The Duchesse de Berry; here Madame speaks about the Regent's children. 2. Mademoiselle de Valois, who later married the Duke of Modena. 3. Louise-Adélaïde, who
became Abbess of Chelles. 4. Mademoiselle de Montpensier, who married Luis of Austria, briefly King of Spain in 1724. 5. Philippine-Elisabeth. 6. Louise Diane, who
married Prince Louis de Bourbon. 7. Louis d'Orléans; by age, he was in fourth place
among the children.

My son does not have enough means to make a great alliance; moreover, who would want to see all these ill-born children have precedence over his own?[1] There are other reasons too, which can be said but not written down. I am still of the old ilk, misalliances are utterly abhorrent to me, and I have noticed that they never turn out well. My son's marriage has spoiled my whole life and has upset my cheerful disposition once and for all.

1. Because her son's wife was the offspring of a double adultery, Madame did not consider these grandchildren to be of equal rank.

Saint Cloud, 8 May 1718

I rather like to see dancing bears; last year the Poles brought some with them, and I sometimes see them here. That reminds me of a funny story that was invented by a high-born girl of the house of La Force.[1] She lived at court for many years and was a lady-in-waiting to Madame de Guise. —The son of a councillor, a very wealthy young man by the name of de Briou, fell in love with Mademoiselle de la Force and married her against his father's will. The father wanted to break this marriage and forbade the son to see the lady and to have any communication with his wife. She bribed a trumpeter and instructed him to tell her husband that as soon as he saw bears and heard the trumpeter play a particular fanfare, he should quickly come down to the bears that would be dancing in his courtyard. Then this lady had herself sewn into a bearskin. When the signal was given, Monsieur de Briou excused himself and went to see the dancing bears. The bear who was his wife joined him and they spoke together for a long time. . . . I have never seen such a clever invention in any novel.

1. The love affairs of Charlotte-Rose de Caumont de la Force (1646–1724) had filled the pages of the *Mercure galant* for years. Mlle. de la Force was a most independent young woman, almost a feminist, and also a talented writer, whose novel *La Reine Margueritte de Navarre* is praised in Madame's letter of 14 November 1720.

Saint Cloud, 9 June 1718

Dearest Luise, today I rose a good hour later than usual because I had gone to bed an hour late yesterday. I did not return from Paris until ten o'clock at night; I had driven there at half past ten in the morning in order to perform a most tiresome and long-winded ceremony in a monastery called l'Abbeye au Bois, namely, the laying of a cornerstone for a new church. I was quite embarrassed, for I was received to the sound of kettledrums, trumpets, shawms, pipes, side drums, and gun salutes. I had to walk through an alley along the foundation with all that noise ahead of me. . . . You can imagine how this attracted the populace. Before this fine procession I had already heard mass with beautiful music at the monastery. At the place for the foundation stone the priests sang three psalms in Latin and also recited some prayers of which I did not understand a word. The place was raised, all covered with carpets, and on top of that they had put an armchair under a dais; that is where I had to sit. I was brought the stone, which had my name written on it, and in the center lay my medal; after they had thrown cement on it, I had to smear it all around. Then they placed another stone on top, and I had to give my blessing over it. I had to laugh; what a powerful thing it is, my blessing. Having done this, I handed the stone to the first officer of my household, namely my *chevalier d'honneur,* Monsieur de Mortagne, and sent him to the lowest part of the foundation, where he placed it in my stead, for I could not climb up and down the ladder, as you can well imagine, dear Luise! All in all the ceremony lasted for more than an hour and a half. For after the stone was laid amidst the noise of kettledrums, trumpets, shawms, pipes, and side drums, even cannon fire, a Te Deum was sung with musical accompaniment; this went on and on and did not end until one o'clock.

Saint Cloud, 30 June 1718

Ever since a week ago Sunday it has been raining every morning, but in the afternoon the weather is fine, except yesterday, when there was rain and hail. Apropos of hail: it has ruined seven villages in Lorraine, where it has devastated everything; other places were affected too, and they say that hailstones weighing two pounds have come down. My daughter writes that in Lorraine they attribute this to witches. It seems to me a foolish opinion that women and men can hide in the clouds and make hail in order to ruin everything. In Paris no one believes in witches, and nothing is ever heard about them. At Rouen they believe that witches exist, and there is always a lot of talk about them. . . .

There is nothing unusual about a man fooling around and having mistresses; among ten thousand one barely finds one who does not love someone other than his wife. In fact, they are to be praised if they at least speak kindly to their wives and treat them right. . . . Madame de Châteauthiers always says that if one wanted to discourage someone from marrying, one only had to make him or her listen to me, to which the Rotzenhäuserin objects that I was never really married and do not know what it is to be married to a man with whom one is in love and by whom one is loved in return, and that this changes everything and makes all the difference. Then I accuse her of loving carnal intercourse; she gets mad at me, and I make fun of her. . . .

My son is indeed plagued day and night, he is so busy that he can barely eat or sleep; I sometimes feel so sorry for him that it brings tears to my eyes, for he is kind to hundreds of people who do not even appreciate it. More

ungrateful people than those of this country I have never seen in all my life.
. . . The falseness one finds here is simply outrageous. . . . If I were to say
everything that can be said about this, I would have to write a book instead
of a letter. These things sometimes make me very sad.

To HERR VON HARLING

Saint Cloud, 3 July 1718

I fortunately still have a good German stomach that digests everything
properly. Every night I eat a little salad, which surprises the French no end;
they ruin their stomachs by overloading them noon and night. . . .

I think that it is a mark of love to be strict with children. When we reach
the age of reason, we realize why it was done and are most thankful to
those who have done the best for us out of this kind of affection. For by
nature children are inclined toward evil, that is why they must be reined in.
How much I wish that dear Frau von Harling could have stayed with me
until I was married, then I would have turned out even better; I never liked
or trusted Mistress Kolb. But Monsieur Polier was an excellent governor
for me. And the one who taught me the most was the good, honest Weben-
heim; I have been grateful to him as long as he lived.

Saint Cloud, 28 July 1718

I must hurry, for my dinner is served, but only want to say that I have not
received the smoked sausages. Just to prove that people here like them, they
once filched and gobbled up a whole box that was sent to me by our dear
departed Electress. . . . No one here is surprised that I like this kind of food.
I also brought raw ham into fashion, and many other German dishes, such
as sweet and sour cabbage, salad with bacon, red cabbage, also venison, of
which very little is eaten here; all of this I have introduced, also pancakes
with smoked herring. I had taught our dear late King to eat this, and he loved
it. My German mouth is still so keen on our German food that I will not
and cannot eat a single French *ragout*. All I eat is beef, roast veal, leg of mutton, and roast chicken, sometimes partridge and never pheasant. For five
or six weeks I will be without my captain of the guards, because Harling must
take possession of his governorship.[1]

1. After many years of military service, he was appointed military governor of
Sommières.

To RAUGRÄFIN LUISE

Saint Cloud, 4 August 1718

Yesterday in the theater my son told me that the Czar has bribed one of the czarevitch's mistresses; she gave him some letters from the czarevitch in which he wrote that he was planning to have his father assassinated. The Czar called together a large meeting of all the bishops and all the councillors of the realm. When they were assembled he sent for his son, embraced him, and said, "Is it possible that after I spared your life you want to murder me?" The czarevitch denied everything. So the Czar handed the letters over to the council and said, "I cannot judge my son; please do it for me, and let it be done with kindness and leniency, not with severity," and with that he left. The council unanimously condemned the prince to death. When the czarevitch heard this, his fright was so great that I am told he suffered a stroke; but he lost his speech only for a few hours. As soon as he regained his speech, he asked to see his father once more before his end. He came to him, and the czarevitch confessed everything, begging his forgiveness amidst a flood of tears; he lived for another two days and died full of contrition. Just between us, I believe he was poisoned so as to avoid the shame and disgrace of seeing him in the hangman's hands. A horrible story, this; it strikes me like watching a tragedy.

To KAROLINE OF WALES

Saint Cloud, 18 August 1718

As long as I can remember, I have always preferred swords and guns to dolls; I would have dearly loved to have been a boy, and that almost cost me my life, because I had heard that Maria Germain had become a man by jumping.[1] That made me jump so terribly hard that it is quite a miracle that I did not break my neck a hundred times.

> 1. The case of Maria Germain of Vitry-le-François is mentioned in Montaigne's essay *On Imagination*. He reports that there is a song warning girls about the danger of jumping and spreading their legs too far.

To RAUGRÄFIN LUISE

Saint Cloud, 27 August 1718, nine o'clock in the morning

Dearest Luise, I am writing to you today so as not to miss the mail tomorrow, for tomorrow I must go to Paris, where there is great excitement. My son has made the King hold a *lit de justice;*[1] he has called an assembly of the entire Parlement and earnestly enjoined the magistrates in the name of the King not to meddle in the government in any way and to perform only their appointed duties, namely the hearing of cases and the handing down of decisions. . . . Since it is known beyond a doubt that the Duc du Maine and his wife have stirred up the Parlement against the King and my son, he has been removed as the supervisor of the King's education and replaced by Monsieur le Duc;[2] in addition he and his children have been stripped of their previous rank as princes of the Blood. His youngest brother,[3] by contrast, has been confirmed in all his prerogatives for life, since he has conducted himself loyally and well. These men of the Parlement and the Duchesse du Maine are so spiteful and so desperate that I now live in mortal fear that they will assassinate my son. For even before any of this had happened, the Duchesse du Maine made some wild statements and publicly said at table, "They say that I am stirring up the Parlement against the Duc d'Orléans, but I have too much contempt for him to take such noble vengeance against him; I shall find ways to revenge myself differently, differently." This will show you, dear Luise, what a virago she is, and that I have reason to fear for my son's life. The people here are just too full of deviltry, it is no pleasure to live this way. . . .

There is one thing about the house of Austria: they have no gratitude. After all, our Duc de Lorraine and his father have served the Emperor faithfully. Yet as soon as the Duke of Mantua is dead, he thanks them by taking Montferrat and giving it to the Duke of Savoy, even though it rightfully belongs to the Duc de Lorraine.

1. A formal ceremony by which the King overruled the Parlement. Note that the Parlement of Paris, which had earlier ruled in favor of Philippe d'Orléans in refusing to register the late King's will, was now turning against the Regent.   2. The Duc de Condé.   3. The Comte de Toulouse.

To KAROLINE OF WALES

Saint Cloud, 30 August 1718

The Parlement had laid a pretty plan; if my son had waited twenty-four hours longer to remove Monsieur le Duc du Maine from the King, it would have resolved to declare the King of age now, so that everything would have gone through Monsieur du Maine. But my son has stolen a march on them by removing the Duc du Maine from the King and stripping him of his rank. They say that the First President of the Parlement was so shocked that he stood there as if he had seen the head of the Medusa, although no Medusa could have been more furious than Madame du Maine, who proffers wild threats. I understand that at her house there was open talk about giving the Regent such a fillip that he would have to bite the dust. Some people think that the old trollop is rowing in the same boat with her pupil.

To HERR VON HARLING

Saint Cloud, 21 September 1718

As for Monsieur and Madame du Maine, one hears more of their conspiracies against my son every day; it is enough to make one's hair stand on end. I do not believe that the devil in hell can be more wicked than the old Maintenon, her Duc du Maine, and his wife. The latter has said for everyone to hear that her husband, her brother-in-law, and her son are a bunch of cowards without courage; she said that she, although only a woman, would request an audience with the Regent for the express purpose of plunging a dagger into his heart. There you see, Monsieur Harling, this lady's meek spirit, and there you see if there is reason to be concerned about such people, especially when they have so many followers. For their cabal is very strong, it has more than ten leaders, all of them among the richest and greatest lords of the court; and what is even worse, they have a following among the wealthiest lords, all of whom favor the Spanish party, and hence the Duc and Duchesse du Maine, and want to bring the King of Spain here. My son is too smart for them; they want to have someone who can be manipulated to their advantage, and for that the King of Spain is a good choice.

To RAUGRÄFIN LUISE

Saint Cloud, 29 September 1718

All the French love Paris more than anything. I am fond of the Parisians, but I never enjoy being in the city, where nothing is to my liking. The kind of life . . . one leads there and the things one sees and hears are insufferable, and one is always forced to do things one does not want to do. One cannot find rest there either by night or by day and often hears and sees the most annoying things. . . .

It is perfectly true that some women have had blue veins painted on them in order to make believe that their skin is so delicate that one can see the veins. It is also true that there are fewer beauties now than in the past; I believe they make themselves old with their face-paint.

Saint Cloud, 3 November 1718

I shudder with horror at the thought of all the burning ordered by Monsieur de Louvois. I believe that he is now doing some burning of his own in the other world, for he died so suddenly that there was no time for the slightest contrition. He was poisoned by his own doctor, who was later poisoned in his turn; but before he died, the latter confessed everything and told who had made him do the deed. But then it was put out that the doctor had ranted in a fit of fever, because he had accused the old trollop; yet the details were such that there could be no doubt about it. In this man was fulfilled the word of the Scripture, "The measure you give will be the measure you get."

To KAROLINE OF WALES

Saint Cloud, 4 November 1718

The reason why Madame la Dauphine[1] was given so many wild young women
was that almost all of them were kin or allies of the old trollop, who tried
her best to amuse and entertain the Dauphine herself, lest she become bored
and seek other company than hers. —She also liked to have young fellows
in her room in order to amuse the King, who enjoyed watching their noisy
fun and games. They only let the King see their innocent pastimes, the rest
was concealed from him, and he only found out about it after her death.
It was a kind of joke that the Dauphine called the old trollop *ma tante;* the
maids of honor called their governess, Madame de la Motte, *mama;* but if
Madame la Dauphine had called the old trollop mama, this would have
been taken for a declaration of the King's marriage, and so she kept to "ma
tante."

1. The second Dauphine, the Duchesse de Bourgogne.

To RAUGRÄFIN LUISE

Saint Cloud, 24 November 1718

That would be a fine thing, dear Luise, if one only cared about people as
long as one could make use of them. I am glad to say that I am not so calculating, nor so à la mode, dear Luise, and that I shall not become so as long
as I live. I have always lived according to our good old maxims, and I shall die
in the same way. . . .

It is too bad that they have done away with the garden, especially since
in the live hedges along the moat there were a great many nightingales that
sang all night long in the spring. But what has become of the lovely clear brook
that ran through the garden, and by which I so often sat and read on the
fallen trunk of a willow tree? The peasant-folk of Schwetzingen and Oftersheim used to gather around and talk to me, and they were more entertaining
than the duchesses in the *cercle*. And how is it that building is done so poorly
now that entire balconies fall off? As I recall, the Swedish house at Mannheim was only made of wood, yet well-built just the same. . . . I believe that
if I should ever see Mannheim, Schwetzingen, or Heidelberg again, I should
not be able to stand it and would weep myself to death. For at the time
when the dreadful calamities happened there, I was in a terrible state for six
months and more; whenever I closed my eyes to go to sleep, I would see
these towns in flames, then I would start up in terror and weep and sob for
more than an hour. How, then, would I feel if I saw all of this with my own
eyes, also realizing that our father and brother are no longer with us, any
more than my mother! Dear Luise, would you please buy a map of the Heidel-

berg township for me, if you can find one: have it neatly pasted onto a cloth so that it will not tear, send it to me, and let me know what it has cost you!

Mistress Eltz von Quaadt was my brother's and my first governess; she was already quite old. Once she wanted to whip me, for I was rather willful as a child. When she tried to carry me off, I wiggled so much and kicked her old legs so hard with my young feet that she keeled over with me and very nearly killed herself in that fall. Therefore she refused to stay with me, and so I was given Mistress Offeln as my governess; we used to call her Ufflen, and she later married Monsieur Harling in Hanover. When my brother joined the menfolks, Mistress Quaadt retired to her house, where she lived with her sister Marie and two other old maids, who were her cousins. This house was in the suburbs, across from the Herrengarten, and my late brother and I were often taken there to visit these old ladies. Mistress Marie had been our dear Electress's governess.[1] So you see, dear Luise, that I knew the Schönburg property very well. These old maids were still alive when you were born, but you never saw them. All four of them lived to an incredibly old age; they kept a very neat and clean house, their dishes were like in Holland, and they also had a lot of porcelain, which was quite rare at the time. From all of this you can see that I was very well acquainted with the Quaadt ladies.

1. Electress Sophie in her memoirs describes the Quaadt sisters as ugly enough to scare little children.

Having been completely eliminated from participation in the Regency and from a potential succession to the throne, the Duc du Maine and his wife (see Cast of Principal Characters) had for some time been conspiring with certain elements at the Spanish court, notably Cardinal Alberoni, a protegé of the powerful Princesse des Ursins, to transfer the regency to Philip V, a direct descendant of the late King. Such a regency would have been a serious threat to peace, since it would have violated formal international treaties by which Philip V had pledged strict noninterference in French affairs. The "Spanish party" had a considerable following among the nobles of France, who felt that a weak regent (or indeed king!) might permit them to recover some of the power they had lost during the long reign of Louis XIV. The conspiracy was particularly serious in Brittany; the execution of Pontcallec described in the letter of 4 April 1720 was connected with it.

To KAROLINE OF WALES

Paris, 9 December 1718

My son has found himself obliged to have the Spanish ambassador, the Prince de Cellamare, arrested. When he, my son, gave orders to seize a courier, namely the Abbé de Portocarrero, letters of the ambassador found on his person clearly proved a conspiracy against the King and my son. The ambassador was arrested by two councillors of State.

To RAUGRÄFIN LUISE

Paris, 15 December 1718

I have already heard about the ridiculous seraglio kept by the Markgraf of Durlach. According to what I have heard lately of our Germans, be they princes or other lords, they all are as lunatic as if they had escaped from the madhouse. I am quite ashamed of it. But what do the reverend pastors say to such doings? You will tell me that they say just what the confessors say here, and you will be right. Except that in the confession one cannot be punished for things one has not mentioned. As long as wantonness and self-interest prevail, all things in the world are bound to go awry. —During a pause in my writing I have learned that Sandrasqui and Count Schlieben[1] were involved in the conspiracy against my son. The whole thing is upsetting to me, but I am particularly annoyed that Germans are mixed up in this nasty business; I am really ashamed of them.

> 1. Sandrasqui was a brigadier in the French cavalry, Schlieben a diplomat. Madame's doors were always open to "our good, honest Germans," and she felt personally responsible for their behavior.

To HERR VON HARLING

Paris, 22 December 1718

I have come to feel that people are fortunate if they only have to worry about thieves, for these are easier to deal with than those who conspire against their fatherland and want to assassinate their rightful masters. This thing is really frightening. We now know that my whole family was to be assassinated, except my own person because I am—quite without merit—loved by the populace, and it is said that the populace would rise up against the conspirators if any harm came to me; as if killing my son and his children would not harm me. . . . In this world I have more to fear than to hope and therefore look forward to death without dread, for I have placed my trust in my Lord and my Redeemer, and when I am alone I sing, "To thee my Lord I commit my troubles . . ."

To RAUGRÄFIN LUISE

Paris, 29 December 1718, ten o'clock in the morning

Dearest Luise, I meant to write to you two hours ago, but I could not do it, for I am in such a shock that my hand trembles. My son came to tell me that he finally had to arrest his wife's brother, the Duc du Maine, and his wife, for they are the heads of the horrid Spanish conspiracy. Everything has been discovered, proof in writing by the Spanish ambassador's own hand was found, and the prisoners have confessed everything. So it is perfectly true that the Duc du Maine is the head of the conspiracy. Therefore my son was forced to arrest him, his wife, and all their people. The wife, as princess of the Blood, was arrested by one of the King's four captains of the guard, while her husband, who was in the country, was arrested by a simple lieutenant of the guard. That makes a big difference between them. Madame du Maine was taken to Dijon in Burgundy, where her nephew is military governor. Her husband was taken to a small fortress at Doullens, and those of their people who were in the conspiracy were all taken to the Bastille.

Paris, 31 December 1718

The last and the first day of the year are most tiresome; if there were a third such day it would be altogether unbearable. Today I will surely not be able to write. Adieu then, until tomorrow. As soon as I have a chance, I shall wish you a happy New Year.

Paris, 1 January 1719

Dearest Luise, I wish you a happy, peaceful, and healthy New Year, a long life, good health, and everything that you might wish and desire for yourself. . . .

Do not let it worry you, dear Luise, that I arise at six! I go to sleep very early, at half past ten at the very latest, and often I am in bed by ten o'clock, so that I usually spend eight hours in bed, which is enough. Every night I eat a salad; my stomach is good and quite accustomed to this; it never, thank God, gives me any trouble. As long, that is, as I do not eat anything that is prepared with bouillon, that is the only thing that does not agree with me. In sickness and in health I never take any bouillon or broth, for that makes me vomit and gives me indigestion. His late Grace the Elector, our father, once very nearly killed me with it; he thought it was just a whim, and I obediently had to take bouillon every morning for a whole month, which made me throw up (begging your leave, as old Frau von Wolzogen used to say) every morning. Soon I became weak and skinny as a reed. The good, honest Polier finally proved to His Grace that I could stand no more of this, and so instead of bouillon I was given a good bowl of wine soup, but with a lot of vinegar, and that fixed me up, otherwise I would have kicked the bucket. When I first came here, Monsieur and all the servants, and the doctors too, thought that no one could live without broth. Monsieur asked me to try it. I told His Grace what it had done to me at Heidelberg. There was nothing for it, I had to try. I threw up to within an inch of my life. Then Monsieur swore that he would never again ask me to take it. But the oddest part, dear Luise, is that when I have thrown up like this, nothing will settle my stomach as well as raw ham and smoked sausage. I would not dislike soup in itself, but whenever I eat it, my stomach swells up and I start to sweat and feel indigestion, so I just have to stay away from it. . . .

I wept over my son's[1] death for six months; I thought I must go mad. This pain cannot be imagined by someone who has never had a child. It is as if one's heart were torn out of one's body. I do not know how I stood it; it still makes me shudder to think of it. But here the clock strikes eight; I must close against my will for this time, just quickly want to tell you that my son does not know a word of German. But I will have your memorandum translated. The ministers do not know German either, so they could not make the report.

1. Her first-born son, who died at the age of two.

Paris, 5 January 1719

A week ago I told you how it came out that the Duc and Duchesse du Maine were at the bottom of the conspiracy. Since then something else has been learned, which convicts the Duc du Maine. A letter from Cardinal Alberoni to this duke was found, containing these words: "As soon as war is declared, set fire to all your mines." Nothing could be clearer. These are wicked and damnable people. Oh, here they come to tell me something that I am sorry about, namely that the King of Sweden[1] has perished in a storm. I might not feel quite so sorry if my cousin, the prince hereditary of Kassel,[2] were to become King of Sweden. He has immediately concluded a truce with Denmark. . . . I was sure that this dreadful conspiracy of the Duc du Maine against my son would anger you. Here we have two little devils, led by two old witches[3] and supported by two arrant knaves.[4] . . . The duke and the duchess have had letters sent everywhere in order to whitewash themselves and blacken my son. The things that these six persons have thought up to revile my son are unspeakable; they are just too false and malicious. . . . You cannot imagine the kinds of libels against my son they have spread all over Paris and in the provinces and even sent abroad. . . . The people who are my son's enemies . . . have such a great following among all kinds of people that it is hard for me not to fret.

1. Charles XII. 2. Friedrich von Hessen-Kassel, married to the daughter and successor to Charles XII. 3. Maintenon and des Ursins. 4. Cardinal Alberoni and Ambassador Cellamare.

Paris, 8 January 1719

Dearest Luise, a new calamity has befallen us. The entire château at Lunéville[1] has burned to the ground with all of its furnishings on the third of this month at five o'clock in the morning. A barracks caught fire first, the house servants wanted to conceal it, dug a ditch under it, and thought they could put out the fire. But it was close to a woodyard; the wind swept the flames into the wood, which immediately caught fire, then it reached the covered tennis court, from there it got into the roof, and within an hour's time everything was gone. The storage house was the first to burn down. They wanted to save the archives and papers, but this effort cost the lives of a hundred persons. The chapel too, a brand new and, I am told, very beautiful building, lies in ashes. The loss is calculated at fifteen to twenty million. The children[2] were saved and carried out naked except for a little shirt. My daughter, with her legs bare, asked to be carried out in a chair, but her porters trembled so terribly that they could not carry her; so my poor daughter had to walk the whole length of the garden in her bare feet, and there were two feet of snow. . . .

I always treated Sandrasqui better than Schlieben, for I was interested in his career and often recommended him. Schlieben, though, is very intelligent and an entertaining conversationalist; still, I have never recommended him. He sometimes asked me to intercede for him, but I never wanted to do it. Once he said to me, "Your Royal Highness often says, 'Schlieben speaks German well, Schlieben is intelligent,' but never 'Schlieben is an honest man and has a good character.'" I said, "That you speak German well I can hear; that you are intelligent I can notice, but that you have the two other qualities you will have to prove to me, for they are not written on your brow."

1. Town and château near Nancy. 2. I.e., Elisabeth Charlotte's grandchildren.

To KAROLINE OF WALES

Paris, 31 January 1719

The fire at Lunéville was not an accident. It has become known that some people gagged a woman who wanted to shout "fire"; also one man was heard to shout, "I did not set the fire." My daughter thinks that it is the old trollop who wanted to burn all of them, because the man who called out was a former servant in the Duc de Noailles's house. But I rather believe that

the young trollop, the Craon, has something to do with this, for Lunéville
is my daughter's *habitation,* as they call it here, and her future widow's seat.

That you do not receive any letters from England is no wonder, seeing all the
horrendous winds and storms that are blowing now. One storm we had here
eight or ten days ago has wrought some incredible effects; it has carried lead
tiles from a church steeple clear across the water in one village, wrenched
two big, heavy church doors off their hinges and set them bolt upright against
a wall a hundred paces away, turned a weather-cock of the steeple of Saint-
Germain l'Auxerrois on its head, and ripped out a tree, sharpening it at the
bottom and planting it twenty feet deep in the ground as if it had grown
there. If this had happened in the county of Lippe[1] people would believe that
it was witchcraft, but in Paris no one believes in witches or burns them; I
do not believe in any of this myself. . . .

Count Degenfeld[2] has done very well to give my little godchild my name;
I thanked him for it two weeks ago. I would have to be a very odd person
to take it amiss that a child who is my godchild bears my name; that is understood, and it would have been a mark of contempt for my name if it had
not been done.

1. Central German principality.   2. Married to the youngest daughter of Madame's
stepsister Karoline.

To RAUGRÄFIN LUISE

Paris, 26 February 1719

I wanted to find out from him [my son] if it was true that his wife tried to
persuade him to go out at night and attend masked balls.[1] He told me that it
was true and also reported that when he said that he would no longer do it
in order to make me feel better, she replied that her daughter de Berry had
scared me in order to rule him herself, and that he was damaging his reputation by showing fear for his life. I am asking you, dear Luise, can the living
devil in hell be more vicious than this woman? . . . You can imagine how
agreeable it is for me, who have always considered this marriage an abomina-
tion, to come upon such utter perfidy now. . . . My confessor has tried his
utmost to persuade me that there is not the slightest impropriety between
the Duc de Lorraine and Madame de Craon, and that he never ever speaks
to her alone. I laughed right in his face and said, "Father, you can tell this to
the monks in your convent, for they know nothing of the world. But if you
think that this is the way to justify your Jesuit fathers who serve as confessors, you are much mistaken, for everyone knows that they tolerate double
adultery." Père de Lignières remained silent and has not brought up the subject since. . . .

I like to see young people of quality go in for serious studies, but before they become involved in learned matters they ought to give some proof of courage, lest it come out too doctorish. . . .

His late Grace my father always drove to the Heiliggeistkirche accompanied by runners, but never with drums and trumpets; that is not befitting for church. The late King, who was accompanied by drummers and trumpeters in every journey, short or long, never used them for church either.

1. Madame had told her son that roving around in Paris at night would be too dangerous.

Paris, 5 March 1719, seven o'clock in the morning

My sleep is not yet altogether straightened out, but I believe, I believe that I might say like Pickelhering when he plays Mutter Anneken,[1] "That's dear old age for you, it never comes without bringing ailments." Various annoyances no doubt play their part as well, and of these one has more than needed; something new every day, and rarely anything good, as the proverb says. At night I still take an egg yolk beaten in boiling water with cinnamon and sugar, as I did when I had the cough; that curbs the worst hunger. . . .

The present Duke of Zweibrücken[2] is a bad potentate and surely one of the most unpleasant persons in the world in his looks, in his temper, and in everything, that God has ever created. He thinks that he and I resemble each other like two drops of water. It is true that he is better looking than I am. But I flatter myself that I am not quite as unpleasant and rather smarter than he. His wife is a bit feeble-minded; between them they are a pair of ugly, repulsive dears. I am glad that they do not have any children; they would be bound to be mad. I already have enough madmen among my kin in the Rheinfeld line. . . .

My goodness, how things have changed at Schwetzingen![3] I cannot get over it. . . . As I recall, the two round garden beds flanking the building where my brother lived and where we ate did not face the Heidelberg road; instead, it was my apartment that looked straight out on the bridge, and a little to the left was the Heidelberg gate with the avenue; it faced the little woods behind which one could see Heidelberg castle. Turning to the left one came to the church, to the Mannheim road, and also the forest of Ketsch; and turning to the right one came to Oftersheim. That is how it was in my day. I also do not see the three open galleries or balconies in front of the rooms that were there in my time.

1. Figures in the traditional German farces. 2. A remote cousin of Elisabeth Charlotte. 3. The Raugräfin had sent her a map of Schwetzingen.

To KAROLINE OF WALES

Paris, 21 March 1719

The Craon woman was my daughter's maid-of-honor; that is when the duke fell in love with her. At the time Craon was out of favor with the duke because he had cheated him dreadfully at cards; he was to be chased away as a scoundrel. But since he is a shrewd fellow, he soon realized that his master had fallen in love with Mademoiselle de Ligniville, even though the duke kept it terribly secret. Just then the Madame de Lenoncourt, my daughter's *dame d'atour,* died; the duke managed to have the post given to her [Ligniville]. Craon is rich, she poor as a churchmouse, and he proposed to marry the lady. The duke was glad to give her to someone who would go along with his roguish game, and so she became Madame de Craon and then *dame d'atour.* When the old governess of her household died, my daughter thought that she was doing the duke, and Craon too, a great favor by making this woman *dame d'honneur;* this was precisely what brought her into *déshonneur.*

To RAUGRÄFIN LUISE

Paris, 2 April 1719

I shall not march in the procession; my bad knees, thank God, excuse me from all unnecessary ceremonies. Here one can apply the French proverb, "Misfortune has its good side, too." . . .

I am becoming so absent-minded in my old age that I think I shall soon be in my dotage or as confused as our aunt, Princess Elisabeth von Herford,[1] who wanted to use a chamberpot for a mask and said, "This mask has no eyes and stinks." And when Her late Grace played trictrac, she used to spit on the board and throw the dice on the ground.

1. Abbess of the Protestant convent of Herford.

Paris, 16 April 1719, seven o'clock in the morning

In my time in the Palatinate the proverb did not go as it goes now and as you write it, namely that when people are too well off they become a bit corrupt. It went, "When the goat gets too frisky, it dances on the ice and breaks a leg." Here they say that whenever there is a regency, people get too big for their breeches and always go in for rebellion. When the King does not govern, one and all think that they should govern. . . . My son is doing his best, as the proverb says, like one who fiddles by himself. . . .

Schwetzingen would be a better place to live in spring and summer than Heidelberg, for one can take better walks in the forest of Ketsch, which is a very fine promenade if it is still standing, and soon there will be excellent strawberries there. In the little woods between Schwetzingen and Heidelberg the strawberries are very good too, but the best huckleberries are found on the slopes of the Heidelberg hill. None are to be found near Paris; I always get them from Normandy, but they are not as good as at home, much smaller, drier, and sourer than in the Palatinate. The Elector should rebuild Friedrichsburg, then he would be able to lodge all his people, if not in the fortress then at least in the town of Mannheim. . . .

P.S. I just learned that the old Maintenon kicked the bucket last night between four and five. It would have been a great good fortune if this had happened some thirty years ago.

Paris, 22 April 1719

My goodness, dear Luise, you tell me, "One does not tire of hearing these two pastors preach." I must confess to my shame that nothing bores me more than to hear a sermon, I go right to sleep every time; no opium would put me to sleep as surely as a sermon, especially in the afternoon. Nor would I want to go to the French church for the Lord's Supper, for they do it very differently from the Germans, and I do not like it. For one thing they do not have any preparation, and for another they sing the psalms in this old-fashioned French. . . . And it always upset me that they served the sacrament wine in glasses that they washed afterward, as I saw them do in Mannheim; to my mind this made for a lack of decorum in such a holy action and felt as if one were in a tavern rather than in a church and Christian congregation. Nothing will ever keep me from reading my German Bible. I own three very beautiful Bibles: the Merian edition, which my aunt the Abbess of Maubuisson left me, a very fine Lüneburg edition, and one that was sent me last year by the Princess of Oldenburg, the daughter of the Princesse de Tarente. This one has my shape—short, squat, and round. The print and the engravings are not as good as those of the two large ones, quite confused. When I came to France, no one except for me was allowed to read the Bible; a few years later permission was given to everyone. The ecclesiastical constitution that made so much noise here[1] tried to forbid it again, but this could not be done. I laughed and said, "I shall follow the constitution and can truly promise not to read the Bible in French; I always read it in German."

1. This was the papal bull *Unigenitus* (1713), which condemned the Jansenist teachings of Père Quesnel.

Paris, 27 April 1719

The late Princesse de Tarente, my aunt, told me that on the day and at the hour when her uncle the Landgraf Fritz met his end, she was walking in the park at The Hague with Ma Tante the abbess, who at the time was still living with her mother, the Queen of Bohemia.[1] They were walking arm in arm; all of a sudden the Princesse de Tarente let out a scream and said that someone was squeezing her arm very hard. They looked at the arm and saw deep blue marks of four fingers and a thumb. She immediately wrote down what had happened, saying, "My uncle, Landgraf Fritz, must be dead, for he firmly promised to say goodbye to me." This was written down, and it did turn out that he had met his end on that very day.

1. Elisabeth Stuart, Madame's grandmother and wife of the "Winter King."

Saint Cloud, 30 April 1719

What I am sending the dear princess[1] is nothing special, just a few trifles in keeping with my small purse. If it were more ample, I would love to send something better, but as the German proverb so truly says, "Stretch your legs according to your coverlet." The Nürnberg cataplasm that makes one's back itch I would not mind having, for I find that scratching one's back is so pleasurable that many things that are considered pleasurable do not measure up to it.

1. Karoline of Wales.

To FREIHERR VON GOERTZ

Saint Cloud, 4 May 1719

I again reminded my son about Colonel Schwartz.[1] He assures me that he has signed all the papers and has cleared the matter with Monsieur Le Blanc.[2] He tells me that when Monsieur Le Blanc asked him the name of the colonel whose pension he was increasing, my son said, "In German, his name is the opposite of yours [*blanc* means "white"], for his name is Schwartz, which means "black." . . . In Paris I myself recommended this matter to him, and I hope that the Colonel will enjoy this increase in his pension for as long as a woman who died three weeks before I left Paris; she was a hundred and seven years old. We usually have two ladies here who are eighty-three and eighty-four years old, so when these two, Frau von Ratsamhausen, and I ride in a carriage together, the load comes to some three- or four-hundred years. But what can one do, one must either die young or grow old.

1. The Hanoverian magistrate Goertz had asked Madame to help obtain an increase in the pension of Colonel Schwartz. 2. Le Blanc, minister of war.

To HERR VON HARLING

Saint Cloud, 7 May 1719

I do not believe that your nephew will be able to write to you today. For the big thing these days at Saint Cloud is bloodletting. Yesterday it was Frau von Ratsamhausen and I, today it is Harling's and Wendt's turn. Thus, a good

bit of German blood has been shed at Saint Cloud. They took the most
beautiful blood from me, looked like chicken blood.[1]

1. On this occasion, Madame's horses were bled, too!

Saint Cloud, 11 May 1719

There is nothing special about the Maintenon's death, except that she died
like a young person. If people should know each other in the next world, then
this lady will have to choose in that world, where everyone is equal and there
is no difference of rank, whether she wants to be with Louis XIV or with the
lame Scarron. If the King should have learned there what was concealed
from him here, he will be glad to return her to Scarron. . . .

Do not be concerned that I will write a word to England about the Princess of Ahlden;[1] I never tell on anyone.

1. The former wife of the King of England, banished for marital infidelity. She was
the daughter of Georg Wilhelm of Celle ("Godfather") and his mistress, Eleanore
d'Olbreuse.

To RAUGRÄFIN LUISE

Saint Cloud, 13 May 1719

As for my son, it is good of course that he does not enjoy meting out punishment; yet when one is in authority one wields the sword as well as the
scales, and for the sake of justice one must be able to punish wickedness as
well as reward good deeds. . . .

I thought that I had already written to you, dear Luise, that our nun[1]
at Chelles was made abbess. Yesterday a courier was dispatched to Rome
about this matter. I fear that the death of the Maintenon, like that of the
Gorgon Medusa, will keep on producing monsters.

1. Louise-Adélaïde d'Orléans, second daughter of the Regent.

Saint Cloud, 1 June 1719

What is all this ranting against the Heidelberg Catechism? I am sure that
there must be some machinations of priests behind this and would not swear
that the Jesuits have not stirred it up, for they are merciless against other
religions. . . . Discord and quarreling are insufferable to me under all circumstances, but for the sake of peace one really should leave out question eighty.[1]
To tell the truth, this is to put it too harshly and could well have been left
out. For it only stirs up animosity without giving any proof, and one should
not speak so harshly about something that, after all, commemorates the

suffering and death of Christ. The discord and bitterness this creates are worse than the thing itself.

1. This section of the Heidelberg Catechism of the Reformed Church calls the Catholic mass "a denial of the sacrifice and suffering of Jesus Christ and accursed idolatry."

To FREIHERR VON GOERTZ

Saint Cloud, 8 June 1719

At noon I will have some of your smoked goose. Sometimes they are prepared here as a purée; the geese are excellent and incomparably better than those that are sent from Gascony. The sausages are very good too. Every Friday I also eat some of the salmon; I have not yet tried the raw smoked goose. Thank you very much for all these good things. I have a favor to ask of you, namely, since I do not doubt that you will soon return to Hanover, now that the King of England is there again, I would like you to convey my humble thanks to His Majesty for the kind greetings that were brought to me by Mademoiselle de la Lechière and to assure him of my respect. . . .

P.S. I would like to add that I am a bit like Jodelet[1] and take a rather dim view of war. May peace and God protect you. Although the Spaniards have not yet succeeded, there is no way of knowing what may happen in the future. "One must not make fun of the dogs before one is out of the village"—that is my opinion too.

1. Comedy by Corneille.

To RAUGRÄFIN LUISE

Saint Cloud, 8 June 1719

Writing is my greatest occupation; I have no skill and desire for fancy-work and nothing in the world bores me as much as sticking in a sewing needle and pulling it out again. You made me laugh heartily, dear Luise, by saying that my letters are like a soothing balm upon your head. At least this balm will not melt into your beard, as it did with Aaron. . . .

Just between us, a convent is nothing but a poorly kept court. Ma Tante the Abbess of Maubuisson never wanted to have any ladies-in-waiting around her, she said, "I have left the world in order to get away from courts"; so she tucked up her skirts and went around in her convent and gardens all by herself, laughed at herself and everyone around her; she was quite funny, but she also had His Grace the Elector's, our father's, voice, resembled him in her eyes and mouth and in many of her mannerisms, and thereby commanded fear and obedience. . . .

Madame d'Orléans . . . will not be back soon. God forgive me! I am not sorry for it; this is company I can easily do without, and I do not like to deal with deceitful people. Her daughter de Berry and the nun are not deceitful, nor, thank God, is her son; but the mother and the third daughter are masters of deceit. The devil himself is not worse. I am as sick of these people as if I had been stuffed with them by the spoonful, as the proverb goes. Let us speak of something else! This chapter stirs up my bile and I lose my cool head when I speak of it.

Saint Cloud, 9 July 1719

It is a wretched thing when people think that being pious means to believe only what the priests want to put over on them. Our late King was like that; he did not know one word of the Scripture because he was never allowed to read it, and he thought that as long as he listened to his confessor and mumbled his paternosters, everything was fine and he perfectly pious. I often felt quite sorry for him because of this, for his intentions were always sincere and good. But they—the old trollop and the Jesuits—made him believe that if he persecuted the Reformed, this would make up before God and man for the scandal of this double adultery with Madame de Montespan. This is how they deceived the poor gentleman. I often told these priests my opinion about this. Two of my confessors, Père Jourdan and Père de Saint-Pierre, agreed with me.

Saint Cloud, 23 July 1719

Dearest Luise, the thing I had feared so much has finally come to pass at half past two Thursday night; the poor Duchesse de Berry has died. On Thursday I stayed with Her Grace until a quarter to nine; when I thought that she no longer knew me, I left. My poor son stayed after I had left and had an elixir administered to her; this brought her back to her senses and she spoke to him for a long time. Then prayers were said in her room until one o'clock, when she once again lost her senses, although she only expired at half past two, as I said before. She died most calmly and resignedly, saying that since she had reconciled herself with the good Lord she did not desire to live any longer, considering that in this world it is impossible not to sin against God, therefore she would rather die than recover, which is what happened. They say that she died a most gentle death and went out like a light, just like a person falling asleep. She was opened yesterday. . . . On Friday right after dinner I went to Paris and found my son in a sadness that would melt a heart of stone. For he does not want to weep and wants to be strong, and yet tears come to his eyes again and again. . . . We shall be in mourning for three months only. We should have been in mourning for six months and would have used black coaches and liveries, but the new rule for mourning in France has cut everything in half. In mourning for one's father and mother, which used to be for a year, one now wears black and drapes the house for only six months; mourning for brothers and sisters, which used to be six months, is now three months and does not call for draping; I shall have my room draped and use black coaches and liveries. . . . Normally I would not go into mourning at all for a child and grandchild; but since she was, after the King, the head of the entire royal house, in other words *l'ainée,* as they say here, I am to mourn her as a sister. It seems preposterous to me that in France one does not go into mourning for one's children; after all, who could be closer to us? But they have outlandish ways in this country. —Another thing I can never get used to is the buying and selling of offices, which has the consequence that one is served by a person for only three months at a time and changes servants four times a year. What they have learned in three months they unlearn again in the other nine, if indeed they have learned anything. This also makes for dishonest servants, for they buy their charges for profit and hope to make as much as possible from them . . . so this is a fine way to teach them to steal. And since one can only have those who have the money to buy the charges, one gets other people's servants, for their masters give them the money to buy the charges, often to reward them. In this way one cannot say a word in the presence of one's own servants without having it spread to all and sundry. Everyone repeats what he has heard to his master. If someone dies, as has happened here, there is despair among all those who had hoped to make a profit on their charge.

Saint Cloud, 27 July 1719

I do not recall whether I told you, dear Luise, that on Sunday last the King[1] did me the honor of visiting me here and expressing his condolences. On Saturday I shall go to thank His Majesty in formal court attire; however, he has permitted me to see His Majesty without a veil. . . .

The mosquitoes of the Rhine and at Mannheim are more poisonous than those here. I once saw Carllutz with his eyes completely swollen shut by mosquito bites. I also have gauze curtains around my bed, but now that I have such short breath I can no longer stand this, it suffocates me. When Herr Max[2] saw someone go to sleep, he used to scare him by making the whirring noise of mosquitoes, but he also knew how to make a perfect imitation of the nightingale's song with the green part of an onion. . . .

There are many examples of sick persons prophesying in their hallucinations or when they are dying. I heard that my late brother on his deathbed recited all the disasters that have befallen the Palatinate in Latin verses. You knew the Wilder family well, dear Luise, and remember that the oldest son accidentally shot and killed his youngest brother. One of the sisters had come down with an acute fever and kept calling out, "Don't let little Carl be with brother Wilm! He will shoot him," which is exactly what happened a few days later. . . .

It is terribly hard on me that I am no longer allowed to eat at night; but then it is still better not to eat at night than to be sick and have to take a lot of medicine.

1. Louis XV, nine years old at the time.   2. Freiherr von Degenfeld, a brother of Elector Karl Ludwig's second wife.

Saint Cloud, 20 August 1719, six o'clock in the morning

Last night I went to bed at half past nine. . . . I only wrote a few words to a lady in Paris, swallowed my egg, wound my clocks, and then to bed, said the bride, to quote the old saying. Now I am sitting in my room right by my balcony door, which I had opened. There is not the slightest bit of wind; the sky is all covered with clouds, and one cannot see the sun. The weather is very mild now, it is neither hot nor cold. I hope it will rain later. . . .

For God's wisdom and providence we do indeed owe Him praise, glory, and gratitude; He knows better what is good for us than we know ourselves, and I do not understand how anyone can refuse to place his trust in God. . . . I do not have the ambition to become terribly old; I do not desire death, nor do I shrink from it, but I must confess that the thought of becoming so old that one is a burden to oneself or others terrifies me. No one lives without sin, but some are more sinful than others. . . .

It is not enough for a reigning prince . . . to refrain from maltreating his subjects, he must also protect them against wicked priests and not permit anyone to harm them. This has always been my opinion, especially when it comes to ecclesiastical tithes and privileges. If the clerics of Baden also have rights over Kreuznach, there must be more priests and monks there than elsewhere, and of that scum nothing good will ever come. As the German proverb has it, "If you are looking for trouble, take a wife, buy a clock, and strike a priest."

Saint Cloud, 24 August 1719

Dearest Luise, yesterday I drove to Paris and thought that I was in the fires of hell, for I have never lived through a more dreadful heat; every gulp of air was like fire. I believe that if this goes on much longer, man and beast must perish. Some of the oxen that were driven from the country to Paris have dropped dead because there was no water for them in the villages through which they passed. . . .

If one has only one son and loves him with all one's heart, one cannot possibly live without fretting, especially in this country, where there are so dreadfully many wicked people and so few good ones. Whether I speak to my son or whether I whistle, it all comes to the same thing; he never follows my advice, for his confounded, impious flatterers are right on the spot and undo everything. They are a wicked lot, who openly pride themselves in believing in neither God nor His word, a bunch of debauched and blasphemous fellows.[1] . . . They drag him into a wild life under the pretext that he must do something to cheer himself up from his hard work and that otherwise he could not stand it; and here in France they think that everything is tedious except gorging, guzzling, and whoring. . . . Oh my dear Luise, you flatter me too much when you say that the likes of me cannot be found in the whole world; there must be dozens of them.

1. The Regent's drinking companions, who called themselves the *roués*, that is, "those who have been through everything."

This letter contains the first mention of John Law, the Scottish financial wizard who persuaded the Regent to liquidate the enormous public debt by a new technique that became famous—and then infamous—as "Le Système." Madame never claimed to understand this admittedly very complicated stratagem and only described, very vividly, its effects on French society.

Briefly stated, the Système was designed for the double purpose of liquidating the public debt and stimulating French overseas commerce. The first step toward these goals was the founding of a State-owned discount bank, a very bold and innovative undertaking that became positively revolutionary when the bank was authorized to print paper money—the famous billets de banque, of which Madame has so many tales to tell. A year later, John Law founded the Compagnie d'Occident, a trading firm that was granted the monopoly of exploiting the supposedly fabulous resources, especially gold and silver, of the French colony of Louisiana ("Le Mississippi"). In a second phase, the company was also given the monopoly of trade with China and Senegal, as well as the tobacco monopoly. A skillful propaganda campaign persuaded investors that this company would realize huge profits, and its stocks soon began to sell very well; the Regent himself and the Princes of the Blood were among the first investors. In a third phase, Law, who had been appointed controller-general of finances, decided to link the bank and the company. This was the essential step that tied the State finances to a speculative venture and necessitated the printing of ever greater quantities of bank notes. A very great demand for the company's stock dramatically increased the price per share, and when early investors liquidated their debts by paying them off with inflated paper money and also converted their quick profits into land and durable goods, the sight of their prosperity caused a veritable stampede for the possession of shares in the "Mississippi." At the height of the Law Système, the value of the stock had risen from 500 to 18,000 livres per share; the speculative craze extended far beyond court circles and gripped even people of modest means. At this stage, the Regent still backed Law against the traditional financial community and the Parlement of Paris.

In managing his Système, *Law made the cardinal error of assuming that the paper money was covered by the potential wealth of the country's economy and therefore permitting the printing of far more bank notes than could ever be redeemed in coin. When it became clear that the company would not produce fabulous profits, the investors wanted to convert their stocks and bank notes into coin, the supply of which was simply not adequate. The ensuing panic led to the collapse of both the company and the bank. As a result, many investors were ruined, and Law had to flee France. When the dust settled, the public debt had indeed been reduced by about half, but the financial experiment had failed, leaving an enduring prejudice against paper money that retarded the development of French banking for a century. (Based on Louis Bergeron,* Les Revolutions européennes et le partage du monde *[Paris, 1968], 50–58.)*

Saint Cloud, 31 August 1719

In the last six days nothing new has happened here but a lot of financial things about which I cannot tell you because I do not understand them. I only know that my son has found a means through an Englishman by the name of Monsieur Law (but the French call him Monsieur Las) to repay all of the King's debts this year. . . .

Thank God I still have a good constitution and bounce right back. I am afraid I shall live only too long, for I have a greater horror of very old age than of death itself. . . . At the point I have reached, one cannot possibly be good looking; my sixty-seven years certainly do show. In public I do not appear so, dear Luise, but in fact I am thoroughly sad. . . .

Where does the Elector lodge at Mannheim, now that the citadel and the château are gone? I imagine he uses the tollhouse at the Neckar Gate. I remember that sixty-one years ago I once visited Mannheim with His Grace the Elector. At the time the citadel had not yet been built (you and Caroline were not yet born, but Carllutz was already born), and we stayed in the tollhouse, which had tiny little rooms. That was my second journey; before that I had been to Neustadt, and I remember that my late brother and I rode together in the same coach, with our governor and governess; and when a tree hit the top of our coach, we nearly died with laughter. . . . I also went to Mergenthal[1] once; what I liked best there was a tiny roof garden on the second story, it was full of flowers and very cleverly made.

1. "Mergenthal" is Mergentheim.

Saint Cloud, 3 September 1719

Laughter has become a rare commodity with us, although the Rotzenhäuserin laughs more easily than I do. On Friday last my son came here and made me rich. He said he feels that my income is too small and therefore increased it by 150,000 francs; and since fortunately I do not have any debts, this has come just at the right time to put me at ease for the remainder of my life. . . .

Our dear Princess of Wales is, it seems to me, always in good humor and cheerful. May God keep it this way. I myself feel that old age drives off pleasure. I too used to be of a cheerful disposition, but the loss of many loved ones and other distressing things, my son's marriage and what has resulted from it, all of this has deprived me of all joy and pleasure.

The Mouchy[1] was surely the most unworthy favorite one has ever seen; she cheated, deceived, and robbed her princess wherever she could. She was of very low birth, too; her grandfather on the maternal side was my late husband's field-surgeon. . . . The mother is not much good either; after she was widowed she kept house for years with a married man. One can say that all of this adds up to stinking butter and rotten eggs. One funny thing that this Mouchy did was to rob her own lover, the Comte de Rioms.[2] Madame de Berry had given this man many gifts of jewels and money. He put everything in a box, which he left at Meudon, and his dear Mouchy stole the box and walked off with it. This strikes me as funny. Here one can say what His Grace our late father used to say in such cases, "Make it up, dirty dogs!" . . .

My son's financial dealings and his hard work benefit the young King greatly, for when my son took over the regency the King was in debt to the tune of 200 thousand million,[3] but, God willing, everything will be liquidated a year from now. My son has found an Englishman by the name of Monsieur Law who knows all about finances; he has helped him do it.

1. The favorite of the recently deceased Duchesse de Berry. 2. Lover of the Duchesse de Berry and of the Mouchy, among others. 3. This is surely a fabulous figure; modern historians estimate that the public debt at the end of the reign of Louis XIV amounted to about 2 billion livres, and that more than half of the gross income of the State treasury (200 million) was earmarked for the servicing of this debt.

Saint Cloud, 17 September 1719

We arrived at Chelles at half past nine;[1] my grandson the Duc de Chartres was already there. A few minutes later my son came, and shortly thereafter Mademoiselle de Valois[2] arrived. Madame la Duchesse d'Orléans[3] had herself bled on purpose so that she would not have to be present, for she and the abbess are not always the best of friends. But even if they were good friends, the mother's natural laziness would not have permitted her to be present because going to Chelles would have involved getting up too early. Shortly after the clock had struck ten we went to the church. . . . After the Te Deum we returned to the convent. At half past eleven I went to table, ate with my son and my grandson the Duc de Chartres. . . . A half hour later our abbess went to table in her refectory, where forty places were set; she ate with her sister

Mademoiselle de Valois and twelve abbesses. It was a funny sight, this bevy of black-clad nuns sitting around the colorful tables, for my son's people had put on a lovely and sumptuous display. The populace was allowed to pilfer all the fresh fruit as well as the relishes. After dinner, at a quarter to four, my carriage came and I left, arriving back here shortly after seven.

1. For the ceremony of Louise-Adélaïde d'Orléans's installation as Abbess of Chelles. 2. Madame's granddaughter, sister of the abbess. 3. Mother of the abbess.

To FREIHERR VON GOERTZ

Saint Cloud, 21 September 1719

Thank you very much for the accounts of the bride's entry into Dresden[1] and the subsequent festivities and also the confirmation of the peace treaty among the crowns of England, Sweden, and Prussia.[2] The former were most entertaining and of the latter I am very pleased to learn. . . . God grant that the northern peace may spread throughout Europe, coming to us as well.

1. On 2 September the Hapsburg princess Maria Josepha, the new wife of Crown Prince Friedrich August of Saxony, had been solemnly received at Dresden. 2. England and Prussia had ended the war against Sweden.

To RAUGRÄFIN LUISE

Saint Cloud, 7 October 1719

It is easy to understand, dear Luise, that I would rather have talked with you than driven to Chelles. In the first place I dislike all convents and their way of life, and in the second place I am quite unhappy that my granddaughter has made the decision to become a nun and abbess; so this spectacle has given me more pain than pleasure. . . .

I thought I told you long ago that Mademoiselle de Chausseraye used to be one of my maids-of-honor; it made me laugh that you thought her place[1] was a convent. She used to be very poor, but she placed everything she had into the Mississippi bank that was founded by Monsieur Law, the Englishman of whom you have heard; in this way she has made a million and is now rich instead of poor; any day now she will buy a large, beautiful estate in the country.

1. The little château "Madrid" in the Bois de Boulogne.

Saint Cloud, 15 October 1719

I already told you on Thursday last how glad I am that my old face[1] has safely arrived. It is not worth much thanks! But I thought, dear Luise, that because you love me, you would like to see what I look like now, especially since you have a picture showing me twenty years ago, which will permit you to judge for yourself that an ugly person can become even uglier with age, just as a beautiful one can become ugly. You should send me a half-length portrait of yourself, so that you can be represented in my cabinet together with your late brother Carllutz, of whom I have a very good likeness. . . . Today I shall say no more except that—measure for measure—I am not giving up my claim to a counterpresent and that I will be very pleased if you can find something new and inexpensive in the way of books or maps at the fair and send it to me. I will gratefully accept it, because I would not want you to give up the good custom of sending me a present from the Frankfurt fair, just as I will not forget the fair of Saint Cloud, for, as the French proverb says, "Small gifts preserve friendship."

1. A portrait.

Saint Cloud, 26 October 1719

All my good, honest compatriots have . . . free access to me, whether in person or in writing. . . . I always like to hear that the good, honest people of the Palatinate still remember me with affection. . . .

Boars' heads are not served upright here as they are at home, they are laid flat and sort of crumpled in a bowl; also they do not use enough salt and spices here. There is no comparison between the ways of preparing them here and in Germany, the meat itself is more flabby here than at home. I much prefer hazel hens to partridges. The hares also are incomparably better in the Palatinate than in this country. . . . I wish I could eat at your house. I would not need any more than what you serve your guests, except that sauerkraut would have to be included, because I love to eat it; but the sauerkraut here is no good, they do not know how to prepare it properly, nor do they want to learn. One thing they do rather well here is stuffed cabbage.

Of course it hurts me to hear that the poor former inhabitants of Heidelberg are being plagued—I almost used the good old Palatine expression "hassled"[1]—so much. What a wretched thing it is that we humans, who only seek to be happy, keep doing our best to make life miserable for one another; how foolish we poor mortals are. Those who let themselves be ruled by priests always do the wrong thing. I thought the Palatine Elector[2] was smarter than to let himself be run by these fellows, and I thought that all the silly things his sister the Empress[3] is doing at the behest of the priests would have served him as a warning not to fall into the same mistake. Moreover, a Prince Elector who has any intelligence at all should remember that the true piety of a ruler consists of upholding law and justice and keeping his word, and he should know that anyone who advises him otherwise cannot be a true or good Christian; therefore, far from following bad advice, he should firmly oppose it. . . .

Some days ago the good Monsieur Law became quite ill from sheer worry and harassment; he cannot find a moment's rest by night or by day and so he finally became ill. No, I do not believe that a more greedy people than the French can be found in the whole world; they can drive you raving mad with their begging in letters and in words, and some of the things they do make me so terribly impatient that I snap at everything that comes close to me like a wild boar. No one could be more intelligent than Monsieur Law. But I would not want to be in his place for all the riches in the world, for he is plagued as much as a soul in damnation.

1. *Geheyt.* 2. Elector Karl Philip. 3. Empress Eleanore, widow of Emperor Leopold I.

I wish you would not accustom yourself to using eyeglasses, they are sure to spoil your eyes, and if one is patient and does not use eyeglasses good eyesight will return. I have proof of this, because I see better now than I did twelve years ago, and yet I have never used glasses. . . . My portrait would not have been worth going to court about; I could easily have sent you another one, for the painter who has painted the one for you, and whose name is Penel, is a young man who will paint for a long time to come. . . . The language of the court is very different from that of the town. So if someone at court speaks as they speak in town, this is called "parler en bourgeois." You will rarely hear a courtier speak in a very elaborate fashion; at court people make a point of being natural. Even the most devious ones act as if they were perfectly natural, but as the jugglers say, "Those who know the art do not betray the master's secrets." I am a truly natural person, and so I can usually spot the false ones right away. Not to be wicked is already to be good, and being good in this way prevents evildoing, for human nature is almost always inclined toward evil. Yet those who let themselves be governed by their reason and have been brought up properly choose virtue. . . . Virtue is not a matter of rank; it is more easily found in the lower than in the highest ranks. For persons of the higher ranks have too many fawners and flatterers who will corrupt them. I do not make any distinction of rank; whenever I find persons of good character, I like to be in their company.

Saint Cloud, 2 November 1719

A few years after Monsieur's death, Alvarez[1] went to Constantinople to trade in jewels; there he grew a big, heavy mustache and adopted the Turkish costume; he looks so funny that I laughed out loud when I saw him, but he can take a teasing. He brought me a fine present from the Princess of Wales, a beautiful golden knife, very well crafted (the sheath is of gold too) and a sealskin box filled with all kinds of well-made microscopes that will amuse me very much when I am in Paris; it is just the present for me. If you had said "salva venia" right away in your last letter I would not have understood, dear Luise, for I do not know a word of Latin; in church they can blab as much Latin as they please, I only pray in German and sometimes in French. The evening prayer here and at Versailles is said in French, and I go to it every day; when the Latin starts up, I read my prayers in German.

1. A merchant, son of an Amsterdam Jew, but brought up as a Christian.

To KAROLINE OF WALES

Saint Cloud, 17 November 1719

My son, Regent though he is, never comes to me or takes his leave without kissing my hand before I embrace him, nor does he sit down in my presence. But otherwise he is not shy and freely talks to me; we laugh and chat together like good friends.

To RAUGRÄFIN LUISE

Saint Cloud, 23 November 1719

Dearest Luise, the day arrived late today; I did not have the lights taken away until eight o'clock, for the fog is so thick that one can see nothing beyond the courtyard. . . .

Chausseraye is quite intelligent, she is always cheerful and always sick. Yesterday I went to see her; she is, thank God, much better than she was and walks around the house now. She looks like a ghost, wears white bonnets, has become very pale, and is clad in a white cotton dressing gown, and since she is tall and slender, she looks just as ghosts are described. I think the White Woman of Berlin must look like that. . . .

A lady whom Monsieur Law did not want to receive thought of a strange maneuver to get to speak to him; she ordered her coachman to upset her carriage before Monsieur Law's door and kept calling, "Coachman, tip us over!" The coachman hesitated for quite a while, but finally obeyed his lady's order and tipped over the carriage right before Monsieur Law's door so that no one could go in or out. Law rushed to the scene, all upset, thinking that the lady had broken her neck or some bones, but when he came to the coach, the lady confessed that she had done it purposely in order to speak to him. . . . Well, that was not so bad, but what six other ladies of quality did from pure greed[1] is really too shameless. They had waylaid Monsieur Law in the courtyard and surrounded him, but he begged them to let him go. They did not want to do it, and he finally told them, "Ladies, I beg your pardon a thousand times, but if you do not let me go I will burst, because I need to piss so badly that I cannot hold out another minute." The ladies answered, "Well then, Monsieur, go ahead and piss, just so long as you will listen to us." He did, and they stayed right with him; this is disgusting, but he himself nearly died laughing. Here you see, dear Luise, what point avarice and greed have reached in this country.

1. I.e., in order to obtain shares of the *Compagnie des Indes*.

Saint Cloud, 26 November 1719

Prince Eugene is perfectly right not to stand for such an ugly accusation[1] and to take the most severe measures against that man Nimptsch. On this point I believe that Prince Eugene is quite innocent, for he is not greedy and has done the right thing. He had left a great many debts here, and as soon as he obtained a post in the Imperial army and received money, he paid off everything he owed to the last penny; even those who had no notes or written promises from him and had forgotten all about it were paid. Oh no, a gentleman who acts so honorably could not possibly betray his master for money; and so I think that the accusation brought by that traitor Nimptsch is altogether unfounded.

1. Court Councillor Nimptsch had accused him of taking bribes.

Paris, 7 December 1719

The poor functioning of the mail often makes one quite impatient. But nothing can be done about it, it will go on just as it pleases the worthy postillions. And you, dear Luise, are quite right to cite the German proverb, "There's no fighting wind and weather." . . .

The Marquise de Foix, who used to be my maid-of-honor and whose maiden name was Hinderson, once had an extraordinary adventure. . . . She became ill at Maastricht and fell into such a dreadful lethargy that she could not move her eyes or anything else, and so it was thought that she was quite dead. She could hear and see perfectly well but, as I said, could not make a sound or move any part of her body. She heard and saw that candles were placed around her bed, along with a big crucifix with two silver candelabras, as is the Catholic custom. Also, the whole room was draped in black with cloth . . . and then someone called for the coffin into which she would be laid. When she heard that she made such a tremendous effort that her tongue was untied, and she called out loudly: "Take away all this stuff and give me something to eat and drink." This scared all the people who were in the room so unspeakably that they fell all over each other. She lived for another three years after that and might still be alive if she had not fallen down a flight of stairs, cutting her head open in many places, and that was the cause of her death. . . .

The brain weakens with time and with old age; that is what is happening to the Palatine Elector now. May God Almighty open his eyes so that my good fellow-countrymen will have peace and quiet, which I wish them with all my heart, and so that all wicked priests may receive their just rewards! The Elector should send all the priests who give him such pernicious advice to the devil; that would put some sense into the others and save the Palatine Elector a religious war.[1] I find King Hiskias's prayer[2] very good and say amen to it with all my heart. . . .

God forgive me! One should not judge others, but I cannot help but doubt that the Montespan and the Maintenon are in Heaven; they have wrought just too much evil in this world; may God have mercy on them! . . .

It is quite incomprehensible what tremendous wealth there is now in France; all one hears is talk of millions. I do not understand a single thing about all of this. Hearing about all this wealth, I think that the god Mammon now rules in Paris.

1. Elector Karl Philipp had begun to persecute the Reformed in the Palatinate.
2. 2 Kings 19:15–19.

Paris, 4 January 1720

Paris makes for the most unpleasant life that can be found anywhere in the world, especially for me. All I have here are botherations and constraints, and there is never anything enjoyable, not even the theater, which is the only pleasure that is left to me in my old age. I just cannot enjoy it here because the Parisians are so boorish that they stand and sit around on the stage in droves, so that the actors have no room to play; it is most annoying. Yesterday we saw a new tragedy that is not too bad; but the actors were held back by all the people.

To FREIHERR VON GOERTZ

Paris, 14 January 1720

Thank you very much for the account of the Czarina,[1] which I find very well written. Her life is clear proof that everyone's destiny is foreordained according to God's will. For all your good wishes for the New Year I thank you and likewise wish you, in addition to continued good health, everything that your own heart desires. I have ended the past year badly and the start of the new year was not much better, for at the end of the year I came down with such a horrendous cough and head cold that three times it looked as if I would choke to death. I was completely without breath for the length of an Our Father, turned black and blue, and thought myself that this was the end of me and therefore recommended my soul to God, but the Almighty did not want me yet. . . .

I never cite anyone and will therefore not say who sent me the pretty account of the Czarina's life.[1] Yet it does her honor, for what I had heard of this lady was much worse than what I read in the description, which I found most entertaining.

1. Catherine I (1679–1727), second wife of Peter the Great.

To RAUGRÄFIN LUISE

Paris, 28 January 1720

Alberoni[1] will not go any further than Genoa, where all the obnoxious characters are gathering now. The Princesse des Ursins is there too; it is too bad that Madame du Maine cannot betake herself as well. I think I already told you that Alberoni wrote to my son, begging his forgiveness and offering to betray Spain. A fine little fellow. He has also declared that all the libelous writings against my son that were distributed under his name came from Paris.

1. Former Spanish cardinal and minister, who had been deposed in 1719.

Paris, 4 February 1720

It is true that Paris and Heidelberg are located on the same latitude, and also in the same ascendant, namely that of Virgo. But I believe that my son's recently deceased doctor, who was a German and a learned man, has found the difference between these two places. His name was Herr Humberg.[1]
He said that once he was walking along, thinking about why the air of Heidelberg is so healthy and that of Paris so very unhealthy, when he happened to pass by a place where workmen were lifting up the cobblestones in order to repave the street with new cobblestones. Where the stones were pulled up, he saw a layer of pitch black sludge underneath. He took some of that sludge, which was a foot thick under the stones, wrapped it in a piece of paper, carried it home, and distilled it. It turned out to be all niter and saltpeter, from which he concluded that when the essence of this is drawn into the air by the heat of the sun, it causes the air to become sharp and harmful. This niter, he said, comes from the many thousands of people who piss in the streets. This reasoning of Herr Humberg's seemed very convincing to me. . . .

I herewith send you, dear Luise, the letter I have written on your behalf to the Palatine Elector. From it you will see that it will not be the fault of my recommendation if you are not paid.

1. Willem Homberg (1652–1715) is known in the history of chemistry as the discoverer of boric acid.

To ELECTOR KARL PHILIPP VON DER PFALZ

Paris, 4 February 1720

May I take the liberty of begging Your Grace most respectfully to take pity on the poor Raugräfin? The Heidelberg treasury still owes her twenty thousand gilders, a paltry sum for as great an Elector as Your Grace but a painful privation for a poor Imperial countess whose only livelihood consists of her revenues from the Palatinate. Your Grace is too generous not to honor her rightful claim, especially since she is the very last of the numerous Raugrafen. I should be most obliged to Your Grace for his kindness in giving strict orders to have the Raugräfin paid.

To RAUGRÄFIN LUISE

Paris, 11 February 1720

Except for my son and Madame de Châteauthiers, I do not know a single soul in France who is absolutely free of selfishness and greed. All the others, without exception, are greedy to the point of making fools of themselves, especially the princes and princesses of the Blood; they have gotten into brawls with the clerks at the bank and into all kinds of other ignominious scrapes. Money rules the world, that is true enough, but I do not believe that there is a place in the world where it rules people more strictly than here.

To HERR VON HARLING

Paris, 29 February 1720

Everywhere one hears of sudden deaths, and Germany is no exception; the Empress Lenore and the Palatine Countess of Sulzbach both died of a stroke. Although this seems to be the fashion for Palatine countesses, I shall do my best not to follow this fashion just yet. But whenever it will be God's will, I would much rather desire a rapid than a slow death. Our dear departed Electress often said in her letters to me that she wished for a death just like the one she had. . . .

The secretary to the Palatine envoy told me the day before yesterday that the religious matters are being cleared up;[1] that is already one effect of the death of the Empress, the Elector's sister; so this is an occasion to cite the French proverb, "Misfortune has its good side, too." The affection for my fatherland is so deeply imprinted within me that it will last as long as I live.

1. I.e., the persecution of the Reformed Protestants.

To RAUGRÄFIN LUISE

Paris, 7 March 1720

How would it be possible to prevent men from pissing in the streets? In fact it is a wonder that there are not entire rivers of piss, considering the huge numbers of people living in Paris. Heidelberg has fewer people than a single suburb of Paris, and the air in Heidelberg is exceedingly good. The two mountains, the Königsstuhl and the Heiligenberg, keep out the very cold north wind and the hot southerly; this makes for a tempered air, which is very healthy. . . .

A man here had 14,000 livres' worth of banknotes in a billfold in his pocket; in a crowd he felt a pickpocket pulling the billfold out of his pocket; he sees who the fellow is and follows him; the pickpocket, realizing that the man he had robbed is following him, begins to run and hides in a narrow passage. But the other, who was also a good runner, gives chase, grabs him by the arm, and says, "Knave, give me back the billfold you stole from me, or I shall have you hanged." This really scares the thief; he reaches into his pocket and gives the man a billfold, whereupon the man happily goes home. The next day when he wants to pay for something, he takes out the billfold but finds it thicker than his own. When he looks at it in broad daylight, it turns out that the thief had made a mistake and that instead of his own billfold containing 14,000 livres, he had given him another, also stolen, containing several millions' worth of banknotes. In examining it the man, who was extremely honest, finds out that this billfold belongs to one of his friends. He joyfully went to see him and jokingly asked him, "What would you give to get back your stolen billfold?" His friend, who was very grouchy about his loss, said, "Listen, friend, how can you joke with me? The loss I have suffered is too heavy to be a joking matter." The friend said, "No, I am not joking. If you give me back my banknotes for 14,000 francs, I will give you your notes, which I have here." The bargain was quickly made. I find it funny that the thief robbed himself, as it were. Every day one hears stories of this kind; but most of them are tragic rather than funny.

Paris, 14 March 1720

I am just returning from the opera and shall swallow my egg to your good health; for this morning I talked to the little secretary to the Palatine envoy. He told me that the Heiliggeistkirche will once again be turned over to the Reformed, and that everything will be done according to the peace treaty. The secretary asked me what my son would say about this, and I replied, "My son will be glad to hear that the Elector abides by the peace treaty; he never approved of the things that have happened and on this point would not have supported the Elector; he has told me so quite plainly." My goodness, did that little man ever open his eyes wide! But I only told him what I had heard from my son himself, and people did him a great injustice to believe that he would approve of such brute force, which directly violates the peace treaty; no, there was no chance of that. My son is not as foolish in religious matters as they think; he is not bigoted and will certainly never let himself be ruled by any Jesuits, that I can guarantee, nor my Excellency either, I promise you.

To HERR VON HARLING

Paris, 31 March 1720

I believe that the devil is altogether out of hand this year with all these assassinations; lately not a night passes but that one finds people murdered for the sake of banknotes. People of high rank have become involved in this ugly and distressing business, among others a handsome young man belonging to the Flemish family of the counts van Hoorne. . . . The count was only twenty-two years old. Monsieur de Mortagne, who was my *chevalier d'honneur,* presented this count to me three or four weeks ago. Mortagne died last Monday morning in his bed and the next day at four in the afternoon the count was executed. This gives rise to mournful thoughts. All of France asked for clemency for the Comte de Hoorne, but my son said that an example had to be made of such a horrid deed, as was done to the great satisfaction of the populace, which shouted, "Our Regent is just." Yesterday again, four fresh bodies were found in a draw-well in the rue Quincampoix.[1] A week ago, two malefactors were burned whose sins were so loathsome and so impious that the court clerk who had to write them down got sick while doing so.

1. The bank was located in the rue Quincampoix.

To RAUGRÄFIN LUISE

Paris, 31 March 1720

Today in the carriage my son told me something that has touched me so deeply that it brought tears to my eyes. He said, "The people are saying something that quite touches my heart; I am very happy about it." When I asked what they had said he replied that when the Comte de Hoorne was broken on the wheel, they said, "Whenever someone does something against the Regent personally, he forgives everything and does not punish him; but when something is done against us, he takes it very seriously and does us justice, as you can see by this Comte de Hoorne." This has so moved my son that, as I said before, it has brought tears to my eyes. That Monsieur

Law does not have any bad intentions is proven by the fact that he is buying many estates and invests all his big money in land, so he will have to stay
in this country.

To FREIHERR VON GOERTZ

Paris, 4 April 1720

On the same day when Comte de Hoorne was broken on the wheel here, four
men of quality had to be beheaded at Nantes because they had been involved in a serious conspiracy. A most curious thing happened with one of
these cavaliers. His name was Monsieur de Pontcallec. Many of the conspirators had escaped by sea and wanted to take Pontcallec with them. But he
told them that it had been prophesied to him that he could die only by the
sea (*la mer*) and that therefore he did not want to embark with them. Standing on the scaffold where he was to be beheaded, he asked the executioner,
"What is your name?" The executioner replied, "My name is La Mer." Pontcallec cried out, "this is my death!" What a curious occurrence.

To RAUGRÄFIN LUISE

Saint Cloud, 21 April 1720

It is quite certain that our Germans used to be virtuous, but now I hear that
they always bring many vices back from France, especially sodomy, which
is dreadful in Paris and brings all other vices in its train. . . . Ever since the
Queen started driving with eight horses I have had as many. The first one to
start this fashion was the recently deceased Duc de la Feuillade. We need
to do this because our carriages are very heavy; it has nothing to do with rank,
and anybody can drive with eight horses. As I said, it is forty years now
that my carriages have been drawn by eight horses, but my calashes usually
have only six. I think it is funny that you, dear Luise, think that I drive
with eight horses because I am the First Lady. I am not overly conceited, but
I do uphold my dignity as I should.

To FREIHERR VON GOERTZ

Saint Cloud, 25 April 1720

On Monday last I duly received your letter of the 12th of this month and
thank you very much for the welcome news you report, namely that my
cousin, the prince hereditary of Hessen-Kassel, has finally received the Swedish crown and has become King.[1] . . . I feel that it is most commendable
and proper that the Queen of Sweden has made her husband King. In this
manner she extricates herself from a great deal of toil and worry, binds
her husband to herself by a strong bond of obligation, and yet retains her
royal rank and estate; in other words, she has the honor without the toil,

which I think is excellent, as is the point that she reserves the right to resume her duties as reigning Queen if my nephew should die. All of this is very well thought out.

1. The Queen of Sweden had crowned her husband, the prince hereditary of Hessen-Kassel, King of Sweden.

To RAUGRÄFIN LUISE

Saint Cloud, 30 May 1720

By yesterday's mail my daughter sent me a memorandum outlining how seventy-five families from the Palatinate are on their way to Orléans, from where they will travel to the Mississippi.[1] The Duc de Lorraine has seen them passing through Lorraine. The enclosed will show you the stages of their journey. This has brought tears to my eyes. I am afraid that Our Lord will severely punish the Elector. If the punishment were to fall only on the confounded priests, I would not mind, but I fear that the Elector himself will have to pay. God grant that I may be mistaken.

1. This was a group of Reformed families who emigrated because of religious persecution.

To KAROLINE OF WALES

Saint Cloud, 31 May 1720

Law, whom people here have worshipped like a god, had to be removed from his post by my son. It is necessary to guard him, for his life is not safe, and the man is terribly frightened.

Saint Cloud, 11 June 1720

I remember the day when the King of England[1] was born as if it were today. I certainly was a willful, forward child. They had put a doll in a rosemary bush and wanted to make me believe that it was the child to whom Ma Tante had given birth; just then I heard her screaming dreadfully, for Her Grace was in great pain; and this did not seem to fit in with the baby in the rosemary bush. I pretended to believe it, though, but hid as if I were playing hide-and-seek with young Bülow and C. A. Haxthausen, squeezed into Ma Tante's reception room where Her Grace was in labor, and hid behind a large screen that had been placed before the door by the fireplace. When the child was born, it was carried to the fireplace to be bathed, and then I crawled out. They should have spanked me, but because it was a happy day I was only scolded.

1. George I of England, the oldest son of Madame's aunt, Sophie of Hanover.

To RAUGRÄFIN LUISE

Saint Cloud, 11 June 1720

I rarely see very much of my son, but last Sunday night and Monday morning I spoke to him for a few moments. I never ever talk to him about affairs of State, nor do I give him any advice, for it is too hard to give others good advice in matters that one does not understand oneself. But as I gather from general rumors, things are still in a very bad way. I wish that Law with his art and his system were at the ends of the world and had never come to France. They are doing me too much honor to believe that things have improved because of my advice. My advice cannot improve or ruin anything because, as I said, I never give any advice in matters of State. But the French are so accustomed to women meddling in everything that it seems impossible to them that I do not meddle, and so the good Parisians, with whom I am rather popular, want to ascribe all improvements to me. I am most obliged to these poor people for their affection, but I certainly do not deserve it.

The smoked sausages still agree with me very well, for I am—thanks be to God—in perfect health, for as long as it may last, because with old women it cannot possibly last too long. I neither desire nor, thank God, fear death and have completely resigned myself to the will of God, and so I sing, dear Luise, as the Lutheran hymn has it, "I place my lot in the hands of God.". . . I too eat a great deal of fruit, but I think that smoked sausage is better for the stomach. I also like fresh sausage, but it seems to me that they are not as tasty here as at home. . . .

Elaborate compliments I find offensive, but polished and courtly manners are most important to me.

To HERR VON HARLING

Saint Cloud, 1 August 1720

I am as tired of all this bank business, be it the Mississippi or the South Sea, as if I had been stuffed with it by the spoonful. I do not understand any of this, and I certainly do not like to see little scraps of paper instead of money and gold. It does not give me pleasure to hear that Germans have made money on the shares, for I see that this only creates avarice, and I would rather see something that incites people to virtuous deeds. Those who have lost money in this bank do not receive much comfort from me when they complain about their losses, because I reply, "That is what comes from greed and always wanting more." I have always been fortunate in that I can amuse myself with innocent pastimes; those who cannot or will not amuse themselves in this way must often suffer bitter boredom.

To RAUGRÄFIN LUISE

Saint Cloud, 4 August 1720

I did not know that Monsieur Rousseau, who painted the Orangerie, was Reformed.[1] He was way up on a scaffold, and since I thought I was all alone in the gallery, I loudly sang the sixth psalm: "Of thy tremendous wrath / that crushes me, alas / deliver me, O Lord / and let thy righteous anger / be changed to mercy mild / the day you judge my sinful heart." I had barely finished the first stanza when I heard someone hurriedly climb down the scaffolding and throw himself at my feet; it was Rousseau himself. I thought the man had gone out of his mind and said, "My goodness, Monsieur Rousseau, what it it?" He said, "Is it possible, Madame, that you still remember our psalms and sing them? May God bless you and keep you in these good sentiments." He had tears in his eyes. A few days later he ran off, I do not know where he went. Wherever he may be, I wish him much happiness and joy. He is an excellent painter of frescoes, and highly respected. . . .

There are few antique medals I do not have already, for I have nearly nine hundred of them. I started out with only 260, which I bought from Madame Verrue, who had stolen them from the then Duke of Savoy. I immediately wrote about it to the present Queen of Sardinia, offering to send them back to the King, but the box had already been ripped open and most of the medals sold. The Queen wrote that she was delighted that I had received at least a few and told me to keep them. They did not cost me much since I bought them by weight, and yet the lot contained a few very rare items. —I like Merian's copper engravings very much, but I think that landscapes are what he does best. I have many of his copper engravings, all the houses of Flanders, Germany, and France he has engraved, as well as all of Switzerland. I have more than nine of his sheets, and also his German Bible and the Four Monarchies.

1. This story, which sounds as fresh as if it had happened the day before, is actually a reminiscence going back to 1687. The landscape and architectural painter Jacques Rousseau (1630–93), a member of the *Académie royale,* had decorated many rooms at the royal châteaux of Versailles, Saint Cloud, Saint-Germain-en-Laye, and Marly. Dismissed from the academy as a Protestant in 1687, he went to Switzerland and Holland but returned a year later, having renounced his Protestant faith.

Saint-Cloud, 8 August 1720

Crossing the sea is a horrendous undertaking, considering that one is liable to arrive in India as well as in England. The late Monsieur was very funny when he told the story of how one day, in the most beautiful weather, he wanted to go for a boatride at Dunkerque. He sat down in the rowboat next to the pilot, who looked downcast, and Monsieur asked him what his trouble was. He said, "A sad memory. It was just a year ago today that, on a day as beautiful as this one, I wanted to take my wife and children for a ride, but there was a sudden storm that led us straight to India, where my wife and children died." When Monsieur heard that he said to the pilot, "Take me back to shore as quickly as possible."

I overslept a bit today, for I did not wake up until six o'clock and said my morning prayer; now it is exactly seven, for I hear the clock strike. So, as the Rotzenhäuserin always sings, it's "Look sharp, my little Johnny." It is true, dear Luise, it is quite true that I am rather well liked by the people, although I do not know why; I do not do them any good or any harm. But in any case, the love of the people cannot be relied upon, it is just too changeable a thing. I confess that I never did like Monsieur Law's system and always wished that my son would not adopt it; I never understood anything about it. That it did away with gold shocked me and seemed fraudulent to me, to tell the truth. . . .

Our Lord did not want our line to rule in the Palatinate, since all of the eight grown sons my grandmother the Queen of Bohemia had borne died without heirs, and even my brother himself had no children. . . . That Mannheim or Friedrichsburg is being rebuilt pleases me; still, I would not want to see Heidelberg abandoned. . . . At Heidelberg . . . the air is excellent, and so is the water.

The rumors that are spread in Paris are a thousand times worse even than what can be read in the newspapers. This very morning I received an unsigned letter saying that next month I am to be burned with all of my household here at Saint Cloud and my son in Paris, so that nothing will be left of him. These are cheery and clever *billets doux* as you can see, dear Luise. I am not afraid for myself, but very much for my son, for these people are just too vicious and hateful. . . .

You would do me a favor if you could find out what has happened to the good, honest, and most able Rousseau. If I recall correctly, someone told me that he is in Switzerland. He paints extraordinarily well in fresco and his designs are beautiful. All those who have seen the Orangerie here have admired his work. This answers your two letters completely.

I lost my high spirits long ago and barely know how to laugh any longer. If the thing I saw yesterday in the theater had happened some years ago, I would have laughed about it for three days. Mademoiselle de la Roche-sur-

Yonne made the funniest somersault; the bench on which she was sitting suddenly collapsed under her and she simply disappeared; they had a hard time pulling her out again. She is big and heavy, and when such people fall it is particularly funny. She herself broke into peals of laughter; at first I was quite frightened because her head had snapped back so hard that I was afraid she had hurt herself, but I felt better when I saw her laugh so heartily.

It seems to me that our good, honest Germans are not quite as eager to do everything for money as the French and the English; they are surely less greedy. Oh Lord, how I detest greed! It certainly is wrong to serve the god Mammon, as the Scripture says, and I believe that this is the most damnable sin, for it is the root of all evil. Our German nobility cannot possibly fatten their pocketbooks as much as the English, for since they are not so greedy, they do not think up all kinds of shenanigans to get money and they consider commerce dishonorable, and that I find estimable.

To HERR VON HARLING

Saint Cloud, 12 September 1720

Yesterday I drove to Paris to partake of a meal that has become a kind of yearly tithe to me; it was given by the Duchesse de Lude, who used to be governess to Madame la Dauphine (the second Dauphine) and is my good friend; she is one of the most excellent women to be found in the world. She gave us a magnificent meal of four warm courses and one course of fruit and relishes, but since I do not eat relishes, this part was a mere table ornament for me. After we had played hocca[1] for a few hours, I called on the King; from there I went to the Palais Royal, and after I had visited with my son and his wife I went to the theater with my four grandchildren. . . .

I think that it is very nice for the King of Prussia to be so polite with the ladies; nothing is more befitting to great lords, and it shows that they have been well brought up and are free of boorish pride. No one could be more polite than our late King was; in this respect His Majesty's children and grandchildren did not resemble him at all. I have always been of the opinion that the highest positions do not make for the happiest and most agreeable life. . . .

Alberoni has stolen 198 bottles of champagne that were sent to the King of Spain; he only gave His Majesty two bottles and a piece of cheese, the rest he sold and kept the money for himself. He also presented a bill stating that the war had cost twenty-eight million and was paid the entire sum; when the bill was examined it turned out that the war had cost only one million and that he had pocketed the other twenty-seven. For this alone he deserves the gallows.

1. One of the few card games that Madame played occasionally.

To RAUGRÄFIN LUISE

Everyone should keep these great truths firmly in his head that we were not put into this world (I mean by Our Lord) in order to follow our caprices and do only what can serve to amuse us, but in order to further God's glory. Therefore we should always strive to live in such a manner as to set a good example to our fellow man and to avoid causing scandal to the best of our ability. In this we are helped by the short prayer taken from one of the psalms, which in my early childhood the good Frau von Harling, my governess at the time, taught me to say morning and night, "Oh Lord forsake me not, lest I forsake thee."

Saint Cloud, 14 September 1720

I do not remember who it was, but someone recently asked me whether in my time at Heidelberg there were as many thunderclaps as we are having now and whether this is why I am not afraid of thunder. I laughed and said, "I am too accustomed to heavy thunderstorms to fear those here, which are not severe at all. In such an event all one can do is to resign oneself to God's will and for the rest one should keep calm without upsetting oneself by useless fear." But I do find that this year there has been more thunder than we have heard in many a year; last year when it was so dreadfully hot we had very little thunder, except one fairly heavy storm on the day when the Duchesse de Berry died. I do not know whether in the next world too cannon are set off to celebrate the arrival of great lords, but I do not think so. The wine cannot possibly be good this year, for the cooking month, that is August, has been too damp and cold. Here everything costs three times as much now as it did a year ago. It is incredible how costly everything has become; what used to be 30 francs is 100 now, and everything is sky-high. I do not demand anything from the King or my son, let alone from Monsieur Law; but I do like to be paid exactly, so that my servants do not suffer want. So far, I am happy to say, I do not owe anything to any merchants or anyone, and it would upset and grieve me very much if I had to go into debt. That reminds me of something that once made me laugh quite heartily. When the late King was still alive and the Duchesse du Maine was spending such horrendous sums on lavish parties, theater performances, ballets, fireworks, and so forth, she and her husband sent for the superintendent of my household because they were jealous that I was keeping up my rank and asked my superintendent, "Tell us, how does Madame manage not to make any debts? After all, she is not rich." My superintendent coolly replied, "Madame is never extravagant; she only spends what she can afford, and in this manner she does not owe anything and does not have to borrow." To this they had no reply, and they dismissed him. . . .

Monsieur Law's young daughter is bound to make a good marriage, for he will give her a dowry of three million, not counting the household furnishings and her personal trousseau. I do believe that if one of the dukes or princes were to press him, he would probably fork over another million or so.

To HERR VON HARLING

Saint Cloud, 22 September 1720

I am quite of your opinion that the old language was more expressive than the French that is spoken now. One would not want to read *Amadis*[1] in present-day French; someone tried to translate Don Quixote into it, but it was not a success. I read Philippe de Comines[2] forty years ago and do not remember his book very well; at the time his style seemed rather naive to me. . . .

Nothing is more full of lies than gazettes and newspapers. Here in France, if one wants to do someone a nasty turn, one asks a third person to write the news one wants to spread on a piece of paper, wraps this around a gold coin, and addresses it "To the gazeteer of Holland," and at the next mail one can be sure to find everything that was on the scrap of paper in the Dutch newspapers. I have never done this myself, but I have often seen others do it. So these papers cannot be too reliable, because partiality is always involved.[3]

> 1. The most famous of the Spanish romances of chivalry; translated into French in 1540. 2. Philippe de Commynes (ca. 1447–1511), author of historical chronicles. 3. For the Dutch newspapers, see also letter of 3 July 1692.

To KAROLINE OF WALES

Saint Cloud, 4 October 1720

My son was much beloved, but since the confounded Law has come here he is becoming more and more hated. Not a week goes by without my receiving horrid threatening letters in the mail, in which my son is treated as the most vicious tyrant.

To RAUGRÄFIN LUISE

Saint Cloud, 2 November 1720

Since the wine of Bachrach is not drunk here before it is seven or eight years old, I will probably not drink very much of this year's Bachracher. God knows where I will be eight years from now, and for all the pleasure that my present life affords me now, dear Luise, I would not be too upset to find out that I will not be here eight years hence. . . .

It is more from spite than from curiosity that the two wicked ministers[1] always want to read my letters. And who would or could stop them? For

all the mail goes through their hands. Nor will they admit it; but the proof
that they are not the only ones to read and divulge my letters is the fact
that Marshals Villeroy and Tessé have complained so bitterly about the things
I said about them in letters to my daughter.

I was pleased with the medal of Messina, my dear, and enjoyed filling this
space in my medal box. I hope that I will soon be able to send you another
present from the Saint Cloud fair. Everything is becoming less costly; one is
beginning to see some gold again, although it is still very high; a louis d'or
is worth 54 francs. But it will go down month by month, so that gradually
everything will return to its former state. God grant it! For I am as tired
of the Mississippi bank and of shares as if I had been stuffed with them by the
spoonful; I shall thank God when I do not hear another word about all this.
You were quite right not to send me an agate box, for I do not need it; I never
ever use snuff, and these little boxes are quite common here. Since when do
you lisp, dear Luise, that you say "Auspürg" rather than Augsburg? Is this
how they now talk in Germany, or was it just a slip?. . . .

I already thanked you for the Czar[2] the day before yesterday, as well as
for the Prince Eugene, but I would like to do it again. Prince Eugene must
be amazingly changed if he now has a long, pointed nose, for he certainly did
not have that in his youth. . . .

The Queen of Spain,[3] who is at Bayonne now, always calls me "Mama"
or "Mamachen." This always embarrasses me, and I do not know how to respond to such endearments, for I am not familiar with this kind of thing;
it was not customary at court and in my day.

1. Torcy and Dubois; the Regent had called the latter, his former tutor, into his
council; he was an able diplomat and served the Regent faithfully.   2. I.e., for a
medal with his image.   3. Maria Anna von Pfalz-Neuburg.

To HERR VON HARLING

Saint Cloud, 14 November 1720

François I never claimed to be a saint and had a most *galant* court. Mademoiselle de la Force has written a pretty novel about this court under the
title *La Reine Margueritte de Navarre;* it is in three small octavo volumes and
makes for most agreeable reading. It takes place at Saint-Germain and not
at Fontainebleau, so François I after his death should be wandering around at
Saint Germain rather than in the galérie d'Ulisse at Fontainebleau. The
Queen Mother[1] had some of the rooms off the galérie d'Ulisse made into an
apartment for herself, and when her chambermaids had to pass through this
gallery at night they saw François I walk around in a green flowered dressing
gown. But he never did me the honor to appear to me. I must not be in
favor with ghosts, because I slept for ten years in the late Madame's room

without ever seeing anything. But the first time that Monsieur le Dauphin[2] slept there, his aunt the late Madame[3] appeared to him. He told me so himself. He felt a call of nature, got out of bed, sat down on his night chair next to the bed and, begging your pardon, relieved himself. As he was working on this, he heard the door to the adjacent salon open (that night there had been a great masked ball in this salon) and saw a bejewelled lady in a brown gown, wearing a beautiful yellow underskirt and lots of yellow ribbons in her hair, come in. Her head was turned toward the window and Monsieur le Dauphin believed that it was the young Duchesse de Foix; he laughed and thought to himself how upset she would be to see him there in his shirt in this little corner and therefore coughed in order to make her face toward him, which the lady did. But instead of the Duchesse de Foix he sees the late Madame, looking just as she did when he saw her last. But instead of scaring the lady, he himself was frightened out of his wits and vaulted back into bed to Madame la Dauphine, who was sleeping. She was awakened by his leap and said, "Why on earth are you jumping like this, Monseigneur?" He said, "Go back to sleep, I will tell you in the morning." The next morning when they woke up she asked him what had made him so upset during the night. He told her his adventure. Madame la Dauphine asked me whether anything had ever happened to me in that room, and I said no. I went to the Dauphin and asked His Grace about it, and he told me word for word what I have just told you. Monsieur le Dauphin insisted all his life that this story was true. What I believe is that Monsieur le Dauphin, who was in the habit of spending a long time on the night chair, fell asleep on it and had this dream that frightened him. Many people are so superstitious because they have been brought up this way in their youth and because they have heard so much about ghosts from their nursemaids.

1. Anne d'Autriche. 2. The first Dauphin, son of Louis XIV. 3. Monsieur's first wife, Henrietta of England.

To RAUGRÄFIN LUISE

Saint Cloud, 21 November 1720

Were the grapes that were sent to you from the Palatinate from Schriessheim? These are usually very good, and I think that they are better than those from the Rohrbach side. I do not think the grapes from Heidelberg are bad for you. I remember that I once devoured so many grapes in the Schriessheim vineyard that my belly swelled up so much that I was unable to walk; but it did not hurt me at all, only gave me an even better appetite for dinner. . . .

I see all the trouble that the confounded Mississippi is causing here. I have such an aversion for all this stuff that I have forbidden all my people to mention either this matter or the constitution[1] in my presence. I do not understand either, but I loathe both of them like a purgative, as Frau von Rotzenhausen always says. I think the devil has invented this thing in order to cast so many people into despair. I do not know what is meant by rising and falling in this matter, nor do I want to learn.

1. The ecclesiastical constitution promulgated by the papal bull *Unigenitus*.

Saint Cloud, 23 November 1720

Today . . . we had this winter's first snow, but it melted right away. That makes me believe that it must be very cold now in Germany and in the Palatinate. Now I no longer wish I were there; I would weep day and night if I were there and must not think too deeply about the olden days, for it always makes me too rueful and sad . . . I have by no means forgotten all the people I knew in my youth and could paint everyone at our old court, young and old.

To KAROLINE OF WALES

Saint Cloud, 26 November 1720

Once at The Hague[1] Ma Tante, our dear Electress, did not go to call on the princess royal,[2] but the Queen of Bohemia[3] did go and took me with her. Ma Tante said to me, "Be careful, Lisette, that this time you do not run around so much that you cannot be found! Be sure you follow right behind the Queen so that she will not have to wait for you." I said, "Oh, Ma Tante will hear about it, I shall be very good." I had often played with the princess royal's son, but I did not know that she was his mother. Having stared at her for a long time, I looked around for someone to tell me who this woman was. Acquainted with no one but the Prince of Orange, I went to him and said, "Would you tell me, please, who is this woman with the horrendous nose?" He laughed and said, "It is the princess royal, my mother." I was struck dumb and just stood there. In order to comfort me, Mademoiselle Hyde led me and the prince to the princess's bedchamber, where we played all kinds of games. I had asked to be called when the Queen was leaving; we were just rolling around on a Turkish rug when I was called. I jumped up and ran to the reception room, but the Queen was already in the anteroom. Without losing a moment's time, I pulled the princess royal back by her skirts, made her a pretty curtsy, stepped in front of her, and followed right behind the Queen, all the way to her coach. Everyone was laughing, I did not know why. When we arrived at home, the Queen went to Ma Tante, sat down on her bed, and said, "Lisette has had quite a day"; then she told her everything I had done, shaking with laughter. Our dear departed Electress laughed even harder than the Queen, called me to her, and said, "Lisette, you have done the right thing; you have avenged us upon the proud princess."

1. When the seven-year-old Liselotte was visiting this city with her aunt.   2. Mary of England, widow of William II of Orange.   3. Liselotte's grandmother.

To RAUGRÄFIN LUISE

Saint Cloud, 28 November 1720

I am popular with the Parisians; it would upset them if I never lived there at all, and so I must sacrifice a few months to the good people. They certainly deserve as much from me, for they like me better than their native princes and princesses; these they curse, while they always wish me God's blessing when I drive through town. I like the Parisians too, they are good people. I am sorry myself that I dislike the air and my dwelling in their city so much. . . .

On a very hot summer day when I was hunting the stag with Monsieur le Dauphin at Saint Leger, we were surprised by a great storm with thunder, lightning, and hail; my skirt was so full of hailstones that it became soaked through when they melted and my boots filled up with the ice-cold water. We were far away from any village and a good three French miles from our coaches; in this way my knees got very cold and have been weak and painful ever since. I have tried a hundred kinds of remedies, and everything helped a little bit in the beginning, but the pain always comes back. Now I no longer bother with anything, and I am neither better nor worse off. I am so old now that there is no point in thinking that I can be cured. . . .

It is true, dear Luise, that anyone who thinks of buying anything now would find prices three times as high as a year ago, especially for gold and jewels. I was offered three times as much as I had paid for some small rings I have; but the offer did not tempt me in the slightest because, fortunately, I am not greedy and only love money so that I can spend it. . . .

If adults lisp, it is because they were not corrected and taught to speak properly when they were young. The second son of the Duc de Luxembourg . . . has such peculiar speech that one can barely understand him. The reason, as his father told me himself, is that he had forbidden the teachers to correct the child's speech, so that he could see how it would turn out.

Saint Cloud, 30 November 1720

It has gone altogether out of fashion to heed the word of God, to have a conscience and to live accordingly. These are simple-minded notions from past years and past ages to which no one pays attention nowadays. They will only find out about this when God duly punishes them. . . .

Oh dear Luise, one does not die of one thing or another, one dies because one's hour has come. For I am firmly convinced that for each of us there is a fixed life span, beyond which we cannot go. It makes no difference therefore whether one is tired of living or not; one will not die a moment sooner or later because of it.

The bubonic plague, which raged in southern France until the summer of 1721, killed some 100,000 people, but it was the last major outbreak in Europe.

Saint Cloud, 5 December 1720

The plague, which had ceased entirely at Marseilles, has started up there worse than ever. I am told that it is also terrible in Poland and has spread to Silesia as well. I am convinced that it will soon be all over Europe. That does not frighten me; nothing will befall me but what God Almighty has in store for me. If I die of the plague I will not die of something else. It would not be surprising if the plague were to come to Saxony, since the King of Poland and his people may well bring it there from Poland.

Paris, 14 December 1720

In this country, and especially in the royal house, princesses are so badly brought up that it is positively disgraceful. If they are attended to they turn out differently; after all, you can see that those who were looked after by me are not that way, for no one could be on better terms with her husband than the Queen of Sardinia[1] is with her king and my daughter with her husband. But if one never corrects children and lets them do exactly as they please between the ages of seven and twenty, nothing reasonable can ever come of it. I have made up my mind not to fret about my Parisian grandchildren any more and to let them carry on however they please. My son's marriage took place against my will, and so I would have to be a great fool to torture myself about all of this. As long as I live I shall treat all of them properly and politely for the sake of peace, but that is it; for the rest I shall live by myself like a small Imperial town. . . .

I do not forget, dear Luise, when I have promised something, for I am mindful of the German saying, "A knave does not keep his word," and as I do not want to become a knave. . . . One must learn early on to speak the truth in small things if one never wants to be caught lying; I am extremely careful about this and detest nothing so much as lying. . . .

Monsieur Law has retired. I do not know yet how things are going with the South Sea Company.[2] I certainly approve when those who are not satisfied with great gains end up losing everything. God forgive me! but I am always glad to hear that stingy people have gotten in trouble by their avarice.

1. Her second stepdaughter. 2. I.e., the shares of that company.

To tell the truth, I am, as the apostle Paul says, neither of Apollos, nor of Paul, nor of Cephas, neither Reformed, nor Catholic, nor Lutheran, but want to be a true Christian to the best of my ability and will live and die in that endeavor. This, dear Luise, is how I truly feel. Adieu! I embrace you with all my heart, and since I never change my mind, you will always be dear to me.

To KAROLINE OF WALES

Paris, 27 December 1720

When he took his leave, he[1] said to my son, "Monseigneur, I have made great mistakes, and have made them because I am human, but you will find no malice or knavery in my conduct." His wife does not want to leave Paris until all his debts are paid.

1. John Law.

To FREIHERR VON GOERTZ

Paris, 29 December 1720

The mails have been dreadfully out of order lately. I have been assured that the reason is a matter of sheer stinginess and that the postmasters do not want to give the poor horses oats, which they find too costly, and feed them only hay. This makes the poor beasts so weak that they cannot run, especially now, when the roads are so bad; but the postmasters do not care whether the letters arrive early or late. They are lucky that I have no authority over the mails, for I would not be as patient as my son. I admire his patience, though I do not know where he gets it, because the late Monsieur had no patience at all, nor can I boast of this virtue, alas. For one desperately needs it in this country.

To RAUGRÄFIN LUISE

Paris, 6 March 1721

The common people of Paris are good, godfearing folk, but what is called the grandseigneurs, that is the princes of the Blood or dukes, all of that is a bunch of good-for-nothings without Christian sentiments, without faith or honor, an ungrateful lot that worships only the god Mammon. Greed and the desire to extort or make money by any means available fills all of their time. I must confess that I am afraid of greedy people who do not believe in God, for they feel free to follow their own fancy and there is no telling how far their wickedness will lead them.

Mannheim is a warm place; I remember that we once ate our evening meal in the Mühlau on the first of May, everything was green already; and then there was such a horrendous thunderstorm that it looked as if heaven and earth must perish. Your mother was scared, but still she could not help laughing at the frightful grimaces that fear wrought on the face of my governess, Mistress Kolb; I thought I would die laughing. . . .

My son's boundless forbearance often makes me so impatient that I feel like stamping my feet. For there is one thing about the French: one can deal with them only if they have great expectations or if they are afraid. With them there is no use looking for gratitude or genuine affection. I have often told my son that I know his nation better than he does; now he admits that I am right. If people are good-natured one achieves more with forbearance than with severity, but this is rare in this country. Their dreadful greed and avarice does not permit it, and the thing that increases their avarice is luxurious living and gambling for high stakes, for that costs a lot of money. That is only the most general reason, but debauchery also helps, for mistresses and favorites must be paid, and that too devours large sums.

I feel for all those who lose their children, for nothing in the world is more painful. The loss of an infant of a few months is more easily borne than when they can walk and talk. When I lost my eldest son, who was almost three years old, I was in such a state that for six months I thought I would go out of my mind with grief.

I am talking about the Pope in the French-Catholic and not in the German-Catholic manner; in France he is not considered infallible, as the Sorbonne has declared, and when the Pope is unreasonable, his opinion is not accepted in France, and moreover everyone is free to speak about it as he pleases. We do not have an inquisition in France. To say "the Holy Father" does not mean anything more here than to say "Pope"; it is just a manner of speaking, and he is not considered holy; but for all that he is a great lord. A bishop of Noyon whom I knew and who was a count and peer never called the Pope anything but Monsieur de Rome; I often laughed about it. I was not fond of the deceased Pope,[1] but for truth's sake I must say that it is quite impossible that the Pope had an affair with the Pretender's spouse.[2] In the first place, he was a man of seventy-three, and in the second place he had such a horrendous hernia that his entire body was open and he wore a silver plaque to hold in his belly and his entrails. That is no state to go in for amorous dalliance, as you can imagine. But that he took an interest in this princess is not surprising; he was her godfather, arranged her marriage, and thought that if the Pretender could regain his throne all of England would once again be in his and the priests' power; therefore he had every reason to take an interest in this princess and her husband. A seventy-three-year-old lover with a silver plaque—a scandalous affair indeed! No French cardinal has a chance of becoming Pope, unless he was born in Italy. The French are right not to want to go to Rome; it costs them a horrendous amount and they have nothing to gain, and so one can believe that they mean it when they say that they are reluctant to go to the conclave.

1. Clement XI had died on 9 March. 2. Maria Sobieska, the wife of James, the son of the deposed James II of England.

Saint Cloud, 26 April 1721

Monsieur Teray[1] knows his business very well and one can trust him, and besides I do what I am supposed to do; yet I am convinced that my hour has been fixed and that I shall not go a step beyond it. As long as I am meant to live, the doctors will always find something that will help me; but once the fatal time that God has foreordained to lead me out of this life has arrived they will be struck by a blindness that will cause everything to go awry. Not that I care; I know that I was born only to die, and so I await that time without impatience but also without anxiety and only beg the Almighty to grant me a blessed end when my hour has come. . . .

All the things one reads in the Bible about life before the Flood and at Sodom and Gomorrha do not measure up to what is going on in Paris. Of the nine young men of quality who dined with my grandson the Duc de Chartres the other day, seven had the French disease.[2] Isn't that disgusting? . . . Most people here find their only comfort in debauchery and distractions; aside from that, they do not want to see and hear anything. They do not believe in a blessed eternity and think that after death there will not be anything, whether good or bad.

1. Madame's physician. Madame liked Monsieur Teray, who endeavored to follow nature as much as possible; also, he did not wear forbidding black robes like the German doctors, but looked "more like a colonel." 2. Syphilis.

To FREIHERR VON GOERTZ

Saint Cloud, 26 April 1721

I have dined off your smoked geese three times already, they are very good and I thank you for them once again, as also for the description of the King of Denmark's absurd marriage,[1] about which I must not say everything I think. No, I must say it, lest it choke me: this is a case that fits the French proverb, "It's the story of the stork, foolish people do foolish work." About the Moscovite feasts: these are certainly wild gorging bouts. I who loathe coffee would starve to death at such a feast. I had a good laugh about this description, for one could not think of anything wilder. The very Turks are not as wild as the Russians. They keep finding some quackery they must do to me. Tomorrow I shall have to take medicine,[2] that is why I am writing today. It is a wretched thing to have reached old age, for one is always bothered by tiresome ailments. My stomach, fortunately, is good, and I can eat all kinds of foods without ill effects. The smoked sausages have not yet arrived. But I thank you in advance. If I were in Moscow, I would simply have to go hungry, for I surely could not eat any of this food except the raw onions. I never heard of more outrageous grub in all my life.

1. A few days after his wife's funeral, King Frederick IV had married his mistress Sophia von Reventloff, having first given her the title of Princess of Schleswig.
2. I.e., purgatives.

To RAUGRÄFIN LUISE

Saint Cloud, 3 May 1721

In everything, including what I eat and drink, I am still altogether German, as I have been all my life. They do not know how to make good pancakes here, because the milk and the butter are not as good as ours; they do not have a sweet taste and are quite watery. The herbs are not as good as ours either, for the earth is not rich but too light and sandy, and that makes for herbs and grass without strength; in this manner the cattle that eat it cannot give good milk, nor can the butter be good, nor the pancakes. And besides, the French cooks do not have the knack for it. How I wish I could eat the pancake made by your chambermaid. I would enjoy it more than all the dishes prepared by my chefs.

I still remember all the psalms and hymns I have ever learned and sing them in my room, also in the coach. I still have my Bible, psalm books, and Lutheran hymnals, so I can sing all I want. I urgently pray God to strengthen my memory, for I feel that it is slipping frightfully; I cannot remember names and believe that I shall forget my own before long. I daily beseech the Almighty to govern my heart and mind in such a way that I will do and think nothing but what is helpful to my salvation, and not to forsake me in my old age. And I end my prayer, after the Our Father, with "Oh Lord, forsake me not, lest I forsake thee."

Saint Cloud, 17 May 1721

Dearest Luise, I am starting early to chat with you, because at eight I must go to church, and right after that I am to be bled, as a matter of precaution, as they say. I let them have their way, and since it has to be, I did not want

to put it off any longer. If I am to give credence to our German calendar
the bleeding will agree with me, for it says that today is the best day of the
year for a bleeding. I will tell you about it, dear Luise, this evening at six
o'clock. But I do believe that it will turn out as the poor Hinderson always
used to say, and that it will make me quite "schlappjes." . . .

Despite all my troubles I did have a good laugh about the Rotzenhäuserin
yesterday, because she is so scared of the poor Marquise.[1] Yesterday she
imagined that she had come and tugged on her coverlet, rustling and puffing
by her bed, and later, when I was in my small dressing room with her, she
imagined that the Marquise was fluttering around her like some white thing.
But I did not see or hear anything, and yet I believe that if the poor Marquise had any reason to come back she would come to me rather than to
Lenor. Her fright really amused me; she says that I cannot see ghosts because
I do not want to believe that they might come; this, she says, annoys the
ghosts and that is why they do not want to come to me. . . .

If it were not for the Duke of Mömpelgard,[2] the Duke of Stuttgart would
surely be the greatest madman in all of Swabia with his seraglio. He makes
a liar out of King Solomon, who says that there is nothing new under the sun
and that everything has been seen before; but to go around followed by
womenfolk dressed as footmen, that is something new indeed, and the idea of
using them as valets and being dressed and undressed by them, that surely
is also a new and unheard of thing.

1. The deceased Marquise d'Alluye, a friend of Madame's.   2. I.e., Montbéliard.

Saint Cloud, 24 May 1721

I rather enjoyed myself when I placed a new medal into my medal cabinet,
it is a Nero. In the ten years I have been collecting medals, my collection
has grown to 957; if God grants me life for a few more years I expect to top
a thousand and hope that what I will bequeath to my son will be, after the
King's medal collection, one of the most beautiful and rarest ones in Europe.
For all my medals are in excellent condition, not worn down at all.

Saint Cloud, 14 June 1721

Dearest Luise, on Thursday last I duly received your letter of 4 June . . . but
since I was writing to you at the time, I probably already told you this,
dear Luise. But what can we do! Old women must always repeat themselves.
My languor is not yet gone, and oh the misery I have in my poor knee; that
makes a bit of a rhyme—don't tell me I am becoming a poet. . . .

Everyone does not think, as you and I do, that our time is fixed. But for
the most part human beings are so arrogant that they seek to figure out
everything with their own reason, and the French nation is given to this even

more than others. I often have to chuckle about this to myself. There is no
need to puzzle one's brains about the exact hour of one's death, for it is no
great feat to figure out that one will soon have to go when one grows old;
as one of the psalms says, "Our life span is seventy years, and if it is long it is
eighty years." So it is clear that a longer life in this world is quite out of the
question and that it would be perfectly useless to fret about it. I certainly never
fail to commend my body, soul, and life to God Almighty three times a day.

Saint Cloud, 19 June 1721

Nothing in the world is more painful than to leave one's fatherland, one's kin,
and one's friends and to go off to a completely strange country where one
does not know the language. . . .

I do not know what pleasure it affords Monsieur de Torcy to regulate the
mail so badly, for Abbé Dubois has let me know that he has nothing to do
with the mails and that they are strictly the Marquis de Torcy's responsibility.
But that is to call them stinking eggs and rotten butter, for one is as bad as
the other, and we would be better off if they were on the gallows rather than
at this court, and the devil knows that they are a pair of gallows birds and
falser than gallows wood, as Lenor always says. If he is curious enough to
read this letter, he will find his praises in it, according to the German proverb:
"Eavesdroppers hear no good of themselves."

Saint Cloud, 10 July 1721

In Italy the life of a princess is full of constraint; anyone who is accustomed
to the free life in Germany will have a hard time putting up with it and, as
they sing in the opera *Isis,* "If there is one thing of value in this world it is
freedom. . . ."

What made me believe that your two nieces do not know German is that
their father, the Duc de Schomberg, did not seem to care about that. The
French-German that people speak here is perfectly dreadful; I would rather
hear English people speak German badly than the French. But I can speak
just as they do. Courtiers often bring me children in order to find out if they
speak well, but usually they speak like this: "Ick hab ein-nen teut-schen
kammer-diener, ick habe teutsch gelern-et." When I hear them talk like that I
lose all patience; the accent of the English comes a little closer than that to
German. If your niece has learned her German from you, it is no wonder that
it sounds a bit Palatine. Herr Benterider[1] says that I speak a mixture of
Palatine and Hanoverian German; I can also do the dialect of Braunschweig,
although I have forgotten quite a bit of it, but I would soon get back into
it if I were to speak it for a few days. . . .

In the last two months I have been drinking a glass of water every morn-

ing, but I top it off with cherries, sometimes sour and sometimes sweet.
I could not possibly eat the black bread here; it is altogether terrible, and
anyone who is accustomed to good black bread, like the kind we used to
eat at Bruchhausen, simply cannot make do with the black bread here.

1. The Imperial ambassador.

According to my way of thinking I cannot consider a person pious if I see
any hatred for his fellow man in him. For Our Lord Christ has insisted on
Christian and brotherly love too strongly to leave any doubt on this point.
Weaknesses are excusable, but not malice. . . .

When I was young I spent many years without any ailments whatsoever;
this I owed to hunting, which, next to God, kept me in good health for
many years.[1] Exercise is very healthy; I hunted on horseback for thirty years
and by calash for ten. As long as Monsieur was alive I rode on horseback,
and since the King's death I have given up hunting altogether; but in that
time I suffered three major illnesses. That is why I believe that in my younger
years hunting kept me in good health. . . .

It is quite rare for a Lorrainer[2] to be intelligent; intelligence is passed down
on the distaff side there, for the women of Lorraine are always smarter than
the men. Lorrainers or Frenchmen, they are all as false as gallows wood, as the
Rotzenhäuserin always says. I have been told by others too that our good
Germans are becoming hideously corrupt and have forsworn the good faith
of the old Germany along with all the virtues that the old Germans had and
that they have adopted all the vices of foreign nations. That irks me very
much. Falseness, malice, and debauchery are particularly ill-becoming in a
German, for since the Germans are not born to these vices they practice
them in their crudest form; so they would do better to keep to the good old
German custom of being honest and sincere as their forbears were. . . .

I am quite of your opinion that whenever someone founds religion upon
politics or mixes the two, like the Lutheran pastor who spoke to you, dear
Luise, that such people do not have a proper religion and will soon be without religion altogether. . . .

Holland to my mind is an agreeable place, and Amsterdam is well worth
seeing. From Utrecht we went to Nymwegen, from Nymwegen to Cleve,
from Cleve to Xanten, from Xanten to Cologne, from Cologne to Bacherach,
where His late Grace our father and my brother came to meet me. We stayed
at Bacherach for a few days, visited Ober-Wesel, and then traveled down
the Rhine to Bingen, and then to Frankenthal, where we stayed for a long
time. I do not know whether I remember all of this correctly, for in fifty-
eight or -nine years one may well forget something. Utrecht is still dear to me,

for I had a very good time there. It is true that if one has seen Holland one finds Germany dirty; but in order to find Germany clean and pleasant one has to travel through France, for nothing is more smelly and piggish than the way Paris is kept. . . .

Apropos of Fontainebleau . . . anyone who is not accustomed to hunting is liable to make some pretty nice somersaults there, but I had fewer falls there than in this vicinity. I think it is because I was so very fond of the place that nothing bad or disagreeable happened to me there; on the contrary, I always enjoyed myself more at Fontainebleau than anywhere else in France. The château of Fontainebleau looks quite German with its large galleries, halls, and balconies. But enough of this, it makes my heart heavy.

1. In another letter from this period, Madame tells the Raugräfin that she has had twenty-six riding accidents. 2. A member of the ducal family of Lorraine.

Saint Cloud, 7 August 1721

What the postmaster of Bern has written is an Austrian style that I do not like at all, for I do not understand half of it. Why does he bother me about the French mail? I have nothing to do with it, so I did not ask my secretary to answer him. That there are people who write a bad and repulsive style does not surprise me, but that this kind of writing is now considered beautiful and admired in Germany upsets me very much and leads me to believe that my poor compatriots are going altogether mad.

Saint Cloud, 25 September 1721

Today we are all wearing formal court dress, for at three o'clock I shall have a ceremony, namely the reception of that confounded Cardinal Dubois, who has received his cardinal's hat from the Pope. I must salute him, make him sit down,[1] and talk to him for a while, which will demand quite a little effort; but then effort and annoyances are one's daily bread here. But here he is, our cardinal, so I shall have to pause. —The cardinal has begged me to let bygones be bygones; he made me the prettiest speech one could ever hear. The man is extremely intelligent, no doubt about it; if he were as good as he is smart, there would be nothing wrong with him. But on this point the devil knows how he is lacking, and one can say as our Count Wittgenstein used to say, "That's the hitch."

1. As a cardinal, Dubois had the right to a *tabouret* in the presence of Madame.

To HERR VON HARLING

This morning I must go to Paris to rejoice with my son and his wife about
the happy news they received on Monday last through a courier from the
King of Spain, who asks my son for the hand of his daughter for his oldest
son, the Prince of Asturias. This will make a very young couple, for the
Prince just turned fourteen on 25 August and Mademoiselle de Montpensier
will only be twelve on 11 December next. All of this I find good and well
and only wish that it did not involve so many visits and compliments that one
is altogether overwhelmed. But this is one of the things to which one can
apply the French proverb, "One must take the burden with the benefits."
Our young bride does not have a name yet; she is baptized of course, but the
ceremony of naming has not yet taken place. The King and I will perform
this ceremony. So before starting out on her journey Mademoiselle de Montpensier will receive three sacraments, baptism, communion, and confirmation; this, I think, is rare. . . .

I am, thank God, very well now, but great strength is not to be expected
at my age; nonetheless I am still able to take an hour's walk. . . . Monsieur
Law will probably leave for Holland, but I do not believe that he will be permitted to go to England, because his name is mud there.

To RAUGRÄFIN LUISE

Saint Cloud, 23 October 1721

Dearest Luise, today I am caught, as the French proverb says, "like a donkey
between two meadows, unable to make up his mind," because I have so
much to say that I do not know where to start. . . .

If I could still accomplish anything and be of service to those who are
dear to me, I would be glad to live on. But alas, I am no longer good for
anything and fear that I shall soon become childish; I am losing my memory
and cannot remember a single name. That is the way to start talking nonsense and to become childish; I shall play with dolls before long, and when
it has come to that one is truly better off dead than alive. Oh dear Luise,
you are deluded by your friendship; unfortunately there is nothing admir-
able about me, and nothing is more ordinary and common than my entire
life. . . . I keep remembering all that I have lost, and my reason is turning
all my joy to ashes. I know that I must resign myself to God's will, but when
all the things one used to enjoy are gone, one cannot help being altogether
dispirited.

Yesterday I went to bed quite early, counted nine o'clock in my bed, and fell asleep right afterward. I only woke up at half past four, when I rang, had a fire made, and the room straightened up. Meanwhile I said my morning prayer and got up shortly after half past five to dress. I put on a good pair of beaver-stockings, a woolen petticoat and over all of this a good, long, quilted dressing gown, which I tie with a big, broad belt. When that is done I have two lamps lighted and sit down at my table. So now, dear Luise, you know my early morning's work as well as I do. Now I shall write until half past ten, and then I will have my honey water brought, wash myself as clean as I can, and rub my hurting knees and my thighs with the *eau vulnéraire* that my doctor has recommended. After that I ring for all my chambermaids and sit down at my dressing table, where all the people of my household, both men and women, come to see me while my hair is being combed and dressed. When my hair is done all the menfolk, except my doctors, barbers, and apothecaries, leave the room; I put on my shoes, stockings, and underpants, and wash my hands. At that time my ladies come in to wait on me; they give me the cloth for washing my hands and my shirt. At this point the whole pack of doctors leaves and the tailor comes in with my dress. I put it on right after I have put on the shirt. As soon as I am laced up, all the menfolk come back, for my *manteau* is made in such a way that as soon as I am laced up I am all dressed, since all my petticoats are tied to the corset with strings and the *manteau* is sown onto the corset; this I find very convenient. When I am completely dressed, which is usually by a quarter to twelve, I go to chapel. The mass lasts at most an hour and a half, and when I return, Junker Wendt, as the first servant of my household, comes to call me to the table. Our meal takes a good hour. On Mondays, Wednesdays, and Saturdays at half past one I go to see Chausseraye at "Madrid"; but if I have some business in Paris I go there on Wednesday or Saturday, stopping at the Carmelite convent, where we hear mass; afterward I call on the King, and from there we go to the Palais Royal to see Madame la Duchesse d'Orléans.[1] Usually my son comes there as well and I dine with all his children and my ladies. My son dines very rarely at noon, for he cannot work with his head after he has eaten and drunk. Later, around three o'clock, I drive out and pay my calls on the princesses of the Blood or our Duchess of Hanover;[2] then it's back to the Palais Royal. On Wednesdays I see a French and on Saturdays an Italian play; when this is over I return to my coach and drive back here; "and so to bed, as the bride said." On Thursdays and Sundays before the church service I go for a ride in the park at this season, and after church in the summer. On Fridays and Tuesdays I do not go out at all, on these days I have too many letters to write to England and Lorraine. On Sunday, Wednesday, and Saturday I read the Bible in the morning. Now you know, dear Luise, all about our life here, just as if you were here with us. . . .

It has often turned out, not only in illnesses but in all kinds of circumstances, that many of the things by which we humans try to forestall misfortune precisely serve to bring it about. This is proof that human foresight is of little use; and yet it is our obligation to take care of ourselves to the best of our knowledge and ability.

1. Madame's daughter-in-law. 2. Benedicta, who had returned to Paris.

Saint Cloud, 22 November 1721

Monsieur le Cardinal Dubois is supposed to make a complete change in the mail service and to straighten out the things that were wrecked by Torcy's avarice and greed. Take the example of the mail to Lorraine: in order to save a courier, he had the trunk thrown into the first stagecoach for Nancy, so that anyone who was curious could read all the letters. He did a lot of stingy things like that while he was in charge of the mails, and he is a true hypocrite, for under the mantle of prayer and devotion he causes as much mischief as ever he can and nothing makes him happier than the chance of doing someone a bad turn. So I am glad that he is no longer in charge of the mails. Although the little cardinal is not much better than the wicked Torcy, he tries to hide his avarice a little better and minds his p's and q's because he is looking for praise. . . .

I love my son with all my heart, and he too treats me very well; I have no complaints about him. But the more I am pleased with him the more it grieves me that I see so little of him and that I have sound reasons to worry about him all the time. To rule a kingdom is a great thing, I grant it. But, dear Luise, think of all the hatred and envy it involves. One would have to be a god to satisfy everyone; those who are not satisfied turn into enemies; in short, there are more bad than good sides to this, and so I have never for a moment enjoyed the idea of my son's regency.

To FREIHERR VON GOERTZ

Saint Cloud, 23 November 1721

Our dear Princess of Wales wrote to me about an exploit of the Czar that reminds me of a scene in the Italian comedy where Harlequin is a prince and gives an audience. The ambassador, who is Spezzafer,[1] makes such horrible grimaces that he frightens Harlequin. Harlequin jumps on the ambassador and knocks everyone into a heap. That is just about what the Czar did, for when the Imperial ambassador arrived he was seated, in full regalia, on a silver throne with a golden table before him. When the audience was over and the ambassador had reached the door, the Czar jumped over the golden throne table and ran out the door after the ambassador. This I call a harlequinade. It is really too bad that this monarch is given to such quirks, for he has many good qualities; but the thing for which I cannot forgive him is his son's death and the manner in which he was poisoned. So far as I am concerned, he is in the doghouse.

1. Figure of the braggart in the commedia dell'arte.

To RAUGRÄFIN LUISE

Saint Cloud, 6 December 1721

Mademoiselle de Montpensier[1] cannot be called ugly, she has smooth skin, pretty eyes, the nose too might do if it were not so narrow, and her mouth is very small. But for all that she is the most unpleasant child I have ever seen in everything, in her manners, her speech, and the way she eats and drinks; it makes one quite impatient to watch her. I certainly did not shed a tear, nor did she, when we said adieu to each other. In Spain I have a stepdaughter, a stepgranddaughter, and now a granddaughter who were or will be Queen of Spain. The best of them all was the stepdaughter, whom I loved with all my heart like a sister, for she could not be my daughter since I was only nine years older. I was still quite childish when I came here, and we played and carried on together along with our dear Carllutz and the little Prince of Eisenach; we often made so much noise that people could not stand to be with us. There was an old lady here by the name of Madame de Fiennes, whom we used to pester mercilessly. She disliked the sound of shooting, and we always tossed firecrackers into her skirts; this drove her wild, and she would run after us trying to hit us, that was great fun for us.

1. Madame's granddaughter who was to marry the Spanish prince.

Paris, 20 December 1721

I much prefer formal court dress to the *manteau,* but now I have to wear it because I am ill, otherwise people would laugh at me. One looks too chambermaidish in the *manteau* to enjoy wearing it. The full skirts everyone is wearing are not at all to my liking, they look unmannerly, as if one had just gotten out of bed. The *manteau,* of the kind that I wear, is nothing new, Madame la Dauphine used to wear it. The fashion of the slovenly skirts was first launched by Madame de Montespan, who used them to cover up her pregnancies. After the death of the King Madame d'Orléans revived it.

Paris, 26 March 1722

I am also on pretty good terms with the King. Yesterday I played a trick on his governors that amused me very much. They are jealously watching the King and always imagine that something is being said against them, but this time I really made fools of them. On the day before yesterday the King had an attack of gas pains; yesterday I went up to the King very gravely and slipped a little note into his hand. The Maréchal de Villeroy became quite upset and asked me most seriously, "What is this note you are giving to the King?" I replied, just as seriously, "It is a remedy for gas pains." The maréchal: "Only the King's first physician may suggest remedies to His Majesty." I said, "In this case I am certain that Monsieur Dodart will approve; it is even written in verse and set to music." The King, quite embarrassed by this exchange, read it to himself and burst out laughing. The maréchal said, "May I see it?" I said, "Oh certainly, it is no secret." What he found in the note were the following words: "When your bowels are disturbed / By vexatious winds / You must not ever keep them there / But rid yourself at once. / So fart! / Fart, there is no better way / To free yourself and them. / Fart! and give them liberty / And you'll be happy too. / So fart!" There was such a roar of laughter in the sitting room that I was almost sorry to have played this trick, especially since the Maréchal de Villeroy was all befuddled about it. This is an old prank from my youth.

Saint Cloud, 13 June 1722

It has been a good hour since we returned from the table. As I was digesting my meal, I watched my newborn canaries eat. I have thirty newborn ones from six adult pairs, one prettier than the next. Here they are telling me that my carriage has arrived, but first I have to fill this sheet. My strength has not yet returned; I cannot walk across the room without panting as if I had chased after a hare. . . .

I do have gold powder, but hyacinth confection I could not swallow. When I had smallpox here they gave it to me, but I almost died from it, for it made me vomit so dreadfully that I thought I must burst. How is it possible that you, dear Luise, can swallow that dreadful stuff? To me it is a veritable emetic and cleans me out top and bottom with such force as if my soul were pushed out of my body. I decided then and there not to take it again as long as I live, because it is worse than any disease. Ma Tante sent me two golden boxes of gold powder, but I never tried it; to tell the truth, I do not like to take anything, whatever it may be, and prefer to be patient.

Saint Cloud, 8 August 1722

They are not telling me, but I can see that they fear that the swelling in my legs and feet might turn into dropsy, which is quite possible, since that is what Her late Grace my mother died of. If I die of dropsy I will not die of anything else. This will have to be as God pleases. . . .

Manners at Hanover were always informal, although our dear Electress would have liked to have seen it otherwise. But Oncle was peculiar that way, and I see that the King his son[1] is not doing any better. . . .

No one in the world owns more and more beautiful paintings than my son; he bought the entire collection of Queen Christina,[2] which she had at Rome and which was highly regarded, as you may have heard. I have often been told that Merian's copper engravings are more highly regarded than his paintings.

1. George I of England.   2. Christina of Sweden.

Saint Cloud, 5 September 1722

Many times a day I commend myself, body and soul, to the will of God, and for the rest I am without anxiety and shall wait to see what God wishes to do with me. . . .

The maps of Mannheim and Schwetzingen will amuse me very much, but also cost me many a sigh by reminding me of the good old days. But the Palatine Elector is too humble to lay himself at my poor, swollen feet!

Saint Cloud, 1 October 1722

Dearest Luise, the day before yesterday rather late I received . . . your package and two welcome letters in good order, along with the map of the Palatinate as well as the small illustrated card and the table of occult signs. All of this has greatly amused me and I thank you, dear Luise, with all my heart. I should love to answer your letter point by point but, dear Luise, I am not yet well at all; I have completely lost my appetite again, my breath is short, and my feet and legs badly swollen. That is why they do not want to permit me to go to bed later than ten o'clock. Still, I must tell you that I consider all the little things I have sent you mere trifles by comparison with the beautiful map, on which I have already taken many walks. I have already wandered from Heidelberg to Frankfurt, from Mannheim to Frankenthal, and from there to Worms . . . and I have been to Neustadt too. My goodness, how all of this brings back the good times of the past, which are gone forever! But your map, dear Luise, will give me pleasure as long as I live. But here they are calling me to go to bed. I embrace you with all my heart and will always love you dearly.

To HERR VON HARLING

Saint Cloud, 3 October 1722

Monsieur von Harling. Since I wrote to you the day before yesterday there has been no change in my state; it will be as God pleases, but I am preparing for my journey to Reims;[1] how it will end, "time will tell." I enclose a letter from your nephew and assure you that in whatever state I shall be, I will always be and remain Monsieur von Harling's sincere friend.

1. On 25 October the coronation of Louis XV was celebrated with great pomp at Reims.

To RAUGRÄFIN LUISE

Saint Cloud, 5 November 1722

I could not possibly answer your letter, both because of my weakness and the continuous hustle-bustle involved in the many ceremonies and in having my children around me all the time, as well as huge numbers of other people, princes, lords, counts, bishops, archbishops, and cardinals. But I do not believe that in the whole world one could see or imagine a more beautiful celebration than the King's coronation. I have been promised a description of it for Saturday. If God grants me life and health until then I shall send you, dear Luise, a full description. My daughter was a bit surprised when she saw me, for she did not want to believe my letters and kept thinking that my illness was only an excuse. But when she saw me at Reims, she was so shocked that her eyes filled with tears; I felt sorry for her. She has handsome children, but I am afraid the oldest will become a giant, for he is already six feet tall and only fifteen years old.[1] The four other children are neither tall nor small for their ages. The youngest, Prince Karl, is what His late Grace our father used to call an odd bird; his mouth runs all the time and he is always in good humor, keeps arguing with his sisters in the funniest way; he is neither handsome nor homely.[2] To my mind the best looking of the three boys is the middle one;[3] of the girls, the youngest is the prettiest, but the oldest one is so well-made that she cannot be considered ugly either.

1. He died at the age of sixteen. 2. Charles-Alexander of Lorraine, later Austrian general and governor of The Netherlands. 3. Franz Stephan, later the husband of Empress Maria Theresa.

Saint Cloud, 3 December 1722

Dearest Luise, the news of my health I have to tell you today will not, I expect, please you at all. I am getting more miserable day by day, and this may well come to a bad end, but I am, thank God, ready for everything and only beg God Almighty to give me patience in the great pain I must suffer day and night, not only because I am so horribly weak but because I am increasingly miserable all over. Whether I will get out of this God alone knows; time will tell, but I have never been as sick as this. The weather here is not bad, but today it is starting to rain, just a little drizzle. I do not think that any kind of weather will be able to help me now. Time, dear Luise, will soon show what is to become of all this. If I get out of this you will always find me as I have been all along. If God calls me to Himself, you must take comfort in the thought that I die without regret or sorrow, happy to leave this world in the hope that my Redeemer, who has died and risen for me, will not forsake me and that since I have kept my faith in Him, He will have mercy on me in my last hour. In this trust I live and die, dear Luise! For the rest, it will have to be as God wishes. Many people complain about coughs and colds now; I am sicker than that and getting worse day by day. I wish that, I wish, dear Luise, that your new companion would tell von Solms . . . Here they are bringing me another of your welcome letters of 21 November, number 83, but I cannot possibly answer it, I am just too sick this . . . But if God grants me life until the day after tomorrow, I shall answer it; all I can say for now is that until my end I shall dearly love you. Elisabeth Charlotte.

This is Elisabeth Charlotte's last letter; she died on 8 December. Raugräfin Luise piously placed this letter in a special leather case, marking it "Last letter from Madame, alas." French writers of journals, letters, and memoirs duly registered the event. Saint-Simon penned one last portrait of Madame, adding that her death had not caused much of a stir at court, except in the heart of the Regent, who wept copiously when he was alone with the duke. A few days before Madame's death, Mathieu Marais in his Journal *gave tribute to her courage and fortitude on her deathbed, describing also the grief of the Regent and reporting a characteristic anecdote: One of Madame's ladies wanted to kiss her hand, but Madame told her, "You may embrace me, for I am going to a country where everyone is equal." In a letter dated 19 December 1722, Joseph Dubois, nephew of the cardinal, gave a description of the formal ceremonies in which the magistracy of the high court, all the constituted bodies of the city of Paris, and the royal court came to present their formal condolences to the young King, the Infanta-Queen,[1] the Regent, his wife, and their son, the Duc de Chartres. Nothing, Dubois wrote, "could be more beautiful than these ceremonies," which "took place in an august manner." After mass the men of the court, 537 of them, dressed in coats festooned with* pleureuses *("weepers"), black crepe bands on their hats, pleated and downturned collars, matte shoes, and great mourning mantles hanging down four or five feet, paid their respects to the King. Louis XV, flanked by the highest officers of his household, stood in the middle of the room, also clad in full mourning, except that the trimmings on his costume were violet. The courtiers entered the King's chamber single file, made*

---

1. The four-year-old fiancée of Louis XV. The Infanta was sent back to Spain a few years later, when relations with Spain had changed. Elisabeth Charlotte was very fond of the child.

him a low bow, and left through an opposite door. In the same manner they called on the Infanta-Queen, the Duc d'Orléans, the Duchesse d'Orléans, and the Duc de Chartres. The Duchesse d'Orléans received the mourners lying on a bed; and even though Madame would have been fully aware that the ceremonial prescribed this symbolic expression of being "prostrate with grief," she might have smiled at the appropriateness of the sight, since she considered her daughter-in-law "the laziest person in the world." In the afternoon the ladies of the court performed the same ritual procession, but they had to enter the various rooms two by two, for otherwise the ceremony would have taken too long. The reason was that the trains of their mantles, attached to their formal court dresses, extended over half the length of the room, so that each pair of ladies had to leave before the next one could enter. Ninety-four ladies (not counting the princesses) called on the royal family. It was, in short, a decorous and highly stylized ceremony in which the royal family and the courtiers participated strictly according to rank. It was one of those occasions that Madame both loved and hated.

On 10 December, her body was borne to Saint-Denis, the resting place of the kings of France and their families. The hearse was preceded, surrounded, and followed by the pages of the King's stables, by the guards and the Swiss soldiers of the Duc d'Orléans, and by his footmen bearing torches. Madame's granddaughter, Mademoiselle de Charolais, and some of the ladies of the court followed in their own carriages, and the service was disturbed by a rather loud quarrel over precedence between Mademoiselle de Charolais and one of the attending duchesses.

The actual burial at Saint-Denis did not take place until 5 February 1723. Here again, the memory of Madame was treated with all the honors to which her rank entitled her: the mass was celebrated by an archbishop assisted by several bishops, and her funeral oration, like that of Louis XIV, was delivered by Père Massillon, now Archbishop of Clermont, a brilliant orator and one of the few preachers who had not put Madame to sleep during her lifetime. Massillon praised her kindness, her loyalty, her frankness, and dwelt at length on her exemplary qualities as a mother.

Grandeur and ceremony apart, perhaps it was Matthieu Marais who found the appropriate words at Madame's death: "The court loses a good princess, and that is a rare thing."

✤ Index

Abortion, 48
Academies, 203
Actors, 109
Address, forms of, 219, 256, 262
Adultery, 225, 232
Affronts, 36
Aging, 65, 83, 193, 197, 226, 236, 242, 264, 265
Air, 151, 163-64, 183, 244, 246
Alberoni (Spanish cardinal), 223, 244, 253
Albrecht Ferdinand, Duke of Wolfenbüttel, 96
Alexandre Louis, Duc de Valois (son of Elisabeth Charlotte): birth of, 9; death of, xviii, 13, 14, 223
Allodial properties, 46
Almanacs, xxv, 144, 265
Amalie Elisabeth, Raugräfin von der Pfalz (Amelise), xxxvii, 160, 178-79
Ambition, 81, 138
Anecdotes told, 30, 71, 74, 79, 99, 105, 140-41, 146, 149, 213, 241, 246, 248, 251
Animals, 143, 273. *See also* Dogs
Anjou, Duc de. *See* Louis XV; Philip V, King of Spain
Anne, Queen of England, 130, 168
Antiquities, 186
Anton Ulrich, Duke of Wolfenbüttel, 97
Appartement, 38-39, 59, 86
Armchair, ceremonial role of, 25, 113, 116
Army, French, 148
Art, Flemish, 122
Ash Wednesday, ceremony of, 129

Assassinations, 247
August the Strong, Elector of Saxony and King of Poland, 104, 153, 166
Austria, house of, 217
Autopsies, 72, 179, 232

Balls, masked, 120
Banknotes, 246, 250
Bastards, royal, 55-56, 91
Bastille, 123, 187, 222
Baylay (court physician), 11
"Bear-cat-monkeyface" (portrait), 9
Beaujolais, Mlle de (granddaughter), 212
Beauty, 88, 109, 141, 157
Beauvais, Chevalier de, 36
Bed, marital, 149
Benefices, 64
Berry, Duc de, xlv, 126, 171
Berry, Duchesse de (granddaughter), xlv, 184, 193, 211, 232
Béthune, Marquis de, 63
Beuvron, Comtesse de, 67. *See also* Théobon, Mlle de
Bible: interpretation of, 94, 114, 121, 137, 199; quotations from, 4, 97, 157, 185, 192, 210, 218, 231, 243, 261, 265, 266; reading of, xxx, 137, 158, 171, 228, 264, 271. *See also* Scripture, difficulty of living up to
Bienséance, xxvi, 43, 87
Bigotry, 71
Bleeding, 41, 65, 229-30, 264-65
Blois, Mlle de (Françoise Marie de Bourbon). *See* Orléans, Duchesse d'
Bocquemar brothers, anecdote about, 99

279

Bonesetter, 102

Books, 140, 144

Bouillon, 222–23

Bourgogne, Duc de, xliv, 112, 126, 165, 188

Bourgogne, Duchesse de: arrival of, in France, 95–96; bad manners of, 113, 160; death of, 187; frivolity of, 136, 219; hypocrisy of, 169; life of, xliv; upbringing of, 110; verbal portrait of, 95

Bracciano, Mme de. *See* Ursins, Princesse des

Brandenburg, Electoral Prince of, 123

Braunschweig-Lüneburg, Duchess Sophie of. *See* Sophie, Electress of Hanover

Braunschweig-Lüneburg, Duke Ernst August of. *See* Ernst August, Elector of Hanover

Bray (court physician), 11

Bread riot, description of, 177

Bretagne, Duc de, xliv

Calendar, Gregorian, 119

Callousness of French royal family, 69

Calvin, Jean, 209

Calvinism, xv

Carllutz, xxxvi, 14, 15, 30; death of, 59–60; memory of, 101, 117, 147; visit of, in France, 9

Carnival: at French court, 129, 162; at Heidelberg court, 129

Catechism, Heidelberg, 230

Catherine I, Czarina, 243

Catholicism: conversion to, xviii, 7, 34, 156, 167, 197; French practice of, 137

Cellamare (Spanish ambassador), conspiracy of, 221–23

Censorship of mail, 34, 37, 52, 56, 61, 80, 87, 147, 157, 159, 193, 207, 255

Ceremonies: Ash Wednesday, 129; baptizing of church bells, 120; christening, 16; coronation, 275; dislike of, 191; installation of abbess, 237; laying of cornerstone, 213; *lit de justice,* 216; marriage, 151; mourning, 133, 232–33, 276; naming of child, 269; receiving of arms, 7; reception of cardinal, 268

Cévennes, Protestants of, 155

Charles, Archduke of Austria, 153

Charles, Duc de Berry. *See* Berry, Duc de

Charles II, King of England, 97

Charles II, King of Spain, death of, 124, 127

Charles XII, King of Sweden, 223

Charlotte von Hessen-Kassel, Electress of the Palatinate, xv, xxxv–xxxvi, 19–20, 30, 49

Chartres, Louis, Duc de (grandson), 182, 212

Chartres, Mlle de (granddaughter), 101, 212

Chartres, Philippe, Duc de. *See* Orléans, Philippe II d'

Châteauthiers, Mme de (lady-in-waiting), 75, 143, 245

Chausseraye, Mlle de (lady-in-waiting), 203, 241

Childbirth, 16, 149, 166, 207, 249

Child rearing, 7

Children: disciplining of, 42, 59; games played by, 26, 249, 258, 272; marriage plans for, 11; upbringing of, 12, 14, 15, 58, 80, 215, 257, 259, 260

Chocolate, 156

Choin, Mlle de, 87, 165

Christening, 16

Christianity: tenets of, 154; true, 261, 267

Christina, Queen of Sweden, 167, 274

Christmas, 33, 39, 184

Church bells, baptizing of, 120

Churches, reunification of, 98

Church services, 144, 145, 155, 158, 166, 186, 228

Clement XI, Pope, 262

Clérambeau, Maréchale de (lady-in-waiting), 35, 36

Clothes, 206, 276. *See also* Fashion

Clysters, 11, 65

Coaches, 348

Coffee, 156

Coiffures, 25, 59, 117

Cold wave of 1709, 170–71

Commerce, disreputable status of, 253

Community, marital, 50, 103. *See also* Marriage contract

Concerts, 38

Condé, Anne-Louise-Bénédicte de. *See* Maine, Duchesse du

Condé, Louis II de Bourbon ("the Grand Condé," "Monsieur le Prince"), xlvi, 11

Condé, Louis III de Bourbon ("Monsieur le Duc"), xlvi

Confession, 221. *See also* Sacraments

Confessors, 92, 127, 232

Conspiracy against Regent, 216–18, 248

Constraints of French royal family, 34, 85
Conti, Louis Armand de Bourbon, xlvi;
    and Poland, 104
Conti, Princesse de, xlv, 43, 87, 119
Convicts, 202
Coquetry, 153
Corneille, Pierre, 22, 84
Coteries, 180
Court dress, formal, 233, 272
Courtiers, French, behavior of, 17–18, 53
Court offices, perquisites of, 177
Coypel (painter), 121
Craon, Mme de, 205, 225, 227
Craon, M. de, 205
Crécy, Maréchal de, 12
Cuckoldry, 87, 205

Dancing, 88, 163, 207
Dauphin, the Grand. *See* Monseigneur
Dauphin, the second. *See* Bourgogne, Duc
    de
Dauphin, the third, death of, 189
Dauphine, Madame la, xliv, 33, 37, 52, 53,
    57; bad health of, 64, 69; death of, 69
D'Avous (treasurer), 183
Death: of Amelise, 178–79; of Carllutz,
    59–60; of Charles II, King of Spain,
    124, 127; of Charlotte of Hessen-Kassel,
    49; of third Dauphin, 189; of Madame
    la Dauphine, 69; of Duc de Bourgogne,
    188; of Duchesse de Berry, 232; of
    Duchesse de Bourgogne, 187; of Elisa-
    beth Charlotte, 276; of A. K. von Harl-
    ing, 142; of F. M. Helmont, 127; of Karl,
    Elector Palatine, 44–45; of Karl Ludwig,
    Elector Palatine, 27–28; of Karl Moritz,
    147; of G. W. von Leibniz, 206; of Leo-
    pold I, Emperor, 159; of Louis XIV,
    199–200; of Louvois, 72–73; of Mme de
    Maintenon, 228; of Marie-Thérèse,
    Queen of France, 40–41; of Monseigneur,
    185; of Monsieur, xviii, 130–34; of
    Polier de Bottens, 186; of Queen of
    Spain, 61; of son, 13, 14, 223; of Sophie,
    Electress of Hanover, 194–96; of Sophie
    Charlotte, Queen of Prussia, 157; of Wil-
    liam of Orange, 144
Death: attitude toward, 108, 234, 263,
    266; fear of, 145, 147, 187; sudden, 218
Debauchery, 53, 90, 104, 210–11, 235;
    varieties of, 161–62
Debt, public, 208
Debts, 128, 254

Degenfeld, Ferdinand von, 46
Degenfeld, Luise von, Raugräfin von der
    Pfalz, xv, xxxvi, 10, 20
Descartes, René, 143
Dévôts, 51, 150; passim
Diet as a remedy, 49
Divorce, 20–22, 50
Dodart (court physician), 273
Dogs, 84, 139, 143, 144, 151, 154,
    167
Dominicans, 127, 142
Dowry of Elisabeth Charlotte, 5
Dragonnades, 64
Drinking, excessive, 115, 116, 123, 147,
    191
Dropsy, 273
Dubois, Guilleaume, Abbé, later Cardinal,
    xlviii, 255, 266, 268, 271
Duchesse, Mme la, xlv, 44

Earthquake, 79
Ecclesiastes, 121
Edict of Nantes, revocation of, 57
Eduard, Prince Palatine, xxxviii
Effiat, Antoine René, Marquis d', xlix,
    36, 48, 55, 56, 63, 65
Eleanore, Empress, 239
Electoral dignity (for house of Hanover),
    79–80
Elisabeth, Abbess of Herford, xxxix, 227
Elisabeth Charlotte, Mademoiselle
    d'Orléans. *See* Lorraine, Duchesse de
Emetics, 41, 131
England, 102; succession to throne of,
    130
English, national character of the, 183
Ernst August, Elector of Hanover, xv,
    xxxviii, 27, 41, 104
Espinoi, Princesse d', 110
Esprit (court physician), 11
Eugene of Savoy, 103, 168, 175, 242
Execution, 248
Exercise, physical, 7, 164, 267
Exotic lands, 157
Eyeglasses, 192, 240

Fairy tales, xxiii, xxiv, 190
Faith, religious, xxviii, 89, 145, 153,
    192, 206
Fancy work, 231
Family ties, 45, 158
Famine, 180
Farces, German, xxiv–xxv, 84

Farnese, Elisabeth, Queen of Spain, xlv, 197
Farting, 80, 273
Fashion, 89, 157
Fasting, 153
Fatherland, loyalty to, 96, 102, 170, 245, 266
Favor, royal, 17, 26, 33, 56, 62, 96, 99–100, 132
Fénelon, François de la Mothe de Salignac, 67, 112, 165
Fever, 52, 131, 212
Foix, Marquise de. See Hinderson, Mlle
Folksong, German, cited, 166
Fontainebleau, 12, 13, 196–97, 256, 268
Food: French, 139, 184, 215, 239, 253, 264; German, 18, 93, 215, 222, 231, 239, 250, 263, 264, 267
Fontanges, Marie Adélaïde Scorailles de Roussilhe, Duchesse de, xlvii, 120
Foundlings' home, 140–41
France, state of, in 1715, 202
Frankenthal, 58
Frederick IV, King of Denmark, 174, 263
French, national character of the, 176, 183, 262
Friedrich I, King of Prussia, 58, 129, 135, 187
Friedrich III, Elector of Brandenburg. See Friedrich I, King of Prussia
Friendship, 24, 37, 100, 117, 158, 219, 269
Funeral, of Mme la Dauphine, 69
Funeral oration, for Elisabeth Charlotte, 277

Gambling, 12, 39, 74, 86, 88, 99
Gazette de Hollande, 255
Gender, dissatisfaction with, 148, 216
George I, King of England, xxxviii, 165, 196, 210, 274; birth of, remembered, 166, 249
Georg Ludwig, Elector of Hanover. See George I, King of England
Georg Wilhelm, Duke of Celle, xxxviii, 11
Germans: ancient virtues of, 248, 267; at French court, 205, 221, 239; Monsieur's dislike of, 90; national character of the, 183, 209
Germany: changing customs of, 97, 153; cleanliness of, 268; loyalty to, 264; nostalgia for, xxii; passim
Ghosts, xxv, 36, 114, 241, 256–57, 265

Gloire, 202, 271
God, nature of, 94
Godchild, 3, 225
Goertz, Friedrich Wilhelm Freiherr von, xxxix, 150
Gonzaga, Anna. See Princesse Palatine
Governesses, 122, 138, 189, 208–9, 215, 220. See also Harling, Anna Katherina von
Governing, art of, 205
Governor: appointment of, for Duc de Chartres, 35
Grace, 145, 161
Grancey, Charlotte de, xlix, 58, 59
Grandchildren of Elisabeth Charlotte: death of three, 185; on Lorraine side, xlii, 211, 275; on Orléans side, xli–xlii, 184, 208–9, 211–12, 260
Gratitude, 18, 43
Greece, 57
Greed, 168, 240, 241, 245, 250, 261
Grief: at death of children, 9, 13, 185, 223, 262; at death of Electress Sophie, 194–96; at death of father, 29; at devastation of Palatinate, 61–62, 219

Hague, The, visit to, 1, 258
Handwriting, 191
Hanover, 120, 273–74
Harling, Anna Katherina von, 2, 80, 83, 137, 142, 215
Harling, Eberhard Ernst Franz von, xxxix, 7, 8, 54, 83, 179–80
Hartsoeker, microscope made by, 176
Haxthausen, C. A., 166
Health, effect of emotions on, 28, 32, 33
Heidelberg, 61, 68, 121–22, 219, 220
Helmont, Franz Mercurius van, xxxix, 93, 94, 127
Henrietta of England, xl, 87, 257
Hierarchy: decline of, at French court, 96, 109, 113; Elisabeth Charlotte's conception of, xxi. See also Precedence, ceremonial; Rank order
Hinderson, Mlle (lady-in-waiting), 10, 242
History, 81, 97, 163, 212
Holland, 267
Homberg, Willem (chemist), 176, 244
Homosexuality, 63, 66, 87, 248
Honor, 44, 56, 66, 104, 242
Hoorne, Comte de, 247
Horseback riding, 9
Horses, 92

Huguenots, persecution of, 112. *See also*
  Reformed, persecution of
Human nature, 240
Hunting, 19, 92, 93, 154, 197, 259
Hunting accidents, description of, 17, 42,
  102, 183
Hymns, German, cited, 111, 118, 142,
  155, 158, 159, 168, 221, 250, 251, 264
Hypocrisy, 89

Ice skating, 127
Illnesses of Elisabeth Charlotte, 49, 60,
  243, 275
Incest, rumors about, 193
Income of Elisabeth Charlotte: in 1671,
  6; in 1689, 63; in 1701, 133, 135–36;
  in 1709, 179; in 1719, 236–37
Inflation (in 1720), 254, 259
Inquisition, 142
Instruments, scientific, 176, 240
Intrigues, xviii, 32, 92

James II, exiled king of England, 61, 70,
  71, 97, 137
Jansenists, 193
Jealousy, 205
Jesuits, 121, 127, 193, 202, 225, 230,
  247
Jewelry, 5, 27, 193
Jourdan (confessor), 10
Justice, 230

Karl, Elector Palatine, xxxvi, 3, 4, 44–45
Karl Eduard, Raugraf von der Pfalz, 147
Karl Ludwig, Elector Palatine: xv, xxxv;
  attitude of, toward his daughter, 19, 99,
  137; death of, 27–29; divorce of, 19–22;
  jocularity of, 65; religious attitude of,
  161; severity of, 122, 222–23
Karl Ludwig, Raugraf von der Pfalz. *See*
  Carllutz
Karl Moritz, Raugraf von der Pfalz, xxxvii,
  64, 109, 116, 147
Karl Philip, Elector Palatine, 239
Karoline, Raugräfin von der Pfalz, xxxvii
Karoline of Ansbach (Princess of Wales),
  156, 197, 210
Kingship, burden of, 248
Königsmarck, Aurora, 97
Kolb, Ursula (governess), 121–22, 215

La Chaise, Père de, 85, 172
La Feuillade, Duc de, 164, 248

La Force, Charlotte-Rose de Caumont de,
  213, 256
Language, French, 240, 255
Language, German, xxx–xxxi, 84, 115,
  118, 142, 143, 148, 170, 266, 268
Lardon, Le (newspaper), 77
La Reynie, Nicolas Gabriel de (minister
  of police), 84
Latin, Elisabeth Charlotte's ignorance
  of, 241. *See also* Church services
La Vallière, Louise de la Baume le Blanc,
  Duchesse de, xlvi, 141
Law, John, 235–36, 237, 240, 248, 249,
  255, 261, 269. See also *Système de
  Law*
Lawyers, 140, 156
Lazarus, resurrection of, 169
Learning, xxvii, 150, 203, 226
Leibniz, Gottfried Wilhelm von, xxviii,
  xxx, xxxi, xxxix, 117, 143, 167, 186,
  202, 203, 206
Lenclos, Ninon de, 107, 108
Leopold, Duc de Lorraine. *See* Lorraine,
  Duc de
Leopold I, Emperor, 41, 58, 127, 159
Lesbianism, 88
Lesdiguières, Duchesse de, 111
Lessons, 1
Letters, writing of, xxix, xxxi, 108, 185
Lettre de cachet, 123
Lever: of Elisabeth Charlotte, 270; of
  Queen of France, 96
Liberty, 266
Life after death, 93, 94, 230
Lignières, Père de (confessor), 172–73,
  225
Lit de justice, 216
Literature, European, familiarity with,
  xxviii
Litigation, 142, 145, 207
Loneliness, 100–101, 108, 144, 152, 158,
  196
Longevity, 151
Lorraine, Chevalier de, xlix, 36, 55, 56,
  205
Lorraine, Duc de, xlii, 111, 118, 205
Lorraine, Duchesse de, xlii; as child, 30,
  33, 42; marriage of, 110–11; marriage
  plans for, 72; married life of, 205; as
  mother, 185; relationship of, with her
  mother, 42, 90, 275; virtue of, 90;
  visit of, in Paris, 210–11; upbringing of,
  110–11

Louis XIV, xiii; absolute power of, 142; appearance of, 204; callousness of, 61, 69, 73; courtly manners of, 172, 253; death of, 199–200; Elisabeth Charlotte's feelings for, xxiv, 28; firmness of, in grief, 164, 185, 189–90; generosity of, 132; ignorance of, in religious matters, 92, 174, 232; mistresses of, 120; piety of, 51, 52, 71; passim

Louis XV, xix, 189, 272, 275

Louis, Duc de Bourgogne. *See* Bourgogne, Duc de

Louis, the Grand Dauphin. *See* Monseigneur

Louis, Prince of Baden, 163

Louis Alexandre, Comte de Toulouse, xlv, 217

Louis Auguste, Duc du Maine. *See* Maine, Duc du

Louise Françoise de Bourbon, Mlle de Nantes, xlv, 44

Louise Hollandine, Abbess of Maubuisson, xxxviii–xxxix, 45, 79, 142, 231

Louvois, François-Michel Le Tellier, Marquis de, xlviii, 72, 168, 218

Love, marital, 92

Luise, Raugräfin von der Pfalz, xxxvii

Lunéville, château of, 224–25

Luther, Martin, 209

Luxury, as source of all evil, 75

Madness, 226

Magnificence, 39, 50, 75, 80

Mail, 31. *See also* Censorship of mail

Maine, Duc du, xlv, 55, 75, 216–17, 222

Maine, Duchesse du, xlv, 217–18, 222, 254

Maintenon, Françoise d'Aubigné, Marquise de, xlvii–xlviii, 64, 66, 82, 91, 107, 108, 128, 135–36, 164, 165, 191, 217, 228, 230; marriage of, to Louis XIV, 53, 56, 172; passim

Makeup, 184, 218

Malplaquet, battle of, 179

"Man in the Iron Mask," 187

Manners at French court, 26

Mannheim, 58, 60–61, 68, 219

Maps, 219–20, 274

Marcin, Marshal de, 164

Maria Anna Christine of Bavaria. *See* Dauphine, Madame la

Marie-Adélaïde of Savoy. *See* Bourgogne, Duchesse de

Marie-Anne de Bourbon. *See* Conti, Princesse de

Marie Françoise de Bourbon, Mlle de Blois. *See* Orléans, Duchesse d'

Marie-Louise d'Orléans, Queen of Spain, 55, 61, 64

Marie-Louise-Gabrielle of Savoy, Queen of Spain, xlv, 138–39

Marie-Thérèse, Queen of France, xliii, 24, 40–41

Marionettes, 73

Marlborough, Mylord, 163, 168, 175

Marly, beauty of, 167, 191

Marriage: attitude toward, 20, 22, 53, 63, 87, 92, 102, 160, 161, 214; ceremony of, 151; of Elisabeth Charlotte, xvi, 152

Marriage contract, 5–6, 50, 103, 137

Marriage negotiations, 5–6

Mary of Modena, exiled Queen of England, 61

Mass, Catholic, 89. *See also* Church services

Massillon, Père, 277

Maubuisson, convent of, 37, 45

Meals at court, 165

Medals, collection of, xxvii, 170, 183, 251, 256, 265

Medianoche, 17, 169

Medical practices, attitude toward, xxv–xxvi, 163. *See also* Bleeding; Emetics; Purging; Remedies

Melancholia, 138, 141, 196, 209

Melusine, 59

Menstruation, 24

Mercure galant (newspaper), 51

Merian (painter), 251, 274

Merode, Mlle de, 127

Microscopes, 203, 240

Miracles, 30, 172–73

Misalliances, 15, 43, 55, 72, 123, 148, 213

Mishmash, 165

Mistresses, royal, 100

Money, shortage of, in France: in 1706, 164; in 1709, 180

Monseigneur, xlv, 35, 52, 58, 72, 93, 98, 113, 185, 257

Monsieur, xl; appearance of, 204; bravery of, 14; callousness of, 101; character of, 114, 121; death of, 130–34; homosexuality of, 81, 90, 91, 98, 106; relationship with, xvii, 41–42, 52, 56, 62, 63, 99, 106, 134; reputation of, 52; selfishness of, 91

Montargis, château of, 154
Montausier, Duc de, 60
Montespan, Françoise Athénaïs de Morte-mart, Marquise de, xlvi, 56, 141, 272
Montpensier, Mlle de (granddaughter), 212, 269, 272
Mortagne (*chevalier d'honneur*), 214, 247
Mosquito netting, 233
Mouchy, Mme de, 237
Mourning attire, 133, 276
Mourning ceremonial, 133, 232, 276

Namur, siege of (1692), 76, 77
Nantes, Mlle de. *See* Duchesse, Madame la
Nassau-Siegen, Prince of, 209–10
Newspapers, 77, 88, 255
Niches, 183–84
Night-stool, 23
Nobility: English, 253; French, 148; German, 143, 253
Novels, 155, 256
Nuns, 45, 199
Nymwegen, treaty of, 27

Obedience, filial, 21, 145
Occult phenomena, xxv, 228, 233–34, 248
Offeln, Anna Katherina von. *See* Harling, Anna Katherina von
Offices, sale of, 98, 140, 233
Olbreuse, Eléanore d', Duchess of Celle, xxxviii, 15, 43
Orange, Princess of, 1, 258
Orange, William of (King William II of England), 23, 61, 70, 73, 97, 98, 117, 123, 130, 144, 258
Orléans, Anne-Marie d', Duchess of Savoy, 55, 138, 188
Orléans, Chevalier d' (illegitimate son of Regent), 182
Orléans, Duchesse d' (Françoise Marie de Bourbon, Mlle de Blois), xli, xlv, 55, 78, 91, 101, 106, 199, 211
Orléans, Louise-Adélaïde, Mlle d', Abbess of Chelles (granddaughter), 212, 230, 237–38
Orléans, Marie-Louise d', Queen of Spain, 55, 64
Orléans, Marie-Louise-Elisabeth d'. *See* Berry, Duchesse de
Orléans, Philippe I d'. *See* Monsieur
Orléans, Philippe II d', Regent, xli; at battle of Steenkerke, 78; at battle of

Turin, 164; as boy, 50–51; campaign of, in Spain, 179; character of, 114; as child, 16, 30; dissolute life of, 90, 104, 106; education of, 65–68; manners of, 241; marriage of, 74–75, 225, passim; popularity of, 248; regency of, 201–3; religious tolerance of, 246–47; shortcomings of, 190–91; talents of, 88, 106, 121, 171, 190, passim
Osnabrück, court of, 4

Pageants, 120
Paintings, 114, 239, 251, 274. *See also* Portraits of Elisabeth Charlotte
Palatinate: devastation of, xviii, 60–61, 62, 64, 81, 151, 168, 219; Elisabeth Charlotte's claims to, 46–47; French incursions into, 11; French occupation of, 105; inheritance from, 50, 57, 64, 91, 103; memories of, 258, 274, passim; princes of, 63
Parabère, Comtesse de (mistress of Regent), 181–82
Paris, city of, 86, 218, 259, 268
Parlement of Paris, 197–98, 201, 216–17
Paul, Saint, 206, 261
Peasants, German, 219
Penel (painter), 240
Pensions, giving of, 99
Perfumes, 207
Peter the Great, Czar of Russia, 102–3, 179, 207–8, 216, 271
Philip V, King of Spain, xliv, 124, 125, 163, 175
Philippsburg, siege of, 58
Philip-Wilhelm of Pfalz-Neuburg, Elector Palatine, 46, 47, 62, 89
Physicians, 7, 11, 41, 45, 58, 64, 140, 156, 187, 189, 273
Pietists, 151–52
Pilgrimages, 117, 119, 150
Pissing in the streets, 244, 246
Plague, 260
Poisoning: of Louvois, 73, 218; of Queen of Spain, 64; rumors about, 188, 197
Poland, 104
Polier de Bottens, Etienne, 170–71, 186, 209
Politesse, 147, 250, 253
Pope, French attitude toward, 119, 137, 262
Populace, Parisian, 70, 75, 77, 108, 177, 221, 250, 252, 259, 261

Portocarrero (Spanish cardinal), 127, 221
Portraits, literary, xxix
Portraits of Elisabeth Charlotte, 6, 10, 24, 117, 124, 238
Prayers, 241, 254, 264, 274
Preachers, 159, 162, 187. *See also* Priests
Precedence, ceremonial, 25, 96, 258, 278. *See also* Hierarchy; Rank order
Predestination, 81, 145
Pregnancy, 7, 14
Presents, 2, 24, 27, 63, 123, 192-93, 229, 238, 240, 256, 274
Priests, 64, 97, 154, 156
Princes: German, 182, 211, 265; true piety of, 29, 239
Princes of the Blood, 245
Princess, ideal, description of, 212
Princesse Palatine (Anna Gonzaga), xvi, 5-6, 172
Punchinello, 73
Purging, 24, 65, 264
Proverbs: French, cited, 38, 93, 103, 148, 158, 175, 180, 227, 231, 239, 245, 264, 269; German, cited, 13, 15, 51, 68, 73, 78, 83, 107, 169, 198, 227, 229, 232, 234, 242, 266

Quaadt, Eltz von, governess, 220
Quakers, 155
Quesnel, Père, 193
Quintessence des Nouvelles, Le (newspaper), 77

Rank order, xix-xx, 160, 165, 222, 230, 240, 276. *See also* Hierarchy; Precedence, ceremonial
Ratsamhausen, Eleanore von, 142, 158, 265
Raugrafen, 20, 29
Reason, use of, 119, 155, 209, 240, 265
Receiving arms, ceremony of, 7
Reformed, persecution of: in France, 107, 108, 115, 176, 232; in Palatinate, 249. *See also* Huguenots, persecution of
Regencies, 227
Regency council, 202
Regency of Philippe d'Orléans, xli, 201, 202-4
Reincarnation, 93, 114, 176-77
Relics, 10, 88, 149, 163
Religion: personal, 71, 161; true, 51, 76, 89, 139-40, 170, 176, 259; varieties of, 156-57; view of, xxi. *See also* Bible; Churches, reunification of; Church

services; *Dévôts;* Faith, religious; Huguenots, persecution of; Miracles; Priests; Reformed, persecution of; Relics; Saints
Remedies, xxv-xxvi, 16, 104, 131, 159, 259, 273
Renown, 129
Reparations for war damages, 104-5
Reputation, 12, 21, 23, 29, 36, 55, 64, 81, 82, 119, 225
Reunion chambers, 27
Rigaud (painter), portrait of Elisabeth Charlotte by, 192
Rioms, Comte de, 237
Roués, 235
Rousseau (painter), 251, 252
Routine, daily: in 1675, 11-12; in 1705, 158-59; in 1721, 270
Royal house, submission of, to King, 184
Royalty, attitude toward, xxiv
Rumors, 85, 90, 188, 193, 197, 252
Russia, 264

Sacraments, 22, 221, 269
Saint-Cyr, school of, 88
Saints, 30, 129, 190
Sancho Panza, 175
Sandrasqui, German courtier, 221
Satire, political, 62, 70, 121, 146, 149, 150, 176, 180
Savoy, Marie-Louise-Gabrielle of, Queen of Spain, 138-39
Saxe, Maurice de, birth of, 97
Saying, German, cited, 63
Scarron, Paul, xlvii, 86, 230
Schlieben, Count (German courtier), 221, 224
Schwetzingen, 219, 226, 227
Science, xxviii
Scripture, difficulty of living up to, 73, 76. *See also* Bible
Secrétaires du roi, 148
Senility, 227, 234, 269
Sermons, 81, 86, 87, 160, 228
Sex, attitude toward, xviii
Siam, King of, 156
Singing in church, 81, 89, 97, 118, 155
Smallpox, 11, 83, 273
Snuff, 199
Sobieski, Jan, King of Poland, 43
Sodom and Gomorrha, 263
Song of Songs, 121
Sophie, Electress of Hanover, xxxvii, 161, 165, 194-96

Sophie Charlotte, Queen of Prussia, xxxviii, 2, 85, 157

Sophie Dorothea, Crown Princess of Hanover, 78, 87, 210

Soul: of animals, 167; immortality of, 94, 114, 143

Spain, court of, 138–39

Spanish succession, war of, 116, 124–27, 144

Spies at French court, 85

Spleen, 14, 129

Splendor, royal, 208

Stage, crowding of, in Paris theater, 86

Starhemberg, Count, 41

Steenkerke, battle of, 77–78

Stones, engraved, 144

Storytelling, xxix. *See also* Anecdotes told

Strasbourg, siege of, 31

Stuart, Elizabeth, Queen of Bohemia, 1, 115, 258

Stuart, James (son of James II), 168, 169, 262

Stuart, house of, xvi

Superstition, 150, 257

Syphilis, 263

Système de Law, 235–36, 238, 241, 245, 250, 252, 256, 257

Tabouret, ceremonial role of, 26

Tea, 111, 156

Teething, 10, 12

Télémaque, 112

Testament: of Charles II, King of Spain, 127; of Karl, Elector Palatine, 46, 48; of Karl Ludwig, Elector Palatine, 48; of Monsieur, 132, 234

Theater: as metaphor, 23; attack upon, by preachers, 85–86, 108; French, xxvii–xxviii, 84, 243; German, xxiv–xxv, 23, 192; Italian, 271–72; love of, 135, 163, 176

Théobon, Mlle de (lady-in-waiting), 35, 36, 42. *See also* Beuvron, Comtesse de

Theology, interest in, xxviii

Thieves, 54, 105

Tissot (court physician), 11

Torcy, Jean Baptiste Colbert, Marquis de, xlv, 150, 157, 207, 208, 255, 266, 271

Toulouse, Comte de, xlv, 217

Tourney at court of Osnabrück, 4

Turenne, Marshal, 11

Turin, battle of, 164

Traveling, xx–xxi, 25, 123, 184, 267

Trier, battle of (1675), 12

Ugliness of Elisabeth Charlotte, 83, 89, 101, 109, 117, 141, 192, 207

Ulrike, Queen of Sweden, 248

Unigenitus, papal bull, 194, 258

Upbringing of Elisabeth Charlotte, xvi

Ursins, Princesse des, xlix, 139, 164, 189, 197

Valois, Mlle de (granddaughter), 211

Ventadour, Mme de, 132, 189

Versailles, château of, xx

Villars, Marshal de, 168

Visits, 198, 253, 269, 270

Vows, religious, 29

Wales, Prince of (son of George I), 210

Wales, Prince of (son of James II), 61

Wales, Princess of (Karoline of Ansbach), xxxiii, 156, 197, 210

Walking, 7

War, 82, 146

Waters, taking of, 72

Weaning, 12, 15

Wendt (*chevalier d'honneur*), 32, 37

Wilhelmine Ernestine of Denmark, Electress of the Palatinate, xxxvi, 3, 11, 19

Will. *See* Testament

Wine, 254, 255

Witchcraft, 163, 214, 225

Wolfenbüttel, court of, 148

Women: honor of, 87; role of, in politics, 204, 250; unfortunate position of, 147

Writing, art of, 185, 186, 231

ELBORG FORSTER has translated numerous historical studies from the French and German, including *Selections from the Annales* (also published by Johns Hopkins).

The Johns Hopkins University Press

A WOMAN'S LIFE IN THE COURT OF THE SUN KING

This book was composed in Centaur and Bembo display and Aldine Roman text type by A. W. Bennett, Inc., from a design by Gerard A. Valerio. It was printed on S. D. Warren's 50-lb. Sebago Eggshell Cream paper and bound in Holliston Roxite A by The Maple Press Company.